Being Untruthful

Herausgegeben von

Monika Fludernik
Stephan Packard

FAKTUALES UND FIKTIONALES ERZÄHLEN

Schriftenreihe des Graduiertenkollegs 1767

Herausgegeben von
Monika Fludernik

Band 9

ERGON VERLAG

Being Untruthful

Lying, Fiction, and the Non-Factual

Herausgegeben von

Monika Fludernik
Stephan Packard

ERGON VERLAG

Umschlagabbildung:

[William Haviland as] Iago [in Shakespeare's Othello]
Photograph, J. & L. Caswall Smith.
London [England] : Virtue & Co., [late 19th century or early 20th century]
https://luna.folger.edu/luna/servlet/detail/FOLGERCM1
~6~6~303855~123829:-William-Haviland-as--Iago--in-Shak

Bibliografische Information der Deutschen Nationalbibliothek:
Die Deutsche Nationalbibliothek verzeichnet diese Publikation in der Deutschen Nationalbibliografie; detaillierte bibliografische Daten sind im Internet über http://dnb.d-nb.de abrufbar.

Gedruckt auf alterungsbeständigem Papier.
Umschlaggestaltung: Jan von Hugo

www.ergon-verlag.de

ISSN 2365-8851
ISBN 978-3-95650-856-1 (Print)
ISBN 978-3-95650-857-8 (ePDF)

Table of Contents

III. Contemporary Extensions: Playing with Facts and the Non-Factual

Introducing the Lie to Narratology: Concepts, Contexts, and Functions of Lying as Non-Factual Discourse

Monika Fludernik and Stephan Packard

This volume engages with the issue of lying, the structure of lies, and the performance of liars across an interdisciplinary range of historical and contemporary perspectives. Its theoretical framework is narratology with its recent interest in factuality. The volume focuses on the relation between lying and other forms of the non-factual, including fictionality.

In 2019, the graduate school Factual and Fictional Narration (GRK 1767)[1] organized a conference on the subject of "Lying and Related Fictions."[2] The topic was chosen in the wake of discussions regarding the range of non-factual discourses and narratives, debates that took their origin in an earlier academic meeting preparing the publication of the handbook *Narrative Factuality* (Fludernik & Ryan 2019). Contributions to the handbook emphasize that not only does non-fiction include a great variety of narratives that are not factual in the prototypical sense of the term, but that, conversely, the field of the non-factual includes a great range of elements outside fiction, if fiction is understood in the generic sense (i.e. literary imaginative narratives, poems, plays and other media such as movies or cartoons).

These asymmetries are grounded in part in the propensity of speakers to mix genres, and in hybrid generic traditions; but also in the often merely implicit double meaning of factuality: *factual* can either refer to a discourse that *should* be concerned with truth, or to a discourse that *is*. Correspondingly, the *non-factual* either signifies a discourse that is *never expected to be truthful* or one that *fails* to be so. What needs to be mapped, then, is a field of normative and descriptive concepts in relations of antonymity, i.e. contrasting semantic opposition (Packard 2019). In this context, the lie, as the most obvious instance of a direct violation of the factual norm, is the logical choice for a paradigm to examine.

Let us start with a definition *ex contrario*: it is worth first pointing out what lies are *not*. Many genres that claim to be factual by virtue of being non-fictional can in fact be demonstrated to deploy fictional strategies and inventive

[1] Graduiertenkolleg 1767 (Faktuales und Fiktionales Erzählen), funded by the German Research Foundation (DFG).

[2] Web: https://www.grk-erzaehlen.uni-freiburg.de/event/tagung-lying-and-related-fictions/.

licenses that render a claim to pure factuality moot. The pragmatics of factual discourses allows for genres and text types in which verbatim quotation is *de rigueur*, and others in which what is being reported may be rendered in condensed and sometimes biased manner. Even documentary journalism employs techniques that are accepted despite their manipulation of the material. Janet Malcolm in her article "A Second Chance" (2020) explains that one convention of respectable journalism, called "the uninterrupted monologue," allows for the representation of an interviewee's utterances on several occasions as *one* monologue supposedly uttered on one occasion. The case of Claas Relotius, a *Spiegel* journalist found guilty of fabricating many of his prize-winning pieces, has led to public scrutiny into some of the guidelines of the *Reportage* as a specifically German genre of journalism. For this subgenre, some textbooks for journalists allow or even encourage the rearrangement of factual information for the purpose of telling a better story, mostly using the strategy of assembling details from different cases and merging them into a constructed story about just one purportedly anonymized person, though this person is actually entirely fictive (Haller 2017; Moreno 2019). Other generic traditions that blur the borders between non-fictional function and fictive reference or ontology flourish in many of our current media formats. In instructional diagrams, for instance, persons will often be represented in a cartoonish fashion, representing types rather than individuals, despite the fact that serious information is being conveyed (Jüngst 2007, Grünewald 2013).

In such contexts, references to the real world are held to be maintained and relied upon, and they are indeed routinely trusted. This first category of fictivity within factual genres and texts involves a license for flouting the rules of factuality. Similarly, fictive suppositions (usually distinguished from imaginative fictions) as well as a number of rhetorical figures and modes like metaphor, hyperbole and irony, operate along comparable lines. Nevertheless, problems may arise (Packard 2017), for example when purportedly factual cartoons reproduce racial stereotypes (Mintz 1979); or when interviewees protest that they do not recognize their own words (Marinos 2001). Such scandals often result in censure for the authors or draftsmen and may feed suspicions against the whole genre.

Non-factuality in factual narratives in our first category embraces an accepted number of contraventions to strict veracity, where these departures from the truth are covered by generic licenses or a relaxing of the rules of literal or referential adequation to the facts. By focusing on the lie, this volume will be concerned with that broad spectrum within factual discourse which is understood to entail a normative expectation of truth or sincerity, and in which that expectation is nonetheless violated. The category also includes a variety of associated phenomena and practices such as forgery, impersonation, acting, dissimulation, fraudulence, and deception in the widest sense of the term –

and even narrative unreliability, wherever it is not employed as a transparent rhetorical device. A third category, that of errors, mistakes, and misunderstandings, doubtlessly deserves attention as well; but for now, we will consider it only insofar as it helps to characterize and distinguish or delimit licenses of untruthfulness from deception.

In literature, deception and lying are to be encountered almost everywhere. Well-known works in the literary canon even explicitly designate their protagonist a liar, for instance Corneille's (1643) and Goldoni's *The Liar* (1750), Henry James's short story "The Liar" (1888), Jean Cocteau's "Le menteur" ('The Liar,' 1949), Stephen Fry's novel *The Liar* (1991; see Fludernik in this volume), and *Jakob der Lügner* ('Jacob the Liar'; 1969); but there are also plays like Tom Stoppard's *The Real Thing* (1982 – note Henry James's "The Real Thing" – 1892) and *Arcadia* (1993) as well as Harold Pinter's aptly named *Betrayal* (1978), in all of which deception plays a key role. Among novels, the best known discussion of lying, forgery and impersonation may be Peter Ackroyd's *Chatterton* (1987; see Groom 2004), but, more recently, Ian McEwan's *Atonement* (2001) has also garnered much interest. Literary fiction in the past fifty years has displayed a keen perception of varieties and performances of lying and duplicity. This can be observed in several notable examples of novels and plays that focus on an analysis of dissimulation, forgery, impersonation and lying, including discussions of plagiarism, forged manuscripts and paintings, fake impersonation and spying as well as the more commonplace lying of false witnesses and adulterous husbands.

The essays in this volume concentrate on lying, but they also consider *practices of dissimulation*, equivocation and faking all the way to forgery. The contributions are taken from a variety of disciplines including philosophy, psychology, history, media studies, Classics, English and American Studies, German and comparative literature, and drama and performance studies. Historically, the essays use examples and case studies that range from Antiquity to the present, though more than a third of the contributions discuss contemporary contexts. This reflects the current relevance of lying in discourses about fake news and "bullshitting" (Frankfurt 2005) deployed in political propaganda and electoral manipulation. As the articles about the early modern period demonstrate (Asch and Berensmeyer in this volume), our present time is not the only one beset by a prevalence of lying and dissimulation; the two most important environments of lying in the Renaissance, however, were the court (politics and politeness) and religion (in the context of the religious persecution of heretics; see Collinson 2002; Berensmeyer & Hadfield 2019). Despite different practices and contexts, some types of non-factual utterance and practices of deception were current in many different periods. In this volume, literature's self-reflexive play with lying and dissimulation is studied in several politically sensitive types of contemporary fiction, but also historically in a variety of earlier texts. These analyses of deception interact with culturally disparate expectations and norms of veracity, but also with legal contexts, social practices, and literary licenses.

On the basis of comparative study, one might have to update current terminology both materially and theoretically. For what has continued to shift, sometimes radically, is not the existence of untruthful utterance (observable universally), but the very disparate historical and cultural connotations which have framed the discussion of deceit and lying. In various settings marked by new cultural and media practices, the lie seems to re-emerge as a new problem, condensing the multifarious discomforts experienced in tandem with these new modes of communication into one key suspicion and indictment, namely that of lacking credibility. (In fact, whenever the lie resurfaces as an explanatory diagnosis, its apparent novelty is an illusion – we have been here before.) Research in sociology has analyzed entire societies from the angle of their negotiation of such suspicion, examining how these societies counter (alleged) deception and deceptive representations. In the framework of systems theory (Luhmann 1997; Baecker 2018, 26-61), sociologists trace a number of surplus phenomena (i.e. supplementary semantic material) linked to three levels of signification. The first of these is the level of basic linguistic reference in oral discourse (prone to be affected by slips of the tongue and imprecise designation in addition to the mistakes arising through mere errors of perception); the second the level of literacy (since writing intrudes ambiguities that are not present in face-to-face communication); and finally there is the level of print culture (which leads to a burgeoning of critical discourses). At each stage of these media innovations, the opportunities for misunderstanding and deliberate misinformation expand and result in renewed attempts to rein in the resulting practices, including that of lying. After the Renaissance, the democratization and secularization of society resulted in shifting the locus of dissembling from the court to polite society and from religious to commercial contexts. Though politics has always been a fertile ground for dissimulation and lying, not least in the work of spies and the secret services, the resurrection of the practice of political manipulation and propaganda in democratic states in the early twenty-first century has brought the issue of the non-factual to the wider public's attention.

1. *Lying and Related Practices*

Lies have attracted a keen interest from scholars in many different disciplines and have done so since times immemorial. Theologically, lying has been associated with Satan, proverbially, the "Father of Lies": "*Lying* is Father to *Falshood*, and Grandsire to *Periury*: *Frawd* (with two faces) is his Daughter, a very Monster: *Treason* (with haires like Snakes) is his kinseman" (Dekker, *Seven Deadly*

Sinnes, cited Hadfield 2017, 93-94). Lying is an act of provocation against God: "Whosoever lieth, witneseth that he condemneth God and therewithal feareth men" ("Montaigne, Essays, II, p. 394" – cited in Hadfield 2017, 17). Biblically, lying was associated with two situations: swearing under oath ("taking the name of the Lord in vain" – third commandment) and "bearing false witness" (ninth commandment). As Hadfield also points out, the 1559 Book of Common Prayer "made children promise" to "beare no malice," not to steal and to keep one's "tongue from evil speaking, liyng and slaunderyng" (cited Hadfield 2017, 17).

Much of the philosophical debate by the church fathers concentrated on the discussion of when it was legitimate to lie or equivocate, with St. Augustine and Kant taking absolutist positions (Bok 1978, 32-7; Carson 2019) and Aquinas adopting a more pragmatic standpoint (Levine 2014, s.vv. Aquinas, Augustus, Kant). The issue under which circumstances it might be justifiable to lie becomes particularly rife in the early modern period when English Catholics were hard put to decide whether or not to swear the Oath of Supremacy (1535) or the Oath of Allegiance (1606). Hadfield's study of lying in the early modern period in fact takes those two acts of parliament as cornerstones for his analysis of this issue for English Protestants and Catholics and links the religious discussion to the prominence of dissimulation in other early modern environments such as the courtly rules of politeness and the operations of rhetoric.

Lying is a near-universal human phenomenon (Nishimura 2019), though inflected culturally and socially. For this reason, it has been a topic of great interest to psychology and brain studies (Bott & Williams 2019, Decker et al. 2019). Guo & Rochat (in this volume) provide an analysis for developmental psychology that combines the psychological with the intercultural perspective by comparing children's lies in China and the USA. Our focus in this section will be on the discussion of lying in its semantic context, in its word field. There are many synonyms and near-equivalents of the lexeme and concept of lying. Scholars have also elaborated several typologies of lying. Let us deal first with semantics.

A key distinction is made between lying and evasion or equivocation, an opposition claimed to be relevant for President Clinton's oath about his relationship with Monica Lewinsky (Hadfield 2017, 21-22; but see Meibauer 2014, 158, who considers Clinton to have lied). In all of these discussions equivocation or prevarication relate to the verbatim utterance and its meanings and implicatures, often supported by the ambiguities of lexical usage.[3]

A second major fault line in the determination of what constitutes a lie (we will come to definitions below) is constituted by the intention to deceive. Because both lies and equivocation are deployed in contexts where deception is

[3] Meibauer (2014, 37) has a table displaying six types of underdeterminacies that lend themselves to deployment in equivocation.

a key objective of the speaker trying to achieve some perlocutionary effect by lying (Meibauer 2014, chapter 3), dissimulation and deceit need not rely on the literal falsity of what is being said nor on the manipulation of ambiguity or on presuppositions that generate false implicatures. Deceit may be deliberate but non-verbal (or at least not focused on a statement that will be taken literally as in an oath, where lying results in perjury). Lying can also be associated with false promises (Arnovick 1999; Mahon 2019b, 37-38), where the sincerity condition of this illocutionary act is being undermined by the intention to deceive the promisee.

A statement's or assertion's truth or untruth (Mahon 34-36) needs to be contrasted with an intent to deceive. False assertions may of course arise due to ignorance or error and are not lies. On the other hand, lying that is not focused on assertions is usually labeled by names such as *dissimulation*, *impersonation*, *fake(ing)*, and more generally *mendacity* and *deceit*. A historically and trans-historically important category of dissimulation is that of *hypocrisy* (Davidson 2004), an attribution of falsity and dissimulation to a person in circumstances where the actual intent to deceive cannot fully be established (self-deception may be in play). Among lies in the linguistic medium that are not intentionally deceptive, rhetorical figures stand out, from metaphor, irony, and hyperbole to litotes – a fact that has been extensively documented in the linguistic literature on lying (Weinrich 1965/2005; Hardin 2019; Claridge 2019; Ortony & Gupta 2019). The most extensively discussed case of the non-factual without intent to deceive is of course fiction, for which Sir Philip Sidney famously proposed that it does not assert anything and hence cannot lie (see Berensmeyer, this volume, as well as Mayer 2003 and Maier 2019).

Another major contrast is established by the literature on lying between "white lies," also called "prosocial" lies, and the negative variant of egoistic or "mendacious" lies (Hornung 2016), i.e. lies meant to benefit the liar rather than the liee (a term coined by Burrow 2020). Prosocial lying is apparently a separate cognitive achievement (see the essay by Rochat & Guo in this volume). White lies are meant to save face, supporting interlocutors' positive self-image (negative face), whereas a lie to preserve one's own self-image (positive face) would be considered an evasion.[4] Terkourafi (2019) provides a categorization of white lies (388-389), which includes the following functions:

(1) saving face;
(2) avoiding tension or conflict;
(3) providing social interaction;
(4) affecting interpersonal relationships;
(5) achieving interpersonal power.

[4] See Brown & Levinson (1978). The term *face* originates with Goffman (1967).

She also introduces more color terms: white lies are contrasted with evil "black" lies. She cites Bryant (2008, 36-37) on the notion of "gray" lies, in which the various factors (intention, consequences, beneficiary, etc.) are at odds with each other, making it impossible to classify them unambiguously as either 'black' or 'white' (Terkourafi 2019, 389). The article goes on to propose blue, red, yellow, and green lies. Blue lies (Fu et al. 2008) are "told to benefit a collective" (Terkourafi 391), and mostly refer to political lies employed to benefit the upholding of the law. Red lies (included in the *Urban Dictionary*) are "told with complete awareness that the other person knows the statement to be false" (392). They therefore correspond to "bold-faced lies" (Meibauer 2014, 107; Sorensen 2007; Carson 2010). Yellow lies, also in current use according to the *Urban Dictionary*, are lies that are meant to cover up embarrassment, and are considered to be cowardly; they are supposed to "protect the speaker" (393). Finally, green lies are ecologically deceptive lies and refer to commercial claims about the alleged ecological qualities of a product (393).

An extensive taxonomy of lies and related practices is provided by Meibauer (2014), who includes the following categories:

- pretending or faking
- lying (insincere lying vs. pretended lying)
- indirect lying
- insinuation
- acting
- reticence
- half-truths
- precondition or presupposition faking
- deliberate ambiguity
- obfuscation
- pretending to lie
- pretending to act/joke (condensing Meibauer 2014, 27-29)

The category of reticence is extremely interesting since it signals that there are "lies of omission" alongside "lies of commission" (Meibauer 2019, 1-2).[5] The possibility of reticence explains the requirement for oaths to speak the "whole" truth (and nothing but the truth). It is also enlightening to note that the act of lying or faking can in turn be faked or performed in acting, thus resulting in a second-level speech act.

We noted above that lying is sometimes considered a perlocutionary act (although the general subsumption of lies in the category of speech acts is controversial, as we will see below). Linguistic analyses of lying often concentrate

[5] See also Meibauer (2019 Intro, 1-2), where he refers to several other taxonomies, among them those by Chisholm and Feehan (1977), Vincent and Castelfranchi (1981) and Bok (1999).

on lying from a speech-act-theoretical perspective since lying is apt to betray the interlocutor's or addressee's trust (Mahon 2019b, 44). Ortony & Gupta (2019), for instance, base their taxonomy on the pragmatics of lying. They distinguish between

(a) False Implicature
(b) Fabrication
(c) False Response
(d) Half-truth
(e) Contrived Distraction
(f) Overstatement
(g) Equivocation
(h) Pretending to Lie (155-56)

Considered in terms of the Gricean cooperative principle (Grice 1975) or the framework of relevance theory (Sperber/Wilson 1996), these categories characterize different strategies of verbal deception. Thus, (a) achieves its goal by uttering a true statement whose implicature leads the addressee astray; (b) invents a "false claim"; (c) responds to a question with an answer which is "in direct opposition to the truth"; (d) "masquerades as the whole truth," but "discloses" only "part of the truth"; (e) manages to change the subject in order to avoid a truthful utterance; (f) exaggerates an aspect of the proposition in order to mislead the addressee; (g) employs an ambiguity to avoid a truthful statement; and (h) has the speaker produce a true assertion but in a manner that will lead the hearer to believe it is a false statement.

Speech act theory has not remained the only approach that considers lying from the perspective of its functions and uses. Besides psychological explanations for the ubiquity of lying, cultural analysis lists a series of typical social settings in which lying occurs or is even practiced with regularity; it also analyzes contexts in which lying is either condoned or even (in particular circumstances) required. Following Snyder (2009), Hadfield (2017, 20) notes the following typical contexts in early modern England in which lying regularly occurs and is commented on by contemporary authors:

- civility and good manners
- the court
- the prince and reason-of-state politics
- moral philosophy
- religious dissent (see Snyder 2009, 19)

The first of these categories coincides with white or prosocial lying, a concern that keeps surfacing in discussions of the insincerity of polite behavior in the seventeenth and eighteenth centuries. Wycherley's *The Plain Dealer* (1676) shows Manly, the eponymous hero, rejecting all flattery and polite lying in favor of plain speech, but the excessive utterance of truthful statements tends to come with the disadvantage of social ostracism, as it already did in Molière's *Misanthrope* (1666), the model for Wycherley's play. As Weinrich shows, Rousseau's notions of sincerity are a direct descendant of the critique of lying associated with polite conversation. (Weinrich's representative of the latter is Marivaux's play *Les Sincères*, 1739.)

Snyder's second area of the exercise of deception is the court, linked to the first on account of the need to behave in (excessively) polite manner, but connected also with the inherent culture of dissembling operative at court both on the part of the courtiers and that of the prince or ruler himself. (On this central factor of dissimulation at court see Asch's essay in this volume.) The subterfuges that become necessary for councilors of state (like those practiced by the figure of Morus in the first part of *Utopia*) and the strategies of deception undertaken by rulers are often linked with the model of Machiavelli's *Il principe* (*The Prince*, 1532), a handbook of political manipulation and pragmatic power politics achieved by means of camouflage and dissemblance (Bakir 2019).

Religious dissent, as already noted, is the primary topic of Hadfield's study of lying in early modern England, and its importance emerges especially in relation to the taking of enforced oaths and to dissidents' answers under interrogation or under the threat of execution. More generally, the religious context invokes the controversialist writings, in which – as in today's *Fox News* versus the *New York Times* or *CNN* – the authors engaging in cross-denominational invectives (Lederer 2007; Bailey 2015) have not only inverted the dichotomous attributes of truth and falsity but also redeploy the same metaphors in reciprocal vilifications. Hadfield quotes a passage from Ben Jonson's *Discoveries*, who glosses the phrase *stare a partibus* ('to stand by one's party') and delineates how political bias determines the speaker's assessment of a person or situation: "Nay, the times are so wholly grown to be either partial, or malicious, that if he be a friend, all sits well about him, his very vices shall be virtues; if an enemy or of the contrary faction, nothing is good or tolerable in him; insomuch that we care not to discredit and shame our judgements to soothe our passions" (Jonson 1906, 28). To the list provided by Snyder one should more generally add the use of guile and deception in one's intercourse with the enemy whether on the battlefield or in diplomacy, a topos current already in antiquity (Mahon 2019a, 14). Clearly, this situation of necessary disguise and lying to the enemy is relevant in later centuries, too, as with the need to lie to the Gestapo during World War II.

Both the context of politeness and that of courtly or religious dissembling do not merely involve the contrast between factual truth and its opposite, the lie. In addition, the performance of mendacity works its poison by an artistry of dissemblance that parallels the *ars celare artem* principle of rhetorical and literary *sprezzatura*. As Helfer (2017, 336, 343) outlines, Castiglione's "famous formulation of the ideal courtier's art of concealing art" (336) suggests that the practices of courtly lying and dissimulation required sophisticated skills of rhetorical and performative acting, whose success depended on the pretense of sincerity in order to hoodwink the hearer into taking the deception for truth. Lying could easily impose on its recipients when they took the performance for a rhetorical display of wit that laid out the truth in a seemingly artless manner:

> Echoing Themistocles' justification about the need for translation to tell the truth [referring to Themistocles' life of Plutarch], [Thomas] Hoby [the translator of Castiglione's *The Courtier* into English] compares language 'to a piece of tapestrie, that beyng spred abrode, discloseth the beautie of the woorkemanship, but foulded together hideth it' (p. 3). (Helfer 2017, 345)

Inverting this process of displaying the truth by unfolding the obscurity of the matter, liars (one might argue) only pretend to unfold the truth but in fact strategically obscure it through misleading clues and artful deceptions.

Further insights afforded by the study of lying in its historical contexts concern the deleterious consequences of a culture of dissembling and duplicity. A general and widespread practice of dissimulation leads to a destabilization of the distinctions between truth and falsity. As Hadfield argues in relation to Shakespeare's *Othello*,

> If everyone told the truth except Iago he might be more readily exposed; he might succeed even more easily. If everyone was conscious that everyone else lied then Venetian society might be more horrible but more secure. What the audience witnesses is a story of lying when the people on stage think they understand the world around them, the limits of their knowledge, and the boundaries between truth and falsehood, but are deluded, a fable for a time of acute paranoia. (Hadfield 2017, 308)

As Hadfield goes on to suggest, the vocabularies of "truth/falsehood and lying," despite the new "*sprezzatura*/recklessness," were not really inventions of the early modern period or that they merely (like *equivocation*) "took on a new significance"; what changed were their much more extensive uses of application (308). At the same time, the Reformation initiated a strife for religious truth that resulted in a contest between theologians and martyrologists (see Collinson 1997) on both sides of the confessional divide keen to proclaim their Truth.

Modern mass media have introduced new contexts for the reach and consequences, and possibly the functions, of the lie by creating the temporally and geographically extended realm of a public sphere fed by print publications in mass circulation (see the essay by Packard in this volume). Extending the theories of cooperative communication, originally mostly oriented towards synchronous (face-to-face) conversation, to asynchronous and few-to-many dissemination of information, additional typologies of the lie have come to complement those described above. The rise of propaganda mirrors the religious and political disputes of early modernity, prominently employed in Christian missionary work as well as in the controversies of the reformation and counter-reformation. As Bussemer (2008, 26-27) notes, it is with its denouncement as a tool of counter-Enlightenment thought that propaganda begins to be associated with the idea of the lie. In a parallel development, the traditional discipline of rhetoric has acquired a dubious reputation and has grown suspect (Barthes 1970). This denigration of propaganda persists despite its having been embraced by the actors of the French Revolution and the workers' movement, and though it has been adopted as a legitimate means of warfare by all parties in both World Wars as well as during the Cold War. (See, for instance, Ferdinand Mount's diagnosis that "deceit and manipulation have been the hallmark of Western policy in the Middle East ever since the Sykes-Picot Treaty" – 2021, 6). In the more narrow sense of propaganda we meet a variety of manifestations in psychological warfare, public diplomacy, and information operations. Bernays's account of Public Relations, which he refers to as propaganda in his study (1928), extends to advertisement, which he sees as a necessary and at least potentially deceitful tool of modern democratic governance.

Propaganda is closely related to the equally changeable concept of ideology. Originally conceived as the science of ideas by the French Enlightenment philosophy of *idéologie*, it was reinterpreted by the politics of Napoleon as a doctrine employing a misleading metaphysics which produces deceptive representations of social relationships and societal structures (see also Williams 2015). Famously taken up by Marx and Engels in their account in *Deutsche Ideologie* (1846), the term ideology has become associated with the suspicion that public discourse and one's common understanding of the social world may be fundamentally flawed; this flaw emerges in deliberate as well as unconscious, but always partisan, misrepresentations and constitutes the core of several incarnations of the political critique of public lying (Adorno 1954). According to these accounts, ideology moreover has crucial repercussions for the analysis of individual psychological development and subjectivation, an area in which political deception and self-deception merge (Žižek 1989, Althusser 1993).

In the most recent research, the ability to manipulate the truth or engage in ideological distortion is considered a commonplace rhetorical tool of the current mass media (Holiday 2013) – or even a lethal threat to the very survival of democracy itself (Applebaum 2020). As Randall Kennedy suggests, the Republican party – after "[f]our years of rage and lies" (Shatz 2021, 26) – "will act calmly, quietly and deliberately to entrench the policies of propelling the degradation of democracy in America" (Kennedy, 27). The further suspicion that the shifted, fragmented public sphere created by the most recent digital networks has allowed the public lie to flourish in the shape of what has been called *fake news* or *postfactuality* remains controversial (Andrejevic 2020). Debate on this topic has produced new typologies of lying. Perhaps most famously, Claire

Wardle in her report on 'Information Disorder' (Wardle & Derakshan 2017) lists seven types of mis- and disinformation:

(a) satire or parody
(b) misleading content
(c) imposter content
(d) fabricated content
(e) false connection
(f) false context
(g) manipulated content

Misleading content (b) is understood as the biased framing of issues or individuals. Imposter content (c) impersonates accepted factual sources, such as politically partisan websites that are formatted to resemble *CNN*. Only fabricated content (d) invents false claims whole cloth. False connections (e) designate cases in which headlines suggest claims that the non-manipulated piece does not endorse. False context (f) describes the misattribution of factual claims. Finally, manipulated content (g) characterizes a strategy in which factual information is conveyed but changes of some important details occur, serving a camouflaged agenda.

Oriented towards distinguishing the merely false from the actively harmful, each of these categories engages deviations from an assumed norm of factuality. It is striking that generic fiction does not figure, even though the first category of satire and parody touches upon literary traditions. Wardle's interest lies in these strategies' potential to deceive the audience, even in the absence of harmful intention. Such deceit can be explained as the direct consequence of a fragmented public sphere, in which the existence of an audience that recognizes a specific rhetorical intent may not entail that a different audience does likewise, opening up the possibilities of their mistaking the piece as factual. As the contributions to this volume will demonstrate, throughout the diverse contexts and histories they engage with, the recognition and denunciation of the lie, and not least the many apologies of its practice, depend on the uncertain delimitations of the act of lying, whose scandalization commonly precedes its definition.

2. *Lying from the Perspectives of Philosophy, Speech Act Theory and Performativity: Facets from a Long and Complex History*

Definitions of lying regularly focus on the utterance of a string of words and the disparity between the expressed lexical meaning and the facts. While some theorists have considered this characterization sufficient, others – sometimes referred to as the 'deceptionists' – add a second necessary criterion, namely that an intention to deceive needs to exist on the part of the speaker. As Montaigne points out, grammarians "say that to tell an untruth is to say something that is false, but that we suppose to be true, and that the meaning of the Latin *mentiri*, from which our French word for lying derives, is to go against one's conscience, and that consequently it applies only to those who say the opposite of what they know [...]" (Montaigne 1958, 30). Colin Burrow cites Bernard Williams, who defines a lie as "an assertion, the content of which the speaker believes to be false, which is made with the intention to deceive the hearer with regard to that content" (Williams 2002, 96; cited Burrow 21).

This logical kind of definition has several disadvantages. For one, it focuses exclusively on utterances or verbal statements. Weinrich (2005) even proposes that individual words can "lie," adducing as an example phrases like *Blut und Boden*, a now universally abhorred National Socialist catchphrase justifying the conquest over Eastern Europe. Secondly, the logical definition of lying assumes that one can recognize the intention of the speaker or the writer, which (as a literary critic) one tends to consider a fiction of communicative convenience. Third, the common argument that the lie asserts or implies the opposite of what is the case is also problematic from a speech act theory perspective, since this equates lying with metaphor and irony – also traditionally defined as 'saying that which is not' – and with fiction (often identified with lying).

In the twentieth century, with the advent of speech act theory, these problems have been treated by recourse to lying as a speech act with the perlocutionary effect of deceiving the addressee. Meibauer (2014) quotes a definition by Saul (2012, 65) that attempts to avoid most of the traditional pitfalls:

Lying (Complete)
If the speaker is not the victim of linguistic error/malapropism or using metaphor, hyperbole, or irony, then they lie iff (A) and (B) holds:

(A) (1) They say that P;
(2) They believe P to be false;
(3) They take themself [sic] to be in a warranting context.

(B) (1) They say something indeterminate across a range of acceptable complete propositions, CP1...CPn;
(2) for each complete proposition in the range CP1...CPn, they believe that proposition to be false;
(3) They take themselves to be in a warranting context.

(Saul 2012, 65; cited Meibauer 2014, 147)

However, though this formula is able to deal with verbal lying in the narrow sense of the term by conceiving of it as a perlocutionary act, i.e. an act accomplished *by* saying something, it takes some liberty with the sincerity condition usually required for successful illocutionary speech acts, i.e. the act accomplished *in* saying something. In singling out (A3) and (B3), this definition emphasizes the Gricean cooperative principle of the Essential Condition that demands speakers commit themselves to the truth of the proposition they are expressing (Searle 1979, 62) – an aspect at stake in cases of indirect lies or false implications (Meibauer 2005), but also symptomatic of the problem that a speaker who lies does not actually accomplish the speech act to which they are pretending.

In distinction from the many ways in which speech acts can be feigned by actors pretending to communicate in literary and aesthetic media – such as actors on stage or authors of fictional narrative –, lies depend on the actual intention of the speaker being not just disregarded by, but hidden from, their audience. This also sets lies apart from various rhetorical devices such as indirect, ironical, or metaphorical speech, in all of which the audience is supposed to appreciate the speaker's departure from the literal truth. While integrating rhetorical speech acts as modifications or complications of the conventions of speech, speech act theorists tend to disregard stage actors' speech-acting, focusing exclusively on the speech act that actors *pretend* to accomplish and assuming they are not engaging in the same speech acts towards their audience. Yet in both cases, felicitous (speech) acting relies on an informed audience that plays along. Deceiving that audience flies in the face of the demands of the prevailing illocutionary act, which can only be considered felicitous if the illocutionary force with which the speaker communicates is recognized by the persons they are addressing. Fundamentally, liars do not cooperate with their victims; and a theory of communication as a cooperative speech act may only go that far in describing the person who lies as a successful communicator (even when they are very successful liars).

As Anne Reboul has pointed out, the

> [...] problem arises with the other side of the illocutionary act, that is with convention: though it is essential to the success of an illocutionary act that the intention at the basis of the illocutionary act should be recognized and hence the illocutionary act should be recognized as such, and for this reason, the intention is conventionally represented in the utterance itself, it is just as essential to the success of the lie that the intention which motivates it shouldn't be recognized and, of course, it is not represented, conventionally or otherwise, in the utterance. Thus, though illocutionary acts and lies are intentional, yet lies are not illocutionary acts because they are not conventional. (1994, 294)

Reboul concludes that lies merely *correspond* to certain speech acts and differ from those similar acts in that the speaker violates the sincerity condition, while hoping that the audience will believe it to have been fulfilled. But perhaps more importantly, liars are *breaking* the convention of the feigned speech act even as they perform the conventionally recognized act of lying.

Once the sincerity condition is bracketed, the question of the speaker's commitment, which the lie violates, becomes much harder to define. Since that violation in fact defines the pragmatic motivation for repudiating lies, an important part of the pragmatic context threatens to be lost when we fail to acknowledge the violation of the conversational sincerity condition. The implications of this problem can be seen most clearly in all those scandals mentioned above where those who failed to speak the truth turn into apologists and defend themselves against the accusation of lying, introducing the finest possible distinctions in order to uphold their claim to have met their obligations of trustworthy speech. For instance, if lies require the speaker to believe their proposition P to be false (A2 and B2 in Saul's definition above), then such a speaker can with impunity assert any proposition whose truth value is unknown to them. This situation needs to be distinguished from the implementation of the canonical Gricean maxim of quality, which stipulates that speakers should have sufficient reason to believe in the *truth* of their propositions.

The requirements that establish belief in a proposition as truthful and those that prove it to be false open a large area of unclaimed ground between them. A proposition can only be unequivocally identified as wrong if it has been falsified. Thus, one will not accuse one's friends of every possible crime or misbehavior under the sun because one does not have sufficient evidence of their innocence. Expanding on Reboul's concept of the corresponding speech act, one could argue that a lie is not a speech act at all, but an act of a very different kind, in which a speaker

- wishes to appear as if they believed P;
- while lacking sufficient cause to believe P;
- and therefore causing the corresponding speech act to fail.

The recognition of intent which is here at stake plays an especially prominent role in performatives, as Searle observes (1969, 47). A more extended understanding of deceit requires a model of such performance and a concept of make-believe to explain practices of lying and dissimulation. Beyond the moral and communicative failure of the insincere speech act, performative accounts of lying are able to describe the conditions under which lies come to fail or succeed. They take note of the situational context of lying, particularly the expectations of addressees or recipients and observers that are based in the institutional, social, and collective frameworks within which lying operates. A performative approach also highlights dissimulation as a *practice* that can be successful or unsuccessful, that can derail. And it tends to underline the techniques or strategies employed in the service of deception.

Linguistic work on lying has been analyzing the strategic use of certain rhetorical figures and the asseveration of truthfulness as key signals of lying (see Weinrich 2005, Meibauer 2018, Claridge 2019). However, a comparison with Nünning's list of signals of unreliability (1997, 1998, 2019) (appropriate also for narrators that *do not intend to deceive*) shows that signals of lying and of unreliability largely overlap. Both contexts in fact do not present unequivocal signs of deception but merely *indices* or possible clues that may support an *interpretation* or *assumption* of a lying speaker or unreliable narrator; they do not provide any clinching evidence except by recourse to the facts (if they can be ascertained): if the facts falsify or undermine the propositions, we do have a case for suspicion or even cause for incrimination. In real life, whether in politics, law or private contexts, the lie can only be established when the speaker is found out: the lie fails to convince in the light of evidence that falsifies the assertions of the liar. In Stephen Fry's novel *The Liar*, the eponymous 'hero' is a congenital liar, but he is found out by his Cambridge tutor when he delivers an essay for his tutorial:

> 'Well constructed, well researched, well supported, well argued . . . '
> 'Oh. Thank you.'
> 'Original, concise, thoughtful, perceptive, incisive, illuminating, cogent, lucid, compelling, charmingly read . . .'
> 'Er – good.'
> 'I should imagine,' said Trefusis [the tutor], 'that it must have taken you almost an hour to copy out.' [...]
> 'Val Kirstlin, *Neue Philologische Abteilung*, July 1973, "The Origin and Nature of the Periphrastic Verb 'Do' in Middle and Early Modern English." Am I right?' (Fry 2011, 47-48)

Here Adrian's pretense to have composed the essay himself is unequivocally exposed as an exercise in plagiarism. However, in real life, contrary evidence may prove to be contested assertion rather than agreed-upon fact for those who hold diametrically opposed world views, as witness the convictions of Trump supporters storming the Capitol as we are writing this text, who are immune to all evidence supporting election results in favor of Joe Biden.

Successful lying depends on a favorable context of reception, and it (ab)uses communicational and social assumptions that ensure business can proceed as usual, whether in terms of cooperative principles (Grice) or relevance theory (Sperber & Wilson). The manipulation therefore is not only one relating to propositions that are false but to implicatures and to the system subtending all communication and exchange among interacting persons and institutions. Dissimulation opens up an abyss between being and seeming; it operates in the manner of treacherous sands that swallow the distinction between truth and falsehood. A performative model of lying ultimately returns to equating the liar with an actor pretending to truth but only performing a deceptive role of authenticity or sincerity. Lying as pretense, as acting, therefore moves the lie into the precincts of fiction, i.e. literary imaginary worldmaking. Whether the failed reference of a lie still establishes a semantic relationship that engages in world building or not is discussed controversially by some of the chapters in this book (Morgenroth, Navratil). Hence, when fiction is censured as an act of lying, this indictment is less convincing (given literature's absent intention to deceive[6]) than the reciprocal thesis, namely that lying is a practice of fictionalizing, of pretense and make-believe.

If so, might lies perhaps achieve productive or even desirable ends? When we turn to the long history of deliberations about lying on the part of philosophers, theologians, and authors of major status, one can observe a series of condemnations of lying, with only a few thoughts about possible justifications for lies in special circumstances, for instance in the story of St. Athanasius' escape from persecution thanks to prevarication (Davis 2017, 65). St. Augustine of Hippo (354-430 A.D.) devoted two short treatises to the issue of lying: *De mendacio* (On Lying) and *Contra mendacium* (Against Lying), written in ca. 395 and 420 respectively. He already distinguished between the "fictitious (*mendax*)" and the misleading ("*fallax*"), which attempts to deceive. Fiction tries to please its audience; "[b]ut he is rightly called a misleader [*fallax*], or misleading, whose business it is that everybody should be deceived [*fallatur*]" (cited Burrow 21).[7] In contrast to later French usage, the Latin *mentiri* is employed by St. Augustine to refer to writers of fiction ("*mentientibus*"), whereas the word *fallacy* in English seems to correlate with unintentionally produced untruth.

One of the most interesting discussions of lying comes from Sir Francis Bacon, who wrote his essay in the wake of Montaigne's deliberations on the subject (see the article by Denery in this collection). Bacon recognizes that lying is not merely a practice of fiction and of self-interest but that it is an enterprise in its own right, engaged in for the delight of producing lies:

> But it is not only the difficulty and labor, which men take in finding out of truth, nor again, that when it is found, it imposeth upon men's thoughts, that doth bring lies in favor; but a natural, though corrupt love, of the lie itself. One of the later school of the Grecians, examineth the matter, and is at a stand, to think what should be in it, that men should love lies; where neither they make for pleasure, as with poets, nor for advantage, as with the merchant; but for the lie's sake. [...] A mixture of a lie doth ever add pleasure. Doth any man doubt, that if there were taken out of men's minds, vain opinions, flattering hopes, false valuations, imaginations as one would, and the like, but it would leave the minds, of a number of men, poor shrunken things, full of // melancholy and indisposition, and unpleasing to themselves? (Bacon 3-4)

The second noteworthy insight of Bacon's is the prevalence of lying, its admixture to any kind of discourse and practice where it serves as the oil that facilitates social intercourse and communication. This significant ingredient in our behavior is then rather abruptly censured by Bacon, thereby exposing the inherent ambivalence that polite lying and the grooming of one's own face and others' faces generates in the moralist:

---

6 Though there are of course texts that pseudofactually proclaim their literal veracity.

7 Burrow cites no source, but the passage can be found online, though references as coming from Augustine's *Soliloquies*. 21 May 2021. https://www.augustinus.it/latino/soliloqui/soliloqui_2_testo.htm.

> [...]; it will be acknowledged, even by those that practise it not, that clear, and round dealing, is the honor of man's nature; and that mixture of falsehoods, is like alloy in coin of gold and silver, which may make the metal work the better, but it embaseth it. For these winding, and crooked courses, are the goings of the serpent; which goeth basely upon the belly, and not upon the feet. There is no vice, that doth so cover a man with shame, as to be found false and perfidious. (Bacon 4-5)

Bacon's proposals come closest to highlighting the usefulness and ambivalencies of lying, though he shrinks from an endorsement of white lies in the manner in which Bernard Mandeville in his parable of the bees praises egotism and greed as profitable to mercantile economy.

So far in our summary, the strategy of legitimating lying has been to condone a modest prevarication or face-saving act of politeness. Justifications of lying acknowledge the sin or harmfulness of lies, but they also draw the reader's attention to some positive or pleasurable uses of the practice, especially in the context of literary composition and imaginative invention. These apologists for fiction and lying all presuppose that the truth is distinguishable from that which is not the truth (falsehood or error), and this positivist assumption only emerges as a problem when the truth cannot easily be ascertained, though it is assumed to exist somewhere (if only one could find it). In fact, the truth is generally conceived of as singular and simple, whereas lies are supposed to be overwhelmingly diverse; they seem threatening in the sheer proliferation of challenges they pose to the preserver of the one virgin truth. As Montaigne observes in "On Liars" (1958, 31): "If, like the truth, falsehood had only one face, we should know the better where we are, for we should then take the opposite of what a liar said to be the truth. But the opposite of a truth has a hundred thousand shapes and a limitless field." There is the threat to be engulfed by the many falsehoods that drown out the voice of the one and only truth. More anxiety-inducing still, one is confronted with so many shapes that *masquerade as truth* (but are falsehoods), and therefore is unable to determine which of these predominantly false 'truths' is the real truth – an insight that anticipates the internet user's dilemma of filtering out real from fake news.

Friedrich Nietzsche and, in his wake, the whole tradition of deconstruction and poststructuralism, added a further turn to the screw of this dilemma by proposing that there is no such thing as the truth: what we consider to be truth turns out to be a very personal and biased perspective on the appearances that we observe (Mayer 2003). Nietzsche's *Umwertung aller Werte* suggested that the truth is blinding and cannot be endured by human subjects: man has had to construct a play of illusions, and the fictions which he has elaborated in order to survive are necessary for man in his interaction with the world. Such radical relativism kills the lie with the truth, since lies can only be considered lies in their deviation from acknowledged truths or facts. Nietzsche's praise of fiction and lying ties in with his assumption that the truth is ugly ("häßlich") and that it is the purpose of art to make truth palatable or tolerable: "Die

Lüge wird somit als eine ernstzunehmende Spielart der Wahrheit gerechtfertigt und die Oberfläche als eine Dimension der Tiefe" (Ingold 2019; 'The lie is legitimated as a seriously version of the truth, and the surface accepted for the dimension of depth'). In *Die fröhliche Wissenschaft* (*The Gay Science*), Book V, section 344, Nietzsche deconstructs science's search for the truth, exposing life to be an aggregate of error, fraudulence, dissimulation, blinding and self-deception ("Irrthum, Betrug, Verstellung, Blendung, Selbstverblendung" – 263). The belief in the truth is recognized to be metaphysical, due to the equation of the divine with truth ("dass Gott die Wahrheit ist, dass die Wahrheit göttlich ist" – 263). And this equation is thoroughly turned on its head by Nietzsche: he proposes that the divine appears in the shape of error, blindness and deception ("Irrthum," "Blindheit," "Lüge" – 264), God being the most enduring lie of all ("Gott selbst sich als unsre längste Lüge erweist" – 264).

Nietzsche's rhetorical ploy was anticipated by Edmund Burke in his famous tract on the French Revolution, in which he excused the trappings of civilized behavior as necessary to hide the ugly reality of man's beast-like nature, using the metaphor of clothes that cover man's nakedness:

> All the pleasing illusions which made power gentle and obedience liberal, which harmonized the different shades of life, and which by a bland assimilation incorporated into politics the sentiments which beautify and soften private society, are to be dissolved by this new conquering empire of light and reason [i.e. the French Revolution]. All the decent drapery of life is to be rudely torn off. All the superadded ideas, furnished from the wardrobe of a moral imagination, which the heart owns and the understanding ratifies, as necessary to cover the defects of our naked, shivering nature, and to raise it to dignity in our own estimation, are to be exploded, as a ridiculous, absurd, and antiquated fashion. (Burke 1993, 77)

Burke's imagery correlates with the praise of polite lying, but it also recognizes the abyss yawning underneath the pleasing illusions of social order, namely that of Hobbesian violence which can only be kept at bay by the fictions of civilization. In this philosophical tradition – in contrast to speech act theory and the standard incrimination of lying – lies are argued to have a useful function that is indispensable to the conduct of human affairs. What we deal with under the banner of truth is therefore always a domesticated version of it, since civilization requires us to conquer our inherent animality.

From this perspective, one moves beyond the singular lie that has been motivated by individual psychology and which can be analyzed linguistically and allows itself to be sanctioned as a single deceptive speech act. Instead, one arrives at the level of a more fundamental and comprehensive practice of dissimulation and deception linked to the ideologies and worldviews of (post)modern society. Well beyond Burke and Nietzsche, and beyond post-structuralist theory, in the climate of 2020, received opinions and generally accepted norms have come under suspicion in the public realm. Just as our despairing search for the trustworthy truth seems to lead to an impasse, our desire for authenticity and sincerity may be doomed to failure and result in blanket mistrust of everybody across the board. As we have seen above, this situation lends itself to a further disruptive consequence, namely the loss of belief in anybody's responsibility for their actions and words, thus voiding the commonwealth of accountability and genuine political agency. Under such conditions, talking about truth becomes hypocritical; the invocation of truths in some quarters becomes a mask or screen behind which power politics can camouflage its fraudulence and duplicities. If the lie is a performance, the discourse about sincerity and truth is likewise a performance – a fact recognized already by William Godwin in his novel *Caleb Williams* (1794), not coincidentally a text reflecting the philosophical and ideological impasses of the French Revolution (compare Fludernik 2001a,b).

3. *Structure of the Volume*

In this volume we have tried to combine theoretical, interdisciplinary, and historical approaches. The volume falls into three parts. In the first, the contributions raise important philosophical and theoretical questions about the nature of lying, deception, dissimulation and fictivity as well as counterfactuality. They do so from a number of disciplines, including psychology, law, literary and media studies. In the second part, the essays we have collected present a number of historical case studies. These cannot by any means provide a comprehensive history of the lie, but they demonstrate its multiple shapes, its ubiquity, and recurrent associations with fictionality, dissimulation, fraudulence, and criminality. The essays cover a range of historical periods from antiquity to the nineteenth century and include contributions from history, philosophy and literary studies. The third and final part of the volume incorporates essays from literary and theatrical studies that address selected contemporary perspectives on the lack of truthfulness in specific discourses where the erosion of trust is felt to be particularly problematic. The relevant contexts include experimental theater, ethnic and migration narratives and literary thematizations of the Shoah.

Part One develops diverse theories of the lie across a number of different disciplines. **Cynthia Guo and Philippe Rochat** introduce readers to some basic information on new psychology approaches to the practice of lying. The article summarizes the most recent psychological research on lying, with a special focus on its relation to the development of self-consciousness in children. By contrasting human practices with strategies of deception in animals, Rochat and Guo provide a background against which prosocial and more overtly selfish lies can be distinguished and demonstrate how these converge in children's concern for maintaining face. The essay argues that lying and deception are basic and common types of behavior; lying can therefore be treated as a defining characteristic of humans.

Frank Schäfer, from a legal perspective, focuses on the status of the lie in German law. As he demonstrates, the lie – except in the case of perjury – does not constitute a key concept within German law. While there exists a general obligation to tell the truth, the lie as such is not codified as an offense – a fact which regularly surprises lay people. Indeed, it is only when lying violates certain other norms, laws or rights that it is penalized. In some cases, dissimulation is acceptable or even required in order to uphold or preserve more important legal principles. In cases where the law fails to punish liars, the only recourse possible is to the censure by public opinion.

Michael Navratil's chapter on counterfactual fiction turns to literary narratives. Drawing on his recent monograph about contemporary counterfactual storytelling in politics, Navratil extends the notion of counterfactuality to the literary genre of alternative history, a genre of the historical novel that delineates history as it did not happen. While counterfactual fictions establish their specific relationship with reality by foregrounding some ways in which the diegetic world differs from what is believed to be true in our world, they also often engage in metafictional reflections that focus on the concepts of truth and lying. Since these metafictional comments usually reinstate a distinction between fiction and truth, implicitly arguing in favor of truthfulness, they contest the fashionable claims of panfictionality or postfactuality.

Stephan Packard takes his cue from the political discourse on fake news or post-factuality to examine the mass media's disposition towards the public lie. He analyzes the public lie from the perspective of an assessment of its specific temporality. Liars in public discourse attempt to seem sincere, yet they must also strategically assume a divided audience: to some sections of their postmodern audience, their lies will seem transparent, while others will take the statements as authentic. Using Hans Christian Anderson's tale of the emperor's new clothes, Packard illustrates that lies may continue to hold sway when they are not publicly challenged. He also links the issue of public lying with the communicative challenges facing public rational discourse that are characteristic of modernity but reshaped by the proliferation of social media networks.

Concluding the first part of the book, **Monika Fludernik** offers a theoretical perspective on liars and lying in literature. She presents a typology of literary lying. Her three categories include a) literature as a form of lying or, put differently, fiction as a lie; b) literary authors as liars and engaging in a pretense of factuality; and c) liars and lying in fictional worlds. Under category c) she lists lying narrators, lying characters, and lying as a central plot element. In the second half of her essay, Fludernik considers the special case of impersonation, devoting in-depth analyses to Sir Philip Sidney's *Old Arcadia* and to Philip Roth's *Operation Shylock*.

The second section begins its series of historical perspectives with **Stefan Tilg**'s treatment of the confluence and differentiation of lies and fiction in Greek and Roman classical authors, namely Hesiod, Plutarch, Lucian, Plautus, Horace, and Ovid, among others. Tilg points out that the issue is as much about terminology as it is about conceptualization. Finally, he addresses problems of lexical semantics and polysemy. The conclusion he draws is that the focus on the author or narrator as the originator of dissimulation is distinctly modern and therefore alien to Antiquity.

Turning to literary lies in the early modern period, **Ingo Berensmeyer** takes us through a detailed reading of William Baldwin's sixteenth-century writings. In particular, he discusses the satirical tale *Beware the Cat*, in which, through a complex narrative structure, cats are presented as storytellers. They elaborate on the virtues and laws of promiscuity, thus complicating the moral reflections that can be found elsewhere in the text. Berensmeyer traces this approach back to Baldwin's earlier writings on fictions or lies and shows that the author makes a case for the usefulness of literary imagination.

Ronald G. Asch's contribution explores the problem of dissimulation and (lack of) trust in inter-confessional relations and politics at the turn of the seventeenth century. Dissimulation as a political strategy does not necessarily imply deceit, but it requires the concealment of one's true convictions. Asch describes how demands for sincere conformity produce a general climate of distrust, especially where declarations of confessional loyalty are concerned.

In his readings of Montaigne and Scudéry, **Dallas Denery** places the two authors in a tradition of truth-telling that ranges from Augustine and the Scholastics to courtly dissimulation and the early Enlightenment. Both Montaigne and Scudéry assume that some deception is a necessary and unavoidable part of human life, thus distancing themselves from the scholastic tradition. They find that social ties are not threatened by lies but rather depend upon a certain flexibility in the representation of facts. At the same time, uncertainty as a consequence of lying is now no longer just a problem of social interaction, but likewise an issue of self-understanding.

Vid Stevanović explores it-narratives as a special case of lying. Works such as Gildon's *The Golden Spy* (1709) or *Adventures of a One-Pound Bank Note* (1819) cast inanimate objects as narrators or focalizers and so give rise to factual suspicion. The reader is faced with a serious epistemological challenge: he or she needs to accept the conventional value of money, which has a material basis in the value of gold, but is confronted with counterfeiting as a recurrent practice. The representation of intrinsic value is tested against the specter of counterfeit coinage. In the figure of counterfeit money and the practice of coining, Stevanović discusses fiction as an analogous practice that is being considered metafictionally in the texts he analyzes.

Concluding the second section, **Katrin Althans**'s reading of Wilkie Collins situates itself at the interface of literary and legal studies. In *The Woman in White* and *No Name*, respectively, Victorian debates about the legal conceptions of illegitimacy, matrimony, divorce, and women's property are examined against the backdrop of the sometimes paradoxical treatment of lies and deception in British law. Collins, Althans concludes, examines both the social and the legal constructions of personal identity. In particular, it is the problem of legitimate and illegitimate children that allows Collins to delineate the problematic relationship between legal fiction and actual deceit.

The third and final part of this volume considers contemporary debates and their treatment of lying. **Daniel Morgenroth** examines the implications of truthfulness, authenticity, and loyalty between actors and audiences in his discussion of a range of recent experimental theater events. Asserting a fundamental connection between performance and lying, his case studies serve to point out new ambivalences and creative relationships between credibility and veracity.

Autobiographical and autofictional narratives are today faced with new demands from current identity politics. Taking his cue from recent scandals involving the ethnic identity of authors composing published US immigrant narratives, **Rüdiger Heinze** explores the limits of what is currently accepted as ethnic fiction and analyzes the shifts in understanding the concept of authenticity. Heinze concludes that fictionality is no longer just a matter of debate in literary studies, but has become entangled in the wider discourse of power relations.

In their close reading of Teju Cole's *Open City*, **Eva Ries** and **Martin Riedelsheimer** reconsider the question whether fiction can lie despite making no overt truth claims. Analyzing unreliable narration in the work, they show that it calls into question normative political as well as quotidian conceptions of truth and falsehood. Thus, they argue, the work explores the relation between truthspeaking and discursive power in a Foucauldian manner by drawing on the notion of *parrēsia*. Ries and Riedelsheimer conclude that Cole's *parrēsiastic* novel does not in fact lie but rather speaks profound truth when it narrativizes untruthfulness. Not only does Cole's novel prominently question the norms that determine truth and falsehood in our everyday and political discourses, it also negotiates the connection between truth and (discursive) power as discussed by Michel Foucault.

Continuing this line of thought, **Tom Vanassche** in the final essay of the volume turns to recent fiction about the Shoah. He focuses on two types of literary strategy, (a) unreliable narrators and (b) documentary fiction. Unreliable narrators suspected of having committed crimes during World War II attempt to excuse their deeds in apologetic autobiography or autofiction. There are also novels that introduce unreliable focalizers. Documentary holocaust fiction, on the contrary, tries to stay as closely as possible within the facts that have been documented in history and trial records. In both perpetrator fiction and documentary novels about National Socialist crime extensive use is made of historical documents about the Shoah. An analysis of the way in which these genres employ the factual material from the historical records showcases the need to persist in moral judgment and evaluation and to expose the unreliability of the narrators of these fictions, but also to question the attitudes of readers.

Acknowledgements

We would like to thank everyone who participated in the 2019 conference and has contributed to this volume of collected essays. In particular, we would like to express our gratitude to the German Research Foundation (DFG) for financing the graduate school, including the conference and this publication. Thanks go also to Hanna Häger and her team for expert organization of the conference. Help with the editing of the manuscript and the stylesheet implementation is gratefully acknowledged. In Freiburg and Cologne the following persons (in alphabetical order) have been involved in the editing process: Nathan Anderson, Gregor Biberacher, Annabell Blank, Tanja Haferkorn, Nadine Menghin, Lars Münzer, and Vesna Schierbaum.

Works Cited

Adorno, Theodor (1954) "Beitrag zur Ideologienlehre." *Kölner Zeitschrift für Soziologie und Sozialpsychologie* 6: 360–375.

Althusser, Louis (1993) *Ècrits sur la psychanalyse: Freud et Lacan*. Paris: Stock.

Andrejevic, Mark Bardeen (2020) "The Political Function of Fake News: Disorganized Propaganda in the Era of Automated Media." *Fake News. Understanding Media and Misinformation in the Digital Age*. Ed. Melissa Zimdras and Kembrew McLeod. Cambridge: MIT Press. 19–28.

Applebaum, Anne (2020) *Twilight of Democracy. The Seductive Lure of Authoritarianism*. New York: Doubleday.

Arnovick, Leslie K. (1999) "Chapter 4. The Expanding Discourse of the English Promise." *Diachronic Pragmatics. Seven Case Studies in English Illocutionary Development*. Amsterdam: Benjamins. 57–71.

Bacon, Francis (1968) "Essay I: Of Truth." *Essays*. Intr. Oliphant Smeaton. London: Dent. 3–5.

Baecker, Dirk (2018) *4.0 oder Die Lücke, die der Rechner lässt*. Berlin: Merve.

Bailey, Michael D. (2015) "Superstition, Dissimulation, and Identity: Discerning False Religion in the Fifteenth Century." *Dissimulation and Deceit in Early Modern Europe*. Ed. Miriam Eliav-Folden. Basingstoke: Palgrave Macmillan. 1–27. Web. 20 January, 2021.

Bakir, Vian, et al. (2019) "Lying and Deception in Politics." *The Oxford Handbook of Lying.* Ed. Jörg Meibauer. Oxford: Oxford Univ. Press. 529–540.

Barthes, Roland (1970) "L'ancienne rhétorique. Aide-mémoire." *Communications* 16: 172–223.

Becker, Jurek (2017) *Jakob der Lügner* [1969]. Berlin: Suhrkamp.

Berensmeyer, Ingo, and Andrew Hadfield (2019) "Mendacity in Early Modern Literature and Culture: An Introduction." *EJES. European Journal of English Studies* 19.2: 131–47.

Bernays, Edward L. (1928) *Propaganda*. London: Routledge.

Bok, Sissela (1999) *Lying: Moral Choice in Public and Private Life*. New York: Vintage.

Bott, Lewis, and Emma Williams, (2019) "Psycholinguistic Approaches to Lying and Deception." *The Oxford Handbook of Lying.* Ed. Jörg Meibauer. Oxford: Oxford Univ. Press. 71–82.

Brown, Penelope, and Stephen C. Levinson (1978) "Universals in Language Usage: Politeness Phenomena." *Questions and Politeness: Strategies in Social Interaction*. Ed. E. N. Goody. Cambridge: Cambridge Univ. Press. 56–311.

Bryant, Erin (2008) "Real Lies, White Lies and Gray Lies: Towards a Typology of Deception." *Kaleidoscope* 7: 23–50.

Burke, Edmund (1993) *Reflections on the Revolution in France* [1790]. The World's Classics. Oxford: Oxford Univ. Press.

Burrow, Colin (2020) "Fiction and the Age of Lies." *London Review of Books* 42.4: 21–25.

Bussemer, Thymian (2008) *Propaganda.* Wiesbaden: VS.

Carson, Thomas L. (2010) *Lying and Deception: Theory and Practice.* Oxford: Oxford Univ. Press.

Carson, Thomas L. (2019) "Lying and Ethics." *The Oxford Handbook of Lying.* Ed. Jörg Meibauer. Oxford: Oxford Univ. Press. 469–482.

Chisholm, Roderick M., and Thomas D. Feehan (1977) "The Intent to Deceive." *The Journal of Philosophy* 74.3: 143–159.

Claridge, Claudia (2019) "Lying, Metaphor, and Hyperbole." *The Oxford Handbook of Lying.* Ed. Jörg Meibauer. Oxford: Oxford Univ. Press. 370–381.

Cocteau, Jean (1949) "Le menteur." *Théatre de poche. Quatorze dessins inédits de l'auteur*. Paris: Paul Morihien. 119–24.

Collinson, Patrick (2002) "Truth, Lies, and Fiction in Sixteenth-Century Protestant Historiography [1997]." *The Historical Imagination in Early Modern Britain: History, Rhetoric, and Fiction, 1500-1800.* Cambridge: Cambridge Univ. Press. 37–68.

Corneille, Pierre (1984) *Le menteur. Comédie* [1643]. *Oeuvres complètes*. Volume 2. Bibliothèque de la Pléiade. Paris: Gallimard. 1–91.

Davidson, Jenny (2004) *Hypocrisy and the Politics of Politeness. Manners and Morals from Locke to Austen*. Cambridge: Cambridge Univ. Press.

Davis, J. Steven (2017) "The Importance of Athanasius and the Views of his Character." PhD thesis, School of Divinity, Liberty University. Web. 21 May, 2021. <https://digitalcommons.liberty.edu/cgi/viewcontent.cgi?article=2678&context=doctoral>

Decker, Alexa, et al. (2019) "Lying, Deception, and the Brain." *The Oxford Handbook of Lying.* Ed. Jörg Meibauer. Oxford: Oxford Univ. Press. 83–92.

Fludernik, Monika (2001a) "Spectacle, Theatre and Sympathy in William Godwin's Caleb Williams." *Eighteenth-Century Fiction* 14.1: 1–30.

Fludernik, Monika (2001b) "Sympathetic Affect and Artful Deception: Rhetorical Ambivalence in William Godwin's Caleb Williams." *Engendering Images of Man in the Long Eighteenth Century.* Ed. Walter Göbel, Saskia Schabio and Martin Windisch. Trier: WVT. 81–96.

Fludernik, Monika, and Marie-Laure Ryan (2019) Ed. *Narrative Factuality: A Handbook.* Revisionen 6. Berlin: De Gruyter.

Frankfurt, Harry G. (2005) *On Bullshit*. Princeton: Princeton Univ. Press.

Fry, Stephen (2001) *The Liar* [1991]. London: Arrow.

Fu, Genyue, et al. (2008) "Lying in the Name of the Collective Good: A Developmental Study." *Developmental Science* 11: 495–503.

Goffman, Erving (1967) "On Face-Work: An Analysis of Ritual Elements in Social Interaction." *Interaction Ritual*. New York: Doubleday. 5–45.

Goldoni, Carlo (2001) *The Liar: A Comedy in Three Acts* [1750]. Trans. Tunc Yalman. New York: Dramatists Play Service.

Grice, Paul (1975) "Logic and Conversation." *Syntax and Semantics*. Ed. Peter Cole and Jerry L. Morgan. Vol. 3. 41–58.

Groom, Nick (2004) "'I am Nothing': A Typology of the Forger from Chatterton to Wilde." *The Victorians and the Eighteenth Century: Reassessing the Tradition*. Ed. Francis O'Gorman and Katherine Turner. Aldershot: Ashgate. 203–22.

Grünewald, Dietrich (2013) Ed. *Der dokumentarische Comic*. Berlin: Bachmann.

Hadfield, Andrew (2017) *Lying in Early Modern English Culture: From the Oath of Supremacy to the Oath of Allegiance*. Oxford: Oxford Univ. Press.

Haller, Michael (2017) *Die Reportage.* Köln: Halem.

Hardin, Karol J. (2019) "Linguistic Approaches to Lying and Deception." *The Oxford Handbook of Lying.* Ed. Jörg Meibauer. Oxford: Oxford Univ. Press. 56–70.

Helfer, Rebeca (2017) "Wit and The Art of Memory in Nashe's *The Unfortunate Traveller.*" *English Literary Renaissance* 47.3: 325–54.

Holiday, Ryan (2013) *Trust Me, I'm Lying. Confessions of a Media Manipulator.* New York. Portfolio.

Ingold, Felix Philipp (2019) "Die Wahrheit ist nackt, aber ihre Blöße vielleicht Verkleidung." *Neue Zürcher Zeitung, Feuilleton* (26 September). Web. 19 May 2021.

Hornung, Melanie (2016) "Classifying Prosocial Lies: An Empirical Approach." *International Review of Pragmatics* 8: 219–246.

Jonson, Ben (1906) *Discoveries* [1640]. A *Critical Edition with an Introduction and Notes on the True Purport and Genesis of the Book.* Ed. Maurice Castelain. Paris: Hachette.

Jüngst, Heike (2007) *Information Comics: Knowledge Transfer in a Popular Format.* Munich: Peter Lang.

Kennedy, Randall (2021) "Cynical Realism." *London Review of Books* 43.2 (May): 24–27.

Lederer, Thomas (2007) *Sacred Demonization: Saints' Legends in the English Renaissance.* Austrian Studies. Salzburg: Braumüller.

Levine, Timothy R. (2014) *The Encyclopedia of Deception.* 2 vols. London: Sage.

Luhmann, Niklas (1997) *Die Gesellschaft der Gesellschaft.* Frankfurt: Suhrkamp.

Mahon, James E. (2019a) "Classic Philosophical Approaches to Lying and Deception." *The Oxford Handbook of Lying.* Ed. Jörg Meibauer. Oxford: Oxford Univ. Press. 13–31.

Mahon, James E. (2019b) "Contemporary Approaches to the Philosophy of Lying." *The Oxford Handbook of Lying.* Ed. Jörg Meibauer. Oxford: Oxford Univ. Press. 32–55.

Maier, Emar (2019) "Lying and Fiction." *The Oxford Handbook of Lying.* Ed. Jörg Meibauer. Oxford: Oxford Univ. Press. 303–314.

Malcolm, Janet (2020) "A Second Chance." *The New York Review of Books.* 24 Sep. 2020. Web. 11 Jan. 2020.

Marinos, Alexander (2001) *So habe ich das nicht gesagt! Die Authentizität der Redewiedergabe im nachrichtlichen Zeitungstext.* Berlin: Logos.

Marx, Karl, and Friedrich Engels (2017) *Deutsche Ideologie: Manuskripte und Drucke* [1846]. Marx-Engels-Gesamtausgabe (MEGA). Ed. Ulrich Pagel, Gerald Hubmann and Christine Weckwerth. 2 vols. Berlin: De Gruyter.

Mayer, Mathias (2003) "Das rechte Leben und das Falsche lesen? Über den Zusammenhang von Literatur, Lüge und Ethik." *Kulturen der Lüge*. Köln: Böhlau. 225–245.

Meibauer, Jörg (2014) *Lying at the Semantics-Pragmatics Interface*. Berlin: De Gruyter.

Meibauer, Jörg (2018) "The Linguistics of Lying." *Annual Review of Linguistics* 4: 357–75.

Meibauer, Jörg (2019) "Introduction: What Is Lying? Towards an Integrative Approach." *The Oxford Handbook of Lying*. Oxford: Oxford Univ. Press. 1–12.

Meibauer, Jörg (2005) "Lying and Falsely Implicating." *Journal of Pragmatics* 37: 1373–1399.

Mintz, Lawrence E. (1979) "Fantasy, Formula, Realism, and Propaganda in Milton Caniff's Comic Strips." *Journal of Popular Culture* 12.4: 653–680.

Montaigne, Michel de (1965) "Des menteurs [1595]." *Essais I*. Ed. André Gide. Paris: Gallimard. 84–89.

Montaigne, Michel de (1958) "On Liars." *Essays*. Trans. J. M. Cohen. London: Penguin. 28–33.

Montaigne, Michel de (1999) "Of Giving the Lie [1580]." *Renaissance Editions*. Transl. John Florio. Oregon: Univ. of Oregon Press. Web. 12 January 2021. <www.luminarium.org/renascence-editions/montaigne/>.

Moreno, Juan (2019) *Tausen Zeilen Lüge: das System Relotius und der deutsche Journalismus*. Berlin: Rowohlt.

Mount, Ferdinand (2021) "Ruthless and Truthless." *London Review of Books* 43.9 (May): 3–8.

Nietzsche, Friedrich (1887) *Die fröhliche Wissenschaft* [1882]. 2nd ed. Leipzig: E. W. Frisch.

Nishimura, Fumiko (2019) "Lying in Different Cultures." *The Oxford Handbook of Lying*. Ed. Jörg Meibauer. Oxford: Oxford Univ. Press. 565–578.

Nünning, Ansgar (1997) "'But Why Will You Say That I Am Mad?' On the Theory, History, and Signals of Unreliable Narration in British Fiction." *AAA [Arbeiten aus Anglistik und Amerikanistik]* 22.1: 83–105.

Nünning, Ansgar (1998) Ed. *Unreliable Narration. Studien zur Theorie und Praxis unglaubwürdigen Erzählens in der englischsprachigen Literatur.* Trier: WVT.

Nünning, Ansgar (2019) "*Unreliable Narration* zur Einführung: Grundzüge einer kognitiv-narratologischen Theorie und Analyse unglaubwürdigen Erzählens." *Unreliable Narration*. Ed. Ansgar Nünning, Carola Surkamp and Bruno Zerweck. Trier: WVT. 3–40.

Ortony, Andrew, and Swati Gupta (2019) "Lying and Deception." *The Oxford Handbook of Lying*. Ed. Jörg Meibauer. Oxford: Oxford Univ. Press. 149–169.

Packard, Stephan (2017) "How Factual are Factual Comics? Parasitic Imaginations in Referential Cartoons." *Science Meets Comics*. Ed. Reinhold Leinfelder, Alexandra Hamann, Jens Kirstein, and Marc Schleunitz. Berlin: Bachmann. 19–27.

Packard, Stephan (2019) "Factualities and their Dependence on Concepts of the Fictional and the Mendacious." *Narrative Factuality*. Ed. Monika Fludernik and Marie-Laure Ryan. Berlin: De Gruyter. 95–110.

Reboul, Anne (1995) "The Description of Lies in Speech Acts Theory." *Pretending to Communicate*. Ed. Herman Parret. New York: De Gruyter. 292–298.

Saul, Jennifer M. (2012) *Lying, Misleading, and What Is Said: An Exploration in Philosophy of Language and in Ethics*. Oxford: Oxford Univ. Press.

Searle, John R. (1974-75) "The Logical Status of Fictional Discourse." *New Literary History* 6.2: 319–32.

Searle, John R. (1979) *Expression and Meaning. Studies in the Theory of Speech Acts*. New York: Cambridge Univ. Press.

Searle, John R. (1969) *Speech Acts: An Essay in the Philosophy of Language*. New York: Cambridge Univ. Press.

Shatz, Adam (2021) "The Four-Year Assault." *London Review of Books* 43.2: 26–27.

Sorensen, Roy (2010) "Knowledge-Lies." *Analysis* 70.4: 608–615.

Snyder, Jon R. (2009) *Dissimulation and the Culture of Secrecy in Early Modern Europe*. Berkeley: Univ. of California Press.

Sperber, Dan, and Deirdre Wilson (1996) *Relevance: Communication and Cognition*. Oxford: Wiley-Blackwell.

Terkourafi, Marina (2019) "Lying and Lie Detection." *The Oxford Handbook of Lying*. Ed. Jörg Meibauer. Oxford: Oxford Univ. Press. 382–396.

Urban Dictionary (2006) "Yellow Lie." Web. 17.5.2021.

Urban Dictionary (2007) "Red Lie." Web. 17.5.2021.

Vincent, Jocelyne M., and Cristiano Castelfranchi (1981) "On the Art of Deception: How to Lie while Saying the Truth." *Possibilities and Limitations of Pragmatics: Proceedings of the Conference on Pragmatics, Urbino, July 8-14*. Amsterdam: John Benjamins. 749–777.

Wardle, Claire, and Hossein Derakshan (2017) "Information Disorder: Toward an Interdisciplinary Framework for Research and Policymaking." *Council of Europe Report DGI* 09. Web. 19 May 2021. <https://rm.coe.int/information-disorder-toward-an-interdisciplinary-frame work-for-researc/168076277c>.

Weinrich, Harald (2005) "The Linguistics of Lying" [1965]. *The Linguistics of Lying and Other Essays*. Seattle: Univ. of Washington Press. 3–80.

Williams, Bernard (2002) *Truth and Truthfulness: An Essay in Genealogy*. Princeton: Princeton Univ. Press.

Williams, Raymond (2015) "Ideology." *Keywords. A Vocabulary of Culture and Society*. Oxford: Oxford Univ. Press. 107–111.

Žižek, Slavoj (1989) *The Sublime Object of Ideology*. London: Verso.

I. Theoretical Approaches to Lying and the Nonfactual

Lying and Self-Consciousness in Human Development

Philippe Rochat and Cynthia Guo

1. *Introduction*

Tricking others to conceal a truth is not proper to humans alone. It is actually pervasive in nature. The survival of both plant and animal species depends on preemptive features that either prevent harm from predators or trick preys. However, these preemptive features are for the most part automatic and evolved characteristics of the species that have been transmitted from generations to generations over millennia, involving either no learning or minimal learning. In humans, deception has a different status compared to other animals: it is *self-conscious*. Here, we want to argue that human deception is uniquely intentional, carrying with it features not found in other animal species. We want to show that children learn to lie and conceal the truth as they become self-conscious and develop a self-conscious psychology that is unique to our species. Lying and deception in children emerge in parallel to their developing capacity to represent beliefs in others, conceal their own feelings, become aware of rules and norms, and particularly as they start to acquire a consciousness of their own reputation.

A first point to clarify is, what does it mean to be self-conscious and to be endowed with the self-conscious psychology that we propose as unique to humans? We posit that we as a species have evolved the unique ability, as well as the propensity, to reflect upon ourselves as objects of contemplation and evaluation, especially through the evaluative eyes of others (Botto & Rochat, 2019; Rochat, 2013). In this chapter, we want to propose that it is mainly this unique human propensity that leads children to deceive others. They do so in a human way, a way that is not found in other species. If our close primate relatives do employ complex tactics to deceive in their deliberate attempts to gain resources, sexual partners, and social ascendance (de Waal, 1982), we humans have additional motives that stem from our self-conscious psychology. In his seminal book on emotions, Darwin (1871) notes that we are the only species capable of blushing and of expressing complex social and self-conscious emotions like shame and guilt. These human self-conscious emotions revolve around a particular concern about our own reputation. This concern also entails some forms of recurrent thinking about how we are perceived and judged by others and what are the public impressions we make, and these go hand in hand with a deep fear of being rejected or scolded by others. We project positive face in order to be liked and gain intimacy with others. Conversely, we avoid negative evaluations. As a rule, we do all we can to promote positive images of the self.

As we have been able to document in empirical studies (Botto & Rochat, 2018; 2019), some first signs of this mark of self-consciousness and deliberate impression management to avoid negative and promote positive evaluation from others emerge already by the end of the second year in human ontogeny. Evaluative Audience Perception (EAP) as measured in these studies parallels other social cognition, in particular language development and the use of personal pronouns. It also coincides with the emergence of symbolic and pretense plays as well as with mirror self-recognition (Lacan's Mirror stage) and with an additional exclusively human touch in the displays of embarrassment, coyness, and in other self-conscious behaviors not observed in other animals (Rochat et al., 2012).

The goal of this chapter is to discuss human deception and contrast it with animal deception. We first briefly review what can be observed in other species. We then turn towards the motives of human deception, looking at how children start to lie, and in particular how their motives to lie and deceive quickly change from what is primarily an avoidance of negative consequences for themselves (i.e., reprimands and punishment) to a concern about their own reputation that is above and beyond explicit selfish concerns. We try to show that prosocial lies, which are commonly perceived as driven by a concern for others, still encompass these self-concerned features. Nonetheless, they are self-concerned only to the extent to which they are meant to protect one's own reputation as potentially assessed by others. In other words, selfish motives may still drive prosocial lies, which are produced to manage social prestige and affiliation, but not simply out of fear of punishment or reprimand. In summary, we try to make the case that the development of other-motivated deception (i.e., motivated by a regard for others) emerging in children by four years of age is another mark of human self-conscious psychology and therefore transcends any other forms of deception found in non-human animals. Lying or deception is a defining feature of what it means to be human – a feature that develops during the preschool years.

2. *Deception in Nature*

Deception in nature is neither a random nor a rare occurrence. Rather, it is a strategy carefully crafted through evolution to maximize the survival and reproduction of a species by exploiting the perceptual systems of other potential predators or prey species. In general, a species that employs a completely honest and transparent communication strategy in relation to other species would presumably not survive. In nature, deception is the rule, not the exception. It appears to be an evolutionary necessity.

Non-poisonous plants often mimic a poisonous one to avoid being eaten by predators (Lev-Yadun, 2006). Floral species mimic the smell, shape, and color of female pollinators to attract male butterflies (Jersáková et al., 2006). Male fiddler crabs have one enlarged claw, an important attribute to win over females in sexual courtship (Bywater & Wilson, 2012). However, these crabs tend to lose their enlarged claw in rivalry combat. At a marked disadvantage for obtaining vital resources in their environment, these clawless crabs by way of adaptive compensation are shown to become more aggressive in combat, 'bluffing' in competition with other intact male conspecifics. Thus, they behave in the same manner as aggressive dogs and chimpanzees, who raise neck hairs to make themselves physically more formidable and threatening.

Deception in non-primate species does not only appear to be instinctive expression of fixed-action patterns, as first described by pioneer ethologists such as Konrad Lorentz or Nikolaas Tinbergen. A growing number of empirical and anecdotal observations reveal much deceptive flexibility in mammalian as well as avian species (Bugnyar & Kotrschal, 2002; 2004; Igic et al., 2015). In addition to automatic responses, there are signs amounting to some level of planning or goal-orientation behind the deception of our evolutionary relatives, both close and far.

Primate research provides much empirical evidence of flexible tactical deception depending on social situations (Hirata & Matsuzawa, 2001; Whiten & Byrne, 1988). For example, in a recent study, Hall and al. (2016) showed the hidden food location to a subordinate chimpanzee, and not to a dominant member of the group, who would certainly get the food in a fight. Data show that the subordinate chimpanzee refrains from walking towards, or even look at the food location in front of the ignorant dominant chimpanzee. In the presence of the dominant, the subordinate hides its excitement and inhibits its desire to move toward the food until it is alone and out of sight of the dominant chimpanzee. The subordinate chimpanzee can be observed to direct its gaze elsewhere in what appears to be a deliberate attempt at deception, even misguiding the dominant peer away from the hidden food. Further observations show that the subordinate chimpanzee will also trick and deliberately guide a dominant but ignorant peer toward the location of less valued food (a cucumber), distracting them away from the location where they know the more desirable food (a banana) is hidden. They systematically defer their consumption of the preferred food to the moment when the dominant peer has departed and they are finally alone (Hall et al., 2016).

This study, as well as many other observations, accounts for the Machiavellian intelligence or systematic social maneuvering documented in many far and close human relatives – who, like us, engage in intense social competition to achieve higher social power (de Waal, 1982). Machiavellian intelligence is not the privilege of humans; other species can be shown to display some forms of intentions, beliefs, and goals that guide them in their deception of others. In the above example, the subordinate chimpanzee is driven by a clear goal: to get to the food before the dominant conspecific. For this, the subordinate may not only strategically conceal its goals but also deliberately misrepresent its knowledge and feign submission to send deceptive signals to the dominant chimpanzee.

3. *Human Antisocial and Prosocial Deception*

Compared to other animals, human deception is often not directly linked to survival or reproduction. We often lie for complex, indirect, and self-conscious reasons in order to maximize our social prestige, to strengthen our social affiliation, and to promote our reputation in the evaluative eyes of others.

Antisocial and prosocial lies are two basic kinds of lies; together, they form a unique feature of our self-conscious species. Antisocial lies are self-serving, creating benefits for oneself or inflicting harm onto others. They are self-protective and self-maximizing, not unlike the Machiavellian manifestations found in other species. In young children, antisocial lies are adopted to avoid reprimands or punishment from others. In contrast, prosocial lies (e.g., white or polite lies) are false and deceptive statements or actions driven by a positive and protective concern for others. Contrary to antisocial lies, prosocial lies are typically valued, promoted, and socially validated, as they are other-oriented and altruistic as opposed to selfish (Talwar & Crossman, 2011). With the exception of hypocrisy, the majority of adult lies are prosocial, and the motives behind prosocial lies are to help, protect, and benefit others (DePaulo & Kashy, 1998).

As we will see next, looking at the developmental literature, it appears that children's first production of antisocial lies precedes the production of prosocial lies. The developmental lag between antisocial and prosocial lies may reveal a distinct dimension of human psychology, namely that of *self-consciousness* or the sense of self as an object of others' evaluation. As we will try to show, the emergence of antisocial lies in children has been associated with the development of theory of mind (the understanding of others' mental states), normative understanding, as well as executive function (the ability to inhibit or conceal overt actions). However, these factors do not seem to account for the developmental lag of prosocial lies, which is considered a unique feature of human deception (see above). Aside from the development of domain-general cognitive capacities like theory of mind, norm understanding, and executive function, this lag needs to be understood in the context of children's developing self-consciousness. With the goal of analyzing this point, we will first briefly review and illustrate what we know regarding the emergence of antisocial as opposed to prosocial lies in children.

4. Antisocial Lies in Children

Converging empirical evidence suggests that children's first lies are antisocial in nature and that children start to tell such lies from around two and a half years onwards (Wilson et al., 2003). For example, in one study, Newton et al. (2000) asked mothers of three- to four-year-old children to keep a detailed diary of their children's deception over a six-month period. These diaries reveal that deception was prevalent by three years of age, and it was most commonly employed by children to avoid physical and psychological discomfort. Consistent with maternal observations, experimental studies reveal a similar developmental origin of deception. In laboratory settings, researchers studied children's spontaneous early lies in the controlled context of a so-called temptation resistance paradigm (Lewis et al., 1989; Evans & Lee, 2013; Talwar & Lee, 2008). In this paradigm, children are put into a tempting situation with the temptation to transgress an explicit rule. For example, a researcher could place an attractive toy on the table and instruct the child participant not to touch it. Due to their limited ability of impulse control, young children often violate the instruction and commit a rule transgression. Following the transgression, researchers ask children questions about the transgression to elicit their deception. Findings from the temptation resistance paradigm converge with results from observational studies and show that children start lying to cover up a transgression from around two and a half years of age (Fu et al., 2018). The same results in relation to age onset were replicated with children across various cultures, in the United States, but also in Australia, China, and West African countries (Carl & Bussey, 2019; Ding et al., 2018; Talwar & Lee, 2011).

The propensity to produce antisocial lies increases with age. In the context of the temptation resistance paradigm described above, four-year-olds and older children show more inclination to forcefully deny a transgression, compared to two-to-three-year-olds who tend to "leak" the truth under adult pressure (Polak & Harris, 1999; Talwar et al., 2004). By seven years of age, the majority of children tend to lie in order to cover up a misdeed (Evans & Lee, 2011; Talwar, Gordon, & Lee, 2007). Overall, children become better at keeping their subsequent verbal statements consistent with their initial lie, as they try to cover up for a transgression. For example, Talwar, Gordon, and Lee (2007) engaged six to eleven years old children in a trivia game and asked them not to peek at the answers when the experimenter left the room. Approximately half the children could not resist the temptation and peeked at the answer, and the majority of them then lied about the transgression. When asked about how they knew the answer, older children were significantly better at feigning ignorance or coming up with another plausible answer (i.e. "I learned it in school!"), whereas younger children often leaked the truth and revealed that they peeked at the answer. Throughout early development, children's ability to control verbal and behavioral leakage continues to improve, making it more difficult for adults to distinguish lies from truthful statements (Talwar & Lee, 2002a).

5. Prosocial Lies in Children

Although children's earliest lies are antisocial, by four years of age, the motivation to lie appears to diversify with the emergence of prosocial lies. Prosocial lies emerge in parallel to antisocial lies, but with an ontogenetic lag of approximately eighteen months (Ding et al., 2018; Wilson et al., 2003).

To capture children's spontaneous prosocial lie production, researchers have adopted a variety of paradigms to probe their naturalistic prosocial lie-telling (e.g. Talwar et al., 2017; Talwar, Murphy, & Lee, 2007; Talwar & Lee, 2002b). For instance, Talwar and Lee (2002b) asked three-to-seven-year-old children to take a photo of the experimenter, who had a noticeable red mark on the nose (i.e. the "Reverse Rouge Task"). When children were asked whether the experimenter looked okay for the photo, the majority of children responded positively. However, when later interrogated by another researcher, most children communicated the truth that the previous experimenter had a red mark on the nose and was not ready for the photo. Therefore, children in the study construed their responses to the first experimenter in contrast to their differing belief that the experimenter was not ready for the camera, telling a prosocial lie in the experimenter's presence.

In another study, four to twelve-year-old children were left alone to find out that the prize they received for playing a game was a disappointing soap bar instead of a toy (Popliger et al., 2011). When later asked by the experimenter whether they liked the gift, children from four years onwards expressed gratitude and appreciation for the undesired gift, hiding their true feeling of disappointment. These children confessed later to their parents that they actually were unhappy and disliked the gift (Popliger et al., 2011). The motive behind the lie was a concern for appearing polite and not hurting the gift-giver's feelings.

Aside from polite lies, it is also from around four years that children are documented to lie with the motive to help others gain rewards and resources. Talwar et al. (2017), for example, engaged four-to-five-year-old children in a competitive game with an adult confederate. The game was set up so that child participants always won, and the confederate always lost. In the last round of the game, the experimenter, who had been observing the game until then, briefly left the room and asked the child to report the outcome of the last round when the experimenter returned. After the child won the last round, the confederate asked the child to falsely report that the confederate had won the last round, so that the confederate could also win a prize. Approximately half of the children lied for the confederate, even though it meant that they would not receive a prize themselves. Together with laboratory studies that probe children's spontaneous production of polite white lies, there is now corroborated empirical evidence that children start to produce prosocial lies by four years of age (Talwar & Lee, 2002b; Talwar, Murphy, & Lee, 2007).

6. *Determinants of Lying in Development*

Children as young as three years may learn that someone is an unreliable informant and henceforth become less inclined to seek information from them (Koenig et al., 2004). The distrust towards informants who deliver untruthful information continues into adulthood, with studies showing that violation of veracity or truth expectations harms cooperation (Lount et al., 2008) and leads to low commitment (Robinson, 1996). The exposure of a lie may harm interpersonal trust and hinder the development of cooperative relationships. But as we have seen, lies can also be a kind of prosocial behavior that expresses altruistic motives and concerns and enhances cooperation, thus constituting an important means of promoting trust in relationships.

Children appear well prepared to detect prosocial inclinations in others. For example, children of the age under one demonstrate a preference for a puppet that helped rather than deliberately thwarted another (Hamlin et al., 2007). Already by eighteen months, children are spontaneously inclined to help others in completing a task (Warneken & Tomasello, 2007; Svetlova et al., 2010). This early natural preference and inclination toward prosocial behavior may represent the root of benevolence which encompasses prosocial lies (Gino & Pierce, 2010; Levine & Scheitzer, 2015). This state of affairs may seem paradoxical considering the fact that the deliberate concealment of truth (i.e., lying) tends to be universally recognized as a moral transgression.

What could explain the developmental emergence of antisocial and prosocial lies, starting by the third year of life? Children's early self-motivated, antisocial lies have been linked to their growing cognitive capacities, including theory of mind, executive function, and normative understanding. Theory of mind is the understanding of others' beliefs and mental states – that someone may experience different desires and beliefs compared to the self, including a different viewpoint or perspective on things (Wellman & Liu, 2004). To tell a lie, a child needs to have some basic understanding that he or she has access to information that the other person does not have – and therefore the other person possesses a mind that is different from his or hers (Talwar & Lee, 2008).

Indeed, studies show that children achieving more sophisticated levels of theory of mind are more likely to lie, in particular, to lie antisocially. Ding et al. (2015) even suggests that the development of theory of mind may cause honest children to start lying for themselves. In their study, Ding and collaborators recruited three-year-old children who did not show any propensity to lie, and randomly assigned them to receive either theory of mind training or a control training in which they learned about the physical properties of objects. In the theory of mind training group, children were presented with multiple story characters who have access to different kinds of information. Subsequently, children were asked questions about each character's belief, and they received feedback from the adult trainer to improve mental state understanding. Following the theory of mind training, these children became significantly more inclined to lie in a hide-and-seek game to win treats. The phenomenon was not replicated for children in the control training group. The study results suggest that the developing appreciation of others' mental states (theory of mind) may be a critical enabling factor of lying in children (Ding et al., 2015; Fu et al., 2017).

Antisocial lying in children has also been associated with the development of executive function, which corresponds to the general ability children develop to plan, decide, inhibit, and monitor their own action in relation to a set goal (Diamond & Lee, 2011). Among executive function abilities, inhibitory control, i.e. the ability to inhibit one's action and temporarily discount one's response in order to achieve a goal, is particularly relevant to lying. Young children are naturally inclined to be impatient, and they often lack inhibitory control. But to produce a lie, one needs to inhibit the desire to leak the truth, and spontaneously produce a false response (Carlson & Moses, 2001). Evidence shows that, indeed, two-to-three-year-old children who are more advanced in inhibitory control are also significantly more likely to lie in the temptation resistance paradigm (Evans & Lee, 2013).

The onset of lying in child development has also been linked to children's understanding of norms and rules, which is typically measured through their propensity to protest when another transgresses a rule as they engage in a competitive game. Using a modified version of the classic temptation resistance paradigm, we implicated two-and-a-half to five-year-olds in the transgression of a third party individual and we found that children's propensity to lie was predicted by their level of norm understanding. Our results suggest that children's understanding of and sensitivity to explicit instructions, rules, and norms may also be an important factor underlying the emergence of early lies. Norm understanding could be a primary source of motivation for a child to start covering up a misdeed to avoid reprimands and punishment.

Finally, parenting styles are also shown to impact children's inclination to lie, in particular, to produce antisocial, self-protective lies. Three-to-six-year-old children with parents who tend to be more controlling and authoritarian, as well as three-to-four-year-old children attending schools with a strict environment of punitive discipline, are shown to be significantly more inclined to tell lies in order to cover up a misdeed (Talwar & Lee, 2011; Wang et al., 2017).

If theory of mind predicts the production of antisocial lies (Talwar & Lee, 2008), it does not appear to be a good predictor of prosocial lies. A few of the studies on this issue have not found any relation between children's theory of mind and their propensity to tell prosocial lies (Li et al., 2011; Talwar et al., 2017). For example, four-to-five-year-old children with more advanced false belief understanding did not show a greater propensity to help another by lying in order to boost the material gain of another individual (Talwar et al., 2017). Similarly, four-to-twelve-year-old children who passed the false-belief theory of mind task were not more inclined to tell a prosocial lie to cover up someone else's transgression (Gordon et al., 2014). Interestingly, children diagnosed with autistic spectrum disorder showing a theory of mind impairment are as likely to produce polite white lies as typical developing children (Li et al., 2011). Contrary to antisocial lies, evidence suggests that theory of mind may not be a critical factor that accounts for children's first productions of prosocial lies, such as white or polite lies.

In contrast to theory of mind, some evidence suggests that the development of executive function could be a better predictor of both antisocial and prosocial lies (Talwar et al., 2017; Gordon et al., 2014). The theory of mind training paradigm (Ding et al., 2015; Fu et al., 2017) is the closest putative evidence of a causal account of what might enable children to produce antisocial lies. However, to our knowledge, there is no equivalent causal account regarding prosocial lies, leaving open the crucial question as to what may explain the developmental emergence of this kind of lies. Prosocial lies go beyond the mere avoidance of punishment and could be, as we will propose next, a cardinal mark of human self-conscious psychology, i.e. of our unique concern for our own reputation and the reputation of our own group (Botto & Rochat, 2018).

7. *Self-Conscious Origins of Lying*

To the extent that human deception is intentional and not accountable merely by evolved instincts or physical features, such as the eyes on butterfly wings that scare off predators or formidable postures adopted to intimidate rivals, it is reasonable to think that some degree of theory of mind, executive function, and norm understanding is required in deception. Minimally, lying as intentional deception does require some construal as to what others may wrongly believe.

It also requires that intentional deceivers restrain themselves from exposing the truth they want to conceal. Finally, it entails some understanding of norms, in particular the expectation that others anticipate being told the truth.

In light of the existing literature (see above), the robust evidence of a developmental lag between the emergence of antisocial (two to three years) and prosocial lies (by four years) strongly suggests that the latter requires an additional competence. As a case in point, we have seen, for example, that the level of children's theory of mind predicts antisocial lies but does not predict prosocial lies (e.g. Li et al., 2011). This might be due to a ceiling effect, namely that all typical developing children would have acquired an understanding of false beliefs by the time they begin to produce prosocial lies (i.e. polite lies, white lies, and blue lies – lies that protect the in-group). The open question is: what might be the missing developmental link that would predict prosocial intents at concealing the truth to protect others from hurting? In other words, what does it take for a child to start lying, not just to avoid reprimands and self-maximize resources, but also eventually to protect, help, and favor others, even at their own cost?

One way to deal with this question is to look at the abundant research literature on possession, sharing, and fairness in development, particularly between the ages of three to five years, as children enter preschools, and as they start to produce both antisocial and prosocial lies (Rochat, 2014). This literature points to the fact that across cultures and social-economic status young children who are asked to share valuable items first tend to self-maximize. However, by five years, children have a significantly greater sense of justice and honesty. They start taking an explicit ethical stance toward others. For example, they spontaneously begin to engage in "costly punishment," sacrificing their own resources and possessions to rectify an injustice (Robbins & Rochat, 2011). They begin to behave with others in mind, not just on the lines of what would amount to immediate self-gratification.

However, it is not clear that the developmental emergence of prosocial lies stands for the development of altruism, i.e., the expression of selfless concern for the well-being of others. The production of prosocial lies could as well be driven by a new developing concern for one's own reputation. The child would then engage in prosocial actions, including prosocial lies, with the ulterior motive of promoting his or her own image for others' evaluation. Rather than being simply altruistic, prosocial lies may at the same time be selfish, though in a more indirect fashion than are antisocial lies. The latter are primarily geared either towards intentionally tricking others with the sole goal of self-maximizing one's profits, or toward covering up misdeeds to avoid reprimand.

The thesis regarding a concern for one's reputation is particularly plausible in light of the fact that when children are documented to produce prosocial lies at approximately four years of age, they are also documented to show explicit signs of caring about their own reputation. By five years, children begin to understand that one way of boosting their own social affiliation is to conform to a majority belief, even if this belief is blatantly false. This strong form of conformity accompanies a new sense of one's own reputation in reference to others (Cordonier et al., 2018). Already by two years of age, laboratory experiments show that children intentionally modify their behaviors to elicit positive evaluations from others. In a series of studies, Botto and Rochat (2018) showed that when the experimenter was watching, fourteen- to twenty-four-month-old children were more likely to engage with a toy that was associated with a positive value previously expressed by the experimenter, rather than one associated with a negative value. The results from the study suggest that by the age of two years, children are already aware of the fact that they are being watched (audience effect) and show concern for how they might be evaluated by an adult who is observing them and who might have either positive or negative reactions toward the object they explore and play with.

This early concern for other's evaluation is even documented in contexts without a real audience. Kelsey et al. (2018) made participating three-year-old children aware of an image of either an eye or a flower in the room, before instructing children to share their resources with others privately. It turns out that children shared more with others when they were aware of the image of a watching eye, but they shared less when they saw an image of a flower. This study provides further support that toddlers are sensitive to others' gaze and potential evaluation, actively trying to promote a positive rather than a negative social evaluation.

Still, this early sensitivity to others' evaluations in young children is quite different from the impression management we observe in adults. For one thing, infants and toddlers seem to care only about how they are evaluated by people with whom they have direct interactions. There is yet no clear evidence suggesting that toddlers may understand the idea of reputation – an abstract representation that can influence how people outside of their immediate social circle perceive and interact with them.

The reputational concern emerging in children by four to five years and indirectly expressed in inequity aversion, costly punishment, strong conformity, as well as the expression of an ethical stance would require a minimum of two basic self-conscious psychological elements. These elements are a) the competent understanding that others can form a shared impression of oneself; and (b) the insight that such shared impression may have prolonged social consequences for one's own social affiliation. This understanding of reputation is different from the sensitivity to others' evaluations that we observe in infants and toddlers. It also appears to emerge jointly with the production of prosocial lies. Some empirical evidence supports this view.

From the time when a majority of children develop a propensity to produce prosocial lies (four to five years, see above), a number of studies using various experimental paradigms also show that children develop an explicit concern for their own reputation (Engelmann et al., 2012; Haun et al., 2014; Hermann et al., 2013; Leimgruber et al., 2012; Piazza et al., 2011). In one such study, for example, Banerjee, Bennett, and Luke (2012) instructed four-to-nine-year-old children to imagine themselves as transgressors of social conventional rules and asked them what they would do following the transgression and the reasons behind it. Children as young as four explicitly expressed their concern about how they might be perceived by others. This concern becomes more prominent and generalized in older children's responses. In particular, Engelmann and colleagues (2013) found that by five years children tend to be less generous in their sharing when the recipient was anonymous as compared to someone they knew they had to interact with in the future. The results suggest that children recognize that the way they behave now may impact future social affiliation and evaluation by others with whom they will interact. Compared to infants and toddlers, by five years children develop a more explicit and future-oriented sense of reputation.

8. *Summary and Conclusion*

With this chapter, we have tried to make the case that deception in human ontogeny needs to be thought of in the context of our uniquely self-conscious psychology. This psychology is a trademark of our species. We reflect upon ourselves through the evaluative eyes of others, and we have a unique concern for what one ought to do in order to be affiliated with others – a concern for reputation.

From an early age, we know that others constantly judge us and that our social affiliation depends on that judgment. Our research shows that as children start passing the mirror mark test, using personal pronouns like I, me, or mine, they also start to strategize about how they present themselves to the world, in particular to the evaluative eyes of others (Botto & Rochat, 2018; 2019). They start to promote positive evaluations from others and avoid negative judgments. They also start to conform to and abide by rules and norms in order to foster their social affiliation and avoid social rejection (Rochat, 2009).

We are a species that cares about reputation. Our reputational concern leads to complex human social emotions such as guilt and shame, both of which are trademarks of our self-conscious psychology, with its first clear manifestations starting in the third year. The word reputation derives from the Latin verb *putare*, to compute or to calculate. It literally stands for the calculation of the impression one projects onto the social world. It entails a secondary 'meta' level of recursive thinking. This meta-level combines one's own self-representation and the imagined representation that others might hold about oneself. This secondary level of recursive thinking (I know that you know that they know etc.) and combined "dual" representation of first and third-person perspectives on the self is the building block of the human self-conscious psychology that children develop and manifest from around two to three years.

Human self-conscious psychology contributes to the beginning of children's careers as deliberate lie-tellers, whose first inclination to deceive others is to avoid punishment or other harmful consequences. But soon after, young children's lies also start to be driven by a concern for their own reputation. We think that it is in the impression management and strategic self-presentation (Goffman, 1959) emerging by two to three years of age that we find the source for the motives behind particular kinds of human deception. This motivation behind the uniquely human deception includes not only the deliberate self-maximizing and self-protective concealment of truth to others, but also, by four years, the deliberate prosocial inclination to conceal the truth to benefit others.

As far as we know, prosocial deception appears to be a human trademark, and we think that it is linked to our species' unique self-conscious psychology. The concern for reputation is a spin-off of the human capacity to generate secondary dual representation about themselves, as well as to compare, hold in long-term memory, and adjust this representation to norms that are shared with others (Rochat, 2018). Recent empirical evidence supports this general idea by showing that theory of mind, executive function, and norm understanding in children predict their proclivity to lie antisocially. Here we propose that another factor driving this development is the concern for reputation – a spin-off of the human ability to generate dual secondary representation about the self through the evaluative eyes of others. In turn, this ability is the expression of a psychology that is uniquely self-conscious, developed by children as they start to speak (Latin *infans*, i.e. without speech). From this point on, communication becomes symbolic and language increasingly syntactic. Children also develop autonoetic (episodic) memory that allows them to archive and revise the imagined impressions of themselves as presumably recorded in the mind of others. They become human: self-consciously proper, caring about reputation, and adept at lying accordingly.

Works Cited

Banerjee, Robin, Mark Bennett, and Nikki Luke (2012) "Children's Reasoning about Self-Representation Following Rule Violations: The Role of Self-Focused Attention." *Child Development* 83.5: 1805–1821. Web. 11 Nov. 2020.

Bateson, Melissa, Daniel Nettle, and Gilbert Roberts (2006) "Cues of Being Watched Enhance Cooperation in a Real-World Setting." *Biology Letters* 2.3: 412–414. Web. 11 Nov. 2020.

Birch, Susan A. J., Sophie A. Vauthier, and Paul Bloom (2008) "Three-and Four-Year-Olds Spontaneously Use Others' Past Performance to Guide Their Learning." *Cognition* 107.3: 1018–1034. Web. 11 Nov. 2020.

Botto, Sara V., Philippe Rochat (2018) "Sensitivity to the Evaluation of Others Emerges by 24 Months." *Developmental Psychology* 54.9: 1723–1734. Web. 11 Nov. 2020.

Botto, Sara V., and Philippe Rochat (2019) "Evaluative Audience Perception (EAP): How Children Come to Care about Reputation." *Child Development Perspectives* 13.3: 180–185. Web. 11 Nov. 2020.

Bugnyar, Thomas, and Kurt Kotrschal (2002) "Observational Learning and the Raiding of Food Caches in Ravens, Corvus Corax: Is It 'Tactical' Deception?" *Animal Behaviour* 64.2: 185–195. Web. 11 Nov. 2020.

Bugnyar, Thomas, and Kurt Kotrschal, K. (2004) "Leading a Conspecific away from Food in Ravens (Corvus Corax)?" *Animal Cognition* 7.2: 69–76. Web. 11 Nov. 2020.

Bywater, Candice L., and Robbie S. Wilson (2012) "Is Honesty the Best Policy? Testing Signal Reliability in Fiddler Crabs when Receiver-Dependent Costs are High." *Functional Ecology* 26.4: 804–811. Web. 11 Nov. 2020.

Cantarero, Katarzyna, Piotr Szarota, Eftychia Stamkou, Marisol Navas, and Alejandra del Carmen Dominguez Espinosa (2018). "When Is a Lie Acceptable? Work and Private Life Lying Acceptance Depends on Its Beneficiary." *The Journal of Social Psychology* 158.2: 220–235. Web. 11 Nov. 2020.

Carl, Talia, and Kay Bussey (2019) "Contextual and Age-Related Determinants of Children's Lie Telling to Conceal a Transgression." *Infant and Child Development* 28.3: n. pag. Web. 11 Nov. 2020.

Carlson, Stephanie M., and Louis J. Moses (2001) "Individual differences in inhibitory control and children's theory of mind." *Child Development* 72.4: 1032–1053. Web. 11 Nov. 2020.

Corriveau, Kathleen, and Paul L. Harris (2009) "Choosing Your Informant: Weighing Familiarity and Recent Accuracy." *Developmental Science* 12.3: 426–437. Web. 11 Nov. 2020.

Cordonier, Laurent, Theresa Nettles, and Philippe Rochat (2018) "Strong and Strategic Conformity Understanding by 3- and 5-Year-Old Children." *British Journal of Developmental Psychology* 36.3: 438–451. Web. 11 Nov. 2020.

Darwin, Charles (1872) *The Expression of the Emotions in Man and Animals.* London: John Murray.

Darwin, Charles (1877) "A Biographical Sketch of an Infant." *Mind* 2.7: 285–294. Web. 11 Nov. 2020.

DePaulo, Bella M., and Deborah A. Kashy (1998) "Everyday lies in close and casual relationships." *Journal of Personality and Social Psychology* 74.1: 63–79.

de Waal, Frans (1982) *Chimpanzee Politics: Power and Sex*. Baltimore: The Johns Hopkins Univ. Press.

Diamond, Adele, and Kathleen Lee (2011) "Interventions shown to Aid Executive Function Development in Children 4–12 Years Old. " *Science* 333.6045: 959–964.

Ding, Xiao Pan, Gail D. Heyman, Genyue Fu, Bo Zhu, and Kang Lee (2018) "Young Children Discover How to Deceive in 10 Days: A Microgenetic Study." *Developmental Science* 21.3: n. pag. Web. 11 Nov. 2020.

Ding, Xiao Pan, Henry M. Wellman, Yu Wang, Genyue Fu, and Kang Lee (2015) "Theory-of-Mind Training Causes Honest Young Children to Lie." *Psychological Science* 26.11: 1812–1821. Web. 11 Nov. 2020.

Engelmann, Jan M., Esther Herrmann, and Michael Tomasello (2012) "Five-Year Olds, but Not Chimpanzees, Attempt to Manage their Reputations." *PLoS One* 7.10: n. pag. Web. 11 Nov. 2020.

Engelmann, Jan M., Harriet Over, Esther Herrmann, and Michael Tomasello (2013) "Young Children Care More about their Reputation with In-group Members and Potential Reciprocators." *Developmental Science* 16.6: 952–958. Web. 11 Nov. 2020.

Engelmann, Jan M., Esther Herrmann, and Michael Tomasello (2018) "Concern for Group Reputation Increases Prosociality in Young Children." *Psychological Science* 29.2: 181–190. Web. 11 Nov. 2020.

Engelmann, Jan M., and Diotima J. Rapp (2018) "The Influence of Reputational Concerns on Children's Prosociality." *Current Opinion in Psychology* 20: 92–95. Web. 11 Nov. 2020.

Evans, Angela D., and Kang Lee (2011) "Verbal Deception from Late Childhood to Middle Adolescence and its Relation to Executive Functioning Skills." *Developmental Psychology* 47.4: 1108–1116. Web. 11 Nov. 2020.

Evans, Angela D., and Kang Lee (2013) "Emergence of Lying in Very Young Children." *Developmental Psychology* 49.10: 1958–1963. Web. 11 Nov. 2020.

Fu, Genyue, Gail Heyman, Miao Qian, Tengfei Guo, and Kang Lee (2016) "Young Children with a Positive Reputation to Maintain are Less Likely to Cheat." *Developmental Science* 19.2: 275–283. Web. 11 Nov. 2020.

Fu, Genyue, and Kang Lee (2007) "Social Grooming in the Kindergarten: The Emergence of Flattery Behavior." *Developmental Science* 10.2: 255–265. Web. 11 Nov. 2020.

Fu, Genyue, Liyang Sai, Fang Yuan, and Kang Lee (2018) "Young Children's Self-Benefiting Lies and Their Relation to Executive Functioning and Theory of Mind." *Infant and Child Development* 27.1: n. pag. Web. 11 Nov. 2020.

Fujii, Takayuki, Haruto Takagishi, Michiko Koizumi, and Hiroyuki Okada (2015) "The Effect of Direct and Indirect Monitoring on Generosity among Preschoolers." *Scientific Reports* 5.9025: n. pag. Web. 11 Nov. 2020.

Gino, Francesca, and Lamar Pierce (2010) "Lying to Level the Playing Field: Why People May Dishonestly Help or Hurt Others to Create Equity." *Journal of Business Ethics* 95.1: 89–103. Web. 11 Nov. 2020.

Goffman, Erving (1959) *The Presentation of Self in Everyday Life*. Garden City, NY: Anchor Books.

Gordon, Heidi M., Thomas D. Lyon, and Kang Lee (2014) "Social and Cognitive Factors Associated with Children's Secret-Keeping for a Parent." *Child Development* 85.6: 2374–2388. Web. 11 Nov. 2020.

Hall, Katie, Mike W. Oram, Mathew W. Campbell, Timothy M. Eppley, Richard W. Byrne, and Frans B.M. de Waal (2016) "Chimpanzee Uses Manipulative Gaze Cues to Conceal and Reveal Information to Foraging Competitor." *American Journal of Primatology* 79.3: n. pag. Web. 11 Nov. 2020.

Hamlin, J. Kiley, Karen Wynn, and Paul Bloom (2007) "Social Evaluation by Preverbal Infants." *Nature* 450.7169: 557–559. Web. 11 Nov. 2020.

Haun, Daniel B., Yvonne Rekers, and Michael Tomasello (2014) "Children Conform to the Behavior of Peers; Other Great Apes Stick with What They Know." *Psychological Science* 25.12: 2160–2167. Web. 11 Nov. 2020.

Herrmann, Esther, Stefanie Keupp, Brian Hare, Amrisha Vaish, and Michael Tomasello (2013) "Direct and Indirect Reputation Formation in Nonhuman Great Apes (Pan Paniscus, Pan Troglodytes, Gorilla Gorilla, Pongo Pygmaeus) and Human Children (Homo Sapiens)." *Journal of Comparative Psychology* 127.1: 63–75. Web. 11 Nov. 2020.

Hirata, Satoshi, and Tetsuro Matsuzawa (2001) "Tactics to Obtain a Hidden Food Item in Chimpanzee Pairs (Pan Troglodytes)." *Animal Cognition* 4.3–4: 285–295. Web. 11 Nov. 2020.

Igic, Branislav, Jessica McLachlan, Inkeri Lehtinen, and Robert D. Magrath (2015) "Crying Wolf to a Predator: Deceptive Vocal Mimicry by a Bird Protecting Young." *Proceedings of the Royal Society B: Biological Sciences* 282.1809: n. pag. Web. 11 Nov. 2020.

Iezzoni, Lisa, Sowmya R. Rao, Catherine M. DesRoches, Christine Vogeli, and Eric G. Campbell (2012) "Survey Shows That at Least Some Physicians are not Always Open or Honest with Patients." *Health Affairs* 31.2: 383–391. Web. 11 Nov. 2020.

Jakubowska, Joanna, and Marta Białecka-Pikul (2019) "A New Model of the Development of Deception: Disentangling the Role of False-Belief Understanding in Deceptive Ability." *Social Development* 29.1: 21–40. Web. 11 Nov. 2020.

Jersáková, Jana, Steven D. Johnson, and Pavel Kindlmann (2006) "Mechanisms and Evolution of Deceptive Pollination in Orchids." *Biological Reviews* 81.2: 219–235.

Kelsey, Caroline, Tobias Grossmann, and Amrisha Vaish (2018) "Early Reputation Management: Three-Year-Old Children are More Generous Following Exposure to Eyes." *Frontiers in Psychology* 9. 698: n. pag. Web. 11 Nov. 2020.

Koenig, Melissa A., Fabrice Clément, and Paul L. Harris (2004) "Trust in Testimony: Children's Use of True and False Statements." *Psychological Science* 15.10: 694–698. Web. 11 Nov. 2020.

Levine, Emma, and Maurice E. Schweitzer (2014) "Are Liars Ethical? On the Tension between Benevolence and Honesty." *Journal of Experimental Social Psychology* 53: 107–117. Web. 11 Nov. 2020.

Levine, Emma, and Maurice E. Schweitzer (2015) "Prosocial Lies: When Deception Breeds Trust." *Organizational Behavior and Human Decision Processes* 126: 88–106. Web. 11 Nov. 2020.

Lev-Yadun, Simcha (2006) "Defensive Coloration in Plants: A Review of Current Ideas about Anti-Herbivore Coloration Strategies." *Floriculture, Ornamental and Plant Biotechnology: Advances and Topical Issues* 4: 292–299.

Heyman, Gail, Monica A. Sweet, and Kang Lee (2009) "Children's Reasoning about Lie-Telling and Truth-Telling in Politeness Contexts." *Social Development* 18.3: 728–746. Web. 11 Nov. 2020.

Leimgruber, Kristin L., Alex Shaw, Laurie R. Santos, and Kristina R. Olson (2012) "Young Children are More Generous When Others are Aware of Their Actions." *PloS One* 7.10: n. pag. Web. 11 Nov. 2020.

Lewis, Michael, Catherine Stanger, and Margaret W. Sullivan (1989) "Deception in 3-Year-Olds." *Developmental Psychology* 25.3: 439–443. Web. 11 Nov. 2020.

Li, Annie S., Elizabeth A. Kelley, Angela D. Evans, and Kang Lee (2011) "Exploring the Ability to Deceive in Children with Autism Spectrum Disorders." *Journal of Autism and Developmental Disorders* 41.2: 185–195. Web. 11 Nov. 2020.

Lount, Robert B., Jr., Chen-Bo Zhong, Niro Sivanathan, and J. Keith Murnighan (2008) "Getting Off on the Wrong Foot: The Timing of a Breach and the Restoration of Trust." *Personality and Social Psychology Bulletin* 34.12: 1601–1612. Web. 11 Nov. 2020.

Ma, Fengling, Angela D. Evans, Ying Liu, Pacino Luo, and Fen Xu (2015) "To Lie or Not to Lie? The Influence of Parenting and Theory-of-Mind Understanding on Three-Year-Old Children's Honesty." *Journal of Moral Education* 44.2: 198–212. Web. 11 Nov. 2020.

Milinski, Manfred, Dirk Semmann, and Hans-Jürgen Krambeck (2002) "Reputation Helps Solve the 'Tragedy of the Commons.'" *Nature* 415.6870: 424–426. Web. 11 Nov. 2020.

Newton, Paul, Vasudevi Reddy, and Ray Bull (2000) "Children's Everyday Deception and Performance on False-Belief Tasks." *British Journal of Developmental Psychology* 18. 2: 297–317. Web. 11 Nov. 2020.

Palmieri, John L., and Theodore A. Stern (2009) "Lies in the Doctor-Patient Relationship." *Primary Care Companion to the Journal of Clinical Psychiatry* 11.4: 163–168. Web. 11 Nov. 2020.

Polak, Alan, and Paul L. Harris (1999) "Deception by Young Children Following Noncompliance." *Developmental Psychology* 35.2: 561–568. Web. 11 Nov. 2020.

Popliger, Mina, Victoria Talwar, and Angela Crossman (2011) "Predictors of Children's Prosocial Lie-Telling: Motivation, Socialization Variables, and Moral Understanding." *Journal of Experimental Child Psychology* 110.3: 373–392. Web. 11 Nov. 2020.

Piazza, Jared, Jesse M. Bering, and Gordon Ingram (2011) "'Princess Alice is Watching You': Children's Belief in an Invisible Person Inhibits Cheating." *Journal of Experimental Child Psychology* 109.3: 311–320. Web. 11 Nov. 2020.

Robbins, Erin, and Philippe Rochat (2011) "Emerging Signs of Strong Reciprocity in Human Ontogeny." *Frontiers in Psychology* 2: n. pag. Web. 11 Nov. 2020.

Robinson, Sandra L. (1996) "Trust and Breach of the Psychological Contract." *Administrative Science Quarterly* 41.4: 574–599. Web. 11 Nov. 2020.

Rochat, Philippe (2009) *Others in Mind: Social Origins of Self-Consciousness*. Cambridge: Cambridge Univ. Press.

Rochat, Philippe (2013) "The Gaze of Others." *Navigating the Social World: What Infants, Children, and Other Species Can Teach Us.* Ed. Mahzarin Banaji and Susan Gelman. Oxford: Oxford Univ. Press. 205–211.

Rochat, Philippe (2014) *Origins of Possession: Owning and Sharing in Development*. Cambridge: Cambridge Univ. Press.

Rochat, Philippe (2018) "The Ontogeny of Human Self-Consciousness." *Current Directions in Psychological Science* 27.5: 345–350. Web. 11 Nov. 2020.

Rochat, Philippe, Tanya Broesch, and Katherine Jayne (2012) "Social Awareness and Early Self-Recognition." *Consciousness and Cognition* 21.3: 1491–1497.

Rochat, Philippe, Maria D.G. Dias, Guo Liping, Tanya Broesch, Claudia Passos-Ferreira, Ashley Winning, and Britt Berg (2009) "Fairness in Distributive Justice by 3- and 5-Year-Olds across Seven Cultures." *Journal of Cross-Cultural Psychology* 40.3: 416–442. Web. 11 Nov. 2020.

Sheskin, Mark, Coralie Chevallier, Stéphanie Lambert, and Nicolas Baumard (2014) "Life-History Theory Explains Childhood Moral Development." *Trends in Cognitive Sciences* 18.12: 613–615. Web. 11 Nov. 2020.

Silver, Ike M., and Alex Shaw (2018) "Pint-Sized Public Relations: The Development of Reputation Management." *Trends in Cognitive Sciences* 22.4: 277–279. Web. 11 Nov. 2020.

Sperber, Dan, and Nicolas Baumard (2012) "Moral Reputation: An Evolutionary and Cognitive Perspective." *Mind & Language* 27.5: 495–518. Web. 11 Nov. 2020.

Svetlova, Margarita, Sara R. Nichols, and Celia A. Brownell (2010) "Toddlers' Prosocial Behavior: From Instrumental to Empathic to Altruistic Helping." *Child Development* 81.6: 1814–1827. Web. 11 Nov. 2020.

Sylwester, Karolina, and Gilbert Roberts (2010) "Cooperators Benefit through Reputation-Based Partner Choice in Economic Games." *Biology Letters* 6: 659–662. Web. 11 Nov. 2020.

Talwar, Victoria, and Angela Crossman (2011) "From Little White Lies to Filthy Liars: The Evolution of Honesty and Deception in Young Children." *Advances in Child Development and Behavior* 40: 139–179. Web. 11 Nov. 2020.

Talwar, Victoria, Angela Crossman, and Joshua Wyman (2017) "The Role of Executive Functioning and Theory of Mind in Children's Lies for Another and for Themselves." *Early Childhood Research Quarterly* 41: 126–135. Web. 11 Nov. 2020.

Talwar, Victoria, Heidi M. Gordon, and Kang Lee (2007) "Lying in the Elementary School Years: Verbal Deception and Its Relation to Second-Order Belief Understanding." *Developmental Psychology* 43.3: 804–810. Web. 11 Nov. 2020.

Talwar, Victoria, and Kang Lee (2002a) "Development of Lying to Conceal a Transgression: Children's Control of Expressive Behaviour during Verbal Deception." *International Journal of Behavioral Development* 26.5: 436–444. Web. 11 Nov. 2020.

Talwar, Victoria, and Kang Lee (2002b) "Emergence of White-Lie Telling in Children between 3 and 7 Years of Age." *Merrill-Palmer Quarterly* 48.2: 160–181. Web. 11 Nov. 2020.

Talwar, Victoira, and Kang Lee (2008) "Social and Cognitive Correlates of Children's Lying Behavior." *Child Development* 79.4: 866–881. Web. 11 Nov. 2020.

Talwar, Victoria, Kang Lee, Nicolas Bala, and R.C.L. Lindsay (2004) "Children's Lie-Telling to Conceal a Parent's Transgression: Legal Implications." *Law and Human Behavior* 28.4: 411–435. Web. 11 Nov. 2020.

Talwar, Victoria, and Kang Lee (2011) "A Punitive Environment Fosters Children's Dishonesty: A Natural Experiment." *Child Development* 82.6: 1751–1758. Web. 11 Nov. 2020.

Talwar, Victoria, Susan M. Murphy, and Kang Lee (2007) "White Lie-Telling in Children for Politeness Purposes." *International Journal of Behavioral Development* 31.1: 1–11. Web. 11 Nov. 2020.

Wang, Lamei, LiqivZhu, and Zhenlin Wang (2017) "Parental Mind-Mindedness but not False Belief Understanding Predicts Hong Kong Children's Lie-Telling Behavior in a Temptation Resistance Task." *Journal of Experimental Child Psychology* 162: 89–100. Web. 11 Nov. 2020.

Warneken, Felix, and Emily Orlins (2015) "Children Tell White Lies to Make Others Feel Better." *British Journal of Developmental Psychology* 33.3: 259–270. Web. 11 Nov. 2020.

Warneken, Felix, and Michael Tomasello (2007) "Helping and Cooperation at 14 Months of Age." *Infancy* 11.3: 271–294. Web. 11 Nov. 2020.

Wellman, Henry M., and David Liu (2004) "Scaling of Theory-of-Mind Tasks." *Child Development* 75.2: 523–541. Web. 11 Nov. 2020.

Whiten, Andrew, and Daniel W. Byrne (1988) "Tactical Deception in Primates." *Behavioral and Brain Sciences* 11.02: 233–273. Web. 11 Nov. 2020.

Williams, Shanna, Kelsey Moore, Angela M. Crossman, and Victoria Talwar (2016) "The Role of Executive Functions and Theory of Mind in Children's Prosocial Lie-Telling." *Journal of Experimental Child Psychology* 141: 256–266. Web. 11 Nov. 2020.

Wilson, Annie E., Melissa D. Smith, and Hildy S. Ross (2003) "The Nature and Effects of Young Children's Lies." *Social Development* 12.1: 21–45. Web. 11 Nov. 2020.

Unlawful and Lawful Lies

Frank L. Schäfer

1. Introduction

> An impostor in German Parliament is spectacular – but [...] is not an isolated case. In times of online applications and career portals on the Internet, the bending of biographies has become a mass phenomenon. Applicants invent hobbies, exaggerate the portfolio of former positions and forge qualifications and degrees. In the wake of automated application procedures, many companies have opened their doors to fraudsters and swindlers. (Michler 2016, trans. FLS)

This press commentary concerns a member of the German Federal Parliament (*Bundestag*) who throughout several legislative periods had deceived voters about her qualifications by means of a largely fictitious curriculum vitae. I will discuss this case in greater detail below. Michler takes the incident as an opportunity to examine recruitment practices in private companies and to describe fake CVs as a mass phenomenon. Wherever money and prestige are involved, the risk of lies increases. Often, such lies lead to serious legal consequences.

This article examines the question of how the German legal system classifies lies and whether in exceptional cases it permits lying as lawful behavior (overview: Depenheuer 2005). Generally, one would tend to discuss such lies under the label of 'white' lies rather than 'lawful' lies. The legal review that I will conduct in this essay will provide the basis for a narratological analysis. The narratological analysis will not focus on the largely straightforward case of the unlawful lie, but on the exceptional case of the lawful lie. The question to be examined is how this special case fits into the system of factuality and fictionality. We will see that a lawful lie may shift the boundaries between factuality and fictionality.

2. Definition and Relevance of Lies in the German Legal Context

In the German legal system, the lie remains unclassified as a legal term. Instead, statutes use more concrete descriptors, such as a victim "induced to make a declaration of intent by deceit" (section 123[1] Civil Code)[1] or "by causing or

[1] Unless otherwise stated, the statutes cited are those of the German legal system. Quotations by articles/sections, paragraphs (number in first brackets) and sentences (number in second brackets). – The English translations of the German statutes are taken from

maintaining an error under false pretences or distorting or suppressing true facts" (section 263[1] Criminal Code; "einen Irrtum erregt oder unterhält"). In the first case, the legislator emphasizes the liar's intention, in the second case the act of deception. In many cases the legal system punishes lying with drastic sanctions: prison sentences for fraud (section 263 Criminal Code), voidability of a contract on the grounds of deceit (section 123 Civil Code) or damages for the tort called "intentional damage contrary to public policy" (section 826 Civil Code). All these cases fall under the uncodified definition of a lie as a deliberate assertion of false facts.

On an objective level, the mere fact of a lie does not presuppose that another person suffers from entertaining a false belief or is necessarily damaged by it. A lie is no less a lie if the person meant to be deceived recognizes the deceit and is therefore not actually deceived. The question, then, is whether an attempted deception should still be sanctioned. Section 263(2) of the Criminal Code punishes the mere lie if the offender aims to benefit from it even though he or she fails to obtain a pecuniary benefit from the victim. The example of fraud in criminal law teaches us that the lie and the intention to defraud somebody are treated as separate cases. Section 263 of the Criminal Code distinguishes between "causing or maintaining an error ["einen Irrtum erregt oder unterhält"] by pretending false facts or by distorting or suppressing true facts" on the one hand and, on the other, the "intent of obtaining for himself or a third person an unlawful material benefit." For a fraudster to be punished, s/he must not only lie willfully but must also act with the intention of enrichment.

Although statutes do not use the word *lie*, lies are very much part of the legal discussion and thus appear in judgements and legal literature. The discussion about the protection of lies at the level of basic rights clearly shows this. The expression of opinions falls under the basic right to freedom of expression in article 5(1)(1) of the Federal Constitution (*Grundgesetz*). Whereas lies concern verifiable facts, expressions of opinion are based instead on personal values. Factual statements can be true or untrue; the understanding is that a judge can determine their truthfulness on the basis of evidence. Opinions, on the other hand, cannot be true or untrue; rather, they are well-reasoned or ill-considered. There is, nevertheless, an intersection between statements of facts and opinions: the basic right to freedom of expression also includes the reference to true facts which are opinion-related and thus contribute to the formation of a public opinion (BVerfGE 61, 1, 8).[2]

---

the Federal Ministry of Justice at https://www.gesetze-im-internet.de/. They are therefore official translations.

2 For decisions, first the court and then the reference is quoted. The abbreviations can be found in the appendix. – From 2007 onwards, German decisions are cited according to the initial page plus recital, the older decisions according to initial page plus cited page.

As for lies, by contrast, the judiciary and the prevailing conservative academic view in law exclude lies from the protection of the freedom of expression because they are not a legitimate means of expression in society (BVerfGE 99, 185, 197; BVerfGE 54, 208, 219). A lie cannot contribute to the democratic process of forming public opinion (Grimm 1995, 1699). Therefore, the legal system regularly sanctions the dissemination of false facts as opposed to that of offensive opinions, which are only prohibited in exceptional circumstances. Of course, this procedure is not undisputed. A more liberal view seeks to extend the scope of the protected freedom of expression to lies (Schmidt-Jortzig 2009, section 162 recital 22). Following this argument, if opinions fall under protection regardless of their content, then this must also apply to facts. This view draws attention to the problem that it is often difficult for the audience to distinguish between untrue and true statements of fact and between opinions and statements of fact. According to this line of argument, lies fall under the basic right of freedom of expression. However, when set against conflicting basic rights (e.g. the rights of defamed parties), the right to freedom of expression is considered less important and the legislator may therefore prohibit lies from being condoned under the umbrella of the freedom of expression. Despite their disparate underlying premises, both views on the treatment of lies – the conservative and the liberal – in the end arrive at the same result, namely that lies are usually forbidden.

Below the level of constitutional law lies are also an important issue, but again they do not function as a term distinguishing lawful and unlawful behavior. The argumentative starting point is the duty to tell the truth in legal contexts. A lie violates the duty to speak the truth and triggers a sanction. Otherwise, legal (as well as social) relations would collapse, since they presuppose a reliance on true facts. But this understanding is not without exceptions. As we will see in what follows, the legal system in some exceptional cases actually justifies lying so that no sanction applies. In other words, the permitted lie is treated like a true statement. For lawyers, the relevant boundary is therefore not between a false statement (lie) and a true statement, but between permitted and prohibited statements.

How does this differentiation relate to the lie as an object of the protection of basic rights? Whoever follows the conservative view and excludes the lie from the freedom of opinion and expression must protect the lawful lie by means of other basic rights such as the general right of personality (*Allgemeines Persönlichkeitsrecht*). On the other hand, whoever accepts the lie under the freedom of opinion will *a fortiori* include the permitted lie under this basic right. In both cases, the lawful lie enjoys priority over the principle of honesty in the course of business or legal affairs.

3. *Lawful Lies: Job Applications*

Let us now look at possible exceptions to the implicit legal ban on lying, starting with labor law. Lawful lies in labor law specifically concern the job application process. The starting point for the differentiation between unlawful and lawful lies can be found in section 123(1) of the Civil Code: "A person who has been induced to make a declaration of intent by deceit or unlawfully by duress may avoid his declaration." Thus, a person who has been induced to enter into a contract by deception can cancel the contract retroactively, as if this contract had never existed. The legislator assumes that the fraudulent deception in section 123(1) of the Civil Code is always unlawful:

> In response to the suggestion to delete the word 'unlawfully' in paragraph 1, it was first stated by general agreement that it referred only to the case of duress and not to the case of fraudulent deception, since the unlawfulness of the latter was self-evident. (Mugdan 1899, 965)

However, legal practice has shown that a lie does not always have to be unlawful but may be permitted in exceptional cases. A lawful lie therefore does not entitle the deceived person to nullify the contract. For this purpose – that is, to nullify the contract – the judge must reduce the scope of section 123(1) of the Civil Code, such that the lawful lie no longer falls under its provision, contrary to the section's wording. This restriction of the norm ensures a symmetry of deception with duress, which explicitly requires the threat to be unlawful (Armbrüster 2018, section 123 Civil Code, recital 19).

Section 123 of the Civil Code is also applicable in labor law, since the general contractual provisions of the Civil Code apply to this special area of the law. In principle, an employee must answer questions from the employer truthfully. This duty of truth is a concretization of the duty of loyalty, which already exists at the stage at which an employment contract is being negotiated (BAGE 15, 261, 263). The applicant must therefore provide truthful information about her/his professional qualifications and other relevant facts. In some cases, however, the job candidate is not obliged to tell the truth. This is the case, for instance, when the question violates anti-discrimination laws and puts a candidate at an unlawful disadvantage.

As will be seen, the exceptions in labor law which permit a lie lack a common denominator. The individual cases differ greatly in their scope. First, the strongest case: during pregnancy, the female candidate has a nearly absolute right to lie. The prospective employer is not permitted to ask a candidate about existing or planned pregnancies during the job interview. This question is to be regarded as inadmissible discrimination on the grounds of gender and therefore violates the prohibition of discrimination in sections 1 and 7 of the General Act on Equal Treatment. Section 1 of the General Act on Equal Treatment mentions gender along with race, ethnic origin, religion, belief, disability, age and sexual orientation. Direct recourse to article 3(2) of the Federal Constitution on equal treatment is therefore unnecessary from the outset. Recent case law expands the gender-based prohibition of discrimination in order to improve the protection of women. This prohibition is applicable in cases exclusively concerning women applying for a job (BAG NJW 1993, 1154, 1155) but also in cases in which the employment prohibition under the Maternity Protection Act bars a pregnant woman from working upon employment (ECJ [2001] ECR I-6993). It also comes into play if a candidate is to be hired for a limited period and cannot work for a substantial part of the contractual term due to pregnancy (BAG NZA 2003, 848-849).

In almost all other cases, candidates have only a limited right to lie because the employer's interest partially outweighs the potential interest of the employee. Most important here are cases of acute and chronic diseases, drug addiction and infections, religious affiliation, party and trade union membership, previous convictions as well as financial situation.

As regards diseases, the judiciary extensively limits the scope of lawful questions in order to protect the sphere of privacy. According to strict case law, only the following questions are allowed:

> Is there an illness or an impairment of the state of health which limits the aptitude for the intended job permanently or periodically? Are there any infectious diseases that do not impair performance but endanger future colleagues or customers? Is an incapacity to work to be expected at the time of commencement of employment or in the foreseeable future, e.g. due to a planned operation, an approved cure or also due to an acute illness that currently exists? (BAG NJW 1985, 645)

Equally strict are the requirements for questions regarding religious denomination, trade union membership and party affiliation. Questions on these issues are only permitted when someone applies to a church, party or to another so-called *Tendenzbetrieb* [special interest group], in which educational, artistic, political or scientific goals are inherent in the constitution of that company or employing agency (see section 9 General Act on Equal Treatment). Applicants for a management position, however, must disclose a Scientology membership because this organization is argued to attempt to penetrate executive levels with its members (OLG Stuttgart NJW 1999, 3640, 3641).

In other areas, the right to ask questions depends on the specific job. Section 164 of the Social Code IX states: "Employers must not discriminate against severely disabled employees because of their disability. For details see the provisions of the General Equal Treatment Act."[3] However, it is not considered discrimination if a disabled person cannot carry out a specific job because of her/his disability and the future employer asks for a disclosure of the applicant's disability. In the case of criminal convictions, a candidate must disclose previ-

[3] No official translation available.

ous convictions that raise doubts regarding her/his suitability for the job in question (BAGE 91, 349, 353: police officer concealing a fine for driving an uninsured vehicle). More rigorous requirements apply to managers. Owing to the societal pressure to serve as role models – indeed, to follow rules almost unconditionally – managers are obligated to disclose all previous convictions. In addition, there are two cases which concretize the requirement of disclosures for criminal convictions. Section 53 of the Federal Central Criminal Register Act stipulates that an offender does not have to disclose minor convictions or convictions that are to be deleted. Conversely, a candidate must state previous convictions without being asked to do so if a legally binding conviction will lead to the imminent imposition of a prison sentence of several months (LAG Frankfurt am Main NZA 1987, 352, 353).

4. *Lawful Lies: Criminal Trials*

4.1. Prelude: Lies in Criminal Law

Criminal law in many circumstances punishes lies. A justification of lying only applies in the rarest of cases. The law's quite comprehensive protection of truth demonstrates forcefully that lies are considered to be fundamentally inadmissible; in many cases, they are not merely treated as a kind of wrongdoing with consequences under private law but are considered worthy of criminal prosecution. Nevertheless, there remain many loopholes for the lie if it does not violate a prohibition of criminal law.

For easier comprehensibility, I will briefly introduce the most important crimes that deal with lies. Fraud in all its forms is at the heart of criminal sanctions which involve lying. In addition to general fraud (section 263 Criminal Code), the following are all punishable offenses wherein the offender lies to others: computer fraud (section 263a Criminal Code), subsidy fraud (section 264 Criminal Code), capital investment fraud (section 264a Criminal Code), insurance fraud (section 265 Criminal Code) and obtaining credit by deception (section 265b Criminal Code). Section 263 of the Criminal Code protects individual assets (BGHSt 34, 199, 203). In addition, section 264a of the Criminal Code ensures the functionality of the capital market (BGHZ 116, 7, 13); section 265 of the Criminal Code the functionality of the insurance industry (BGHSt 60, 15 recital 53); and section 265b of the Criminal Code the functionality of the credit market (BGHSt 60, 15 recital 42). Section 264 of the Criminal Code serves the general interest in development of effects and the freedom of the state to strengthen the economy, and only indirectly protects assets (BGHSt 59, 15 recital 53). Other fraudulent offenses such as sports betting fraud (section 265c Criminal Code) presuppose lies, but do not mention them in their wording. False testimony (section 153 Criminal Code), perjury (section 154 Criminal Code), false accusation (section 164 Criminal Code) and intentional defamation (section 187 Criminal Code) are additional crimes requiring a lie. The protected legal interests here range from public to private commitments. Criminal offenses related to politics are discussed below in sections 5 and 6 of this article.

The criminality of the so-called Auschwitz lie deserves special attention, since the lawmaker criminalizes a specific lie, namely the denial of the Holocaust. Section 130(3) of the Criminal Code states:

> Whoever publicly or in a meeting approves of, denies or downplays an act committed under the rule of National Socialism of the kind indicated in section 6(1) of the Code of Crimes against International Law in a manner which is suitable for causing a disturbance of the public peace incurs a penalty of imprisonment for a term not exceeding five years or a fine.

This criminal offense entertains a complicated intersection with the freedom of expression: on the one hand, opinion-related facts are treated like opinions (freedom of expression principle); on the other hand, lies about facts (Auschwitz) are excluded from toleration. In the case of an opinion-forming lie, these two principles come into conflict (Huster 1996, 487-488). In the case of the Auschwitz lie, the offender deliberately denies a historical fact (the extermination of millions of European Jews), but this happens within an ideological, opinion-forming framework relating to the National Socialist worldview. In the case of the Auschwitz lie the legislator resolves the described conflict in favor of the duty to speak the truth in order to prevent the poisoning of public opinion.

4.2. Lies in Criminal Trials

If you are looking for a right to lie and thus for lawful lies in criminal law, then criminal proceedings are the first port of call. In the area of criminal law, the main issue lawyers discuss is that of the accused's right to lie in a criminal trial. Roman law already formulated the principle of *nemo tenetur se ipsum accusare*, that no accused person needs to incriminate herself/himself before the public prosecutor or the criminal court (Holzhauer 2012, 325 ff.). Today, section 136(1)(2) of the Code of Criminal Procedure transforms this principle into a binding rule: "He [the accused] shall be advised that the law grants him the right to respond to the charges or not to make any statement on the charges and the right, at any stage, even prior to his examination, to consult defense counsel of his choice." However, if the accused does not remain silent but makes a statement, s/he has no unlimited right to invent untrue facts in order to exonerate herself/himself. The Federal Court of Justice formulates this as follows: "If the accused violates the general penal laws in the course of his interrogation by untrue statements, he can be punished for this" (BGHSt 60, 198 recital 37). The defendant commits criminal offenses such as those of false accusation (section 164 Criminal Code) or intentional defamation of a third person (section 187 Criminal Code) by denying her/his own guilt and simultaneously accusing another person. S/he therefore enjoys only a partial right to lie. However, judges have left one small loophole for a defendant: the judiciary has not yet decided on the situation in which the accused untruthfully designates another person as the only alternative perpetrator (BGHSt 60, 198 recital 33). In this case, it could be argued that the defendant has no choice but to accuse another person in order to enforce her/his right to deny her/his own guilt. Consequently, one could conclude that the accused must remain unpunished because of this dilemma (criminal offense on the one hand or self-incrimination on the other). By contrast, law enforcement authorities are not permitted to lie to the accused in order to convict her/him of a crime. Section 136a of the Criminal Procedure Code prohibits certain methods of examination, amongst them "deception."

5. *Lawful Lies: Election Campaigns*

In the sphere of governance, almost lawless spaces exist next to areas with a qualified duty to tell the truth. Nevertheless, freedom from legal sanctions does not mean freedom from sanctions in general. As the following example shows, law and politics form a unity here: where law ends, the almost equally effective quasi-normative social rules of politics begin. During election campaigns politicians may make unfulfillable promises to their voters, and they may interpret the state of public finances more positively than would an auditor. Such an act of so-called voter deception is socially outlawed in Germany. When politicians resign from their office after the public has learned the truth, they do so not for legal reasons, but on account of political tactics, or they bow to public morality. It would therefore be wrong to speak of a general right of politicians to lie. Although the lie does not entail a legal sanction, it results in a political or social sanction, the severity of which may in individual cases well reach the level of a criminal penalty. (See also Packard in this volume.)

Politicians only become liable to legal sanctions in a normative, legal sense if they cross certain legal barriers. Examples are various specific cases of electoral fraud. This includes the falsification of election results according to section 107a Criminal Code, of election documents according to section 107b Criminal Code and the act of deceiving voters according to section 108a Criminal Code. The offense of 'deceiving voters' is very narrowly defined in section 108a of the Criminal Code: "Whoever, by means of deception, causes another to be mistaken as to the content of their declaration upon casting their vote or, against their will, not to vote or to cast an invalid vote [...]." Voters must be mistaken about the content of their vote at the ballot box, a mere error of motive is not sufficient. When politicians deceive voters by making false promises during the election campaign, this in no way fulfills the requirements of said offense.

6. *Lawful Lies in Political Candidacies*

The curriculum vitae of politicians forms the last case in which one can find a right to lie. In contrast to the accused person in a criminal trial, however, this right to lie is not based on the principle of *nemo tenetur se ipsum accusare*, but on the fact that criminal laws do not punish certain lies from the outset. Politicians are, for example, allowed to add to their curricula vitae inexistent legal exams. Such a lie is treated merely as another case of so-called voter deception, which is not a crime in the sense of criminal law (see above, section 5). The federal laws on presidents, ministers and parliamentarians set no minimum requirements for professional qualification, so there is no duty of honesty regarding certain qualifications. This distinguishes Germany from countries such as Turkey, where according to article 101 of the Turkish Constitution (as of 2018) only those persons can become president who have successfully completed their university studies.

In some cases, the German legal system produces legal results, which – at first glance – laypersons might describe as ethically questionable: the press reported the case of a Member of Parliament (*Bundestagsabgeordnete*) who had fabricated almost her entire curriculum vitae and falsely pretended to be a certified lawyer. After the fraud had been uncovered, the Public Prosecutor's Office refrained from opening an investigation because the Member of Parliament had not committed a criminal offense (Public Prosecutor's Office Essen, press release 27 November 2016): the Member of Parliament had not illegally held a title (section 132a Criminal Code), nor had she committed fraud (section 263 of Criminal Code), deceived voters (section 108a Criminal Code) or falsified documents (section 267 Criminal Code). However, legality is by no means a synonym for the absence of all kind of sanctions. Apart from the law, the social sphere has its own rules, but they are not legal ones. As with electoral deception, the lie is socially outlawed; when somebody has been caught lying, the public and political colleagues regularly call for the fraudster's resignation. In the afore-mentioned case, the Member of Parliament ended up resigning from her parliamentary mandate; no court had imposed a criminal penalty on her before or after her resignation.

In comparison with politicians, civil servants must observe the truth much more closely. Since civil servants are subject to a duty of loyalty to the state, section 7(1) of the Federal Civil Servants Act stipulates that only those may be appointed as civil servants "who offer the guarantee to stand up at all times for the free democratic basic order in the sense of the Basic Law." The hiring authority may require applicants to answer questions about any current or former activities in or for anti-constitutional organizations or political parties including foreign secret services, political organizations of the former GDR or the State Security Service of the former GDR. This applies even if no court has as yet established the unconstitutionality of the respective organization or the Federal Constitutional Court has not yet banned the respective anti-constitutional party (BVerfGE 39, 334, 357 ff.). Moreover, after entering the civil service, officials are not allowed to lie to their superiors or to any other person about administrative proceedings.

7. *Philosophical and Ethical Perspectives*

In the context of legal philosophy and ethics, instead of speaking about a legal lie, it would be better to refer to a white lie. The white lie may be lawful in individual cases, but ethically it remains a borderline case. In labor law, for example, job candidates may find themselves constrained to employ a white lie when no other practical means are available to defeat unlawful questions. Those who tell a white lie will suffer a conflict of conscience; they are forced to behave like actors on stage; their employment begins with a lie (Benecke 2018, paragraph 33 recital 158). But the disclosure of the truth could have led to their exclusion from the application process. Discriminated candidates would then have to engage in a lengthy lawsuit suing for the desired employment contract under section 21(1)(1) of the General Act on Equal Treatment.

The philosophy of law devotes itself extensively to the dilemma of the white lie. Immanuel Kant's essay "On a Supposed Right to Lie from Altruistic Motives" (1797) deserves special attention. In his remarks, Kant responds to a contemporary opinion that limited the duty to speak the truth. The argument was that not every person has a right to truth, suggesting that the corresponding duty to speak the truth was also limited. Kant, on the other hand, advocates an absolute duty of speaking the truth. He distinguishes between truth as an epistemological category (*Wahrheit*) and truthfulness (*Wahrhaftigkeit*) as a theorem of reason. Kant derives the absolute character of this truthfulness from his categorical imperative: "To be truthful (honest) in all declarations is therefore a sacred command of reason prescribed unconditionally, one not to be restricted by any conveniences" (Kant 1797, 307; trans. Gregor 1996, 613). According to Kant's philosophy of law, every lie is to be considered an injustice. Although Kant has shaped the present-day German legal system like no other philosopher, his rigorism did not prevail in this respect. As we have seen, the current German legal system in certain cases recognizes the white lie as a legal means of communication.

8. *A Narratological Perspective*

After examining the various fields of law and the ethical implications of the lie, one might wonder what insight narratology can gain from the legal distinction between unlawful and lawful lies. Lies could be relevant in the context of the boundaries between fictionality and factuality. In general, it should be noted that the concepts of factuality and fictionality, as well as their relationship to each other, are highly controversial (see Fludernik & Ryan 2020; Klauk & Köppe 2014). Whoever equates the word *fiction* with 'falsehood,' 'deception' or the term *lie* under the umbrella of a pan-fictional metatheory (Zipfel 2001, 21) could be misled into identifying the lie as an instance of fictionality. However, this is by no means a compelling conclusion. To the extent that narrative theory avoids or excludes a pan-fictional metatheory, it considers the lie primarily as linked to factuality (Martínez & Scheffel 2016, 12). Fictionality does not aspire to truth and therefore cannot fail at it; more pertinently, an audience consciously reading something *as fiction* is not deceived.[4] A lie, by contrast, lays claim to the truth. Therefore, while lies may appear in fictional narratives (see the essay of Fludernik in this volume), they do not serve the function of establishing or upholding the fictionality of the text.

However, here is not the place to decide such a complex question as the classification of lies in general. We are only concerned with the status of lying in the field of the law. The law belongs to the realm of factuality and also aims to be factual. The law is characterized by its normativity, i.e. by the imposition of binding commands in the form of rules. Legal practitioners apply the law, and the law thus has very real consequences. A lie can result in criminal punishment, for example for perjury. This distinguishes the legal system from literature, where lies often, but not always (see e.g. ideological literature), have no effect on the real world.

On the other hand, the law makes use of many fictions which might seem equatable with cases of fictionality. However, a closer look at legal fictions reveals that these follow their own rules (Stern 2017; see also Althans in this volume). In the German legal system, legal fictions are merely a special type of reference transposed from one norm to another. They should in no way be treated as instances of fictionality. The thesis that the law primarily aims at factuality is therefore to be maintained. On the other hand, despite this premise, the issue of fictionality should not be brushed aside overhastily. For instance,

[4] My thanks to Stephan Packard for this insight.

one could propose the lawful lie as a case in which the boundary between factuality and fictionality begins to shift. This case study opens up a space for the hybridization of lies, especially for the framing of fictionality from the perspective of factuality (see the example about answers to questions about an applicant's pregnancy as discussed below), and for other areas in which the two categories shade into one another.

In this connection, it is not the unlawful lie that is of primary interest. The unlawful lie often remains undetected: the victim of the lie does not recognize it and continues to be deceived; s/he is therefore subject to an illusion. Communication is no longer grounded on a fact-based level, but the parties still maintain the claim to truth. The liar does not openly denounce the consensus on truth. S/he perpetuates the claim to factuality of her/his narration towards the other party and the outside world.

With the lawful lie, on the other hand, matters are not so simple. Forbidden questions about pregnancy in labor law provided a first example. Even laypersons with only basic knowledge of the legal system know that candidates do not have to answer unlawful questions truthfully when applying for a job. This is especially true for experienced members of a company's human resources (HR) department. Nevertheless, such forbidden questions about pregnancy occasionally appear in legal practice. Either the HR manager asks the question in order to deter female applicants, or the HR manager wants to test the reaction of the applicant. The HR manager may expect only a rule-compliant answer, but not the truth. To the extent that both sides recognize the right to lie, there is a tacit consensus between the parties regarding the illegality of the question and consequently the possibility of a lie. The female candidate is evaluated not for the truth of the information she provides about her presumed pregnancy, but for the convincing or unsuccessful performance with which she denies a possible pregnancy. The female applicant's narration about her pregnancy is fictional, since the veracity of her statement about her pregnancy is no longer important. A doctor could theoretically verify a pregnancy, but such a verification would be of no lawful use. Nevertheless, the fictional story remains embedded in a factual narrative act. If the candidate does not get the job because of her answer to the pregnancy question, she can file a complaint for discrimination. Vice versa, the employer must not dismiss an employee because of her lie when s/he becomes aware of her pregnancy. In this respect, too, the lawful lie has real consequences.

By contrast, let us look at the case of a defendant's lie at her/his trial. Here both the narration and the story contained therein are factual. If the criminal judge is unable to clarify the facts of the case by other means of evidence, s/he must base her/his decision on the accused's story according to the principle *in dubio pro reo* ("in case of doubt for the accused," presupposed in section 260 Criminal Procedural Code). This presumption of innocence dates back to the sentence *favorabiliores rei potius quam actores habentur* ('defendants are rather favored than plaintiffs') of Roman law (Digest 50, 17, 125). The judge has to apply this presumption even where s/he doubts the truth of the narrative, since the account given has to be treated as fact-based. For her/his judgement the judge must rely on the defendant's statement (even if it is a lie) until s/he can *prove* that it is a lie.

What is the difference between a defendant's lie and a pregnant job applicant's lie? In the case of the right to lie about pregnancy, the question which precedes the narrative is forbidden; in criminal proceedings, on the other hand, the defendant's negation of guilt is not based on any forbidden question. Therefore, from a legal perspective, a proven lie harms the defendant, but it does not harm a pregnant woman. Moreover, while the question regarding the applicant's pregnancy has to be excluded from the application procedure as a whole, the defendant's false statement may even be included in the main narrative of the case presented by the judge. Our consideration of the legal aspects of lying thus leads to a decisive distinction for the narratological analysis of lies. The stronger right to lie in cases of pregnancy suspends the factual claim to true communication, whereas the right to lie in criminal proceedings does not.

The example concerning pregnancy in job interviews reveals how the boundaries between factuality and fictionality are connected to the right to lie. The external framework (the job interview as a speech act, recruitment or rejection) remains factual. Within this framework, however, the lie can be considered a fictional narrative act. This form of embedded fictionality clearly distinguishes such a type of legal lie from the literary lie, which belongs to the realm of pure fictionality (at least in the prototypical sense of fiction). In this respect, considering legal lies, one is justified in speaking of a shifting of the border between factuality and fictionality. From an interdisciplinary point of view, the law could therefore be argued to contribute to the testing of narratological concepts of factuality and fictionality.

9. *Conclusions*

The German legal system is based on the truth of information. This goes hand in hand with the duty to tell the truth. In exceptional cases, however, (white) lies are permitted. The boundaries between permitted and prohibited actions therefore do not separate true statements from lies, but rather distinguish lawful behavior (lawful lies and true statements) from unlawful behavior (unlawful lies). Thus, the legal system treats lawful lies like true statements. A permitted lie from the outset either remains without sanctions, or there is a justification for the lie which bars any sanction. Examples of such lawful lies come from labor law, the political sphere bordering on public law, criminal law and criminal procedural law. They illustrate lies in job interviews, in political election campaigns, in political candidacies and in criminal trials.

For narratology, this right to lie is important when we examine concepts of factuality and fictionality and the interdisciplinary applicability of narratological categories. Many of the examples discussed above (like the defendant's right to lie) confirm the classification of the lie as belonging to the realm of factuality. In the case of the pregnancy of a job applicant, however, the right to lie means that the (untruthful) narrative in which the applicant denies being pregnant shifts from the factual to the fictional realm. While lies in literature (by characters) are factual in nature within the fictional world, in this special case of a legally permitted lie, the lie is fictional. Nevertheless, this fictionality remains embedded in a factual context, and such permitted lies have real legal consequences.

Works Cited

Armbrüster, Christian (2018) "§ 123 BGB." *Münchener Kommentar zum Bürgerlichen Gesetzbuch*. Ed. Franz Jürgen Säcker et al. 8th ed. Munich: C. H. Beck. N. pag. Web. n. d.

Benecke, Martina (2018) "Faktische Bindung des Arbeitgebers durch Begrenzung seiner Informationsmöglichkeiten ('Grenzen des Fragerechts')." *Münchener Handbuch zum Arbeitsrecht*. Ed. Heinrich Kiel et al. 4th ed. Vol. 1. Munich: C. H. Beck. N. pag. Paragraph 33. Web. n.d.

Depenheuer, Otto (2005) Ed. *Recht und Lüge*. Münster: LIT Verlag.

Fludernik, Monika, and Marie-Laure Ryan (2020) Ed. *Narrative Factuality: A Handbook*. Berlin: De Gruyter.

Grimm, Dieter (1995) "Die Meinungsfreiheit in der Rechtsprechung des Bundesverfassungsgerichts." *Neue Juristische Wochenschrift* 48: 1697-1705.

Holzhauer, Heinz (2012) "Geständnis." *Handwörterbuch zur deutschen Rechtsgeschichte*. Ed. Albrecht Cordes et al. Vol. 2. Berlin: Erich Schmidt Verlag. cols. 325-335.

Huster, Stefan (1996) "Das Verbot der 'Auschwitzlüge', die Meinungsfreiheit und das Bundesverfassungsgericht." *Neue Juristische Wochenschrift* 49: 487-491.

Kant, Immanuel (1923) "Über ein vermeintes Recht aus Menschenliebe zu lügen." [1797] *Werke*. Ed. Königlich Preußische Akademie der Wissenschaften. Vol. 8. Berlin: De Gruyter. 423-430. English translation by Mary J. Gregor (1996). *Immanuel Kant: Practical Philosophy.* Cambridge: Cambridge Univ. Press. 606-616.

Klauk, Tobias, and Tilmann Köppe (2014) Ed. *Fiktionalität: Ein interdisziplinäres Handbuch*. Berlin: De Gruyter.

Martínez, Matías, and Michael Scheffel (2016). *Einführung in die Erzähltheorie.* 10th ed. Munich: C.H. Beck.

Michler, Inga (2016) "Bewerbung gefälscht: So sichern sich Betrüger lukrative Jobs." *Welt Online* 22 July: N. pag. Web. 11 November 2019.

Mugdan, Benno (1899) Ed. *Die gesammten Materialien zum Bürgerlichen Gesetzbuch für das Deutsche Reich.* Vol. 1. Berlin: R. von Decker's Verlag.

Press Officer of the Public Prosecutor's Office Essen. "Die Staatsanwaltschaft Essen hat von der Einleitung eines Ermittlungsverfahrens gegen Petra Hinz gemäß § 152 Abs. 2 der Strafprozessordnung abgesehen." Essen: Public Prosecutor's Office Essen, 27 September 2016. Web. 17 November 2019.

Schmidt-Jortzig, Edzard (2009) "Meinungs- und Informationsfreiheit." *Handbuch des Staatsrechts.* Ed. Josef Isensee and Paul Kirchhof. 3rd ed. Vol. 7. Heidelberg: C. F. Müller. 875-908.

Stern, Simon (2017) "Legal and Literary Fictions." *New Directions in Law and Literature.* Ed. Bernadette Meyler and Elizabeth Anker. Oxford: Oxford Univ. Press. 313-326.

Waton, Alan (1985) Ed. *The Digest of Justinian.* 4 vols. Philadelphia: Univ. of Pennsylvania Press.

Zipfel, Frank (2001) *Fiktion, Fiktivität, Fiktionalität: Analysen zur Fiktion in der Literatur und zum Fiktionsbegriff in der Literaturwissenschaft.* Berlin: Erich Schmidt.

Cases

BAG NJW 1985, 645. German Federal Labor Court. Decision 7 June 1984. File 2 AZR 270/83. *Neue Juristische Wochenschrift* 38 (1985), pp. 645 f.

BAG NJW 1993, 1154: German Federal Labor Court. Decision 15 October 1992. File 2 AZR 227/92. *Neue Juristische Wochenschrift* 46 (1993), pp. 1154-1156.

BAG NZA 2003, 848. German Federal Labor Court. Decision 6 February 2003. File 2 AZR 621/01. *Neue Zeitschrift für Arbeitsrecht* 20 (2003), pp. 848 f.

BAGE 15, 261. German Federal Labor Court. Decision 7 February 1964. File 1 AZR 251/63. *Decisions of the Federal Labor Court,* vol. 15, edited by the members of the Federal Labor Court. Berlin: De Gruyter, 1966, pp. 261–270.

BAGE 91, 349. German Federal Labor Court. Decision 20 May 1999. File 2 AZR 320/98. *Decisions of the Federal Labor Court,* vol. 91, edited by the members of the Federal Labor Court. Berlin: De Gruyter, 2000, pp. 349–358.

BGHSt 34, 199. German Federal Court of Justice. Decision 22 October 1986. File 3 StR 226/86. Decisions of the Federal Court of Justice in Criminal Matters, vol. 34, edited by the members of the Federal Court of Justice and the Federal Attorneys. Cologne: Heymanns, 1988, pp. 199–203.

BGHSt 60, 15. German Federal Court of Justice. Decision 8 October 2014. File 1 StR 114/14. *Decisions of the Federal Court of Justice in Criminal Matters*, vol. 60, edited by the members of the Federal Court of Justice and the Federal Attorneys. Cologne: Heymanns, 2016, pp. 15–37.

BGHSt 60, 198. German Federal Court of Justice. Decision 10 February 2015. File 1 StR 488/14. *Decisions of the Federal Court of Justice in Criminal Matters*, vol. 60, edited by the members of the Federal Court of Justice and the Federal Attorneys. Cologne: Heymanns, 2016, pp. 198–204.

BGHZ 116, 7. German Federal Court of Justice. Decision 21 October 1991. File II ZR 204/90. *Decisions of the Federal Court of Justice in Civil Matters*, vol. 116, edited by the members of the Federal Court of Justice and the Federal Attorneys. Cologne: Heymanns, 1992, pp. 7–14.

BVerfGE 39, 334. German Federal Constitutional Court. Decision 22 May 1975. File 2 BvL 13/73. *Decisions of the Federal Constitutional Court*, vol. 39, edited by the members of the Federal Constitutional Court. Tübingen: Mohr Siebeck, pp. 334–391.

BVerfGE 54, 208. German Federal Constitutional Court. Decision 3 June 1980. File 1 BvR 797/78. *Decisions of the Federal Constitutional Court*, vol. 54, edited by the members of the Federal Constitutional Court. Tübingen: Mohr Siebeck, 1981, pp. 208–223.

BVerfGE 61, 1. German Federal Constitutional Court. Decision 22 June 1982. File 1 BvR 1376/79. *Decisions of the Federal Constitutional Court*, vol. 61, edited by the members of the Federal Constitutional Court. Tübingen: Mohr Siebeck, 1983, pp. 1–13.

BVerfGE 99, 185. German Federal Constitutional Court. Decision 10 November 1998. File 1 BvR 1531/96. *Decisions of the Federal Constitutional Court*, vol. 99, edited by the members of the Federal Constitutional Court. Tübingen: Mohr Siebeck, 1999, pp. 185–202.

ECJ [2001] ECR I-6993. European Court of Justice. Decision 4 October 2001. File Rs. C-109/00. Tele Danmark A/S/Handels- og Kontorfunktionærernes Forbund i Danmark. [2001] *European Court Reports* I–6993.

LAG Frankfurt am Main NJW 1987, 352. Regional Labor Court Frankfurt am Main. Decision 7 August 1986. File 12 Sa 361/86. *Neue Zeitschrift für Arbeitsrecht* 4 (1987), pp. 352–354.

OLG Stuttgart NJW 1999, 3640. Higher Regional Court Stuttgart. Decision 22 June 1999. File 12 U 3/99. *Neue Juristische Wochenschrift* 52 (1999), pp. 3640 f.

Abbreviations

BAG	Bundesarbeitsgericht = Federal Labour Court
BGHSt	Entscheidungen des Bundesgerichtshofes in Strafsachen = Decisions of the (German) Federal Court of Justice in Criminal Matters
BGHZ	Entscheidungen des Bundesgerichtshofes in Zivilsachen = Decisions of the (German) Federal Court of Justice in Civil Matters
BVerfGE	Entscheidungen des Bundesverfassungsgerichts = Decisions of the (German) Federal Constitutional Court
ECJ	European Court of Justice
ECR	European Court Reports
LAG	Landesarbeitsgericht = (German) Regional Labour Court
NJW	Neue Juristische Wochenschrift = New Weekly Law Journal
NZA	Neue Zeitschrift für Arbeitsrecht = New Journal for Labor Law
OLG	Oberlandesgericht = (German) Higher Regional Court

Translation of Statutes

Note: The English translations of the German statutes are taken from the Federal Ministry of Justice at https://www.gesetze-im-internet.de/. They are therefore official translations.

Criminal Code

Section 107a: Fraud in connection with elections

(1) Whoever votes without being entitled to do so or brings about an incorrect election result or falsifies the result in another way incurs a penalty of imprisonment for a term not exceeding five years or a fine. [...]

Section 263: Fraud

(1) Whoever, with the intention of obtaining an unlawful pecuniary benefit for themselves or a third party, damages the assets of another by causing or maintaining an error under false pretences or distorting or suppressing true facts incurs a penalty of imprisonment for a term not exceeding five years or a fine. [...]

Section 263a: Computer fraud

(1) Whoever, with the intention of obtaining an unlawful pecuniary benefit for themselves or a third party, damages the property of another by influencing the result of a data processing operation by incorrectly configuring the computer program, using incorrect or incomplete data, making unauthorised use of data or taking other unauthorised influence on the processing operation incurs a penalty of imprisonment for a term not exceeding five years or a fine.

Lying in Counterfactual Fiction: On the Critical Function of Metafactuality

Michael Navratil

1. Introduction

By choosing the word *postfaktisch* [postfactual] as Word of the Year in 2016, the Society for the German Language (*Gesellschaft für deutsche Sprache*) reacted to a general unease in the public sphere; namely, to the feeling that in the political arena, i.e. in the wake of Brexit, the rise of Pegida and AfD (the right-wing Alternative for Germany), and of the candidacy of Donald Trump for the office of US president, commonly agreed-upon truth was losing its hitherto unquestioned prominent status in the political arena. Increasingly, an appeal to emotions – no matter how irrational – seemed to replace a reference to facts, thus undermining the possibility of effectively exposing political lies. The importance and dangers of so-called post-truth – as well as of closely associated phenomena such as fake news, 'alternative facts,' conspiracy theories, and populism – have supplied a key topic of both political and academic debate in recent years.

Turning to the domain of literature, one of the likely fellow-travelers of post-truth is *counterfactual fiction*, defined as works of fiction that consciously alter commonly known facts about the real world within their respective storyworlds. Especially scholars who are sympathetic towards postmodernism tend to draw a link between post-truth and counterfactual fiction. Moritz Baßler, for example, when commenting on the political implications of counterfactual, parahistorical fiction in general, and on Richard Kelly's apocalyptic movie *Southland Tales* (2006) in particular, arrives at the following conclusion:

> Die Bilder von *Southland Tales* sprechen [...] eine klare Sprache: Jede fiktionale Vervielfältigung der Historie ist geradezu harmlos gegen die medialen Paralogien der Jetztzeit. Die Anspielung auf George W. Bushs kontrafaktische Begründung für den Irakkrieg macht das parahistorische Potenzial der Mediengesellschaft nur allzu deutlich. Der medial erweiterte Thesaurus unserer Handlungscodes hat sich hier eindeutig durchgesetzt; zu irgendwelchen einfachen Unterscheidungen von Faktizität und Fiktionalität führt kein Weg zurück. (Baßler 2010, 272)

> [The images of *Southland Tales* speak a clear language: every redoubling of history must appear harmless when compared to the medial paralogies of our own time. The reference to George W. Bush's counterfactual justification for the war on Iraq renders all too obvious the parahistorical potential of a society dominated by the media. The medially enriched thesaurus of our behavioral codes has evidently prevailed here; there

> can be no return to any simplistic differentiations between facticity and fictionality.] (my translation)

Baßler links the growing popularity of parahistorical rewritings of history in various fictional media – apart from *Southland Tales*, his examples include Christian Kracht's novel *Ich werde hier sein im Sonnenschein und im Schatten* (2008) and Quentin Tarantino's movie *Inglourious Basterds* (2009) – with the apparently diminishing importance of references to factual truth in the discourse of politics. In a world heavily influenced by popular media, Baßler argues, the differentiation between what is true and what is false proves increasingly difficult to determine. In this context, Baßler points up early manifestations of post-truth and connects them with the aesthetic phenomenon of counterfactual fiction.

One may, however, ask whether the various forms of nonfactuality that Baßler touches upon in his article are really all that similar. If one defines counterfactuality as that "propositional disposition" which assumes something that is "known or believed to be obviously false" (Albrecht & Danneberg 2011, 14), then clearly the justification of the Bush administration for the invasion of Iraq cannot be classified as an instance of counterfactuality, but rather constitutes a direct lie. Also, the construction of counterfactual storyworlds evidently depends on a clear distinction between fact and a deviation from fact: after all, if there simply were no facts to begin with, it would not be possible to counterfactually deviate from them. If this chain of argument is true, however, counterfactuality would not, as Baßler suggests, undermine the "differentiations between facticity and fictionality" (my translation) – or rather between the factual and the non-factual, as Baßler seems to have the ontological distinction between truth and falsehood in mind here. On the contrary: by presupposition, counterfactuality would support these distinctions.

The issue is further complicated by the fact that works of counterfactual fiction often additionally discuss political lies and other instances of nonfactuality at the level of their narrative content. Kelly's movie, which deals – among a myriad of other topics – with political ideologies, conspiracies, and the dubious anticipation of political events in religious scriptures and popular culture, is a pertinent example. Evidently, the relationship between counterfactuality and lies is more intricate than Baßler has it with his postmodern levelling of different forms of nonfactuality.

In this paper, I want to explore the relation of counterfactual fiction to lies in greater detail. I will start my discussion of counterfactual fiction with a brief research report on counterfactuality in general. I will then provide my own definition of counterfactual fiction. This definition significantly expands upon existing definitions of fictional counterfactual storytelling in that it is not restricted to a certain sub-genre of the historical novel – namely the alternate history novel – but can cover variations of real-world facts in different narrative genres and fictional media. Following the elaboration of the specific reference structure of counterfactual fiction, I will try to differentiate counterfactual fiction from lies. The second part of my paper is concerned with the phenomenon of *metafactuality*: reflections about truth and lies *within* counterfactual storyworlds. Such metafactual reflections are very commonly found in counterfactual fiction; however, as far as I can see, their function has not so far been a topic of extended scholarly discussion. I suggest that the main function of such metafactual elements lies in their ability to emphasize the importance of truth or, to put it differently, to criticize post-truth. I will illustrate this critical function of metafactuality on the basis of a brief interpretation of Quentin Tarantino's *Inglourious Basterds*. In the final part of my paper, I want to draw on some concepts from cognitivist narratology, specifically on the theory of the *willing construction of disbelief* (punning on Coleridge) as suggested by Richard J. Gerrig (1993, 230), in order to substantiate my claim that metafactuality is ultimately truth-supporting.

2. *Counterfactuality: A Brief Research Report*

Counterfactual fiction forms part of the more general phenomenon of counterfactual thinking, which is by no means limited to the arts.[1] Counterfactual thinking seems to be a common practice of human reasoning (Roese & Olson 1995, vii). In everyday life, the feeling of regret, for example, is regularly based on counterfactual considerations of the type *If I had only done x rather than y* (Gilovich & Medvec 1995, Roese & Morrison 2009, 17). Similarly, attributions of guilt and responsibility often involve counterfactual reflections, such as, *If you had arrived on time, we wouldn't have missed our train* (Roese & Morrison 2009, 18, 20).

Different forms of counterfactual thinking have for decades been the focus of research in a variety of scholarly disciplines. In analytic philosophy, *counterfactual conditionals* (conditionals with a non-factual if-clause) have been a topic of discussion since the middle of the twentieth century.[2] In the theory of history, the usefulness and methodological merit of counterfactual scenarios ('What if Napoleon had won the battle of Waterloo?') has been a staple of debates for some fifty years now.[3] Since the 1990s, an increased interest in counterfactual thinking and counterfactual storytelling has developed across a multitude of

[1] The following discussion of the research history and the definition of counterfactual fiction draws on my own research in the context of my PhD thesis: *Kontrafaktik der Gegenwart. Politisches Schreiben als Realitätsvariation bei Christian Kracht, Kathrin Röggla, Juli Zeh und Leif Randt* (forthcoming).

[2] The term *counterfactual conditional* was originally introduced by Nelson Goodman in 1947.

[3] Edward Hallett Carr notoriously dismissed the discussion of "the might-have-beens of history" as a mere "parlour-game" (Carr 1961, 91). One of the most influential defenses

additional areas, including psychology, cognitive linguistics, theoretical physics, political studies, and the social sciences.[4]

Researchers today generally agree that the functions, uses, and even definitions of counterfactual thinking vary across disciplines and contexts of use. Andrea Albrecht and Lutz Danneberg, in reference to counterfactual imaginations, remark that "[d]epending on the context, their function can be critical, affirmative, explanatory, heuristic, illustrative, or pedagogical. Counterfactual imaginations can be used to solve problems, analyze notions, and facilitate conclusions" (Albrecht & Danneberg 2011, 16). It therefore seems reasonable to discuss counterfactual thinking specifically within its respective area of use. In this article, I will focus on the structure and uses of counterfactual storytelling in the domain of art and, more specifically, fictional narratives.

In literary studies, discussions of counterfactual storytelling to date have concentrated primarily on the genre of *alternate history*, that is, novels or other fictional media that present a version of history which significantly differs from the received version of the past.[5] Prominent genre examples include Philip K. Dick's *The Man in the High Castle* from 1962 (Nazi Germany and Japan win World War II) and Robert Harris's *Fatherland* from 1992 (Nazi Germany wins World War II), Christoph Ransmayr's *Morbus Kitahara* (a counterfactual realization of the Morgenthau plan) and Thomas Brussig's *Helden wie wir* (an alternative explanation of the fall of the Berlin wall), both from 1995, as well as Philip Roth's *The Plot Against America* (Fascists take over America) from 2004. In recent years, the genre of alternate history has been notably popularized by the adaptation of Dick's novel as a web television series (2015–2019), and by Quentin Tarantino's highly meta-reflexive take on the genre in his movies *Inglourious Basterds* (2009) and *Once Upon a Time in Hollywood* (2019).

Most studies on the alternate history novel focus on its relation with other subgenres of the historical novel, its links with postmodernism,[6] and its sup-

---

of counterfactual thinking in history is Alexander Demandt's short book on the topic (Demandt 1984). For an extended research discussion see Richard J. Evans (2013).

4 An overview of different approaches to counterfactual thinking can be found in the edited volumes by Roland Wenzlhuemer (2009) and Dorothee Birke et al. (2011).

5 The most prominent monographs on the topic are the following: Helbig (1988), Rodiek (1997), Hellekson (2001), Rosenfeld (2005), Widmann (2009), Singles (2013). There have also been attempts at describing all fictional worlds as counterfactual by drawing on possible world semantics. David Lewis, for example, suggests "to analyze statements of truth in fiction as counterfactuals" (Lewis 1979, 42). This approach, however, does not allow for an analysis of counterfactual texts in the narrow sense or individual counterfactual elements in works of fiction. Catharine Gallagher rightly emphasizes: "Possible-worlds theorists tend to classify all fictions as counterfactuals, enlarging the latter term beyond usefulness for a study of explicitly counterfactual genres" (Gallagher 2011, 333).

6 The relation of alternate history to postmodernism is highly ambivalent. Gavriel D. Rosenfeld notes: "It is, fittingly enough, still a matter of speculation why the fascination with alternate history has grown in recent years, but it seems to be the byproduct of broader political and cultural trends. To begin with, the new prominence of alternate

posed interconnectedness with constructivist theories of historiography, such as the narrative constructivism of Hayden White.[7] This emphasis on questions of genre and intellectual history, however, has set aside a discussion of the basic reference structure of counterfactual elements, which every scholarly consideration of counterfactual texts has to be grounded on implicitly or explicitly.[8] As a consequence of this overall indifference to the fundamental reference structure of counterfactual fiction, there have also been no attempts at a theoretically sound differentiation between counterfactual elements and other nonfactualities in works of fiction, nor have there been extended considerations of counterfactual storytelling in genres other than the historical novel.

3. *Counterfactual Fiction: A Definition*

Instead of treating fictional counterfactual writing in the context of genre theory, I want to provide a new perspective on counterfactual fiction from the vantage point of narratology and the theory of fiction. I propose the following definition:

> *Counterfactual fiction designates elements within fictional media which are characterized by a significant variation of real-world facts.*[9]

All the key terms in this definition will have to be further elaborated in the following paragraphs.

The limitation of counterfactuality to *fictional media* is central to my concept of counterfactual fiction since one needs to differentiate counterfactual fiction

---

history reflects the progressive discrediting of political ideologies in the West since 1945. [...] Closely tied to the death of political ideologies in promoting the upsurge of alternate history is the emergence of the cultural movement of postmodernism. While alternate history clearly predates the rise of postmodernism, the latter movement has certainly enabled the former to move into the mainstream" (Rosenfeld 2005, 6–7).

7 This common association of Hayden White's theories with the genre of alternate history seems misguided to me. As White himself states, his theories are not concerned with the (willful) creation of new historical information – as alternate history texts clearly are – but rather with the interpretation, narrativization, and evaluation of past events (White 1999, 2).

8 This preference of questions of genre over considerations of basic reference structures is familiar from the study of fantastic fiction. Marianne Wünsch (1991, 12–13) has pointed out that every typology of fantastic texts first has to rely on an understanding of the basic structure of fantastic elements. The same, I claim, is true for counterfactual elements. Ansgar Nünning's influential typology of the historical novel (1995), for example, significantly does not feature the alternate history novel as a separate subgenre of historical novels but rather discusses counterfactual references as a narrative device that can be employed in different kinds of historical novels – and, I claim, also beyond historical narratives.

9 *Counterfactual fiction* is my suggested translation for the concept I introduced as *Kontrafaktik* in German (Navratil 2019).

from other uses of counterfactual thinking, for example, in everyday life or in scientific discourse. (Although factual forms of counterfactual thinking are not discussed at length in this article, I would like to propose the term *counterfactuality* as an umbrella term for all manifestations of counterfactual thinking and writing. The term *counterfactual fiction* would then refer only to fictional, and the term *counterfacticity* only to factual manifestations of counterfactuality.) As there is a strong link between fictionality and narrativity (Fludernik 1996, 39; Zipfel 2001, 56–58), counterfactual fiction will typically surface in narrative form: in novels, fictional movies, comics, and drama.

Since fictional narratives always produce fictional worlds/storyworlds (Ryan 2007, 29; Ryan 2014; Wolf 2017, 260), the reference structure of counterfactual fiction can be described as a relation between elements of two worlds, one of them designated as real and the other one designated as fictional. Elements of counterfactual fiction establish a special kind of two-level reference: an indirect or implicit reference to a certain fact in the real world and a direct or explicit reference to the variation of this very fact in the fictional world. This counterfactual, *transfictional double-reference*[10] can always be paraphrased in terms of a comparison of the following sort: *While x is true of y in the real world* (e.g., Nazi Germany has lost the war), *in the fictional world, by contrast, z is true of y* (Nazi Germany has won the war). Text interpretations which focus specifically on counterfactual fiction will always try to attribute hermeneutic value to precisely such transfictional double-references.

Another way of grasping the reference structure of counterfactual elements would be to describe it as a form of *determinate negation* ('bestimmte Negation'): counterfactual fiction deviates from fact, but not in order to constitute a world independent from concrete information about the real world,[11] but in order to present a hermeneutically significant variation of that very information. Often, this counterfactual variation serves as a means of commenting on, evaluating, or criticizing the very real-world facts from which it deviates.

The term *variation*, then, is meant to highlight that one is concerned with a deviation from real-world fact that dialectically maintains a connection with the original fact. Much like variations in music, in counterfactual fiction it is not merely the final result of the variation that is of interest but also the

10 Unfortunately, the theory of fiction features two different notions of 'transfictionality.' Marie-Laure Ryan (2008) and Richard Saint-Gelais (2008) use the term to refer to an element that crosses over from one fictional world to another (a more felicitous name for this phenomenon might have been *interfictionality*). Wolfgang Künne on the other hand defines the term 'transfictional' as follows: '"[W]ir verwenden jeweils zwei konkrete singuläre Terme, und (nur) einer von ihnen ist fiktional.'" [We are using two concrete singular terms, (only) one of which is fictional. – My translation] (Künne 1983, 295; see also Künne 1995, 155–161) When describing the double-references of counterfactual fiction as transfictional, I am using the term in Künne's sense.

11 This may be the case for fantastic fiction, which might also explain the often-formulated reproach of 'escapism' directed against fantastic texts.

connection of the variation with its original 'theme,' that is, the respective real-world facts. As Neal J. Roese and Mike Morrison put it (albeit for counterfactual thinking in psychology): "If reality is the theme, and counterfactual is the variation, then the juxtaposition of the two embodies a combination of the joy of recognition with surprise at something novel" (Roese & Morrison 2009, 22).

My definition of counterfactual fiction does not focus on entire texts or genres, but instead on the reference structure of specific *elements* within fictional worlds. Much as with fantastic elements in, for example, fantasy novels, counterfactual elements usually only make up a small portion of all the elements in a given text. Even in a classical alternate history novel such as Philip K. Dick's *The Man in the High Castle*, most individual elements – characters, settings, plot lines etc. – are not strictly speaking counterfactual but rather realistic or even simply factual.

Focusing on individual elements is advantageous insofar as it allows for much more precise text analyses than overarching genre designations or text typologies. While it may be still pragmatically useful to refer to texts that very prominently feature counterfactual elements as 'counterfactual texts,' one should always keep in mind that such a designation works on the principle of metonymy, overgeneralizing a certain feature belonging to the fictional world which is not actually a property of all of its elements.

The concept of *significance* allows for a differentiation between counterfactual fiction and other kinds of nonfactualities, for instance mistakes and 'simple' – that is: non-significant – inventions in works of fiction. Fictional narratives may contain incorrect information about the real world, such as, for example, wrong street names in a real city. As long as these instances of false information do not play any role in the interpretation of the given work, however, they should not be regarded as counterfactual elements but rather as insignificant mistakes (Huemer 2010, Lamarque 2015, 375). Similarly, mere fictional inventions – that is, inventions within fictional works that are covered by the convention of fictionality – for the most part cannot be regarded as counterfactual elements. Anna Karenina, for example, is an invented character, but the interpretation of Tolstoy's novel does not depend on the fact that most of its characters are fictitious, nor are these characters commonly regarded as fact-altering variations or disguised versions of real people (as in a roman-á-clef): it is not the comparison with a real-world counterpart that renders the figure of Anna Karenina interesting, but rather her story and fate as such. In counterfactual fiction, by contrast, deviation from real-world facts is significant for the interpretation of the given work precisely *as a variation*.

It should also be noted that significance is here treated as an essentially *hermeneutic* category. As such, it is dependent on the knowledge and interpretational framework of a given reader. Readers must have a certain knowledge of real-world facts in order to be able to recognize deviations from them in a work of fiction, since these facts are not (reliably) provided within the work itself but have to be deduced by inference (Winko & Jannidis 2015). Furthermore, such variations of facts have to be regarded as significant in the context of a specific interpretation of a given work in order for them to count as counterfactual. Counterfactual fiction thus cannot be considered as a static text structure – like meter in a poem –, but should be regarded as an interpretational hypothesis with a greater or lesser degree of plausibility and intersubjective acceptability.

The emphasis on *real-world* facts is crucial for differentiating counterfactual fiction from intertextuality. There is significant structural overlap between counterfactual and intertextual fiction: both usually entail a reference to two distinct worlds, texts, or frames of reference (Hrushovski 1984) as well as an interpretative comparison between those two referents. However, the intertextual allusions to, say, Homer's *Odyssey* in James Joyce's *Ulysses* cannot be regarded as counterfactual as they do not serve the purpose of rewriting real-world facts but rather of establishing a link with a previous text.

Facts. The definition of truth and its preconditions are notoriously controversial philosophical issues. Much of the philosophical debate about truth, however, is only of limited interest to literary studies (Zipfel 2001, 104; Köppe 2014, 48). The term *fact*, as it pertains to counterfactual fiction, relates to a conventional or pragmatic understanding of truth: the relevant facts implied in counterfactual fiction can be defined as those *specific* and *conventionally accepted* pieces of information about the real world – or, to use Umberto Eco's term, those elements of the encyclopedia (Eco 1994, 120) – that readers are likely to know as part of their geographical, historical or cultural knowledge. The information, for example, that there is gravity on earth does not lend itself to counterfactual variation, as this information is of a very general nature; a fictional variation of this information – that is: a world without gravity – would not so much constitute a case of counterfactual, but rather of fantastic fiction. Also, the facts in question have to be of such a kind that their variation in a work of counterfactual fiction clearly changes their truth-value. The nature of love or the existence of extraterrestrial life, for example, are not appropriate 'facts' for counterfactual variation, since there is no commonly accepted understanding about these particular aspects of reality.

Owing to their high level of specificity and conventionality, facts about history are particularly suitable for counterfactual variations. Counterfactual fiction, however, may also be based on biographical facts (for example, in autofictional narratives or in the roman à clef), on social or political tendencies of the present (in dystopias), or on information about certain aspects or agents of public life (in satire). Unlike the alternate history genre, for which the employment of counterfactual elements is a defining feature, these other genres do not of necessity include counterfactual elements; however, as texts of these other genres often implicitly refer to highly specific real-worlds facts by presenting an artistic variation of these very facts, they too lend themselves to an investigation through the lens of counterfactual fiction.

The dystopian genre can serve as an example here. Often it may be plausible to read a dystopian text about, for example, a totalitarian state regime as a mere *allegory* about the dangers of just any totalitarian state, or as *speculative fiction*, that is a text laying out possible, plausible, and preferably avoidable paths for the prospective development of a given society. In both cases, an emphasis on counterfactual elements would not be central to the respective interpretation. However, dystopian texts oftentimes establish implicit references to very specific events, actors, or simply facts of the past or, more often, the present. By focusing on these specific counterfactual variations of facts, one goes beyond a reading of dystopian texts as mere political allegories or as more or less plausible models for the future. Instead, one focuses on the (critical) light that a certain real-world fact and its counterfactual variation within a particular fictional world shed on one another when considered together.[12]

4. A Note on Counterfactual Fiction vs. Lies

Works of counterfactual fiction and lies share one obvious characteristic: they are both untrue, in the sense that their propositions do not hold for the real world. Their pragmatic status, however, is markedly different. Lies are characterized not only by their untruthfulness, but also by an intention to deceive: a liar is not simply a person who utters false information (if this were the case, all poets would have to be regarded as liars, as Plato indeed claimed), but a person who utters false information with the intention that this information be taken as true by their listeners or readers. This latter specification precisely does not hold for counterfactual fiction (nor, in fact, counterfactuality in general). Unlike lies, counterfactual scenarios never entail an intention to deceive. Counterfactual thinking generally and works of counterfactual fiction in particular derive their specific epistemic, evaluative, or aesthetic potential from the shared understanding that a particular proposition is untrue (Albrecht & Danneberg 2011, 14). Another way of putting this would be to say that counterfactuality reflexively draws attention to its own falsehood. This special property of counterfactuality will be of great importance when discussing the function of lies,

12 The relevance of counterfactual thinking for the genre of utopia/dystopia has variously been noted, but for the most part without consequences for the ensuing interpretations or text typologies. Birte Christ notes: "Surprisingly [...] the classical literary utopia in the tradition of Thomas More and, more widely framed, speculative fictions with a utopian impetus have so far not been explored from the perspective of counterfactuality. [...] Here is an entire literary genre which may be read afresh from the perspective of the studies of counterfactuality [...]." (Christ 2011, 220–221).

ideologies, and conspiracy theories within the storyworlds of counterfactual fiction.

Another difference between counterfactual fiction and lies should be noted. As mentioned above, the comparison between real-world fact and a counterfactual variation thereof always crosses the barrier between two worlds. Lies, on the other hand, only refer to the particular world in which they are told. While the interpretation of counterfactual fiction always involves a transfictional crossing between worlds, lies can be uttered, described, or unveiled world-immanently. In this respect, lies work like metaphors, which likewise share certain features with counterfactual scenarios (Danneberg 2006, 75), but are also non-world-connecting (Eco 1992, 262).

5. Metafactuality

Facts and deviations from facts are constitutive of the phenomenon of counterfactual fiction. Interestingly, many works of counterfactual fiction additionally address the question of fact and falsehood at the level of their narrative content (Hellekson 2001, 30–31). Within their storyworlds, works of counterfactual fiction regularly discuss topics such as lies, the constitution of truth, or the manipulation of facts. For such diegetic thematization of truth and lies within counterfactual worlds, I want to suggest the term *metafactuality*.

Metafactuality designates any discussion of truth, lies, and related topics within counterfactual storyworlds.

One of the best-known examples of metafactuality is the book within a book (Hawthorne Abendsen's *The Grasshopper Lies Heavy*) in Philip K. Dick's alternate history classic *The Man in the High Castle* (1962), a novel that, like so many works of twentieth-century alternate history, is based on the counterfactual premise that Nazi Germany has won the war. In the counterfactual storyworld of Dick's novel, a book is circulating which describes the victory of the allied nations, the capture and trial of Hitler, and the rise of the British Empire as the world's dominant power. The structure and the various world-relations between Dick's novel, the book within a book, and the real world can be illustrated in the following way (the letter 'F' being a shorthand for 'fact'):

Figure 1: Metafactuality in Philip K. Dick's *The Man in the High Castle*

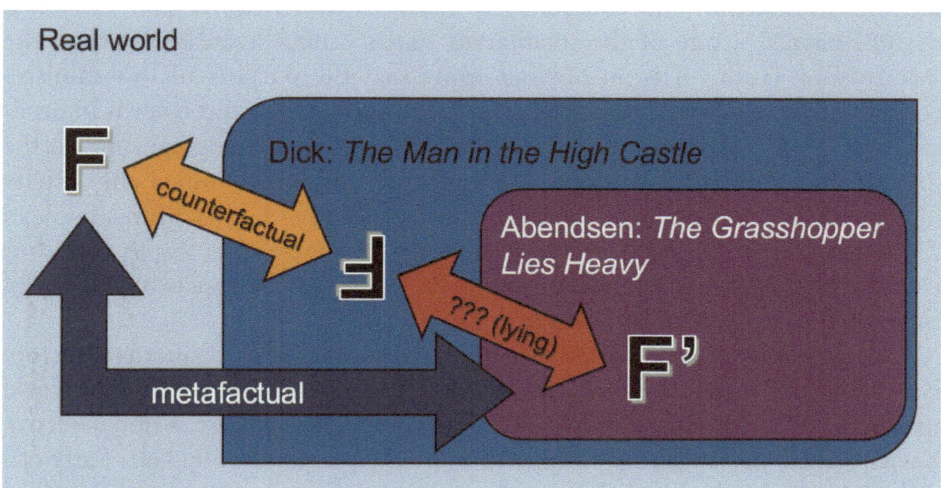

It may at first seem as though *The Grasshopper Lies Heavy* constitutes a simple counter-counterfactual reversal of the counterfactual world presented in Dick's novel (Helbig 1988, 90). However, upon closer consideration, it turns out that the world mapped out in Abendsen's book significantly differs from the real world, so that this meta-variation (Abendsen's book) of the counterfactual variant of reality (Dick's book) does not simply bring the reader back to reality, but rather constitutes yet another world in its own right. More significantly still, the pragmatic status of *The Grasshopper Lies Heavy* remains unclear: at different stages in the novel, Abendsen's book is ascribed the status of a work of counterfactual fiction, a work of propaganda, and of a prophecy. Given this epistemically dubious status, *The Grasshopper Lies Heavy* can be related to other, less obvious metafactual elements of Dick's novel. *The Man in the High Castle* abounds in discussions about different kinds of nonfactuality, for example the ideologies of racism and antisemitism, the forgery of art, and political conspiracies. None of these elements, however, can be adequately described as counterfactual, that is, as openly altering facts; instead, they address questions of deception, delusion, and lies. Thus, the status of *The Man in the High Castle* as a work of fiction does not so much provide the framework for a counter-counterfactual – and hence, meta-reflexive – discussion of the book's own genre, but rather heightens the reader's attentiveness to different kinds of nonfactuality, which in the framework of Dick's novel are, for the most part, politically hazardous.

The (apparent) counter-counterfactual reversal of fictional truth constitutes but one possible manifestation of metafactuality. Metafactual reflections can take on a variety of forms. For example, in George Orwell's *Nineteen Eighty-*

Four (1949) – which can be interpreted as a counterfactual variation on the horrors of Stalinism and consequently classified as a work of counterfactual dystopianism[13] –, one of the totalitarian state's central agencies is called the 'Ministry of Truth.' It is an obvious irony that the purpose of this ministry consists not in establishing facts but rather in forging historical records in order to make them compatible with the ever-changing political dogma: truth in the denomination of this institution is a deliberate misnomer hiding the activity of lying conducted by its civil servants. Much like the book-within-a-book in *The Man in the High Castle*, the metafactual element in *Nineteen Eighty-Four* thus clearly draws attention to questions of truth, lies, and – the anachronistic use of the term is well justified here – fake news.

A third example of metafactuality, again from the genre of alternate history, is Robert Harris's novel *Fatherland*, depicting yet another counterfactual world in which the Nazis have won the war. The novel's protagonist, Kripo-detective Xavier March, investigates a number of murders of high-ranking Nazi Party officials. As is gradually revealed in the novel, these Nazi officials were all involved in planning the genocide of the Jews, a historical event of which only few Germans are aware in the novel's fictional world. By successively murdering the architects of the 'Final Solution,' the Nazi party is trying to obliterate the last traces of the Holocaust. Yet again, the metafactual element does not simply mirror the counterfactual setup of Harris's novel at the diegetic level; instead, the truth-related issue thematized in *Fatherland* clearly concerns forged history, more specifically, denial of the Holocaust.

6. *The Critical Function of Metafactuality*

As with counterfactual fiction in general, it seems tempting to read metafactual elements through the lens of postmodernism, thus interpreting them as narrative devices that emphasize the relativity of truth. This is, however, a reading that in my view ought to be rejected. Firstly, for their very constitution, counterfactual storyworlds rely on a clear distinction between what is true and what is false, since the existence of truth – whatever its exact status may be – is a precondition for any counterfactual departure from fact. Secondly, as was elaborated above, metafactual elements in counterfactual worlds themselves are usually not counterfactual. In relation to the counterfactual world within which they are located, metafactual elements tend to take on the status of direct

[13] As was noted above, such a counterfactual reading of dystopian texts has to go beyond an interpretation as general political allegory or speculative fiction. Instead, it would have to focus on the counterfactual connection between concrete elements in the real world – in Orwell's case: specific features of the totalitarian regimes of his own day, or, in the case of consciously anachronistic readings, any other time or society – and their variation within the fictional world of *Nineteen Eighty-Four*.

lies or other kinds of deceptive nonfactuality: they are, for example, concerned with forged historical records, distorting ideologies, and with the manipulation of the media.

These metafactual lies within counterfactual storyworlds are, of course, deceptive only for the fictional characters in that work of fiction. For readers or viewers in the real world, they are clearly recognizable as being at odds with truths about the respective storyworlds. Metafactual elements often use this very informational gap between the knowledge of fictional characters and that of actual readers for literary effect: in relation to the real-world readers or viewers, metafactual elements emphasize the very process of lying or, to put it differently, comment on the generation of post-truth. Metafactual elements in counterfactual worlds thus do not promote the legitimacy of a post-factual world view; rather, they *stage* post-truth in order to draw attention to its falsity, thereby exposing it to criticism. This critical staging of post-truth is all the more effective as it takes place within the framework of counterfactual fiction, that is, in texts that, in themselves, already draw attention to the distinction between truth and falsehood. It is this, as it were, reflexive attention to different forms of truth and falsehood that accounts for metafactuality's ability to expose lies for what they are. In short: metafactuality frequently serves as a narrative device for criticizing lies, post-truth, and other deceptive nonfactualities, thus affirming the importance of truth.

7. *Quentin Tarantino: Inglourious Basterds*

This truth-affirming function of metafactuality can be illustrated by a brief analysis of one of the most prominent works of counterfactual fiction from recent years: Quentin Tarantino's counterfactual war movie *Inglourious Basterds* (2009). Tarantino's movie presents a number of storylines set in the years between 1941 and 1944. At the heart of the plot is a fictitious Jewish-American Guerrilla army named 'Inglourious Basterds,' led by Lieutenant Aldo Raine, which hunts down German soldiers in Nazi-occupied France; another protagonist of the movie is SS-detective Hans Landa, called the 'Jew Hunter,' who is in turn trying to hunt down the Basterds. During the first night of one of Joseph Goebbels's movies in a French cinema – a glamorous event attended by Adolf Hitler himself –, some members of the Basterds manage to infiltrate the cinema and shoot Hitler, Goebbels, and most of the gathered Nazi notables. Two other terrorist acts are committed in parallel: the French-Jewish cinema owner Shoshanna Dreyfus and her black lover Marcel set fire to the cinema. And, in addition to this, the entire building is blown up by a charge of dynamite placed in the Führer's box by Hans Landa. The movie thus stages a symbolically charged triple annihilation of the Nazis elites, carried out by a Jewish guerilla army, a French survivor of the Holocaust, and a German dissident.

With regard to the topic of metafactuality, it is the third plot line which is most important. When the 'Jew Hunter' Landa realizes that a German victory is becoming unlikely and that consequently he might well find himself standing before a Jewish tribunal, having to justify his crimes, he decides to make a deal with the Basterds and the English government: he will assist in the assassination of Hitler and the entire Nazi elite. In return for his collaboration he demands – apart from a considerable material compensation – that all his crimes committed as a Nazi officer should be presented to the public as mere acts of camouflage. Additionally, he wants to be elevated to the status of a war hero who played a major role in the overthrow of the Nazi rule of terror. By posing the somewhat laconic question "What shall the history books read?," Landa presents Aldo, the head of the Basterds, with an ethical conundrum. Aldo can either support a scandalous historical lie, thus implicitly justifying the heinous crimes committed against the Jews, but by so doing also help end the war. Or he can insist on the truth, thereby risking that the war goes on for several more years, claiming millions of lives. Tarantino's movie, which is itself a prime example of counterfactual fiction, thus metafactually tackles the topics of forged history, opportunistic realpolitik, and the conflict between utilitarianism and an ethics based on principles, a conflict which in the concrete case is all the more pressing as it relates to the total signifier 'Auschwitz.'

Ultimately, the movie opts in favor of truth. Initially, the Basterds agree to the deal with Landa, the Nazis are killed, and Landa himself is taken away from the city. However, before releasing Landa, the Basterds do to him what they have done to all their Nazi prisoners: with a huge butcher's knife, they carve a swastika into his forehead (an act of cruelty which is shown as one of the movie's final scenes). Tarantino's movie thus clearly rejects the possibility of a post-factual distortion of the truth; on the contrary, the truth is visibly inscribed onto the very body of the liar for everyone to see. As with Orwell's Ministry of Truth, the central function of the metafactual element – in the case of *Inglourious Basterds*, a proposed distortion of the memory of the Holocaust – seems to reside in its emphasis on the abiding importance of truth, no matter what the political circumstances. It is one of the many ironies of *Inglourious Basterds*, then, that this very defense of historical truth is itself based on a lie, namely on the Basterds' betrayal of their pact with Landa to leave him unharmed after his surrender. Tarantino's movie thus ultimately suggests that lying *to* a mass murderer in order to ultimately reveal a politically more substantial truth is quite a different thing from lying *about* the Holocaust.

8. *Metafactuality as 'Willing Construction of Disbelief'*

At the end of my paper, I would like to substantiate my reading of metafactuality as truth-supporting by drawing on some concepts from cognitivist narratology. Empirical studies, of course, are not necessary for rendering hermeneutic claims plausible; also, since the writing of this paper did not involve experimental research, I do not wish to make any definite claim as to the accuracy of my hypothesis. All I wish to do here is lay out yet another path for the study of metafactuality that future research may or may not follow.

Many theorists of fiction today tend to regard fictionality not as a property immanent to certain objects but rather as a certain pragmatic stance one takes towards narratively constructed worlds (Lamarque & Olsen 1994; Köppe 2014). In this view, it is not a specific quality of texts and other media that renders them fictional but rather the 'institution' of fictionality, that is, a certain set of conventions that govern the modalities of reception. One key aspect of this mode of reception, to use Samuel Taylor Coleridge's famous definition, is the "willing suspension of disbelief" (Coleridge 1834, 174): when reading a work of fiction, we as readers are usually indifferent as to the real-world reference of the apparent assertions made in it. Put more simply: we do not really mind whether what is said is true or false.

This interpretation of fictionality has often been associated with an autonomist view of art, namely the belief that what a work of fiction states as true is completely independent of what is true in the real world. However, in recent years, this autonomist view has been called into question (Blume 2004, 16–34). Not only do genres like the historical novel evidently depend on real-world facts (as do, of course, works of counterfactual fiction). Cognitivist narratologists such as Richard J. Gerrig, Deborah Prentice, and David N. Rapp have also suggested that at a basic cognitive level, fictional texts are processed no differently from factual texts and that, as a consequence, fictional texts may have a significant effect on readers' real-world beliefs. In his seminal study *Experiencing Narrative Worlds*, Richard J. Gerrig writes:

> I suggested that there is no processing distinction between the serious and the non-serious assertions of nonfiction and fiction. [...] And I suggested that all information is understood as true until some is unaccepted. My general conclusion is that fictions will fail to have a real-world impact only if readers expend explicit effort to understand them as fictional. (Gerrig 1993, 240)

Regardless of the fact that readers may well be familiar with the institution of fictionality, the presentation of information in fictional media oftentimes affects their beliefs about the real world – unless this process of 'spontaneous' learning is actively interrupted. In this view, it does not take an effort to believe what is said in a work of fiction, as human beings seem to have a natural propensity to believe; it rather takes an effort *not* to believe (Rott 2013).[14]

Drawing on these empirical findings, Gerrig reformulates Coleridge's claim of the "willing suspension of disbelief" as the "willing construction of disbelief" (Gerrig 1993, 230, 240). While Coleridge suggests that, when reading fiction, we have to suppress our natural impulse to notice instances of falsity, Gerrig in contrast proposes that we spontaneously take what is said to be true, even when we read or see it in a work of fiction (Gerrig & Gagnone 2020, 142). Only in a second step are the beliefs generated through works of fiction – if the need arises – critically evaluated: "the only experiential distinctions between fiction and nonfiction are those that readers effortfully construct" (Gerrig 1993, 240). This effortful construction of disbelief may be initiated by, among other things, certain strong markers in the text that emphasize the fictitious nature of some of the properties of a fictional world. For example, there is evidence that fictional worlds which are clearly non-realistic – such as the storyworlds of science fiction and fantasy genres – are less likely than realistic texts to affect readers' real-world convictions (Rapp et al. 2014, 67–68; Gerrig & Gagnon 2020, 142).

I have no space here to discuss the merits, implications, and possible problems of the theory of willing construction of disbelief at length (but see Zipfel 2013, 53–58; Rott 2013). What is important in the given context is that the concept of a willing construction of (truth-affirming) disbelief may be productively related to my suggestions regarding the general function of metafactuality. If it is necessary to have certain hints and markers in a text in order to recognize an aspect of a fictional world as untrue, the metafactual discussion of lies within works of counterfactual fiction might constitute just such a marker. While counterfactual fiction itself constitutes a form of nonfactuality clearly distinct from lies, it often serves as a framework for a diegetic presentation, problematization, and political critique of lies as well as of other forms of deceptive nonfactuality. Through their epistemic dual structure of a lie within a counterfactual world, metafactual elements actively draw attention to their own truth status – or lack thereof – and may thus function as a means for the willing construction of disbelief.

9. *Conclusion*

In this paper, I have presented a discussion of counterfactual fiction, that is, counterfactual storytelling in fictional media. My definition of counterfactual fiction has focused on its specific reference structure. I have also distin-

[14] The philosophical term for this concept is *negative doxastic voluntarism* (Rott 2008, 2013).

guished counterfactual fiction from lies. In the second half of my paper, I have discussed the use of lies and other nonfactualities within counterfactual storyworlds, for which I suggested the term metafactuality. As I have argued, metafactual elements in works of counterfactual fiction usually do not have the status of counterfactual fiction themselves, but are concerned with deceptive forms of nonfactuality. Metafactuality involves, as it were, 'embedded' nonfactuality, that is, lies *within* counterfactual storyworlds. This emphasis on the distinction between truth and lies highlights works of counterfactual fiction and the metafactual elements within them as privileged artistic forms for the critique of lies, conspiracy theories, and other kinds of deceptive as well as politically disruptive nonfactuality. My thesis that metafactuality is truth-affirming may resonate with empirical findings from cognitivist narratology which emphasize that special effort is needed to refrain from believing in the claims made in works of fiction. Metafactuality, I suggested, may function as a narrative device for initiating a 'willing construction of disbelief.'

The central claim of this article might be summarized as follows: despite their respective links with the general topic of nonfactuality, works of counterfactual fiction and the metafactual elements within them ultimately do not undermine the distinction between truth and falsehood but, on the contrary, emphasize the abiding importance of truth, especially in the political sphere. It may be no mere coincidence, then, that in recent years a fair share of politically engaged works of fiction have been works of counterfactual fiction. These works comprise alternate histories – like Tarantino's *Inglourious Basterds*, the recent web TV-adaptation of Dick's novel *The Man in the High Castle* (2015–2019), and three novels by Christian Kracht (2008, 2012, 2016) –, but they also include the abundant production of dystopian fiction which counterfactually comments on the political developments and ideological trends of our own day. Here one may think of Dave Eggers's *The Circle* (2013), Suzanne Collins's *The Hunger Games* (2008–2010), the web TV-adaptation of Margaret Atwood's novel *The Handmaid's Tale* (first season released in 2017), the dystopian novels of Juli Zeh (2009, 2017), or Michel Houellebecq's infamous novel *Submission* (2015). Perhaps the popularity of these works of fiction is not so much a sign of the ubiquity of postmodern thought, nor yet another indicator for the continual merging of truth and lies in today's political sphere. Their popularity may instead be an expression of a wide-spread desire for art – at least – to affirm the truth. From this viewpoint, counterfactual fiction does not align with the phenomenon of post-truth at all but instead functions as one of art's antidotes to political lying.

Works Cited

Albrecht, Andrea, and Lutz Danneberg (2011) '"First Steps Toward an Explication of Counterfactual Imagination.'" *Counterfactual Thinking – Counterfactual Writing.* Ed. Dorothee Birke, Michael Butter, and Tilmann Köppe. Berlin: De Gruyter. 11–29.

Baßler, Moritz (2010) "'Have a nice apocalypse!' Parahistorisches Erzählen bei Christian Kracht." *Utopie und Apokalypse in der Moderne.* Ed. Reto Sorg and Stefan Bodo Würffel. Munich: Fink. 257–272.

Birke, Dorothee, Michael Butter, and Tilmann Köppe (2011) Ed. *Counterfactual Thinking – Counterfactual Writing.* Berlin: De Gruyter.

Blume, Peter (2004) *Fiktion und Weltwissen. Der Beitrag nichtfiktionaler Konzepte zur Sinnkonstitution fiktionaler Erzählliteratur.* Berlin: Erich Schmidt.

Carr, Edward Hallett (1961) *What is History?* New York: Macmillan.

Christ, Birte (2011) "'If I Were a Man': Functions of the Counterfactual in Feminist Fiction." *Counterfactual Thinking – Counterfactual Writing.* Ed. Dorothee Birke, Michael Butter, and Tilmann Köppe. Berlin: De Gruyter. 190–211.

Coleridge, Samuel Taylor (1834) *Biographia Literaria, Or, Biographical Sketches of My Literary Life and Opinions.* New York and Boston: Leavitt, Lord & Co. and Crocker and Brewster.

Danneberg, Lutz (2006) '"Überlegungen zu kontrafaktischen Imaginationen in argumentativen Kontexten und zu Beispielen ihrer Funktion in der Denkgeschichte.'" *Imagination und Innovation*. Ed. Toni Bernhart and Philipp Mehne. Berlin: Akademie. 73–100.

Demandt, Alexander (1984) *Ungeschehene Geschichte. Ein Traktat über die Frage: Was wäre geschehen, wenn...?* Göttingen: Vandenhoeck & Ruprecht.

Eco, Umberto (1992) *Die Grenzen der Interpretation.* Munich and Vienna: Hanser.

Eco, Umberto (1994) *Im Wald der Fiktionen. Sechs Streifzüge durch die Literatur.* Munich: Hanser.

Evans, Richard J. (2013) *Altered Pasts: Counterfactuals in History.* Waltham, Massachusetts: Brandeis Univ. Press.

Fludernik, Monika (1996) *Towards A 'Natural' Narratology.* London and New York: Routledge.

Gallagher, Catherine (2011) '"What would Napoleon Do? Historical, Fictional, and Counterfactual Characters.'" *New Literary History* 42.2: 315–336.

Gerrig, Richard J. (1993) *Experiencing Narrative Worlds: On the Psychological Activities of Reading*. New Haven, CT, and London: Yale Univ. Press.

Gerrig, Richard J. and Janelle M. Gagnon (2020) "The Factual in Psychology." *Narrative Factuality: A Handbook.* Ed. Monika Fludernik and Marie-Laure Ryan. Berlin and Boston: De Gruyter. 133–147.

Gilovich, Thomas and Victoria Husted Medvec (1995) "Some Counterfactual Determinants of Satisfaction and Regret." *What Might Have Been: The Social Psychology of Counterfactual Thinking.* Ed. Neal J. Roese and James M. Olson. Mahwah, New Jersey: Erlbaum. 259–282.

Goodman, Nelson (1947) "The Problem of Counterfactual Conditionals." *The Journal of Philosophy* 44.5: 113–128.

Helbig, Jörg (1988) *Der parahistorische Roman: Ein literarhistorischer und gattungstypologischer Beitrag zur Allotopieforschung.* Frankfurt o.t.M.: Lang.

Hellekson, Karen (2001) *The Alternate History: Refiguring Historical Time.* Kent, Ohio: Kent State Univ. Press.

Hrushovski, Benjamin (1984) "Fictionality and Fields of Reference." *Poetics Today* 5.2: 227–251.

Huemer, Wolfgang (2010) "Gibt es Fehler im fiktionalen Kontext? Grenzen der dichterischen Freiheit." *Was aus Fehlern zu lernen ist in Alltag, Wissenschaft und Kunst.* Ed. Otto Neumaier. Vienna and Münster: Lit. 211–227.

Köppe, Tilmann (2014) "Die Institution Fiktionalität." *Fiktionalität. Ein interdisziplinäres Handbuch.* Ed. Tilmann Köppe and Tobias Klauk. Berlin and Boston: De Gruyter. 35–49.

Künne, Wolfgang (1983) *Abstrakte Gegenstände. Semantik und Ontologie.* Frankfurt o.t.M.: Suhrkamp.

Künne, Wolfgang (1995) "Fiktion ohne fiktive Gegenstände: Prolegomena zu einer Fregeanischen Theorie der Fiktion." *Metaphysik. Neue Zugänge zu alten Fragen.* Ed. Johannes L. Brandl, Alexander Hieke, and Peter M. Simons. St. Augustin: Academia. 141–161.

Lamarque, Peter and Stein Haugom Olsen (1994) *Truth, Fiction, and Literature: A Philosophical Perspective.* Oxford: Clarendon Press.

Lamarque, Peter (2015) "Literature and Truth." *A Companion to the Philosophy of Literature.* Ed. Garry L. Hagberg and Walter Jost. Malden, Oxford, and Chichester: Wiley Blackwell. 367–384.

Lewis, David (1979) "Truth in Fiction." *American Philosophical Quarterly* 15.1: 37–46.

Navratil, Michael (2019) "Jenseits des politischen Realismus. Kontrafaktik als Verfahren politischen Schreibens in der Gegenwartsliteratur (Juli Zeh, Michel Houellebecq)." *Das Politische in der Literatur der Gegenwart.* Ed. Stefan Neuhaus and Immanuel Nover. Berlin and Boston: De Gruyter. 359–375.

Navratil, Michael (forthcoming) *Kontrafaktik der Gegenwart. Politisches Schreiben als Realitätsvariation bei Christian Kracht, Kathrin Röggla, Juli Zeh und Leif Randt*. Berlin and Boston: De Gruyter.

Nünning, Ansgar (1995) *Von historischer Fiktion zu historiographischer Metafiktion*. 2 vols. LIR, 11–12. Trier: WVT.

Rapp, David N., Scott R. Hinze, Daniel G. Slaten, and William S. Horton (2014) "Amazing Stories: Acquiring and Avoiding Inaccurate Information from Fiction." *Discourse Processes* 51.1–2: 50–74.

Rodiek, Christoph (1997) *Erfundene Vergangenheit. Kontrafaktische Geschichtsdarstellung (Uchronie) in der Literatur.* Frankfurt o.t.M.: Klostermann.

Roese, Neal J. and Mike Morrison (2009) "The Psychology of Counterfactual Thinking." *Counterfactual Thinking as a Scientific Method.* Ed. Roland Wenzlhuemer. Cologne: Zentrum für Historische Sozialforschung. 16–26.

Roese, Neal J. and James M. Olson (1995) "Preface." *What Might Have Been: The Social Psychology of Counterfactual Thinking.* Ed. Neal J. Roese and James M. Olson. Mahwah, New Jersey: Erlbaum. vii-xi.

Rosenfeld, Gavriel D. (2005) *The World Hitler Never Made: Alternate History and the Memory of Nazism.* Cambridge, New York, and Melbourne: Cambridge Univ. Press.

Rott, Hans (2008) "Negative Doxastic Voluntarism and the Ethics of Belief." *Truth and Judgement*. Ed. Patrick Nerhot. Milano: Franco Angeli. 27–49.

Rott, Hans (2013) "Von der Mühe, nicht zu glauben. Fiktionale Texte und negativer doxastischer Voluntarismus." *Fiktion, Wahrheit, Interpretation. Philologische und philosophische Perspektiven.* Ed. Eva-Maria Konrad, Thomas Petraschka, Jürgen Daiber, and Hans Rott. Münster: mentis. 65–106.

Ryan, Marie-Laure (2007) "Toward a Definition of Narrative." *The Cambridge Companion to Narrative.* Ed. David Herman. Cambridge: Cambridge Univ. Press. 22–35.

Ryan, Marie-Laure (2008) "Transfictionality Across Media." *Theorizing Narrativity.* Ed. John Pier and José Ángel García Landa. Berlin: De Gruyter. 385–417.

Ryan, Marie-Laure (2014) "Story/Worlds/Media: Tuning the Instruments of a Media-Conscious Narratology." *Storyworlds Across Media: Toward a Media-Conscious Narratology.* Ed. Marie-Laure Ryan and Jan-Noël Thon. Lincoln, Nebraska: Univ. of Nebraska Press. 25–49.

Saint-Gelais, Richard (2008) "Transfictionality." *Routledge Encyclopedia of Narrative Theory.* Ed. David Herman, Manfred Jahn, and Marie-Laure Ryan. London and New York: Routledge.

Singles, Kathleen (2013) *Alternate History: Playing with Contingency and Necessity.* Berlin and Boston: De Gruyter.

Wenzlhuemer, Roland (2009) Ed. *Counterfactual Thinking as a Scientific Method.* Cologne: Zentrum für Historische Sozialforschung.

White, Haydn (1999) *Figural Realism: Studies in the Mimesis Effect.* Baltimore, Maryland: Johns Hopkins Univ. Press.

Widmann, Andreas Martin (2009) *Kontrafaktische Geschichtsdarstellung. Untersuchungen an Romanen von Günter Grass, Thomas Pynchon, Thomas Brussig, Michael Kleeberg, Philip Roth und Christoph Ransmayr.* Heidelberg: Winter.

Winko, Simone, and Fotis Jannidis (2015) "Wissen und Inferenz. Zum Verstehen und Interpretieren literarischer Texte am Beispiel von Hans Magnus Enzensbergers Gedicht *Frühschriften*." *Literatur interpretieren. Interdisziplinäre Beiträge zur Theorie und Praxis.* Ed. Jan Borkowski. Münster: mentis. 221–250.

Wolf, Werner (2017) "Transmedial Narratology: Theoretical Foundations and Some Applications (Fiction, Single Pictures, Instrumental Music)." *Narrative* 25.3: 256–285.

Wünsch, Marianne. *Die Fantastische Literatur der Frühen Moderne (1890–1930). Definition – Denkgeschichtlicher Kontext – Strukturen.* Munich: Fink, 1991.

Zipfel, Frank (2001) *Fiktion, Fiktivität, Fiktionalität. Analysen zur Fiktion in der Literatur und zum Fiktionsbegriff in der Literaturwissenschaft.* Berlin: Erich Schmidt.

Zipfel, Frank (2013) "Imagination, fiktive Welten und fiktionale Wahrheit. Zu Theorien fiktionsspezifischer Rezeption von literarischen Texten." *Fiktion, Wahrheit, Interpretation. Philologische und philosophische Perspektiven.* Ed. Eva-Maria Konrad, Thomas Petraschka, Jürgen Daiber, and Hans Rott. Münster: mentis. 38–64.

Waiting for the Emperor's New Clothes: The Temporal Order of the Public Lie

Stephan Packard

"The President of the United States is not a crook." In Robert Anton Wilson's *Schrödinger's Cat* trilogy (1979, 191), this aphorism, echoing Richard Nixon's apodictic self-apology in 1973, is attributed more generally to "The President of the United States" and quoted in parallel with that older proposition, "All Cretans are liars," attributed here to "Empedocles the Cretan." The juxtaposition suggests that some of the irritation associated with the Liar's Paradox should apply to affirmations of truthfulness as much as it does to a universal and self-referential statement of deception. But the equation of the Cretan and the politician is ostensibly false: a purely logical puzzle that arises only through self-reference is replaced by an inquiry into the pragmatics of speakers' self-presentation in factual assertions. It is precisely because all factuality depends on speakers' sincerity that the same speakers can never categorically exclude the possibility of insincerity. If the President's protestation of his own reliability is taken to be infelicitous, this will not be due to a syntactical conundrum, but on account of the pragmatics of political and public discourse.

This chapter deals with the tensions within those pragmatics. It examines some features of public lies by looking at the conditions of their possibility. My central claim is that the general pragmatics of public communication lies at the root of both the familiar, time-worn frustrations with popular deceit and of the more recent denouncements of 'fake news' and 'postfactuality.' In addition, I propose that it is not some recently declining interest in facts or the effects of new, digital, and networked means of communication (as is often claimed) that are primarily responsible for the named effects but the same general pragmatics of public communication. Social media are not the determining cause of a burgeoning distrust in politics, but, as I will argue, connect with the shifting parameters of political discourse in quite specific ways.

I begin by pointing out the importance of the temporal order of the public lie by looking at an established literary treatment of deception and power, namely Hans Christian Andersen's "Keiserens nye Klæder," 'The Emperor's New Clothes' (1837). I use this parable as a paradigm for the analysis of political deceit and its relationship with different orders of propaganda. I will argue that the public lie endures as long as public censure remains inconclusive (section 1). On this basis, I go on to delineate some further properties of the public lie, distinguishing it both from private lies and from literary fictions and focusing on its dependence on divided audiences (section 2). Finally, I briefly consider the changing conditions for the public lie which have been produced due to the digital transformations of the public sphere (section 3).

Of course, the Cretan Liar's Paradox, at least in the popular form repeated by Wilson, is not a paradox at all. Deliberately or by providential mistake, Wilson in fact happens to hint at this by having one Empedocles – instead of the traditional Epimenides (Russell 1908) – deliver the statement, attributing it to the wrong Cretan. In the assertion that all Cretans are liars, the apparent contradiction is easily solved by assuming that this one Cretan, in this one instance, is telling one simple and deliberate lie, or at least commits a fortuitous mistake of his own. Contrary to his claim, not all Cretans lie, much less do they do so all the time. His proposition in this instance *need* not have been false – but it is, precisely because the next thing he or any other Cretan says might as well be true. The more rigid Liar's Paradox demands that speakers indict their own speech as false even as it is performed: 'I am lying right now.' More elegantly, it can do away with the self-reference to the speaker altogether and is then expressed by a self-referential statement: 'This sentence is false.' By making these distinctions, one can clarify what makes the political lie and the irritation it causes a substantially different matter than the Liar's Paradox: the public lie depends on imagining the speaker's performance, and on classifying speakers as belonging to particular groups of political identity or allegiance. In fact, the Epimenides of tradition had a reason to decry the lying Cretans, which focuses the intension and thus limits the extension of his statement: he was protesting his countrymen's erection of a tomb to Zeus, whom he considered immortal (cf. Harris 1907). Hence, the intended pragmatic meaning of 'all Cretans' obviously excluded the speaker, despite the imprecise syntax.

Our tendency to confuse the logical and the political irritation with one another is in itself illuminating. Rather than being willing to face political conflict, we seem all too ready to pretend that some intractable logical problem complicates the expectation of truth in public statements. Why else would we even assume there is a point to Empedocles' ill-formulated aphorism in the first place? Why should we assume a difficult problem where a less complicated reading is available? Why were we willing to recognize in the simple case of a patently false statement a more fundamental logical problem that was not even there? I believe that the answer lies in our desire to avoid the censure of the lie. We would rather plunge into logical aporia and consider that truthfulness is generally self-contradictory, than assume that this one fictitious Cretan, or one given President of the United States, were deliberately deceiving their audience. But for how long can the reality of the lie be evaded?

1. *Waiting for Truth: The Times of Postfactuality and the Emperor's New Clothes*

"Es heißt ja neuerdings, wir lebten in postfaktischen Zeiten." 'Nowadays people claim that we live in postfactual times': in these words, Germany's Chancellor Angela Merkel, summarized a pessimistic diagnosis of the times. This was as early as 2012, in a public address reacting to her party's recent defeat at the state elections in Berlin (*Der Spiegel* 2016). Four years later, *Oxford Dictionaries* named *post-truth* the word of the year. In the ensuing media attention, *The Washington Post* associated this phrase directly with the Trump campaign for the Presidency. An editorial on the subject was illustrated with a picture from the Clinton/Trump debates (Wang 2016), and accused Donald Trump – well, not quite of being a liar. Instead, the article chose circuitous paraphrases such as "Trump's relationship with the truth was, well, complicated" (Wang 2016). In the editorial, which discusses false public statements, public trust in politicians, and truth-checking from many different angles, the word *liar* does not appear once, and *lie* only in a citation from another source, which again avoids a direct attribution:

"We concede all politicians lie," wrote conservative columnist Jennifer Rubin; "[n]evertheless, Donald Trump is in a class by himself" (Wang 2016, citing Rubin 2016). Putting Trump "in a class by himself" is an indictment of sorts, yet it still seems to grant the man more leniency than would his direct condemnation as a liar; the phrase suggests that whatever Trump might be doing to the truth is not quite mendacity, but something else.

To be fair to *The Washington Post*, it eventually became one of the few major news media outlets that called President Trump a liar without equivocation. But others were more reluctant to follow, and even the *Post's* delay is interesting. When *Der Spiegel* reported on the *Oxford Dictionaries*' decision, they quoted Merkel's statement from four years earlier in order to argue that postfactuality was an older, more general affair, and one less directly tied to any particular speaker's abuse of the truth. Merkel had continued by saying, 'Supposedly that means that people are no longer interested in facts but are instead only following their emotions' ["Das soll wohl heißen, die Menschen interessieren sich nicht mehr für Fakten, sondern folgen allein den Gefühlen"]. Later she would often argue vehemently that people still had to rely on the truth in order to make relevant decisions. But in Berlin in 2012, she yielded to the supposed expectation of feelings over facts, accepting that 'it would be illogical to counter [others' postfactual attacks] with facts' and proposing that she 'would instead offer an emotional response of her own in return' (Fischer 2016; "[...] nun wäre es unlogisch, dies mit Fakten zu kontern" and: "Ich will dem also meinerseits mit einem Gefühl begegnen"; all translations by S.P.). All of these formulations shift the perception of a problem with factuality from individual responsibility to a more general public atmosphere. In this manner, by deploying a critique of society which superficially appears to be more radical, any direct challenge to the powerful individual who has told a lie is avoided.

Following this line of argument, one can demonstrate that the idea of post-truth rehearses a story about a society which has grown disinterested in facts, while others might tell a story about liars fabricating so-called facts. I here propose that we should look very carefully at these stories' treatment of the truth. Since the post-truth narrative makes claims about truth conditions, it participates in the explicit discursive mechanisms by which we construct truth, as Michel Foucault has famously argued (Foucault 1971, esp. 12-14). Postfactual discourse, then, might or might not be characterized by an actually diminishing interest in facts but *is* characterized by a topical interest in such a change – and by a pragmatic hesitancy to call out liars.

We are dealing with a narration on three levels. On the base level, one person makes a public claim, saying that something happened, and narrates that event. On an intermediate level, a second source cites and frames this claim, telling us that the original speaker presented facts in such a manner so as to 'engage in a complicated relationship with the truth' – or in some other fashion avoiding the direct accusation of deceit. On a third overarching level of discourse, many such instances are summarized or conflated and either criticized or justified as being a phenomenon of the 'post-truth era.' The narration on the second level chooses to tell a postfactual story of the lie committed on the first level; the narration on the third level presents a story about what we might call *post-truth, i.e. the quality of speaking postfactually*. The discourse of postfactuality is necessarily nested between the lie and the indictment of a whole society that allows for it to pass unchallenged. In order to describe untruthful claims uttered in specific instances, it deploys a category that differs from the label of the lie and adopts that category from a tale about a general decline of the public sphere's rational quest for truth.

By narrating postfactuality as a gradual decline, tales of post-truth refocus the generalized lack of truthfulness temporally rather than individually: they tell us that our age has become less truthful, rather than that certain people have. In 2012, Angela Merkel spoke of 'postfactual times'; and after the *Oxford Dictionaries* had declared *post-truth* the word of that year in 2016, Amy Wang in the *Washington Post* responded by stating: "It's official: Truth is dead. Facts are passé." Yet she then continued: "And this sentiment – 😂 – is so last year" (Wang 2016). This assertion both points out that the moment for the catastrophe of factuality might already have passed and, more generally, ascribes it to postdigital communication as characterized by the use of the smiley laughing tears. If there is a specific time of postfactuality, it can be found on either the third or the second level of the encompassing narrative – and on each level either as a discursive event of storytelling or as the time of the event told in the story. On the third level, the narrative of a society losing its interest in truth is told at a certain point in history and, through this telling, suggests that the loss of that interest supposedly occurred at a certain historical juncture. On the second level, each framing of a non-factual statement as postfactual rather than as a lie occurs at a particular point in time, but also refers to the lie, which happened at another time (usually earlier, though a narrator can also expect others to deliver fake news in the future). (While the first level also engages with a temporal order in making a false claim about an event that supposedly happened at some point in time, this does not affect the protestations of postfactuality.)

If there is a specific time for postfactuality, then, this might be the case because so many lies are being told at that moment; or because so many critics tend to frame lies evasively at that time; or because a society has supposedly succumbed to postfactuality at that time; or because a society is diagnosed as having done so at a particular time. The question of whether postfactuality is a new phenomenon can thus be asked in a series of four questions: did people in the past not lie as much as they do today? Did they not hesitate to call out liars as they do today? Or, if they did hesitate, was that hesitation less systemic? And: is the diagnosis of postfactuality entirely new – have we not heard it before?

Certainly, despair over people's failing investment in truth is far from new. As Dallas Denery notes in this volume, Montaigne connects the mere wearing of clothes, which cannot help but relate to the changing styles of fashion, with a person's willingness to change their opinions and identity as readily as their style of clothing. More generally, the common criticism of discourse at court is associated with the attention to dress and surface appearances, and the decline of a trust in rhetoric goes along with the stories of a decline in political discourse (Barthes 1970). The thesis of such a decline associates the shift to post-truth discourse with the rise of a certain political structure; it therefore also allows one to imagine that shift as political rather than temporal. The fundamental link of power to the conditions of truth-telling goes back to antiquity's conception of *parrhesia*, the act of speaking truth to power. In 1983 Foucault outlined the characteristics of the *parrhesiastes*, the speaker of *parrhesia*, in his lectures on "Discourse and Truth" at Berkeley (Foucault 2019). The *parrhesiastes* is a person who enjoys a long-established credibility or expertise, and who now takes a special risk by uttering the truth: someone who speaks out, obeying a moral duty to the truth, who criticizes power, and who does so without resorting to rhetorical manipulation or finesse. *Parrhesia* thus relates to two temporalities of truth, both pragmatic rather than historical. The *parrhesiastes* enjoys a long-established role as truthful authority. Previously, the parrhesiastes' statements have been accepted as true. The most recent statements place the parrhesiastes in temporary danger, foregrounding a moral in addition to an epistemological relation to truth. The opposition between repeated proofs of truthfulness and then one punctual moment of endangered truth speaking highlights the temporality of parrhesia, not by ascribing them to a historic point in time when truth-telling was still possible, but by describing the pragmatic temporalities of duration involved in each case: the question is not *when*, but *for how long* one needs to do *parrhesia*. The transient circumstances of power make *parrhesia* special. Preceding the modern public sphere, it was then arguably a specific feature of the political sphere to provide a test for a speaker's dedication to truth. The idea of *parrhesia* already assumes that to speak truth under such circumstances is a rare exception rather than the rule, even though, or precisely because, it constitutes a moral duty. From this perspective, mendacity is expected to rule in regular speech under the condition of dangerous power, and *parrhesia* interrupts this expectation and this regularity at unique moments. Here it is therefore not a matter of turning away from the truth at a certain point in time, but of exceptionally speaking the truth though the circumstances suggest that lying might be safer. Of course, silence would be safer still; but the moral duty involved posits silence as complicity. The question of whose responsibility it is to break their silence and say the truth is of special importance to the pragmatics of the public lie, as we will see in greater detail below.

One famous account of the ubiquity of falsehood and its interruption through truth is Hans Christian Andersen's "Keiserens nye Klæder," 'The Emperor's New Clothes,' first published in 1837. Andersen proffers his political parable in the shape of a fairy tale purportedly written for children, and affixes to the ruler the ostensibly timeless title of emperor. Thus Andersen denies his critique any explicit positioning in a particular historical moment (notwithstanding possible Aesopian interpretations). In the famous tale, an emperor and his court are tricked by a charlatan tailor to believe in the existence of an invisible textile perceptible only to the wise. When the emperor is clothed in his new robes (which do not exist), both the court and the people pretend that they can see these garments. This dissimulation expands in space and time until there is a large public procession at which all the people get to gaze at the naked, supposedly clothed emperor. Then, finally, one person in the crowd, a child, points out the truth: "'But he isn't wearing anything!' said a little child." ["'Men han har jo ikke noget paa!' sagde et lille Barn." – 1837, 111]. So far, this situation is only connectable to the classical role of the *parrhesiastes* if one assumes that childlike innocence corresponds to an established authority for knowing the truth. Far from concluding the dominion of the lie, however, the emperor's public exposure merely tests it. For Andersen does not end his tale with the child's pronouncement. While the call is taken up by the crowd, the child's father distances himself from the indictment ("Herre Gud, hør den Uskyldiges Røst" – "Dear God, hear the voice of the innocent"), and eventually the power structure persists, if under strain and held hostage to the lie:

> "But he isn't wearing anything!," cried the whole crowd at last. The Emperor cringed, realizing they were right, but he thought, "I must make it through this procession." And the chamberlains went and carried the train of the dress which was not there at all. ["Men han har jo ikke noget paa," raabte tilsidst hele Folket. Det krøb i Keiseren, thi han syntes, de havde Ret, men han tænkte som saa: "nu maa jeg holde Processionen ud". Og Kammerherrerne gik og bar paa Slæbet, som der slet ikke var. – 1837, 111. Trans. S.P.]

From anecdotal evidence, it appears that many people seem to remember the story ending several lines earlier, believing that the child's cry resulted in a new, more factual consensus. And indeed Andersen is clearly interested in the punch line that exposes the lie, letting the liars know that they have been exposed *as* liars. But that is not the only point of the tale, for the lie has yet to be officially acknowledged. Though the lie has been called out, it still continues to rule, leaving the people in the story and Andersen's readership equally uncertain as to the eventual outcome. The emperor's power is not curtailed in any obvious way; his followers show their support even more obviously than before, repeating the same lie. The people, indispensable participants in the communicative assemblage, have heard the denouncement, and have perceived the lie, but no consequences devolve from their realization: even after the crowd has begun chanting, the emperor's procession goes on. I argue that it is in this ambivalent temporality, with the falsehood exposed but only partially acknowledged, that the public lie lives, defined by its duration and not by any specific point in history. Rather than arising through a huge societal upheaval, as the story of post-truth would have it, postfactual discourse has its place in a specific constellation defining the relation between power, the public, and falsehood, and linked to the time while the lie endures. That lie will not survive forever but, for the moment, it avoids conclusive censure.

Just as the concept of *parrhesia* can be defined in part by its two situational temporalities, i.e. established authority and transient danger, the extended avoidance of conclusive censure characterizes the public lie. This at once sets the public lie into potential relation to *parrhesia*: a successful *parrhesia* could eventually put an end to the public lie. Less optimistically, we might have to wait for the displacement of some power structures to settle some matters of post-truth, which can only happen once open censure has become less dangerous. In either case, placing the problem in its proper pragmatics, namely its political context, invites comparison with other forms of political speech-under-power, i.e. propaganda (e.g. Bussemer 2008). As more recent theories of propaganda have emphasized, primarily in discussions of China's public media control (Roberts 2018), 'hard' propaganda can be set apart from 'soft' propaganda. While the latter emphasizes attempts to change the public's mind – often by manipulative means –, hard propaganda does not need to be believed. Instead it demonstrates the superiority of a certain power, usually a government, to uphold a blatant lie by means of the mere threat of repressive consequences for any parrhesiastic interruption (Huang 2018). Indeed, lending their support, even public support, to the false claims of those who wield power can be a most effective shibboleth for followers to prove their loyalty: no one would be likely to repeat the obvious falsehood except with this intention. Note that the distinction between hard and soft propaganda needs to be contrasted with the division between 'strong' as opposed to 'weak' propaganda (Fahlenbrach 2018). According to this more traditional and still useful conception, strong propaganda can be diagnosed when a dictatorship censors different opinions so successfully that its own propaganda becomes more effective in convincing the public of the regime's truth than the criticisms of dissidents countering the official arguments. Hard propaganda, on the other hand, is effective in the face of convincing opposing views. It survives even as the crowd chants that the emperor is naked; the falsehood persists *despite* opposition rather than due to its absence.

Andersen's tale may stand as a simple paradigm of this kind of discourse. A closer look at actual examples in public communication will serve to further differentiate the relationships between such untruth, recognized lies, standards of truth, and licences of fiction in the public sphere. In addition to censure, interventions in the time of lies include attitudes of feigned innocence, of aesthetic interruption, and of the fictionalization of mendacity.

2. *Dividing the Audience: Lying in Private, in Public, and in Literature*

Several decades ago, conspiracy theories appeared in popular literature at least as widely as they did in works of political esotericism. Even then, the borders of fictionality could be put to the test by successful popular tales. Several years prior to the *Schrödinger's Cat* trilogy quoted at the beginning of this chapter, Robert Shea's and Robert Anton Wilson's much more infamous *Illuminatus!* trilogy (1975) delighted those readers and reviewers who understood this "ultimate conspiracy book" (according to *The Village Voice* quoted on the book cover) as a fantastical pop novel about, among many other topics, political gullibility in the waning years of student protests and New Age counterculture. Yet less than a decade later, George Johnson (1983) discussed the trilogy's preposterous claims among those conspiracy theories that contributed to the rise of a paranoiac New Right in American politics. Should one regard this result as a defeat of Wilson's rhetorical intent or consider it as a triumph of the original fiction, particularly seeing that Wilson went on to embrace the opportunity for sequels, hoaxes, and continued esoteric communication in his many subsequent publications?

If a fiction that is abused as a factual statement can be said to amount to a lie, it is the abuse, not the original imaginary content, that is responsible for the deceit; this draws our attention to the distinction between successful communication and the very different felicity conditions of deceit. However, one might also suspect that the enjoyment of that imaginative conspiracy is apt to support the factual lie to the same degree as it did the seemingly harmless fiction. If it is funny, intriguing, or interesting to imagine a certain conspiracy in jest, this might also provoke interest in the same theory when presented in all apparent sincerity. In both cases, the entertainment qualities perhaps contribute to the popularity of a public statement, which in turn constitutes one of the measures of such a statement's success. The same measure probably applies to most public lies.

A second infelicitous interaction between fiction and lies in public discourse may arise in contexts where apologies for lying reformulate those lies as rhetorical ploys. As recent discussions of fiction and factuality have emphasized (see Fludernik and Ryan 2019, as well as Fludernik in this volume), in many rhetorical figures and strategies that appear outside traditional literary fiction, the conditions of strict truth claims are suspended. Apologies based on rhetoric need not take as blatant a form as the infamous defense presented by US Senator Jon Kyl's spokesperson for the senator's false claim during a 2011 Senate debate. He had proposed that "well over 90 percent of what Planned Parenthood does" (Reeve 2011) supposedly consisted in abortions. The senator, as his spokesperson qualified, had "not intended" the (utterly false) number of 90 percent "to be a factual statement but rather to illustrate that Planned Parenthood, an organization that receives millions in taxpayer dollars, does subsidize abortions" (Reeve 2011). While the context of a Senate debate might invite expectations that speakers will indulge in strong rhetoric, the precise statistical number given would seem to many to suggest a factual intention. But perhaps not to all – at least, the senator's spokesperson believed that there was some value in recasting the statement as merely illustrative. If that value does not consist in believability, it could instead be said to lie in a negotiation of postfactuality: it cites a presumably general category of non-factual communication in order to frame this concrete, factually false statement as something other than a lie.

Of course, 'not intended as a factual statement' has since then become one among many sarcastic or acerbic descriptors of political mendacity – though the phrase seems to have originated in legal discourse defining libel and slander in courts of law. Even in that context, however, the most traditional forms of fiction, such as the storytelling in a published novel, do not necessarily constitute a full defense, as a New York Trial Court notes in an oft-cited decision from 2003:

> For a fictional character to constitute actionable defamation, the description of the fictional character must be so closely akin to the real person claiming to be defamed that a reader of the book, knowing the real person, would have no difficulty linking the two. Superficial similarities are insufficient. (New York Trial Court 2003)

While the court's opinion outlines conditions for committing defamation in fiction, these conditions are not commonly met in fictional prose, nor did the court believe they had been met in the individual case in question. The definition proceeds from an established concept of fictionality in the literary field. However, where the distinction between public fiction and public lies becomes unclear, so too might questions of responsibility and liability.

Similarly, one can point to a third kind of ambivalence that can arise around a public statement of proven falsehood without the speaker's malicious intent having been sufficiently clarified. A person who believes in the accuracy of the falsehood they affirm might be considered innocent. However, since subjective belief is fundamentally intractable where subjective statements are dubious, this standard is difficult to apply. Legal discourse again offers a solution by introducing the concept of "reckless disregard for the truth," a protection against the abuse of free speech that limits First Amendment rights in US law. As the Supreme Court affirmed in 1964, upholding the conviction of Louisiana District Attorney Jim Garrison for having publicly maligned the conduct of eight judges of the Parish's Criminal District Court in 1964, "the knowingly false statement and the false statement made with reckless disregard for the truth do not enjoy constitutional protection" (Parish's Criminal District Court 1964). In the most favorable scenario, the application of the test for neglect could render the question of deliberate falsehood moot. Even if the speaker did not actually know the truth, in some circumstances it would have been up to them to confirm the facts. Within the framework of speech act theory, ideal cases in which speakers are able and obliged to perform a reliable testing of the truth of their statements are also those that most forcefully meet the felicity conditions for truthful assertions in the first place: I can only fully assert as fact that which I am likely to know for a fact.

However, all too often circumstances are not ideal. One can in fact distinguish between two different concepts of success determining the pragmatics of lying. Though lies are communications and hence fundamentally cooperative acts, they seem to succeed when listeners come to grief and to fail as soon as interlocuters arrive at understanding each other's intentions. This of course stands in opposition to Paul Grice's cooperative principle (Grice 1975), usually assumed to hold for all speech acts. J.R. Searle in his seminal publications on speech act theory seems to exclude the very idea of a successful lie by means of a normatively, i.e. ethically, narrowed concept of success that disregards vicious intent by implication as always already infelicitous. Searle deals with lies in two ways: as an arguable *infelicity condition* of sincere assertions (Searle 1969) that violates the positive condition of sincerity (Stokke 2018); or as a distinction from fiction, mentioned but in passing when discussing the latter (Searle 1975). The illocutionary force of a standard assertive speech act requires not only that the sincerity condition be met, but that the sincere communicative intent of the speaker become transparent to the audience. As soon as that happens, the liar whose true intentions have been found out must have failed (see also Reboul 1995, Marsili 2020). So a liar communicates, and a liar might (viciously) succeed; but a liar's success is not successful communication, for the latter is a co-operative act in which actors may only succeed together.

The noted kinds of ambivalence all relate to another obvious challenge involved in trying to characterize and possibly censure a lie, setting aside the restrictions imposed by political power. At first, this challenge may appear to be epistemological: how may we ever know that a statement is definitely false, and how may we know with any certainty that the speaker lied on purpose or acted out of negligence? The very conditions under which lies are most likely to prosper, namely where truth and real motivations are hard to discern, are also those that make it difficult to objectively establish the mendacious nature of a statement. We find ourselves confronted with a latency problem not dissimilar to the one encountered in censorship studies, where the very nature of the phenomenon we seek to explain makes it hard to establish in the most important cases: where censorship is most effective, it leaves no trace. The problem cannot be solved; but, as with the problem of the political lie hiding behind the Cretan paradox, some clarity can be arrived at by shifting from the epistemological issue to an assessment of communicative pragmatics. Rather than despairing that we cannot with any certainty ascertain truth or motivation, we can instead ask who is in a situation to ascertain it, to want to do so, and to say so publicly. In following this angle of analysis, I therefore propose a three-step examination of the different positions that speakers as well as audiences find themselves in when encountering (a) the private lie (from which derive our more naïve assumptions about lying); (b) the public lie proper; and (c) the (equally public) nature of traditional, published literary fiction. By giving an account of the perspectives of the different actors involved in each constellation, we may arrive at a fuller appreciation of one key feature of the public lie: its duplication of audiences.

Consider first the private lie. A liar deceives an audience, which consists of a limited amount of persons. The lie could be considered strategically (albeit not ethically) successful if the audience never realizes that it exists at all. The speaker is likely aware of the deceit (although successful self-deception could be considered a most effective preparation for lying to others). The audience will eventually hope to become aware of it. In this situation, any ambivalence would be epistemological and based on suspicion. Pragmatically, the audience will have to proceed either as if sincerity or as if insincerity has been established. The two imaginable audiences, the one that believes the lie and the one that does not, are positioned in direct contrast to each other. The lie flourishes as long as audiences remain undecided whether to believe the statement or not.

For lies presented in fiction (see Fludernik in this volume), we habitually assume a privileged audience, for whom the epistemological problem is less intractable. The reader may, for instance, have access to the innermost thoughts of characters (Zunshine 2006), especially in modern(ist) narratives, or to a narrator who provides them with certainty about who is lying and who is telling the truth. By no means are these privileges extended in all fiction; but wherever they do apply, the information presented is by its very status incontrovertible. It is precisely because the fictive events are part of a fiction that no other source than the author can ever contradict them. This situation significantly differs from the case of private lies in the real world, where outside sources become decisive tools in approximating a reliable decision on truthfulness.

So in the case of fiction, audiences often are better equipped to decide on the validity of a statement. Moreover, they are also under less pressure to do so. This contrasts with private lies, where a particular audience has to make a decision on whether to believe or disbelieve a statement, because that decision informs their subsequent actions. One type of fictional narration for which even a competent audience does remain in doubt is unreliable narration (Phelan 2005). Here, we are famously faced with two or more options. Often, an audience will realize each option in turn, moving from one interpretation of the tale to another as they re-assess the reliability of a narrator as well as that of various characters. Sometimes, both interpretations are indefinitely held in the balance. In such cases, the undecided audience contents itself – happily or not – with entertaining the possibility of either option. They may even conclude that the doubt is to be maintained permanently, and aesthetically intended. But for each of these variations, the audience is relieved from any pragmatic need to decide.

Yet all of these privileges afforded to the audience of a fictional story rest on the assumption that a competent literary audience is reading the text under the assumption of reading fiction. However, this need not always the case. There are two imaginable audiences of fiction, one that recognizes a text as fiction and one that does not. Most literary criticism only considers the first case; the second audience falls victim to the same misunderstanding that affected some of the readers of *Illuminatus!*: they take the fiction to be the literal truth about their own world. It is precisely at this point, as soon as more than one audience co-exists, that we move from fiction to the public lie.

For the public lie, decisions do have to be made, at least by some audiences, and third sources are as crucial as in the case of private lies. Yet, while different audience responses logically exclude one another in the realm of the private lie (you either believe or do not believe the assertion), in the public sphere such responses need not be mutually exclusive in practice, since different groups may come to simultaneously hold contradictory stances. The crucial difference is that for literary texts audiences may simulate different viewpoints and suspend their resolution. In the public sphere, different judgements of factual public statements are realized by different actual audiences: some will believe a statement while others do not. One might argue that there is a third case in which a statement is known but not considered relevant to certain parts of the public, a situation which allows them to engage in the epistemic restraint of the fiction reader. Even though, epistemologically speaking, such audiences are faced with the pure dichotomy typical of private lies, they in fact have the practical option of suspending their decision, perhaps indefinitely – not in the manner of literary suspense but of disinterested détente. It is in this context that the basic affordances of the public lie seem to suggest that audiences are no longer interested in truth but only in emotions – just like readers of some traditional literary fictions. The distance that a public audience sometimes enjoys from the issues under discussion, even though they are real, here appears to have much the same effects as the ontological distinction between audience and fictional characters in literature: for the uninterested public, it is as if some public debates concern problems out of this world.

The simultaneity of several distinct *realized* audience stances is decisive for the fundamental difference that distinguishes public lies from equally public literary fiction (where the differences in judgment are suspended), and equally from mendacious private deception (in which a decision must be made). A much discussed paradigmatic case is that of the successful public hoax. Here one part of an audience is entertained not only by the deceptively persuasive false account as a successful fiction, but also by the inappropriate reaction of another part of the audience that believes the lie. Françoise Lavocat (2019) has examined the literary version of such hoaxes as 'pseudofactual narratives,' in which the problem becomes one of recognizing fiction. But this genre of fictional hoaxes takes its name from actual hoaxes, real and usually criminal acts that are familiar from the limited, private sphere of communication and consist in a deception enacted by a perpetrator upon a victim. By contrast, the public hoax is different from the private hoax and from the literary lie in the following respect: the public hoax wants to be recognized as pseudofactual by some members but not by all of its audience. One vastly effective case (Graff 2004) of a public hoax was engineered by the performance group "The Yes Men." They staged an interview with what appeared to be a spokesperson for the international company Dow Chemical. Claiming to speak for the company, the actor supposedly took responsibility for the gas leak at the pesticide manufacturing plant which devastated the community in Bhopal, India, in 1984, and promised remuneration – neither of which Dow Chemical had ever done. This placed the corporation in the difficult position of having to re-affirm, publicly and over and over again, that they did not intend to take responsibility for their actions and saw no moral obligation to do so. The hoax has been hailed as creating "discursive leverage" for the survivors and their descendants (Owen

2011), and as a case of "utopian politics" or "satirical fake news" (Reilly 2013). But this appreciation of the hoax would be impossible if it had simply been allowed to stand, or if it had been fully transparent to all imagined audiences. It was only because the hoax was sufficiently convincing to trigger a retraction from Dow Chemical, and yet sufficiently transparent to be recognized as a performance, that it escaped the sanction of an outright lie under libel law.

This example also demonstrates that some of the different audience reactions might well themselves be feigned. Where different stances are realized at the same time, they can be performed by different actual groups among a fractured audience, or by the same members of the audience in different contexts or at different times. Whether or not any of the journalists questioning actual Dow Chemical spokespersons about the company's policy were truly uncertain about the veracity of the Yes Men's claims, or whether they simply played their part as a cover for rhetorically indirect critical interviews, is a moot point. Eventually, it is a matter of whose responsibility it was to check the facts in the first place and to clarify the confusion. In this respect, the case could be interpreted as similar to the standards applied in the legal concept of reckless disregard for the truth, also geared to deal with public assertions: we want to know not only who knew, but who should have known the truth. In the case of the Dow Chemical hoax, that responsibility was seen to rest less with the performers than with the corporation they had impersonated. Criticism of the Yes Men's hoax – including self-criticism from members of the group itself – has focused on drawing attention to yet another segment of the public, namely those first- and second-generation survivors of the disaster in Bhopal who briefly believed in the vindication of their claims and in financial compensation only to be disappointed once more. From this ethical angle, responsibility has been relocated back to the Yes Men, and it is for this reason that they again found themselves accused of lying.

Meanwhile, a second group of similar performers has sprung up, who sometimes co-operate with the Yes Men, and who ironically embrace the label 'The Good Liars.' In 2020, they publicly announced that they were "teaming up to draw attention to voter suppression tactics ahead of the 2020 U.S. Election by doing a series of actions/stunts/pranks and releasing videos and images of them in order to transform people from apathetic viewers into motivated voters" (*Center for Artistic Activism* 2020). This rendering of hoaxers as 'good liars' amounts to a defense of hoaxing in parallel to the defense of false statements in fiction; more pertinently, it draws upon the fact that *some people* recognize the activists' actions *as fiction*.

More importantly for our concerns here, the public lie in general seems to prosper through the existence of fragmented audiences, even though (unlike the hoax) it cannot call upon literary and performative fiction as its defense. Any story about the rise of a 'post-truth era' assumes that, while many have abandoned an interest in truth, the conveyors of that story still embrace that interest and believe that they are able to distinguish between lies, errors, and controversial facts. On the third level of the 'post-truth' narrative, an omniscient narrator resurfaces, confidently telling us that one audience was deceived, another was not, and so on. The postfactual framing of conflicting claims has always already decided the very questions that are in fact impossible to decide.

Public lies need to be understood in the context of long-established issues surrounding the very concept of the public itself. In the Habermas model (2013; see also Imhof 2011; Imhof et al. 2013), the public sphere is tied historically to its production through media technologies and practices. Yet this bourgeois ideal has long been counterpointed in criticism by emphases on the particularity of differing interests, giving rise to distinct public spheres (Fraser 2007). It has also been pointed out that the marginalization and exclusion of some communities goes hand in hand with an invisible imposed disciplinary generalization ('normalization' – *Normalisierung* according to Link 2017) of the characteristics of the core group, the included. Moreover, the supposed rationality of the public sphere's non-violent debates is called into question by its dependence on the systematic pressures of media production and consumption (Luhmann 2017). Protestations of post-truth generally assume a fragmentation of the public sphere to various degrees. Even Angela Merkel's claim that 'the people are no longer interested in facts' suggests that some people, herself included, continue to be. Very often, accusations are much more acerbic and partisan, attributing a belief in, or even support of, fake news solely to the political opponent or enemy.

The label *fake news* itself has undergone a radical change of denotation. Originally used to refer to a genre of satire – realized, for example, by the Yes Men as well as in satirical fake news shows such as the famous *The Daily Show* –, it is now employed as an indictment of actual deceit. Yet, even when celebrating a triumph over 'fake news,' public discourse tends to paint a picture of a fragmented public. After Donald Trump had lost the re-election, Michael Tomasky asked, "What did the Democrats win?" Answering his own question, he told a story of a population that has overcome a notorious liar, but only at the cost and through the means of society fracturing into different segments with incompatible perceptions of reality:

> But even if Trump himself fades, it's hard to see the changes he has effected being undone. No one else will be quite as brazen as Trump, but he and his 73 million votes have taught the party that created him a great deal. [...] You can lie and lie and lie and invert and pervert the truth endlessly, and half of the media and country will be onto you, but the other half will pick up on your cues and rearrange their understanding of the world to suit yours, and together you will fight the other half to a rough draw,

> even on a matter as serious as the effective negligent homicide of tens of thousands of Americans, if not more. (Tomasky 2020, 40)[1]

The issue of the public lie, then, tests our assumptions about the public sphere itself. Even before the rise of the classical mass media, which Habermas suspected of dismantling the rational public sphere of the bourgeoisie, the relationship of the public to mendacity and truth-telling could sometimes seem contradictory. While Montaigne in his reflections on courtly dissimulation maintained that, once returned home, he could revert to virtuous truth (Montaigne 1965, 504; see Denery in this volume), Kant surprises readers even today with his quite different view. In the famous *Was ist Aufklärung?* (1784), he argues that "the *public* use of reason must always be free, and it alone may bring about enlightenment for man; but its *private use* may often be quite narrowly restricted, without hindering the progress of enlightenment too much" ["der *öffentliche* Gebrauch seiner Vernunft muß jederzeit frei sein, und er allein kann Aufklärung unter Menschen zu Stande bringen; der *Privatgebrauch* derselben aber darf öfters sehr enge eingeschränkt sein, ohne doch darum den Fortschritt der Aufklärung sonderlich zu hindern" – 1962, 57; translation S.P.]. For Kant, the 'private' use of reason attaches specifically to what we might call public office. Kant still seems to conceive of such office as being primarily responsible to a ruler (the court) rather than 'the public,' thus pertaining to a courtly rather than a public understanding of social communication. To this conception of the public, the new bourgeois public sphere of the 'scholar' ["der Gelehrte"] is seen to be opposed. Such historical transformations, however, lend even greater urgency to the question: what new transformations are taking place now, and how do they affect the extended temporality and the divided audiences of the public lie?

3. *Finding New Touchstones: Brief Notes on the Public Lie in Social Networks*

It has not been my intention to give a comprehensive account of what has recently been called fake news. Instead, I have focused on showing that many of the features associated with fake news and corresponding claims about 'postfactuality' and 'post-truth' relate to some fundamental aporias of public communication and are linked to analogous characteristics of the public lie. As I have suggested, public lies are destroyed only in the process of a successful and collectively affirmed act of censure. If we want to investigate whether the new digital social media have contributed to a new rise of public mendacity, as is so often proposed, we might ask whether consensual censure becomes easier

[1] My thanks to Monika Fludernik for pointing me to this example.

or harder to effect in the public sphere through the involvement of social networks. I argue that there are at least three areas in which the felicity conditions of consensual censure are shifted by these new formats of communication: the subject positions that can formulate such censure and to whom such censure may be addressed; the fragmentation of a public sphere in which consensus could be reached; and the growing ontologies of the lie that are situated in social media's many layers of incessant self-observation and commentary.

What are the necessary requirements for a successful public censure of a lie? One requirement is that subject positions must exist from which censure can be formulated and to which it can be addressed. Fundamentally, a political power shift is required that removes protection from the liar. But while public critique itself can make such a shift more likely to occur, it would be naïve to believe that shifts in opinion alone suffice to topple power structures. As a consequence, one could assume the causes for the inhibition of censure to lie outside of, or to be only indirectly affected by, social media. However, the arrival of consensual public censure may be deferred by the limited or suspended obligation to intervene that characterizes debates in social media, in which curation is often either absent or automated and unlikely to explicitly engage with the content of ongoing discussion. One should therefore ask: to whom should such censure be addressed? Who will feel responsible to voice it? Which audience can it hope to reach on social media?

At the same time, a fragmented public will prolong the life of public lies. Consensual public censure requires some preliminary agreement about the places in which a public consensus can be expressed, constituting a second requirement for the successful destruction of a public lie. Social media have convincingly been associated with the fragmentation of the public sphere from a number of different points of view: on account of their differentiated control of access (Bauman 2016; Bauman & Lyon 2013); due to the splintering of social networks (van Dijk & Poell 2013); because they provide new staging platforms for various factions (Boutyline & Willer 2017); and due to their algorithmic reproduction of inequalities (Metcalfe & Dencik 2019) which result in vastly different scales and modes of participation (Rudolph 2019). The idea of the so-called "filter bubble" (Pariser 2011), in which the algorithmic pre-selection of news provides each of us with an individual account of the world, is unconvincing. It has been justly criticized as a technological red herring that follows an oversimplified understanding of networked homophily (Chun 2018), which creates networked virtual neighborhoods of similar users, and exposed as a misconception of the actual experience of "filter clashes" (Pörksen 2018).

In a world of filter clashes as opposed to bubbles, the ideas and perceptions of those with different political associations are by no means hidden from each other's eyes. Instead, one is constantly and frustratingly confronted with their always already scandalized representation. One is tempted to view proponents of contrary opinions with an enmity that could be compared to what Jacques Rancière (2005) has called "la haine de la démocratie," 'the hatred of democracy.' From that perspective, political opponents are represented as those deplorable individuals who instantiate all the accusations which enemies of democracy direct at democracy's alleged tendency towards mob rule, thus spoiling the universality of rational discourse and individual freedom for the rest of us. But this hateful and partisan imagination is itself not new: it has been with democracy, its enemies and its defenders, at least since the political treatises of Plato and Aristotle. At least since the eighteenth century, the imagination of incompetent *other* audiences has been inscribed into classical, modern mass media with their absent and silent majorities of consumers. Already in the early periods of consumer society, the situation frequently occurred in which one audience felt concerned about the use that other, more helpless readers might make of, say, a novel. Such anxieties then give rise to recriminations against those other audiences, and these others are branded as juvenile, female, lower class, uneducated, racially different, or stigmatized in different ways. Rancière concludes that such a hatred of democracy is connected to the rise of technocracy, in which factual expertise leaves little room for democratic debate to arrive at its own decisions. If Rancière is right, the rise of such a machinery of political othering, rather than being the result of new digital social media, should perhaps more fruitfully be considered as a concurrent development.

A third and equally important requirement of successful consensual censure for lies is an agreement about what defines lies in the first place. Social media introduce a complicated network of self-observation at many levels, with users developing new and growing ontologies to describe the communicative acts of their peers. While this discourse can be helpful to pinpoint the nature of deceitful communication, it can also be abused to obscure the issue. Here the concept of postfactual discourse, i.e. third-level storytelling about the decline of a public interest in truth, can do as much damage as it can help. Research into 'fake news' or disinformation has provided many valuable accounts on how to characterize lies, with Claire Wardle's proposals having perhaps attracted the greatest public attention. Diagnosing a rise of disinformation disorder (rather than postfactuality), Wardle (2018) offers "definitions" as "tools [that] will give you the words you need to talk about information disorder." These include a list of "7 types of mis- and disinformation" (on the definition of these categories see the introduction to this volume):

- satire or parody
- misleading content
- imposter content
- fabricated content
- false connection

- false context
- manipulated content (Wardle & Derakshan 2017)

The value of such research is obvious and undeniable. However, we should not expect – nor does Wardle do so – that such an analysis will solve those parts of the problem that are not primarily definitional. In looking at this taxonomy, one is reminded of Shakespeare's Touchstone, who in Act V, Scene iv of *As You Like It*, at Jaques' request, names "in order [...] the degrees of the lie":

> O sir, we quarrel in print, by the book; as you have books for good manners. I will name you the degrees: The first, the retort courteous; the second, the quip modest; the third, the reply churlish; the fourth, the reproof valiant; the fifth, the counter-check quarrelsome; the sixth, the lie with circumstance; the seventh, the lie direct. All these you may avoid but the lie direct and you may avoid that too, with an 'if'. I knew when seven justices could not take up a quarrel, but when the parties were met themselves, one of them thought but of an 'if', as, 'if you said so, then I said so'; and they shook hands and swore brothers. Your 'if' is the only peacemaker; much virtue in If. (Shakespeare 2006, V, iv, 337).

Perhaps not coincidentally, the different degrees of the lie emerge as various ways to avoid quarrels even as they are enumerated; and the avoidance of the "lie direct" turns into the avoidance of the censure of the lie, with a happy suggestion for solving quarrels by rephrasing dissensus as hypothesis. One could therefore propose that a purely technical explanation of public lies might threaten to merely conceal political dissensus. Similarly, to connect too readily the current bouts of public disinformation with specific media conditions of the latest social media is equivalent to succumbing to a reductive techno-determinism; the problem is in fact an issue of political agency and responsibilities. Political motives drive and protect public lies; understanding the precise nature of the technology that shapes these lies and the categories that distinguish them may help to differentiate between a variety of such lies; but this analysis should not distract us from exposing and confronting the political motives underlying public lying.

Works Cited

Andersen, Hans Christian (1837) "Keiserens nye Klæder." *Eventyr. Fortalt for Børn* 1.3. Copenhagen: Reitzel. 107–111.

Barthes, Roland (1970) "L'ancienne rhétorique. Aide-mémoire." *Communications* 16. 172–223.

Bauman, Zygmunt (2016) *Strangers at Our Door.* Cambridge/Malden: Polity.

Bauman, Zygmunt and David Lyon (2013) *Liquid Surveillance.* Cambridge/Malden: Polity.

Boutyline, Andrei, and Robb Willer (2017) "The Social Structure of Political Echo Chambers: Variation in Ideological Homophily in Online Networks." *Political Psychology* 38.3. 551–569.

Bussemer, Thymian (2008) *Propaganda*. Wiesbaden: VS.

Center for Artistic Activism (2020) "The Good Liars: Making Voter Suppression Personal." 2 Nov. 2020. Web. 26 Apr. 2021. https://c4aa.org/2020/11/the-good-liars-making-voter-suppression-personal.

Chun, Wendy Hui Kyong (2018) "Queerying Homophily. Muster der Netzwerkanalyse." *Zeitschrift für Medienwissenschaft* 10.18. 131–148.

Der Spiegel (2016) "'Postfaktisch' ist internationales Wort des Jahres." 16 Nov. 2016. Web. 26 Apr. 2021.

Fahlenbrach, Kathrin (2018) "'Schwache' und 'starke' Propaganda als Teil liberalen und anti-liberalen Protests." *Online-Propagandaforschung*. Ed. Bernd Zywietz. N.d. Web. 26 Ap. 2021. https://www.online-propagandaforschung.de/index.php/schwache-und-starke-propaganda-als-teil-liberalen-und-anti-liberalen-protests.

Fischer, Sebastian (2016) "Das Signal." *Der Spiegel*. 19 Sept. 2016. Web. 26 Apr. 2021.

Fludernik, Monika, and Marie-Laure Ryan (2019) "Factual Narrative: An Introduction." *Narrative Factuality: A Handbook*. Berlin: deGruyter. 1–27.

Foucault, Michel (1971) *L'ordre du discours*. Paris: Gallimard.

Foucault, Michel (2019) *Discourse and Truth*. Ed. Henri-Paul Fruchaud and Daniele Lorenzini. Chicago: Univ. of Chicago Press.

Graff, Vincent (2004) "Meet the Yes Men who Hoax the World." *The Guardian*.16 Dec. 2004. Web. 26 Apr. 2021.

Grice, Paul (1975) "Logic and Conversation." *Syntax and Semantics* 3: *Speech Acts*. Ed. Peter Cole and Jerry L. Morgan. New York: Academic Press. 41–58.

Habermas, Jürgen (2013) *Strukturwandel der Öffentlichkeit. Untersuchungen zu einer Kategorie der bürgerlichen Gesellschaft*. Frankfurt: Suhrkamp.

Harris, J. Rendel (1907) "A Further Note on the Cretans." *The Expositor* 7.3. 332–337.

Huang, Haifeng (2018) "The Pathology of Hard Propaganda." *The Journal of Politics* 80.3. 1034–1038.

Imhof, Kurt et al. (2013) Ed. *Stratifizierte und segmentierte Öffentlichkeit*. Wiesbaden: Springer VS.

Imhof, Kurt (2011) *Die Krise der Öffentlichkeit. Kommunikation und Medien als Faktoren des sozialen Wandels*. Frankfurt/New York: Campus.

Johnson, George (1983) *Architects of Fear: Conspiracy Theories and Paranoia in American Politics*. Los Angeles: Tarcher.

Kant, Immanuel (1967) "Beantwortung der Frage: was ist Aufklärung?" [1784] *Was ist Aufklärung?* Ed. Jürgen Zehbe. [1784] Göttingen: Vandenhoeck & Ruprecht. 55–61.

Lavocat, Françoise (2019) "Pseudofactual Narratives and Signposts of Factuality." *Narrative Factuality. A Handbook*. Ed. Monika Fludernik and Marie-Laure Ryan. Berlin: deGruyter. 577–592.

Link, Jürgen (2017) "Populismus zwischen Normalisierung und Denormalisierung." *Populismus: rechts, links, Mitte*. Ed. Jürgen Link and Rolf Parr. *Kulturrevolution: Zeitschrift für Diskurstheorie* 72.1.

Luhmann, Niklas (2017) *Die Realität der Massenmedien*. 5th ed. Wiesbaden: Springer.

Marsili, Neri (2020) "Lying, Speech Acts, and Commitment." *Synthese*. https://doi.org/10.1007/s11229-020-02933-4. 26 May 2021.

Metcalfe, Philippa, and Lina Dencik (2019). "The Politics of Big Borders: Data (In)justice and the Governance of Refugees." *First Monday* 24.4.

Montaigne, Michel de (1965) *The Complete Essays of Montaigne*. Trans. Donald M. Frame. Stanford: Stanford Univ. Press.

New York Trial Court (2003) *Carter-Clark v. Random House.* 768 N.Y.S. 2d 290.

Owen, Louise (2011) "'Identity Correction' The Yes Men and Acts of Discursive Leverage." *Performance Research* 16.2. 28–36.

Pariser, Eli (2011) *The Filter Bubble. How the New Personalized Web Is Changing What We Read and How We Think*. London: Penguin.

Parish's Criminal District Court (1964) *Garrison v. Lousiana*. 379 U.S. 64.

Phelan, James (2005) *Living to Tell about It*. Ithaca: Cornell Univ. Press.

Pörksen, Bernhard (2018) *Die große Gereiztheit: Wege aus der kollektiven Erregung*. München: Carl Hanser.

Rancière, Jacques (2005) *La haine de la démocratie*. Paris: La Fabrique.

Reboul, Anne (1995) "The Description of Lies in Speech Acts Theory." *Pretending to Communicate*. Ed. Herman Parret. New York: deGruyter. 292–298.

Reeve, Elspeth (2011) "Kyl's 'Not Intended to Be a Factual Statement' Also Not a Statement." *The Atlantic*. 22 Apr. 2011. Web. 26 Apr. 2021.

Reilly, Ian (2013) "From Critique to Mobilization: The Yes Men and the Utopian Politics of Satirical Fake News." *International Journal of Communication* 7. 1243–1264.

Roberts, Margaret E. (2018) *Censored: Distraction and Diversion Inside China's Great Firewall.* Princeton: Princeton Univ. Press.

Rubin, Jennifer (2016) "How the GOP Became Indifferent to Lies." *The Washington Post*. 26 Sept. 2016. Web. 26 Apr. 2021.

Rudolph, Steffen (2019) *Digitale Medien, Partizipation und Ungleichheit. Eine Studie zum sozialen Gebrauch des Internets*. Wiesbaden: Springer VS.

Russell, Bertrand (1908) "Mathematical Logic as Based on the Theory of Types." *American Journal of Mathematics* 30.3. 222–262.

Searle, John R. (1969) *Speech Acts: An Essay in the Philosophy of Language*. Cambridge: Cambridge Univ. Press.

Searle, John R. (1975) "The Logical Status of Fictional Discourse." *New Literary History* 6.2. 319–332.

Shakespeare, William (2006) *As You Like It*. Ed. Juliet Dusinberre. London: Bloomsbury.

Shea, Robert, and Robert Anton Wilson (1975) *Illuminatus!* Trilogy. New York: Dell.

Stokke, Andreas (2018) "Lying, Sincerity, and Quality." *The Oxford Handbook of Lying* Ed. Jörg Meinbauer. Oxford: Oxford Univ. Press. 134–148.

Tomasky, Michael (2020) "What Did the Democrats Win?" *New York Review of Books*. 17 Dec. 2020. 36–40.

van Dijck, José, and Thomas Poell (2013) "Understanding Social Media Logic." *Media and Communication* 1.1. 2–14.

Wang, Amy (2016) "'Post-truth' Named 2016 Word of the Year by Oxford Dictionaries." *The Washington Post*. 16 Nov. 2016. Web. 26 Apr. 2020.

Wardle, Claire (2018) "Information Disorder: The Definitional Toolbox." *First Draft*. 6 Jul. 2018. Web. 26 Apr. 2020. https://firstdraftnews.org/latest/info disorder-definitional-toolbox/.

Wardle, Claire, and Hossein Derakshan (2017) "Information Disorder: Toward an Interdisciplinary Framework for Research and Policymaking. Council of Europe Report DGI(2017)09." Strasbourg: Council of Europe.

Wilson, Robert A. (1988) *Schrödinger's Cat* Trilogy. New York: Dell.

Zunshine, Lisa (2006) *Why We Read Fiction: Theory of Mind and the Novel.* Columbus: Ohio State Univ. Press.

Games of False Identity: Liars and Lying in Literature

Monika Fludernik

There exists an extensive literature on the equation of imaginative fiction with lying and likewise on the legitimation of fiction that tries to counter that accusation.[1] What so far has remained fairly underresearched is the *representation of lying* in literary texts, especially the treatment of liars and the analysis of plots that turn on lying and deception. What is lacking is a consideration of the use of lying and liars in fiction *in general* rather than a study of these *in particular genres* (e.g. the detective novel) or *in individual texts*. Thus, as is well known, the conycatching tales of the early modern period or the picaresque novel are genres that, like detective fiction, for obvious reasons include trickery on a grand scale, with key protagonists lying, dissimulating, and cheating as well as forging, betraying people, and even engaging in libel and slander. In addition, lying is encountered frequently in the realistic novel in connection with the adultery plot; after all, extramarital affairs cannot be managed without subterfuge and deceit. Since dissimulation occurs extensively in strategic military operations and of course in spying, fiction that is concerned with war and the secret services likewise contains a fair share of lying in its widest sense of the term. Hence, the connection between lying and genre is well documented in literary studies.

Besides these generic contexts in which lying and dissimulation are rife, individual novels and plays (as well as films and of course other media) sometimes feature a particularly heinous lie that results in serious consequences, or acts of deceit and betrayal that blight the lives of the other characters. Though there is much critical discussion of these plot incidences and the (immoral) character of liars and cheaters in the literary criticism on these *texts individually*, a comparative analysis of lying in literature as such does not yet exist.

In what follows I would like to propose a preliminary typology of lying in literature and will then provide a case study of a particular subcategory of dissimulation, namely that of impersonation, especially focusing on texts from the Renaissance and the twentieth century. Like marital infidelity, impersonation is a form of deceit that involves the dissimulator in lying, but it additionally extends to more general pretense and to play acting. Since this

[1] For instance, a list of traditional pro-fiction arguments includes the following: fiction does not assert, it is playful make-believe, its truth lies in the depiction of human nature and in moral teachings, literature provides a testing ground for possible, but not currently actual scenarios. See also Berensmeyer in this volume.

volume is concerned with lying as non-factuality in a wider sense of the term, impersonation seems to be a useful example case to bring out key features of deception involving more than verbal disingenuity.

1. *A Typology of Literary Lying*

Where does lying play a role in literary texts? For convenience sake, I will focus on novels and drama, excluding poetry and verse narration.[2] Besides featuring verbal lying (i.e. uttering a proposition that does not correspond to the facts), this essay will centrally deal with impersonation, i.e. the enactment of false identity, and will also consider other forms of deception such as forgery, faking, and deceit. The term *lying* is thus used in a wider sense of the word, focusing on non-factuality rather than the assertion of untruth.

An initial distinction must be made between (A) *literature* (or fiction) *as lying* and (B) *lies and lying in literature*. (A) is usually considered a global matter but may be mirrored within literature as well. Inside literary texts, *literature as lying* can be thematized both in the critical or philosophical reflections of the narrator persona of a text and in the reflections or musings of characters. The theme of fiction as lying can also be the thematic focus of a narrative as a whole, appearing not only as an argument proferred by the narratorial persona but also as played out in a plot that is self-reflexively concerned with deception. An example of such a story is Henry James's "The Real Thing" (publ. 1892), a text that deals with an illustrator who sketches the aptly named Monarchs, a high-class couple come down in the world and who pose for the first-person narrator in order to make some money. Paradoxically, though the Monarchs are "the real thing," the illustrator finds he fails to produce the right kind of illustrations and succeeds much better with a model that does not look like nobility at all but allows his imagination to transform her into a semblance of the genuine article. The implicit message is that art needs to lie in order to signify truth. The narrator's reflections take us directly to the mystery of fiction, i.e. aesthetic invention, which 'speaks the truth' while 'lying' in a factual assessment of the represented situation.

Under category B, lying in literature, let us first turn to ***authors who lie***. A literary text (as a whole) may lie when the author proclaims a text to be his own work, while it is actually the product of some other person's pen. Put differently, we are then confronted with a case of blatant plagiarism or theft of

---

[2] Although much of what I am discussing is applicable to other media besides literary prose fiction, film and drama, this essay concentrates on the novel with a few additional remarks on films. In lyric poetry I cannot conceive of lying except in cases where the speaker of the poem calls himself a liar or accuses the addressee (mostly the beloved) of deceit. Verse narrations of course function like prose narratives and both Chaucer and Spenser's *Faerie Queene* include cases of lying and dissimulation.

authorial property. Forgery (Ossian's poetry as published by James Macpherson) is another comparable example. On a different level, autobiographical narratives more recently have caused scandals because of their departure from the facts in key aspects of their life stories. The most famous such case is that of Binjamin Wilkomirski's *Fragments* (1995). These memoirs of a holocaust survivor turned out to be a fiction composed by the Swiss Bruno Dössekker. In this instance, the lies of the author included the pretense that the text was autobiographical, hence factual, and the adoption of a Jewish persona and name by the Swiss-German non-Jewish author. Partial incorrectness may equally give rise to controversy as was the case with Rigoberta Menchú's autobiography (1984) or James Frey's *A Million Little Pieces* (2003). Menchú was accused of exaggerating her status as a victim and Frey of fictionalizing his story of addiction. (A more complicated situation is studied by Tom Vanassche in this volume.) The genre of the memoir or autobiography sets especially high standards of truthfulness and therefore often gives rise to controversies.

The fact/fiction divide can also be transgressed creatively when a fictional text pretends to be factual (as in Hildesheimer's novel *Marbot* [1981; see Cohn 1999], which fakes the genre of biography, by seemingly telling the life story of a real historical person) and in the much more common case of a supposedly historical or even scientific work that is pure fiction, i.e. invention. In the long view, a history that turns out to be fiction may not raise too many eyebrows; it can be read as a historical novel. Scientific fake, on the other hand, results in a scandal, as did the Sokal affair (see Hilgartner 1997). Here the author, the physicist Alan Sokal (Sokal 1996), pretended that he was engaging in scientific argument but in actual fact was producing scientific nonsense; he was lying by inventing statements that were intended to imitate poststructuralist cultural criticism, entrapping the scientifically uneducated reader (as well as the referees of the peer review process, as it turned out), and thereby successfully exposed a particular kind of cultural criticism as nonsense and some cultural critics as unable to recognize such pseudo-scientific drivel due to their lack of scientific knowledge or training.

The inverse type of lying (fact masquerading as fiction) has also recently aroused some interest, namely the production of apparently fictional texts, which turn out to be factual and therefore render themselves liable to lawsuits of libel and defamation. Such romans-à-clef have been analyzed in Johannes Franzen's *Indiskrete Fiktionen* (2018).[3] The authors in Franzen's example texts pretend that their novels are fiction, i.e. invention, and that they are therefore not constrained to safeguard their characters' reputations. However, when these characters turn out to be very thinly disguised contemporary celebrities, court injunctions have the possibility to suppress these texts. (One may recall that

[3] See also his essay "Contested Inventions: Fictionality and Ethics" (2020).

the literary fame of Thomas Bernhard started with the publication of his novel *Holzfällen* in 1984 [trans. *Woodcutters* 1987], a work that the court decided could be taken to slander one of his Viennese acquaintances.)

Lying texts or authors are also familiar from contexts in which novels, supposedly written by a woman for a female (feminist) audience, turn out to have a male author; or where the author assumes the identity of a particular ethnic or sexual minority, impersonating a role that is later exposed as deliberately mendacious. The best-known such scandal is that of Virago's publication of a collection of short stories by "Rahila Khan" (*Down the Road, Worlds Away*, 1987); the author of that penname later emerged to be a native Englishman named Toby Forward (Ruthven 2001, 23-24). In such acts of deception, authors try to profit from a particularly fashionable literary market niche to cash in on their fake identity. Readers buying these books as the 'genuine' article – a novel by, say, a Maori author – feel cheated since their interest in the book had significantly depended on the authenticity of the ethnic authorship. The strategy of using pennames that increase the likelihood of getting published is, however, a common one in literary history, used widely in the work of political dissidents and women authors publishing anonymously or under (male) fake names.

At the same time, it needs to be underlined that fiction likes to play with identities and with the fact/fiction dichotomy. It is therefore inevitable that the playful misleading of the reader must be considered a legitimate literary strategy. Moreover, one also needs to emphasize that imagining the perspective of people from different cultures, sexes or orientations and from different ethnicities comes within the purview of the fundamental project of the empathetic literary imagining of others, whether these others are from a different class or culture or sex. Taking literary texts to lie when they pretend to convey a perspective closed to a Western or WASP author on account of the reigning identity politics (only Maoris may write about Maoris, etc.) therefore impacts on current practices of literary censorship and constrains authors to assume false identities if they wish to write about certain subjects and get published.

In all of the examples I have discussed so far in my first category (B1), the text as a whole is taken to be a lie, a forgery or an act of a treacherous deceit; and this deception is ascribed to the responsibility of the author(s). My next category is that of **lying *within* literature** (B2) (see Figure 1). As a narratologist, I subdivide this articulation of deceptive discourse into the *levels* on which the lying occurs. Hence, for novels, one can distinguish

- lies proferred by the narrator persona;
- lies by the characters; and
- lies as a major plot element.

Fig. 1. Lying and Literature

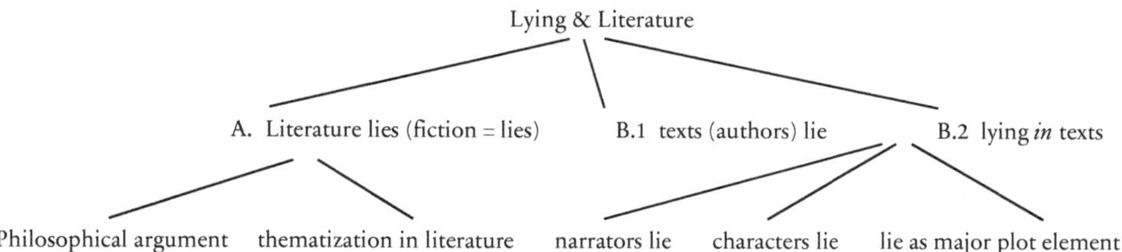

In drama and film, there is usually no narrator persona (stage managers also on the whole do not lie). However, there are some cases of visual presentation in film that deliberately deceive viewers into the belief that they are watching what actually happens/ed, only to disabuse them later on. (Hitchcock's *Stage Fright* [1950] is the classic example, in which Jonathan's visual flashback turns out to be a lie. See Elsaesser 2009.)

Lying Narrators have already been the topic of narratological research on unreliability. The narratorial strategies of deliberate deception of the reader are, however, rare and more frequently acts of omission of information rather than statements misleading the reader (Nünning 1997, 1998a, 1998b; but see Yacobi 2001). The detective story, with an authorial narrator persona, is one of the key genres in which omission functions to delay the readers' recognition of who is the murderer. In fact, though there may be an overt narratorial persona in the text, this persona is usually taken to be a mouthpiece of the author, and the deceptive omissions are condoned as useful enhancements of suspense.

Unreliability is a term mostly reserved for first-person narrators, and lying first-person narrators are few and far between, with the famous *The Murder of Roger Ackroyd* (Agatha Christie 1926) a particularly fine instance. In that novel, Dr. Sheppard, the narrator, is the murderer, and he tells a version of events that leaves out his deed, only confessing the murder in his final suicide note after his guilt has been discovered by Hercule Poirot. Another well-known narrator liar is Will Self in Martin Amis's *Money* (1984); however, this narrator does not merely repeatedly deceive people, he is also himself tricked and deceived. A third lying character one could mention is Tarquin Winot in John Lanchester's *The Debt to Pleasure* (1996); here the ulterior dark purposes of the narrator persona are disguised by his entertaining narration, which tends to obscure what is actually happening.

The most self-deceiving, unreliable narrator, however, is a narrator who is naïve, unintelligent or biased and who therefore fails to report what happens in an adequate fashion, violating Gricean maxims of quality and manner. As Phelan & Martin (1999) have suggested, such a narrator may be underreporting (not telling the whole truth), underinterpreting (deliberately avoiding implications of actions and events) or underevaluating (desisting from criticizing or praising events and actions within standard frameworks of morality or conventions of behavior). Phelan & Martin's example, Ishiguro's *The Remains of the Day* (1989), is an excellent illustration of self-deceit: the butler who does not want to own up to his own failings. John Fowles's *The Collector* (1963), too, has a very unreliable narrator-diarist, Frederick Clegg (there is also the reliable diarist, his victim Miranda Grey), and in this case the narrator's story is a pathological case study in which the true enormity of his actions never quite registers in his mind. He lies to his hostage, but to the reader only to the extent of presenting his abnormal actions as perfectly normal.

Many novels also center on lies or acts of deception in the past (or about the past), whose uncovering constitutes the *major plot element*. The lie is therefore one uttered by a *character*. Kristy Woodson Harvey's *Lies and Other Acts of Love* (2016) is a recent example of such a tale, but Henry James's *The Golden Bowl* (1904) or George Eliot's *Silas Marner* (1861) could also serve as famous instances of this type of narrative. As in *Silas Marner*, an innocent person may be framed by a lie. (*The Count of Montecristo* is another example, with Edmond Dantès going to prison in consequence of a lie.) Novels with this kind of plot do not need to have a first-person lying narrator (like the unreliable Briony in McEwan's *Atonement*, 2001).

Quite frequently, narrators who are suspected of being unreliable cannot be unequivocally pinned down as liars. Is the governess in James's *The Turn of the Screw* (1898) a neurotic spinster who imagines seeing ghosts or are there really ghosts? When the lie is a plot element, it is usually established as a lie in the course of the liar's (liars') exposure. However, there are cases in which the question of lying remains unresolved, as it does in James's "The Figure in the Carpet" (1896). In that story everything turns on the discovery of the delusive 'figure.' We never arrive at a solution of the mystery and keep wondering whether that figure does exist (but is irretrievable) or whether the statement about its existence was a lie meant to entrap the unwary.

Such ambiguities illustrate the point that the line between the truth and its opposites may be difficult to draw. In contrast to Montaigne,[4] a twenty-first century reader will acknowledge that there is no simple truth when it comes to areas of experience that resist objective evidence. Texts like "The Figure in the Carpet" tend to highlight the impossibility of determining a particular state of affairs. Much postmodernist literature additionally likes to create complex layers of reality such that the ontological status of what is being presented remains deliberately undeterminable, or the plot moves from one reinterpretation of events to another. For instance, in Peter Ackroyd's *Chatterton* (1987), the portrait (which is ostensibly one of Thomas Chatterton) turns out to be

4 The reference is to the following passage by Montaigne: "If, like the truth, falsehood had only one face, we should know better where we are, for we should then take the opposite of what a liar said to be the truth. But the opposite of a truth has a hundred thousand shapes and a limitless field" (Montaigne 1958, 31).

one of Meredith posing as Chatterton painted by Henry Wallis (whose painting of the dead Chatterton is well known). Meredith, learning of his wife's affair with Wallis, attempts suicide in the church biographically associated with Chatterton and is rescued by the appearance of Chatterton's ghost. The painting disintegrates when Charles's friend Philip tries to restore it. Likewise, the manuscript which Charles had received from the owner of the portrait of Meredith alias Chatterton (and which pretends that Chatterton faked his death and is now really William Blake) also turns out to be a forgery committed by Chatterton's publisher Mr. Joynson (alluding to the famous publisher Joseph Johnson). The fact that Charles, the discoverer of portrait and manuscript, suffers from a brain tumor and dies suggests that not only forgery and faking but also psychological and mental instability might be adduced as explanation of the events; mental disorder is a theme that echoes the supposed insanity of Chatterton. The novel therefore plots several acts of forgery but ultimately fails to provide an incontestable 'true' version of events.

Some heterodiegetic novels revolve around the *figure of the liar* and could therefore be argued to be studies in the psychology of lying. This is true of Henry James's "The Liar" (1888), a story in which the painter Lyons studies the mendacious husband of Mrs. Capadose and traps the couple in a lie after they have destroyed his painting of the husband (which exposed the colonel's deceitful character): they accuse another person of the deed. James's story is, however, much more sophisticated than this plot summary implies since it suggests that the painter himself is dishonest and a double dealer, out to revenge himself on the wife who has chosen to marry the colonel instead of himself.[5]

The figure of the liar in literature is a classic one from the stock character of the braggart in Greek Comedy's *alazon* onward to Plautus' *miles gloriosus* and the Brothers Grimm story "Twelve Idle Servants" (in which each servant tells an even more hyperbolic story about his refusal to work). Another classic type of liar is the lying manipulator, well known from Molière's *Tartuffe* (1664), Corneille's *The Liar* (1643), Goldoni's *The Liar* (1750) and Sheridan's Joseph Surface in *The School for Scandal* (1777). In these prototypes mendacity combines with intrigues initiated by the liar on the plot level and with the showcasing of hypocrisy as a major character trait in the liar persona.

In what follows, i.e. in the main section of this article, I will continue to concentrate on fictive liars. I have chosen a particular type of deception, namely impersonation, and will study the moral and humorous possibilities linked with pretending to be another person. My examples will be Sir Philip Sidney's *Arcadia* (1580), discussed at length, and Philip Roth's *Operation Shylock* (1993),

---

5 There is some similarity here to George Bernard Shaw's *The Doctor's Dilemma* (1906), in which the husband of Mrs. Dubedat, a painter, is a man who borrows money and never pays it back (he is a liar), and the eponymous hero has a love interest in the wife and deceives her by allowing the husband to die.

briefly mentioning Stephen Fry's *The Liar* (1991) and Julian Symons's *The Belting Inheritance* (1965).

2. *Pretending to be Somebody Else – The Dissimulation of Identity*

Assuming somebody else's identity is equivalent to an act of deception or pretense. This kind of dissimulation comes closest to acting (as on stage); with the difference that there is no knowledgeable audience watching the play. In drama, audiences take the fictional identities of the actors for their 'real' ones; they are part of the fictional world represented on stage. However, within this projected world on stage, a character may assume a fake identity, and therefore the actor plays a double role, impersonating a persona, assuming a disguise, in which he or she pretends to be somebody else entirely. On stage, these situations of assuming a false identity are usually clearly signalled, with the audience in the know and only the other characters being deluded: that is, the deceit operates within the fictional world, but the duplicity of the impersonator is patent to the spectator.

Examples of such impersonation are pervasive, especially in comedy. In Shakespeare, *Twelfth Night* and *The Comedy of Errors* are well-known examples; one can also look at Goldoni's *The Liar* (1750), in which Lelio impersonates a Neapolitan nobleman and later a merchant, but where the audience is early on informed about his real identity as Pantalone's son. Likewise, in Sheridan's *School for Scandal* (1777), the rich uncle Sir Oliver pretends to be a moneylender (Mr. Premium – IV, i), but he only deceives the 'good' nephew, Charles. Later he impersonates a poor relative, Mr. Stanley, asking Joseph Surface for charity (V, i), which Joseph denies him; in the process he lies that he never received any money from his miserly uncle Sir Oliver. In both cases the audience is aware of the disguise and its purpose to test the brothers. Whereas the adoption of a different identity becomes necessary as a strategy of survival in the Shakespeare plays mentioned above, in Goldoni – as in Corneille's *Liar* (1643) – it is an expression of the liar's inherent mendacity in the service of Don Giovanni-like sexual predatoriness. In Sheridan's play, impersonation serves the shrewd testing of the virtue of the two nephews' character. It serves to cut through the deceptive appearances of (hypocritical) virtue (Joseph) and (apparent) licentiousness (Charles).

From drama I now turn to fiction and the analysis of selected narratives.

2.1. Arcadian 'Counterfeiting'

My first case study will be Sir Philip Sidney's *Old Arcadia* (1580), in which the heroes Pyrocles and Musidorus assume, respectively, the characters of the

Amazon Cleophila (Zelmane in the *New Arcadia* of 1590) and the shepherd Dorus in order to woo the two daughters of Duke Basilius, Philoclea and Pamela. (Basilius has retreated to the woods of Arcadia in response to an oracle, and open wooing is not possible.) The situation is therefore one of amorous intrigue, but – unlike the wooing of Lelio in Goldoni's *The Liar* – the two princes in Sidney's pastoral romance do not intend to deceive their ladies but only their father and have (at least initially) entirely honorable intentions of marriage. Nor – in contrast to Lelio or Don Giovanni – are they inveterate philanderers, but youthful heroes who have fallen in love for the first time in their lives.

Much has been written on the issue of deception and dissimulation in the early modern period[6] in a variety of different contexts – the court; politics; politeness; and religion; but the context most relevant to Sidney's *Arcadia* is that of betrayal in love, for which John Lyly's *Euphues* (1578) or some of Shakespeare's sonnets may be treated as comparable. Deception in love, Euphues claims, is a necessity and a right: "No, no, he that cannot dissemble in love is not worthy to live. I am of this mind, that both might and malice, deceit and treachery, all perjury, any impiety may lawfully be committed in love, which is lawless" (1987, 140). However, where Lyly's Euphues – after some soul searching – decides to cheat on his friend Philautus by wooing his beloved Lucilla, and Lucilla in her turn decides to betray Philautus and turn to Euphues (only to abandon him, too), the two princes of Sidney's romance are no such turncoats, and their deceit materializes not in betrayal but in the strategy of impersonation. They engage in gender duplicity (Lobsien 2005, 116; Wald 2014, 89–130) in the case of Pyrocles and social dissembling in the case of Musidorus.

Yet, what makes impersonation a morally extremely problematic act is not merely its assumption of a false identity (which could be treated as a lie), but the subsequent series of dishonest actions and words that become necessary in the wake of the initial deception. Though the first stage of dissimulation of a false identity is therefore presented as a despairing reaction to Basilius' withdrawal from the world, which makes a state visit by the two princes (clearly very acceptable bridegrooms for the daughters) impossible, the subsequent plot of the romance shows the two heroes involving themselves in ever more murky immoral dealings that could be argued to be an illustration of Shakespeare's lilies that fester more than weeds (sonnet 94).[7] As Cleophila recognizes, "deceit cannot be otherwise maintained but by deceit" (Sydney 1580, 181). Castiglione's *sprezzatura*, grounded in "wit, ambiguity, feigning," as

[6] Snyder calls the period the "Age of Dissimulation" (title of Chapter 1). See Snyder (2009), Hadfield (2017) as well as Asch (in this volume).

[7] Or, as Lyly has it, "The pestilence doth most rifest infect the clearest complexion, and the caterpillar cleareth into the ripest fruit. [...] one drop of poison infecteth the whole tun of wine; one leaf of colloquintida [bitter apple] mareth and spoileth the whole pot of porridge; one iron mole defaceth the whole piece of lawn [white fabric]" (94).

Kinney observes, "encourages indirection" and produces "simulation," which is "indivisible from dissimulation" (41). Circumstances conspire to inveigle the princes in a number of deceitful acts and words that corrupt their original honesty and lead to criminal actions and their sentencing in Book V of the text. The happy ending materializes when Basilius awakes from apparent death (the 'poison' he has drunk was actually a sleep potion) and assumes responsibility for the political chaos that his withdrawal from court has occasioned. These developments also save the two princes from execution and seal the return to national (and rational) order by a double marriage of the two love couples.

The behavior of Pyrocles and Musidorus deteriorates significantly between Book I of the *Old Arcadia* and its near-fatal Book V, in which the two young men acknowledge their guilt. However, they refuse to save their own skin by disclosing their real identities, instead out of shame adopting new fake names: Pyrocles now pretends to be Timopyrus, and Musidorus Palladius. They concede that their Arcadian behavior has been unworthy of the reputations of Pyrocles and Musidorus.

To briefly list their shady dealings for readers unfamiliar with the romance: initially, Pyrocles (Cleophila) and Musidorus (Dorus) perform some heroic deeds by rescuing the princesses from a lion and a bear and by putting down an Arcadian riot. Pyrocles is persecuted both by the lustful Basilius and by the lovesick Gynecia (his wife, who recognizes that the Amazon is a man). In order to keep Gynecia from exposing him, i.e. Cleophila (Pyrocles), to be a man in disguise (and thus risking death for having entered the security zone), Pyrocles arranges an assignation with Gynecia in a cave. Under the pretext of a rendez-vous, he likewise lures Basilius to the same place, thus gaining the opportunity to talk to Philoclea and declare his love (and gender) to her. Pyrocles and Philoclea exchange vows of love. Most probably the two lovers sleep with one another (this is what the fool Dametas, who discovers them, assumes and tells the court). Pyrocles knows that Musidorus and Pamela are about to elope and that his cousin is contemplating an invasion of Arcadia to ensure the marriage of the two princes with the two princesses. As the court will later see it, Musidorus has therefore violated the future ruler of the kingdom (Pamela) and conspired to invade the country, an act of treason. Moreover, in retrospect, it appears as if Pyrocles' adoption of the role of the Amazon was a deliberate ploy to infiltrate Arcadia and to engineer the death of Basilius: he stands accused of an attempt at assassination designed as a first step towards the usurpation of the throne. Therefore the assumption of a female fake identity leads Pyrocles into further lying and manipulation against his hosts, and it eventually exposes him to the reasonable suspicion of sedition and conspiracy (treason, usurpation).

In the case of Musidorus disguise as a first step towards dishonesty and criminal action emerges in parallel manner. Rooming as shepherd Dorus with the stupid Dametas, the prince is beset by the unwished-for attentions of Dametas' daughter Mopsa and enervated by the shrew Miso, Dametas' wife. He can only woo Pamela by pretending to woo Mopsa in her presence, yet finally manages to convey to Pamela who he is and to engage her consent to the elopement. For this, he has to evolve a complex combination of deceits in order to get rid of Dametas (sent to dig a hole to get at a buried treasure), Miso (made jealous and sent to town to spy on her supposedly unfaithful husband) and Mopsa (made to believe she will get a wish realized if she remains on top of a tree for a whole night). Musidorus has carefully planned the elopement, arranging for ships in the harbor to take the couple to his native Thessaly and putting his army in readiness. This procedure is clearly treasonous, as is the avowed plan to force Basilius to accept the marriage(s) through blackmail by having Thessaly invade Arcadia. The misbehavior of Musidorus climaxes during the elopement when he fails to restrain his sexual urges and almost rapes the sleeping Pamela, but is prevented when the rioters arrive and kidnap the couple. Though his breaking of his oath to Pamela to preserve her virginity until marriage has not actually resulted in her violation, he very nearly defaults on his promise. Moreover, Musidorus lies to his hosts (Dametas and his family) and plans a coup d'état (though only to force Basilius to agree to the marriages).

Since Sidney's narrative is not (meant to be) realistic, the question what the princes could or should have done in order to get access to the princesses cannot be easily answered. Given that Basilius is afraid of the oracle's predictions and hopes to escape their fulfilment (which of course happens *because* he withdraws from court), the option of seeking him out in their proper persons may really have been impossible for Pyrocles and Musidorus.[8] Where the princes definitely go astray is in the deceit and lying that naturally evolves from their false identities and in the strategies of persuading the princesses to marry (and elope with) them in secret. Although this is nowhere said explicitly, the proper procedure would have been to leave and attempt an official offer of marriage through Pyrocles' father and the available diplomatic channels – presumably with Philanax, who is Basilius' regent. Much of the responsibility lies with Basilius for keeping his daughters prisoner, thus losing their obedience and respect and making them susceptible to allurements of elopement and clandestine marriage. However, in a different fictional world, the two princes could have declared their love in letters, and the continuous lies and dissimulations need not have occurred for so long a period of time.

The nearly tragic ending of the romance likewise results from dissimulation, but also from Basilius' disinclination to accept advice (of Philanax or of his wife Gynecia). As the reader of the text will remember, in Book I Philanax

[8] Dipple argues that Basilius "set up an unnatural circumstance in which Pyrocles and Musidorus were forced to go to absurd lengths and bizarre disguises to accomplish their forthright intention of wooing the princesses" (99).

strongly advises Basilius against his withdrawal to the Arcadian forests. In the scene where Basilius goes to the cave to have a rendez-vous with the Amazon Cleophila, he ends up sleeping with his wife (whom he takes to be Cleophila since she has put on Cleophila's cloak for her assignation with Pyrocles-Cleophila). When they discover each other's identity, they are both ashamed. Basilius insists on swallowing Gynecia's love potion (inherited by her), though she passionately advises against it, and as a consequence falls into a deep sleep which (Romeo-and-Juliet-like) everyone considers to be death, thus seemingly turning Gynecia into his murderess. It is on account of Basilius' death that the two princes appear to be assassins and would-be usurpers of the Arcadian throne. Hence, the pretense that Gynecia is Cleophila (by dressing up in her clothes) and of Pyrocles pretending to be the Amazon has terrible consequences (though the root cause of the alleged murder lies in the adultery that both Basilius and Gynecia intend to commit). Dipple therefore appropriately speaks of the "moral ambivalences [...] that surround the Arcadian nobility and the young princes" (87).

The earlier lies of the princes about their identity now work to their detriment. Instead of resorting to the truth, they continue to counterfeit their identity during the final trial in order to preserve their good name, since they are ashamed of their behavior – and rightly so. Yet it is not merely in taking on yet another disguise that they lie during the trial; they also lie by omission. Pyrocles (alias Timopyrus) pretends that he raped Philoclea (which he did not do; in fact, it is not clear whether they even had sex with one another, though the text implies they did), and Musidorus (alias Palladius) remains silent regarding his attempted or contemplated rape. On the other hand, the dishonesty they display at the trial is offset by their princely demonstration of courage, though that performance cannot conquer the suspicions that Philanax has introduced into his accusations. In fact, Philanax's prosecution sophistically turns each mitigating factor into yet another argument against the princes, for instance by assuming that they have stolen their jewels and clothes and therefore only counterfeit their nobility. The defendants are therefore unable to gain credence for their valid arguments against the prosecution. The punishment of liars is upon them: the two lovers have lied, and now they cannot be believed.

Yet the lies and impersonations that the princes engage in are the consequence of their love, and the text figures both love and impersonation in the terminology of counterfeiting. The first mention of counterfeiting occurs in the description of Philoclea's beauty in her painting, in which she is "drawn as well as it was possible art should counterfeit so perfect a workmanship of nature" (11). Shortly afterwards, Musidorus wonders about "some Amazon Cleophila that hath counterfeited the face of my friend" (17), while Pyrocles declares he will "seek to counterfeit" an Amazon (19). (In Book III, Musidorus even calls Pyrocles a "counterfeit courtesan" – 148.) When Musidorus has also assumed another identity, Pyrocles-Cleophila even suspects this "counterfeit[ing]" is to mirror to him the "deformity of [his] passions" (38). The unsavoury nature of counterfeiting likewise emerges from Gynecia's "knowledge of Cleophila's counterfeiting which [...] fortified her unlawful desires" (51). The first eclogues take up again the image of counterfeiting by comparing coining and poetic composition ("glosses of deceits" – 58). In the rest of the romance, counterfeiting does not merely refer to impersonation but also to Dorus' "counterfeit[ing] of the extremest love" to Mopsa (87), to the scorn feigned by Cleophila towards the advances of Basilius and Gynecia (85) and to the royal couple's strategy of feigning sleep prior to the adventure of the cave (see also 147). In Book V, the concept of counterfeiting reverts to the meaning of falsity and impersonation.

This is not the place to discuss the trial of Book V in detail (see Dipple 1970, McCoy 1979, Stillman 1986, Beier 1989). Philanax, besides condemning the princes in advance ("this venomous serpent" – 335; "this wolvish shepherd, this counterfeit prince" – 346) and turning their defense arguments to their disadvantage, also engages in deceit by suppressing the letters of the princesses. Euarchus, Pyrocles' father (who acts as the judge) is likewise at fault, since he is swayed by Philanax's misrepresentations and biased arguments (Dipple: "a case partially presented and dimly understood" – 93); and he errs on the side of overfulfillment of the letter of the law rather than on the side of clemency. In the end, the princes ("both virtuous and guilty" – Dipple 93) prove their nobility by their behavior and repair their heroic status.[9] Not only do they think first of their ladies rather than themselves and then intercede one for the other, pleading mercy not for their own life but for that of their friend and cousin. They also desist from trying to sway Euarchus from his mistaken draconian course of judgment, accepting their death sentence with equanimity and courage and, in the case of Pyrocles, with exemplary filial obedience to the father's decision.

What is interesting in the framework of my discussion of lying is the fact that the arguments of the romance center on two antitheses: between reason and passion, and appearance and reality. Both of these dichotomies come into play in the oracle. In Book I, Basilius is overcome by passion (fear) and does not follow the very reasonable counsel of Philanax. The oracle is also an instance of misleading or specious signification which serves to obscure the meaning that will emerge only later in the story. The text can therefore be argued to thematize ambiguity and the limits of rational behavior, giving to chance or Fortune the important role that, rationally and ideally, should be played by

9 The guilt of the princes is hinted at right at the beginning when the love-sick Pyrocles does not dare to look Musidorus in the face, "armed with the very countenance of the poor prisoner at the bar whose answer is nothing but 'guilty'" (Sidney, 16). The prison of love image recurs in the romance, already in Pyrocles's rejoinder to Musidorus' reproaches in which he declares himself to be both sick and a prisoner for life (22).

human reason and plain appearance. Though the oracle does not lie, it sets in motion the series of impersonations and pretenses that nearly result in catastrophe.

Indeed, Sidney's Arcadia is not such an ideal realm of retreat from the evil of the court, usually considered typical of Renaissance notions of pastoral romance. Unlike the Forest of Arden, Duke Basilius' pastoral retreat houses the legitimate ruler but not as exiled king; although the eclogues focus on shepherds playing their instruments and discoursing on love, the songs are actually philosophical arguments about passion versus rationality. Moreover, the one shepherd who is described at length is Dametas, who could be called an anti-pastoral character on account of his greed, stupidity, and love of intrigue. More importantly still, the two riots of the story, the one put down by the princes in Book II and the one raised by the noblemen (amongst others) in Book IV, transport the problems of the real world (how to rule the masses) directly into the supposedly peaceful pastoral realm, canceling Arcadia's constitutive alterity. Basilius' retreat may not be the court, but it is beset by the same problems of social unrest that sway the masses in ordinary states, re-posing the question of good (or inadequate) rulership within the pastoral heterotopia. The Shakespearean theme of good monarchical rule is omnipresent in the text and attaches not simply to Basilius but to Cleophila's speech pacifying the mob and to Euarchus' judging of the accused princely malefactors. And, metaphorically speaking, it also involves the theme of self-government and self-control so signally absent in the behavior of the two princes.

These arguments lead us to see the roles adopted by Pyrocles and Musidorus as well as by Basilius not merely as deceptive but as self-deceptive and symbolic: Basilius pretends to be a shepherd, but this equals a renunciation of his royal status and the assumption of the role of a subject. Pyrocles' Amazonian disguise implicitly comments on his effeminization through surrender to the irrationality of love; and Musidorus' apprenticeship with Dametas reflects his lowly instincts – he allows himself to be ruled by a person who is very much his inferior. The fake identities assumed by the princes and the pseudo-pastoral role adopted by the duke result in the inevitable betrayal of their best selves, forcing them into behavior that they would otherwise have avoided and becoming, for Philanax, a model "of disguisers, falsifiers, adulterers, ravishers, murderers, and traitors" (346). Or as Sheridan's Joseph Surface remarks: "Sincerely I begin to wish I had never made such a Point of gaining so very good a character – for it has led me into so many curs'd Rogueries that I doubt I shall be exposed at last" (Sheridan II,ii; 248).

2.2. Postmodernist Ploys

Let me now turn to more modern texts. As we have seen in the case of Ackroyd's *Chatterton* above, in the twentieth century, outside comedy, impersonation moves to deal with situations in which alternative identities become increasingly difficult to distinguish, and the question of ontology outweighs issues of epistemology – quite in accordance with Brian McHale's distinction between modernism and postmodernism (1993 [1987]). Traditionally, as I noted, the reader is in the know and the deceived dramatis personae are deluded and have to figure out who the man or the woman really is, eventually uncovering the assumed identity.

This is naturally a prominent motif in detective fiction, one which may be handled with some sophistication. For instance, in *The Belting Inheritance* (Symons 1965), the first-person narrator, Christopher, relates how, ten years after the end of the war, a stranger arrives at Belting, Lady Wainwright's country house, and claims to be her beloved son David. It turns out eventually that the claimant is not David, who really died in the war, but his brother Hugh. Hugh had to escape from England in the wake of being responsible for his business partner Sullivan's death (who had discovered that he had defrauded him of the profits of the business to pay for his gaming debts). He then posted his name as a war casualty and is now trying to regain the inheritance under his brother's name. Ironically, there is no family fortune to distribute, Lady Wainwright has spent it all, and her children's hatred of the intruder was therefore pointless.

Stephen Fry's *The Liar* (1991) takes lying and impersonation one step further by combining so many levels of reality and so many roles enacted by a number of different characters that what eventually emerges as 'real' threatens to be yet another fiction. Since the plot of this text is extremely complex, let me reduce it to the two series of impersonations that figure prominently. On the one hand, there is the eponymous liar Adrian Healey, whom we meet as a pupil in public school and later as a student at Cambridge, studying with Professor Trefusis. Initially, Adrian's lies are related to plagiarism and his homosexuality, but later he tells Trefusis a long story about being a male prostitute in Piccadilly and having been to prison for drugs found on him and belonging to his patron. However, that story is undermined when we learn that he has been spying under cover for his uncle, who is in the secret services. Adrian moreover produces a forgery of an unknown Dickens manuscript, combining his own experiences as a male prostitute with a study of Victorian pornography. Trefusis, also a liar, is a man with many faces. He initially appears to be an eccentric don, who causes a scandal for being surprised in a lavatory with another man, but on the sabbatical abroad, on which he invites Adrian to join him, it emerges that he is involved in the MI5 and trying to extricate a Hungarian invention from the hands of the Russians (the lavatory was the tryst for receiving secret material). Yet even this account of Trefusis's identity (and those of the inventor and his brother traumatically killed before Adrian's eyes) turns out to be a fiction produced by MI5 members, including Adrian's uncle, for their own entertainment.

Fry's novel is much more postmodernist than Symons's detective tale. The various impersonations are apt to mislead the reader and seem obscure to some of the characters, too. In the end it even emerges that Trefusis must have known Adrian from his school days and that he therefore is the prime manipulator. The novel displays a typically postmodernist inclination for merging fact and fiction, with autobiography (stories the characters tell about their lives) turning out to be unreliable, deliberately untruthful and even entirely made up. The text therefore again demonstrates the affinity between impersonation and lying, though from the opposite direction than in the *Old Arcadia:* here lying involves impersonation, where Sidney illustrated that impersonation necessitates lying. The novel extends the practice of lying beyond the adoption of fake identities into plagiarism and forgery as well as secret services manipulations of apparent reality.

My main example in this section, Philip Roth's *Operation Shylock. A Confession* (1993), could be argued to complicate in radical manner the already overcomplex constellation that Fry offered to us. Thus, the central act of impersonation is that of the author-narrator, who is confronted with a doppelgänger and in turn impersonates that doppelgänger; this alter ego calls himself Philip Roth, but the narrator jocularly refers to him as Moishe Pipik. We thus have a situation (familiar from many autofictional texts[10]) in which the real author, Philip Roth, writes ostensibly about himself and his own experience, yet this story is actually fictional, with the author impersonating himself in the first-person narrator persona 'Philip Roth.' The novel was the final text in a plan for a quartet with the title *Two-Faced. An Autobiography in Four Acts*, as shown in a 1990 draft in the Library of Congress (Gooblar, 35); its title invokes "deception and betrayal," though Gooblar associates the deceit with "writing non-fictional depictions of other people" (35). As Gooblar notes, Roth in a 1984 interview thematized the "writerly skill of impersonation" and praised Witold Gombrovicz for "introduc[ing] himself as a character, using his own name" (43). This pattern familiar from other Roth novels is complicated by the narrator's loss of identity due to having taken the postoperative drug Halcion, resulting in the Philip Roth of the story no longer recognizing himself. This split personality syndrome then becomes exacerbated by the encounter with Moishe Pipik, who claims to be Philip Roth and expounds the anti-Zionist doctrine of diasporism (Jews should return to the diaspora). In the course of the story, Philip Roth finds out more about his impersonator and ends up

[10] On autofiction see, among others, Asthoff (2008) and Jones (2010). See also Rüdiger Heinze's essay in this volume.

impersonating him as part of a secret service action, into which he has been pressured by the Israeli secret services. There is therefore a doubling or duplication of the double to be observed in this novel.[11] As Cohen observes, "Roth's abiding preoccupation with fictive alter egos, counter-selves, and doubles" can be treated as the result of a "logic of endless deception" (2007, 82).

The theme of lying and impersonation is additionally mirrored in the text by the key political event of the historical 1986 trial of Ivan Demjanjuk, accused of being the concentration camp guard 'Ivan the Terrible' in Treblinka. Demjanjuk claimed not to be Ivan the Terrible and to have been saddled with a false identity. In fact, historically, Demjanjuk was confronted with a doppelgänger figure coming to haunt him. The death sentence against Demjanjuk was lifted by the Supreme Court of Israel in 1993 (the year Roth published the novel) when it was found that Ivan the Terrible had been one Ivan Marchenko, resulting in the release of Demjanjuk and his return to the USA. (Demjanjuk was later sentenced for his complicity in the deaths of inmates in the Sobibor extermination camp.)

In addition to these two plots, the narrator's contact with the Palestinian George Ziad, whom Brostoff regards as another alter ego of Roth's, should be mentioned. Brostoff insightfully comments that Ziad's name should be connected with "his own never-mentioned double, Edward Said" (2019, n.p.).[12] Ziad, the diasporic Palestinian returned to Palestine, is the inverse image of Roth, the American diasporic Jew. Many additional intertextual doubles have been proposed for the novel. Harold Bloom, for instance, suggested that "Philip Roth's shadow self or secret sharer is not [Pipik]; it is Shylock" (Bloom 1993, 48; Safer 2010, 169). This is followed up on by Haselstein in relation to the Demjanjuk trial, which, she argues, "is juxtaposed to Shylock's trial and to the trial of the Palestinians 'Roth' had witnessed earlier" (2011, 67). The extensive discussion of diasporism in the novel, proposed by the fake Roth, Moishe Pipik, serves as a disorienting factor. As Carpi comments in her insightful article on the functions of diasporas in *Operation Shylock*, the narrator Roth's breakdown due to the drug Halcion "is an image of the effects of diaspora on a person who does not consider himself any longer at home in the world. The effects of the pill are similar to those caused by a diaspora consciousness" (Carpi 2017, 195).

The novel therefore mirrors several acts of lying and impersonation, but undercuts and radicalizes the deceptive quality of impersonation by making the distinction between truth and fiction or real and fake identity porous if not

---

[11] See Cohen (2007) on the importance of the double in Roth's work. Greenberg (1997) also points out that Roth's oeuvre abounds in scenarios of doubling (Nathan and Henry Zuckerman in *The Counterlife*) and of impersonation such as the 'passing' of Coleman Silk, the protagonist in *The Human Stain*. On impersonation in Roth see also Shostak.

[12] Said was a good friend of Roth. See Shatz (2021, 30).

undecidable.[13] The ostensible reason for Roth to be in Israel, his interviews with Aharon Appelfeld, adds one more layer to the deliberate erosion of the fact/fiction divide, since Appelfeld is a holocaust survivor who also fictionalizes his own experiences during the holocaust. As one of the victims of the Shoah, he is therefore a kind of doppelgänger for Demjanjuk, but also serves as a foil to the ruling retributive atmosphere during the trial, since Appelfeld distances himself from the pursuit of justice against the perpetrators. (The title of the book, derived from the secret service action in which the narrator is later involved, has also been taken to refer to the Demjanjuk trial and to criticize it as excessive in the manner of Shylock's revengeful comportment in Shakespeare.)[14]

What Roth accomplishes in his fiction is the undermining of the distinction between lying and veracity. The narrator persona may be reliable, unreliable or self-deceiving. His impersonator, likewise, may be a forger of identities or deluded in the manner of Dössekker-Wilkomirski. In a telephone conversation with the narrator early in the novel, Aharon Applefeld remarks,

> "Yes, and the madman [the impostor] undoubtedly believes that in New York and London and Connecticut there is a madman [i.e. Roth] pretending to be him."
> "Unless he's not at all mad and knows exactly what he is doing." (Roth 1994, 33)
> Is he mentally so damaged that he truly believes that my history is his; is he some psychotic, some amnesiac, who isn't pretending at all? If every word he speaks he means, if the only person pretending here is me ... (43)[15]

Only the narrator's deliberate adoption of the role of his alter ego equals an *intentional act of deception*. The situation therefore emphasizes the sliding scale between veracity and deception and poses both epistemological and ontological challenges to the characters and to the readers. Roth the narrator encounters a radical uncertainty about what is and what is not real. Tricking Pipik in the role of Pierre Roget, the journalist, 'Roth' believes he has been outwitted ("He knows, I thought, hanging up. He knows perfectly well who I am" – 48); yet, as it turns out, it is Pipik who has been deluded: "'But – then – that was *you*,'

13 On the "probing" of the "permeability of the borders between fact and fiction" see Gooblar (2008, 34), who argues that Roth uses a "'hall of mirrors'" and "explor[es] the ways in which non-fiction may be just as unreliable a representation of reality as fiction" (34).

14 But see also Hayes (2014, 187-9) on the Freudian ramifications of the uncanny in connection with Shylock and the doppelgänger figure in the novel. Haselstein, in her insightful article, observes on both the "parallel between the Jewish state and Venice in their treatment of the Other" and on the negative stereotype of Shakespeare's villainous Jew and its after-effects in pogroms and the holocaust (as outlined by Supposnik in the novel – Roth 1994, 274-5) (Haselstein 2011, 66-67). She also suggests that the "conflict between 'Roth' and Smilesburger is thus defined as a conflict between Shylock and Shylock – but also a conflict between Antonio and Antonio [...]" (66).

15 Original dots. In this telephone conversation with his double, Roth is pretending to be Pierre Roget, "a French journalist based in Paris" (Roth 40).

he cried. '*You* were Pierre Roget. You tricked me!' And he slumped over in his chair at the horror of the discovery, pure commedia dell'arte" (82; original emphasis). The trauma of impersonation is, precisely, that one no longer knows who is the other person and who one is oneself. Later in the book, Roth even believes that his act of impersonation was "a Halcion hallucination" (176). At the end, Pipik voices his anguish against 'Roth' by exclaiming: "*He*'s the fake, *that's* the irony, *he's the fucking double*, a dishonest impostor and fucking hypocritical fake" (367; original emphasis). As Cohen suggests, by doubling the double, 'Roth's' "claim to truth" is "void[ed]" and results in "an annihilation of the self" (2007, 91).

Roth's "proliferation of doubles" (Gooblar 2008, 46) can be interpreted as a postmodernist strategy of playing games with ontology. As Haselstein observes, "Roth's signature as a writer is a blending of the realist novel with artistic self-portraiture, which defines reality as a stage for a playful mise-en-scène of the author's personal preoccupations and obsessions" (2011, 49). The metafictional element in the text is foregrounded both in the narrator's comments (for instance when he talks about the story being "frivolously plotted, overplotted, for his taste altogether too freakishly plotted, with outlandish events so wildly careening around every corner [...]" – Roth 1994, 245), but there is also implicit metafiction in the dialogue, as when Aharon Applefeld in the novel remarks, "He has less talent for impersonating than you have" (107). In addition, the actual roles of characters display dizzying levels of dishonesty, dissembling and role-playing: "Ziad may be an Israeli informer [...], and the Jewish civil rights lawyer of the Palestinians may be an Israeli secret agent" (Haselstein 62).

The levels of fictionalizing and proclaiming fictions to be facts and querying the factual as possibly fictional are numerous. In the final pages of the book when Roth the author-narrator is told by Smilesburger to cut out the last chapter of his manuscript for security reasons, 'Roth' accuses Smilesburger of being a "highly entertaining deceiver" (Roth 1994, 387) – a label obviously appropriate to his own and Pipik's fictionalizing. Smilesburger, who admits to having recruited Philip "perhaps even with a false enticement" (386), asks him to produce fiction instead of fact, a request which Philip counters with "'If I were to do as you ask, the whole book would be specious. Calling fiction fact would undermine everything'" (387). This is as much as to say: since the book has pretended to be factual, writing a fictional account would falsify everything and be deceptive. However, as the "Note to the Reader" at the end of the book demonstrates, lying is certainly something Roth is doing, and in the manner of the Cretan liar: "[...] the names, characters, places, and incidents either are products of the author's imagination or are used fictitiously. Any resemblance to actual events or locales or persons, living or dead, is entirely coincidental. This confession is false" (399). As Safer points out (2010, 161), the reference of "this" in the final sentence is radically ambiguous: it may refer *either* to the proposition in the penultimate sentence, thereby denying the fictionality of the text – this being the most obvious meaning – *or* to the subtitle of the novel, *A Confession*, therefore underlining the fictionality of the novel: a false or lying confession is fiction.

In *Operation Shylock*, fraudulence and delusion or illusion (after all, this is fiction) rub shoulders with one another, and the moral issues arising from these ambiguities fail to be resolved except in dizzying spirals of uncertainty. Though referring to Roth's novel *Deception* (1990), Cohen shrewdly comments that "the affair [in this context: the play with identities] remains permanently suspended between fiction and reality, such that to read the novel is to be condemned irremediably to deception" (2007, 82). The seriousness of the impersonator's pretense is in fact present only to the audience – for the first-person narrator this whole affair is a personal trauma and material for writing. But the death sentence for Demjanjuk and the Israeli policies affecting Palestinians are spelled out in actual and prospective bloodshed and therefore hint at a context in which the game of identities ceases to be merely provocative postmodernist entertainment.[16]

3. *Conclusion*

In this essay I have tried to establish that imposture leads to lying just as lying may lead to imposture. One can therefore consider the assumption of a fake identity to be part of a scale of dissembling and lying, with the intention of deceit adopting more or less verbal forms or affecting behavior and action to a more or less extended degree.

Focusing on the practice of impersonation, I have discussed how the moral denunciation of lying and deceit ("counterfeiting") in the early modern period has been displaced by an emphasis on role-playing with (deceitful) identities in modern and postmodern literature, which displays and cultivates the 'art of lying' propounded by Oscar Wilde. In both of the texts that I have discussed in detail, dissimulation and impersonation are *performances* that go wrong. In Sidney, the performance is linked to *sprezzatura*; in Roth, to the postmodernist aesthetics of indeterminacy.

---

16 By contrast, Gooblar sees the seriousness of Roth's text in its "claiming to be factual, thus implicating, exposing and invading the privacy of Roth" (46): "Roth, who, in his past three books, had examined the consequences of this sort of exposure from the position of the writer, now finds himself on the other side of the conflict, powerless to determine the way his story is told" (47). Gooblar argues that the need for "out-Pipiking Pipik" results from the realization that 'Roth' as an excellent stylist is outmaneuvered by the banal impersonator (47). His manner of hitting back is the attempt to produce a "counterplot in which to subsume the Pipikesque imbecility" (Roth 1994, 246).

In the first section of the essay I have proposed a typology of lying in literature and suggested that generic frameworks are especially relevant to the deployment of lying characters in works of literature. Though, on the level of the plot, i.e. the fictional world, as soon as a liar enters the stage, questions of veracity and conventions of truthfulness are being debated explicitly and implicitly, it is with lying and deception on the narratorial and authorial level that the issue of conversational maxims of quality (Grice) and their infringement acquires the most urgency. However, if novels adopt a postmodernist questioning of ontology and engage in performances of postmodernist self-reflexive play and autofictional destabilization of the boundaries between fact and fiction, then one can bracket serious moral implications and 'lying' becomes the accepted norm of the imaginary act of producing fiction.

Works Cited

Ackroyd, Peter (1993) *Chatterton* [1987]. London: Penguin.

Amis, Martin (1986) *Money: A Suicide Note* [1984]. London: Penguin.

Asthoff, Jens (2008) *Autofiktion*. Kultur & Gespenster, 7. Hamburg: Textem-Verlag.

Bernhard, Thomas (2010) *Woodcutters* [1984]. Trans. David McLintock. New York: Vintage International.

Beier, A. L. (1989) "Changing Depictions of Popular Revolt in Sixteenth-Century England: the Case of Sidney's two *Arcadias*." *The Journal of Medieval and Renaissance Studies* 19.1: 15–33.

Bloom, Harold (1993) "Operation Roth." *New York Review of Books* 22 April: 45–48.

Brostoff, Ari M. (2019) "The Double Allegiance: Philip Roth and the Question of Zion." *Post45*. 12 April. Web.

Carpi, Daniela (2017) "Cultural Mobility and Diaspora: The Case of Philip Roth's *Operation Shylock*." *Diaspora, Law and Literature.* Ed. Klaus Stiersdorfer and Daniela Carpi. Berlin: Walter de Gruyter. 187–204.

Christie, Agatha (1951) *The Murder of Roger Ackroyd* [1926]. Harmondsworth: Penguin.

Cohen, Josh (2007) "Roth's Doubles." *The Cambridge Companion to Philip Roth.* Ed. Timothy Parrish. Cambridge: Cambridge Univ. Press. 82–93.

Cohn, Dorrit (1999) "Breaking the Code of Fictional Biography: Wolfgang Hildesheimer's *Marbot*." *The Distinction of Fiction*. Baltimore: Johns Hopkins Univ. Press. 79–95.

Corneille, Pierre (1984) *Le menteur. Comédie* [1643]. *Oeuvres complètes*. Volume 2. Bibliothèque de la Pléiade. Paris: Gallimard. 1–91.

Dipple, Elizabeth (1970) "'Unjust Justice' in the *Old Arcadia.*" *Studies in English Literature, 1500-1900* 10.1: 83–101.

Eliot, George (1996) *Silas Marner: The Weaver of Raveloe* [1861]. Ed. David Carroll. London: Penguin.

Elsaesser, Thomas (2009) "The Mind-Game Film." *Puzzle Films. Complex Storytelling in Contemporary Cinema*. Ed. Warren Buckland. Malden: Wiley. 13–41.

Fowles, John (1963) *The Collector*. Boston: Little, Brown & Co.

Franzen, Johannes (2018) *Indiskrete Fiktionen: Theorie und Praxis des Schlüsselromans.* Göttingen: Wallstein Verlag.

Franzen, Johannes (2020) "Contested Inventions: Fictionality and Ethics." *Travelling Concepts: New Fictionality Studies*. Ed. Monika Fludernik and Henrik Skov Nielsen. Frankfurt: Peter Lang. 45–67.

Frey, James (2003) *A Million Little Pieces.* New York: Talese/Doubleday.

Fry, Stephen (2011) *The Liar* [1991]. London: Arrow Books.

Goldoni, Carlo (2001) *The Liar: A Comedy in Three Acts* [1750]. Trans. Tunc Yalman. New York: Dramatists Play Service.

Gooblar, David (2008) "The Truth Hurts: The Ethics of Philip Roth's Autobiographical Books." *Journal of Modern Literature* 32.1: 33–53.

Greenberg, Robert (1997) "Transgression in the Fiction of Philip Roth." *Twentieth-Century Literature Online* 32.1: 33–53. Web.

Grice, Paul (1975) "Logic and Conversation." *Syntax and Semantics*. Ed. Peter Cole and Jerry L. Morgan. Volume 3. 41–58.

Hadfield, Andrew (2017) *Lying in Early Modern English Culture: From the Oath of Supremacy to the Oath of Allegiance.* Oxford: Oxford Univ. Press.

Haselstein, Ulla (2011) "Diasporic Doubles: Philip Roth's Operation Shylock." *Re-Framing the Transnational Turn in American Studies.* Ed. Winfried Fluck et al. Hanover, NH: Dartmouth College Press. 49–71.

Hayes, Patrick (2014) *Philip Roth: Fiction and Power*. Oxford: Oxford Univ. Press.

Hildesheimer, Wolfgang (1981) *Marbot: eine Biographie.* Frankfurt: Suhrkamp.

Hilgartner, Stephen (1997) "The Sokal Affair in Context." *Science, Technology, & Human Values* 22.4: 506–522.

Hitchcock, Alfred (1950) Dir. *Stage Fright.* Warner Brothers.

Ishiguro, Kazuo (1989) *The Remains of the Day*. London: faber & faber.

James, Henry (2001) "The Figure in the Carpet" [1896]. *Selected Tales*. Ed. John Lyon. London: Penguin. 284–313.

James, Henry (1963) "The Liar" [1888]. *The Novels and Tales of Henry James*. Vol. 12. New York: Scribner.

James, Henry (2001) "The Real Thing" [publ. 1892]. *Selected Tales*. Ed. John Lyon. London: Penguin. 204–224.

James, Henry (1995) *The Turn of the Screw* [1898]. Ed. Peter G. Beidler. Boston: Bedford Books of St. Martin's Press.

James, Henry (2009) *The Golden Bowl* [1904]. London: Penguin.

Jones, E. H. (2010) "Autofiction: A Brief History of a Neologism." *Life Writing: Essays on Autobiography, Biography and Literature*. Ed. Richard Bradford. Basingstoke: Palgrave Macmillan. 174–84.

Khan, Rahila (1987) *Down the Road, Worlds Away*. London: Virago Upstarts.

Kinney, Arthur F. (2005) "*Utopia*'s First Readers." *Challenging Humanism: Essays in Honor of Dominic Baker-Smith*. Ed. Ton Hoenselaars, and Arthur F. Kinney. Newark: Univ. of Delaware Press. 23–53.

Lanchester, John (1996) *The Debt to Pleasure*. London: Picador.

Lobsien, Verena Olejniczak (2005) "'Transformed in show, but more transformed in mind': Sidney's *Old Arcadia* and the Performance of Perfection." *Performance of the Sacred in Late Medieval and Early Modern England*. Ed. Susanne Rupp and Tobias Döring. Amsterdam: Rodopi. 105–117.

Lyly, John (1987) *Euphues: The Anatomy of Wit* [1578]. Ed. Paul Salzman. *An Anthology of Elizabethan Prose Fiction*. Oxford World's Classics. Oxford: Oxford Univ. Press.

McCoy, Richard C. (1979) *Sir Philip Sidney. Rebellion in Arcadia*. London: Harvester Press.

McEwan, Ian (2003) *Atonement* [2001]. New York: Anchor Books.

McHale, Brian (1993) *Postmodernist Fiction* [1987]. London: Routledge.

Menchú, Rigoberta (1984) *I, Rigoberta Menchú: an Indian Woman in Guatemala* [1983]. London: Verso.

Molière (1977) *Tartuffe* [1664]. Ed. Hugh Gaston Hall. London: Arnold.

Montaigne, Michel de (1958) "On Liars." *Essays*. Penguin Classics. Trans. and intr. J. M. Cohen. London: Penguin. 28–33.

Nünning, Ansgar (1997) "'But why *will* you say that I am mad?' On the Theory, History, and Signals of Unreliable Narration in British Fiction." *Arbeiten aus Anglistik und Amerikanistik* 22: 83–105.

Nünning, Ansgar (1998a) Ed. *'Unreliable Narration': Studien zur Theorie und Praxis unglaubwürdigen Erzählens in der englischsprachigen Erzählliteratur*. Trier: WVT.

Nünning, Ansgar (1998b) "*Unreliable Narration* zur Einführung: Grundzüge einer kognitiv-narratologischen Theorie und Analyse unglaubwürdigen Erzählens." *Unreliable Narration*. Ed. Ansgar Nünning, Carola Surkamp and Bruno Zerweck. Trier: WVT. 3–40.

Phelan, James, and Mary Patricia Martin (1999) "The Lessons of 'Weymouth': Homodiegesis, Unreliability, Ethics, and *The Remains of the Day*." *Narratologies: New Perspectives on Narrative Analysis*. Ed. D. Herman. Columbus: Ohio State Univ. Press. 88–109.

Roth, Philip (1986) *The Counterlife*. London: Penguin.

Roth, Philip (1991) *Deception* [1990]. New York: Touchstone.

Roth, Philip (1994) *Operation Shylock. A Confession* [1993]. New York: Vintage.

Ruthven, Kenneth K. (2001) *Faking Literature*. Cambridge; New York: Cambridge Univ. Press.

Safer, Elaine (2010) "Operation Shylock: The Double, the Comic, and the Quest for Identity." *Playful and Serious: Philip Roth as a Comic Writer*. Newark, DE: Univ. of Delaware Press. 152–180.

Shaw, George Bernard (1960) *The Doctor's Dilemma* [1906]. Harmondsworth: Penguin.

Shatz, Adam (2021) "Palestinianism." [Review of Timothy Brennan's biography of Edward Said, *Places of Mind*, London: Bloomsbury 2021]. *London Review of Books* 43.9 (6 May): 25–30.

Sheridan, Richard Brinsley (1989) *The School for Scandal* [1777]. *Sheridan's Plays*. Ed. Cecil Price. Oxford: Oxford Univ. Press. 217–300.

Shostak, Debra (1997) "The Diaspora Jew and the 'Instinct for Impersonation': Philip Roth's Operation Shylock." *Contemporary Literature* 38.4: 726–54.

Sidney, Sir Philip (1994) *The Old Arcadia* [1580]. Oxford: Oxford Univ. Press.

Snyder, Jon R. (2009) *Dissimulation and the Culture of Secrecy in Early Modern Europe*. Berkeley: Univ. of California Press.

Sokal, Alan D. (1996) "Transgressing the Boundaries. Toward a Transformative Hermeneutics of Gravity." *Social Text* 46/47: 217–252.

Stillman, Robert E. (1986) *Sidney's Poetic Justice:* The Old Arcadia, *Its Eclogues, and Renaissance Pastoral Traditions*. Lewisburg, PA: Bucknell Univ. Press/London: Associated Univ. Presses.

Symons, Julian (2018) *The Belting Inheritance* [1965]. British Library Crime Classics. London: The British Library.

Wald, Christina (2014) *The Reformation of Romance. The Eucharist, Disguise, and Foreign Fashion in Early Modern Prose Fiction*. Berlin: deGruyter.

Wilde, Oscar (1982) "The Decay of Lying – An Observation" [1891]. *Critical Writings of Oscar Wilde* [1969]. Ed. Richard Ellmann. Chicago: Univ. of Chicago Press.

Wilkomirski, Binjamin (1996) *Fragments: Memories of a Wartime Childhood* [1995]. Trans. Carol Brown Janeway. New York: Schocken Books.

Woodson Harvey, Kristy (2016) *Lies and Other Acts of Love*. East Rutherford: Penguin.

Yacobi, Tamar (2001) "Package Deals in Fictional Narrative: The Case of the Narrator's (Un-)Reliability." *Narrative* 9: 223–229.

II. Historical Perspectives:
Lies, Fictions, Dissimulations

'Lying' as a Term for 'Fiction' in Graeco-Roman Antiquity

Stefan Tilg

1. Introduction

Ancient Greeks and Romans had a number of terms to express notions similar to our contemporary concept of 'fiction.' 'Fiction' here shall be understood not in its narrow modern sense as 'prose fiction' or 'novels' but in its more general meaning of an invented story with invented characters. While the quality of being invented also applies to lies, the fictional story differs in the contexts of its production and reception. It is told without the intention of deceiving and it is not taken as actual fact by its audience.[1] Ancient authors could more or less imply such a concept by the word *mŷthos*[2] ('myth,' as a general manner of speaking rather than referring to concrete 'mythical' stories), by the Aristotelian idea of what is 'possible' in poetry as opposed to the factual events of historiography (e.g. *Poetics* 9), or by rhetorical definitions of *argumentum* and *fabula* (relating to more realistic and more fantastic kinds of invented stories, e.g. Cicero, *De inventione* 1.27). Perhaps surprisingly, however, another viable terminological choice in referring to fiction was also what a standard translation would render as 'lie,' Greek ψεῦδος (*pseûdos*) and Latin *mendacium*, together with their verbal and adjectival cognates.

Often the use of these terms for both fiction and lying has been seen as evidence of a lack of the concept of 'fiction' in the sense described above. After all, the idea of a 'lie' points to the factual discourse of truth and falsehood, in which utterances are always liable to fact-checking. Fictional discourse, by contrast, is characterized by the irrelevance of truth-value – fact-checking of fictional stories simply misses their point. Familiar quotations seem to support an easy trajectory from the Greek "the poets lie a lot" (*pollà pseúdontai aoidoí*, ascribed to Solon) to Sidney's "the Poet, he nothing affirmes, and therefore

[1] I am aware of the fact that there is some linguistic and philosophical dispute about the significance of deceiving in lying (e.g. Meibauer 2015 and various contributions in Meibauer 2019). My impression is, however, that arguments against deception as a defining characteristic of the lie come out at something rather similar (e.g. intentional 'concealment') to deceiving. In any case I think these technical nuances do not matter much for my approach to practices in ancient literature and intellectual culture.

[2] The original Greek has throughout been transliterated into Roman script according to the rules of the *New Pauly* (Leiden: Brill 2002–2011).

never lyeth."[3] Classical scholars have to some extent agreed with that broad trajectory (e.g. Gill 1993) or have designed their own, more elaborate accounts in which the 'invention of fiction' (as opposed to the discourse of truth and lies) takes place at different stages of antiquity itself – for instance, Rösler (1980; 2014) identifies Aristotle as the turning point; Hose (1996) looks at the Roman first century B.C. Studies of the more general issue of the relation of literature and lying (e.g. Mecke 2015; Maier 2019) do not focus on the historical dimension and historical terminology of the problem, nor do they account for the paradoxical fact of the use of terms of lying in referring to concepts of fiction.

In my own approach, I argue that 'lying' has always been an option for saying 'fiction,' and I discuss why that may be the case. I focus on the main Greek and Roman terms for lying (*pseûdos*, *mendacium*) and on their deployment in contexts that suggest we are dealing with fictional rather than factual discourse. I do not of course mean to imply that all occurrences of *pseûdos*, *mendacium* and similar terms should now be translated as 'fiction,' nor do I claim that what we call 'fiction' was not also discussed in terms of truth and falsehood. But I think there exist enough passages where a translation of a Greek or Latin lexeme denoting a 'lie' with 'fiction' is warranted and this suggests a more complex picture than the customary trajectory leads one to believe. This article falls into two major parts. In a first step (section 2), I lay out some major passages in Greek (2.1) and Latin (2.2) and discuss their terminology of 'lying.' In a second step (section 3), I propose a number of accounts for the paradoxical idea of 'lying' as fictional discourse: lexical semantics and natural language polysemy (3.1), similar usage in other languages and epochs (3.2), and the author-centered model of fiction in antiquity (3.3). All translations are from the current Loeb editions if not indicated otherwise.[4] The resulting inconsistencies in the translations of *pseûdos*, *mendacium*, and related terms of lying – for instance, 'lie,' 'invention' or 'fiction' – is deliberately preserved in order to highlight the broad range of interpretations.

---

3 Solon's dictum is transmitted as a kind of proverb in a number of ancient passages, see Feddern 2018, 495–7 for a full account. Sidney's statement can be found on p. [G4^{v}] of the first edition of *An Apologie for Poetrie* (London: Olney, 1595). The now standard title *Defence of Poetry* harks back to the title of the second print, published later in the same year (*The Defence of Poesy*, London: Posonby, 1595).

4 The Loeb Classical Library, published by Harvard University Press, is the best-known series of accessible, bilingual Greek and Roman texts in the English-speaking world. I also add at this point that references to ancient texts follow the classical way of citing book/paragraph numbers and poem/line numbers rather than page numbers of individual editions.

2. *Selected Passages*

Recent studies of the shades of meaning of *pseûdos* (Mesturini 2018) and in particular of the ancient discourse of fiction (Feddern 2018) provide a great deal of helpful material, especially since the available dictionaries of ancient Greek are not comprehensive enough to bring out the nuances of fiction in *pseûdos*. For Latin *mendacium* and its related verb *mentiri*, however, the entries in the *Thesaurus Linguae Latinae* are extremely useful. With the exception of Hesiod, whom I include because of his early date and his prominence in discussions about lying, my selection focuses on passages in which words for 'lying' implicitly or explicitly seem to refer to larger communicative processes (from sender to receiver) and to the conventions of fiction. From time to time, I will call these conventions (synonymously) the 'fictional pact' or the 'fictional contract.'

2.1. Greek

Hesiod, *Theogony* 26–8

This famous and difficult passage comes from one of the oldest works of Greek literature, Hesiod's poem about the genealogy of the gods (*c*.700 BC). It is usually quoted as proof for an exclusive focus on truth and falsehood in archaic Greece, but in fact it may well point to an understanding of the nature of fiction. In the extended prologue of the poem, Hesiod, in his role of a shepherd, reports his encounter with the Muses when tending his lambs on the slopes of Mount Helicon. He recalls them addressing him with an insult and a revelation:

> Field-dwelling shepherds, ignoble disgraces, mere bellies: we know how to say many false things similar to genuine ones (*ídmen pseúdea pollà légein etýmoisin homoîa*), but we know, when we wish, how to proclaim true things (*alēthéa*).

The standard interpretation of this passage is that Hesiod, as a champion of rational enlightenment, draws attention to the dangers of mixing up truth with falsehood passed off as truth, i.e. lies. On this account, the lying Muses should be read as an image for lying poets. These poets would in particular be represented by Homer, who comments in *Odyssey* 19.203 on a deceptive story that Odysseus, still incognito, tells to Penelope: "Thus he made the many falsehoods of his tale seem like the truth" (*íske pseúdea pollà légōn etýmoisin homoîa*). The verbal similarity to *Theogony* 27 is obvious and there is no denying that, in Homer, Odysseus tells a lie. Moreover, scholars have often been under the impression that there was a stark generic divide between Homeric epic, meant for entertainment, and Hesiodic didactic poetry, meant to convey the truth. Nietzsche pithily summarized the point in his 1874 lecture on the history of Greek literature (*Kritische Gesamtausgabe* II.5, 1995, 54): "Lügengesang ist homerisch, Wahrsang hesiodeisch" ['the lying song is Homeric, the true song Hesiodic.']. As first discussed by Stroh (1976) and recently corroborated by Feddern (2018), however, this viewpoint suffers from dubious assumptions (even leaving the vexed questions of the date of Homer and Hesiod and of their relative priority out of account).

In antiquity, didactic poetry was hardly ever separated from epic poetry, and there is no evidence for a reading of the *Theogony* as a 'factual' didactic poem before the eighteenth century (unsurprisingly so, considering the wild stories about the gods that Hesiod presents). In fact, the long opening section of the poem concerning the Muses does not focus on truth but on the 'sweetness' of the Muses' voice (e.g. lines 39–41), the pleasure they elicit in the hearers (e.g. lines 65–67), and on the rhetorical power of their song (e.g. line 98: poets with the gift of the Muses may allow sorrows to be forgotten and turn unhappiness into happiness). While the speaker in Homer, Odysseus, is a notorious liar, the speakers in Hesiod are the Muses, daughters of Zeus, who are revered as the fountainhead of all literary pleasure. It would be difficult to believe that the Muses, goddesses of the highest authority, should introduce themselves by insisting on the negative power of 'lying'. Rather, everything they say serves to underline their own praise of themselves. Hence, when they say that they know many falsehoods (*pseúdea*), they are much more likely to mean something positive, and the easiest way of accounting for their utterance would therefore be to assume they are referring to the power of fiction. When the Muses say that their 'false things are similar to genuine ones,' they are unlikely to refer to any notion of realism relating to the historical world or even to a set of traditional beliefs about the gods (which would be a preposterous claim considering the fantastic nature of large parts of the *Theogony*). Instead, they presumably refer to the coherence and internal plausibility of their stories, a pivotal quality in many later discussions of fiction in Greek literature (as pointed out by Feddern). And when the Muses finally say that they also can, when they wish, proclaim true things, they are praising their ability to mix invented and non-invented elements in their story – just as, in principle, any piece of fiction could claim to do. I am not concerned here with the question whether the *Theogony* is presented as a fictional narrative with factual elements or, inversely, as a factual narrative with fictional elements. What matters in our context is the acknowledgement of fiction under the metaphoric trappings of a lie. If my reading of the passage is correct, the programmatic explicitness with which truth and lies are mixed into a new fictional whole at the very moment in which the poet is invested by the Muses might be regarded as the declaration of a fictional pact *in nuce*.

Plutarch, *How the Young Man Should Study Poetry*

While some doubts about the correct reading of Hesiod's passage will always remain, things become more straightforward with some later authors. A particularly interesting work in our context is Plutarch's essay *How the Young Man Should Study Poetry* (first/second century AD; transmitted in and quoted after the collection of Plurarch's essays titled *Moralia*). Like his philosophical model, Plato, Plutarch takes a moral approach to fiction and finds it to have certain educational and ethical risks. He is especially concerned about readers mistaking fiction for fact and mixing it up with reality. Plutarch's response to these risks, however, differs significantly from Plato's. While Plato, for short, advocates the banning and censoring of fiction (at least those parts of it that cause moral harm), Plutarch recommends responsible reading that is aware of the nature of fiction. To analyze the peculiarities of fiction, he distinguishes between intentional and unintentional *pseûdos* on the part of the poets. None of these untruths is to be equated with a lie. The unintentional *pseûdos* simply encompasses mistakes by the poet. Intentional *pseûdos*, on the other hand, corresponds to what we would more appropriately call 'fiction' (*Moralia* 16a–b):

> [poets tell *pseûdos*] intentionally, because for the purpose of giving pleasure and gratification to the ear (and this is what most people look for in poetry) they feel that the truth is too stern in comparison with fiction (*pseûdos*). For the truth, because it is what actually happens, does not deviate from its course, even though the end be unpleasant; whereas fiction (*pseûdos*), being a verbal fabrication, very readily follows a roundabout route, and turns aside from the painful to what is more pleasant.

Whatever Plutarch may mean exactly by the 'roundabout route' of fiction, the gist of this passage seems to be that fiction is freer and more malleable than the brute facts of reality. According to Plutarch, the poet has every right to invent, not a lie but another (more satisfying and more pleasurable) version of reality. And this is not done to deceive readers, as long as they, too, are aware of the fabricated status of such stories (*Moralia* 16d–e):

> Whenever, therefore, in the poems of a man of note and repute some strange and disconcerting statement either about gods or lesser deities or about virtue is made by the author, he who accepts the statement as true is carried off his feet, and has his opinions perverted; whereas he who always remembers and keeps clearly in mind the sorcery of the poetic art in dealing with falsehood (*pseûdos*), who is able on every such occasion to say to it: "'Device more subtly cunning than the lynx' [a line from a lost and anonymous tragedy], why knit your brows when jesting, why pretend to instruct when practising deception?" will not suffer any dire effects or even acquire any base beliefs, but he will check himself when he feels afraid of Poseidon and is in terror lest the god rend the earth asunder and lay bare the nether world.

The language of lies and deception is here paradoxically employed to challenge the fictional competence of the reader. Fiction, more dangerous than the "lynx," will be tamed if readers know how to approach its particular playfulness ("when jesting," the Greek verb is *paízein*) and beguilement ("when practising deception," the Greek word is *exapatân*). As Feddern (2018, 505) remarks, in our context both phrases readily lend themselves to associations with modern concepts of fiction: playfulness is often invoked by modern studies as a crucial characteristic of fiction, with Walton's (1993) *make-believe* being one of the most prominent examples. And the idea of feigning assertions 'as if' they were true is at the heart of 'pretense' theories of fiction such as inaugurated by Searle (1975; on which see also 3c, below).

That the idea of 'deception' is here aligned with the fictional competence of the reader also emerges in a closely preceding passage. There, Plutarch maintains that the 'deception' of poetry works only with intelligent addressees in the first place (which is also a nod to the son of Plutarch's addressee, described as a clever boy who will take profit from the present work; *Moralia* 15d):

> For the element of deception (*tò apatēlón*) in it [sc. poetry] does not gain any hold on utterly witless and foolish persons. This is the ground of Simonides' answer to the man who said to him, "Why are the Thessalians the only people whom you do not deceive (*ouk exapatâis*)?" His answer was, "Oh, they are too ignorant to be deceived by me"; and Gorgias called tragedy a deception wherein he who deceives is more honest than he who does not deceive, and he who is deceived is wiser than he who is not deceived (*hó t' apatêsas dikaióteros toû mḕ apatḗsantos kaì ho apatētheìs sophôteros toû mḕ apatēthéntos*).

The famous passage from Gorgias (fifth/fourth century BC), often referred to as an early version of Coleridge's 'willing suspension of disbelief' (e.g. Rösler 2014, 375–378), corroborates Plutarch's basic idea; namely, that a "foolish person," who takes fiction at face value, cannot even begin to enter into the game of make-believe. Once the game has started, as Plutarch points out in *Moralia* 16d–e (quoted above), players have to be careful not to be carried away by the pretense.

Fables

A genre often discussed in ancient theory as displaying *pseûdos*, meaning 'fiction,' is the fable. Our main body of theoretical texts is here constituted by the *progymnasmata*, manuals of prose composition preparing students for a subsequent full-fledged rhetorical education.[5] These manuals typically consist of a series of instructions for certain elementary literary and rhetorical exercises (e.g. how do you go about composing an ekphrasis?). Among the texts' exempla or exercises, the fable is the only literary genre that occurs, probably because it was short and popular in education. Moreover, it always takes the first place in the series of exercises with only one exception (in which the fable comes

[5] Kennedy 2003 presents the extant texts – from the first century AD to late antiquity – in English translation; my quotations follow this translation.

second). Everyone studying rhetoric (at least by imperial times) must have been exposed to the theory of the fable as presented in the progymnasmata. This theory is usually introduced by a standard definition, as, for instance, phrased by our earliest author, Theon (72): "A fable is a fictitious story (*lógos pseudễs*) giving an image of truth," with the "image of truth" pointing either to an allegorical level or to internal plausibility. Now, in the case of the fable it was obvious that its *pseûdos* was not meant to deceive. Any educated person could see that stories about speaking animals and the like were invented and demanded to be read and interpreted differently from factual narratives. This is why some authors of progymnasmata expand the basic definition to say that it was "admittedly," i.e. openly, "made up of falsehoods" (Nicolaus 6; the Greek word for 'falsehood' again being *pseûdos*). Along these lines, Theon (76) says that if one were to refute a fable ('refuting' being a progymnasmatical exercise of its own), it would make no sense to attack its 'lying,' "since even the fablemaker himself acknowledges that what he writes is false and impossible [*pseudê kaì adýnata*]." The attack could only aim at a lack of internal plausibility or the uselessness of the moral lesson. The 'admitted lie' is thus evoked as a generic convention of fiction; the progymnasmata assume a reading in accordance with the fictional pact.

Lucian, *True Stories*

The same idea of the 'admitted lie' is playfully adopted in Lucian's *True Stories* (second century AD). The central paradox of these stories, in which Lucian recounts embarking on a fantastic journey leading as far as the moon, is of course that they are anything but 'true.' As the author explains in his preface, he models his fantastic journey on a series of travelogues by various historians and ethnographers which were passed off as fact though he finds them hard to believe. His satirical literary counter-project is explained as follows (1,4; the Greek word for 'lie,' 'lying' is always *pseûdos* and the verb *pseúdesthai*):

> Therefore, as I myself, thanks to my vanity, was eager to hand something down to posterity, that I might not be the only one excluded from the privileges of poetic licence, and as I had nothing true to tell, not having had any adventures of significance, I took to lying. But my lying is far more honest than theirs, for though I tell the truth in nothing else, I shall at least be truthful in saying that I am a liar. I think I can escape the censure of the world by my own admission that I am not telling a word of truth. Be it understood, then, that I am writing about things which I have neither seen nor had to do with nor learned from others—which, in fact, do not exist at all and, in the nature of things, cannot exist. Therefore my readers should on no account believe in them.

Although Lucian revels in the language of lying, he is clearly inviting readers to enter into what we would now call a fictional contract.

2.2. Latin

Hose (1996) observes that Latin *mendacium* is more closely tied to the idea of deceit than its Greek equivalent *pseûdos*. Based on this observation, he argues that the Romans needed new words for 'fiction' and found a solution by splitting up the concept of *pseûdos* into two technical rhetorical terms: *fabula*, meaning a more or less fantastic invention which is manifestly false; and *argumentum*, meaning a story that, although invented, could actually have really happened. Hose's reasoning raises a multitude of problems which need not be discussed in our context. Here, I would only like to demonstrate that *mendacium* and the related verb *mentiri*, even if they are in general closer to our 'lie' than *pseûdos*, can still mean 'fiction.' Hose, as will be seen, interprets his (meagre) evidence too narrowly. His only substantial example is a passage from Plautus' comedy *Pseudolus* (191 BC), to which we now turn.

Plautus, *Pseudolus*

As with all Roman comedies, the plot of this story is somewhat complicated. Suffice it to say that it is about a plotter, the slave Pseudolus, whose habit of contriving intrigues is even reflected in his very name ('the little liar,' derived from Greek *pseûdos*). For one of his major schemes in the play, Pseudolus badly needs 20 minas, a sum equivalent to 2,000 drachmae. Since he does not have this sum, he plays out his scam with hypothetical money. In our passage, he reflects on this in a soliloquy (401–405):

> You have neither a starting point for beginning your web nor fixed limits for finishing it. Yet just as a poet, when he takes writing tablets, looks for something that doesn't exist anywhere, but finds it nonetheless and makes likely what is a lie [*mendacium*], I shall now become a poet: even though the twenty minas don't exist anywhere, I'll find them nonetheless.

On the face of it, one could argue (with Hose) that if Pseudolus, the liar, compares himself to a poet inventing a 'lie,' the poet must also be a liar, like Pseudolus. But this is only one way of interpreting the passage, which I think fails to acknowledge its playfulness. On the one hand, all that is said about the poet is that he invents: he 'looks for something that doesn't exist' and makes a plausible story out of it. Although this proceeding is called *mendacium*, it does not necessarily follow that deception is implied. In fact, to conclude this from the use of the word *mendacium* would be a *petitio principii*. When Pseudolus compares his own deceitful plotting with the poet's *mendacium*, this could just as well be a case of comic incongruence, in which the distance between the comic character and his would-be model, the poet, is ironically highlighted. On the other hand, Pseudolus' reflection on poetry invites a meta-literary and meta-dramatic reading and thoughts about the status of play in which we see him. Audiences might ask themselves, whether Plautus in some way corresponds to Pseudolus, and whether the drama they are watching (or reading) is in fact a 'lie.' However, whereas the characters in the narrated world may be deceived by Pseudolus, the audience is not. Spectators (and readers) see Pseudolus explicitly explaining and dissecting his 'lie' to them. If Pseudolus stands for Plautus, Plautus is offering them a fictional contract.

Later Poets: Horace and Ovid

Indirect confirmation for the reading of *mendacium* as fiction in Plautus comes from a number of later passages in Roman poetry. These, as I will show, seem to continue Plautus' usage rather than break away from it (as Hose suggests).

Horace's *Ars poetica* (14 BC) is to this day cited as one of the main ancient authorities on poetics. In a passage in praise of Homer's incomparable ability to 'forge' a coherent and plausible story, the verb *mentiri* ('to lie') is used (151–152):

> and so skilfully does he [Homer] invent [*mentitur*], so closely does he blend facts and fiction [*sic veris falsa remiscet*], that the middle is not discordant with the beginning, nor the end with the middle.

The verb may be specifically motivated by elements of fantastic fiction such as the Scylla and Charybdis or the Cyclops episodes, which are referred to in the immediate context. A rudimentary sense of 'lying' would then consist in the invention of elements that are physically impossible and hence 'incredible.' But it is still the notion of contractual fiction that is appealed to. Far from deceitful lying, *mentiri* here emphasizes Homer's imaginative capability, much appreciated by his reader, Horace.

Ovid (43 BC–AD 17) twice refers to *mendacia vatum*, 'the lies of the poets,' implying a sense of disillusion. In one of his love elegies, *Amores* 3.6.17–8, he addresses a river which closes off the way to his beloved, and he wishes he had some fantastic device like Perseus' winged shoes to cross the water: "But the wonders whereof I speak are false tales of olden bards [*mendacia vatum*]; no day e'er brought them forth, and no day will." Similarly, in a passage from his poem on the Roman calendar, *Fasti* 6.253–254, Ovid prays to the goddess Vesta and explains that although he felt her presence he did not see her: "Not indeed that I saw thee, O goddess (far from me be the lies of poets! [*mendacia vatum*])." While these passages, on the face of it, appear to discredit fiction as lies, it is important to keep in mind that they are uttered in moments of disillusion (add in the second case a taboo about seeing gods). Their larger implication is that inventing supernatural phenomena is simply what poets do, as an established practice. It is ironic that few poets exploited this convention to the extent Ovid himself did – one only has to think of all the fantastic stories in the *Metamorphoses*. Therefore, what could be read as an attack on fiction turns out to be a playful invocation of its convention. This convention is openly addressed in *Amores* 3.12.19, where Ovid claims that poets cannot be treated like witnesses in court: "And yet 'tis not the custom to heed the poet's witness." This is one of a number of ancient topoi of 'poetic licence,' for which, in terms of lying, also see Pliny, *Letters* 6.21.6: "Poets are permitted to lie" (*poetis mentiri licet*; my translation). Ovid illustrates his claim with a catalogue of fantastic creatures and events, drawn from poetry.

Finally, in the apology that Ovid directed to Augustus during his exile we have another example of the relatedness of *mendacium* and fiction emerging from Ovid's terminology. In a passage where the poet attempts to distance himself and his moral real-life character from his risqué literary work (the latter being the alleged reason for his banishment), he maintains that "most of my work, unreal (*mendax*) and fictitious (*ficta*), has allowed itself more licence than its author has had" (*Tristia* 2.355–356). The adjective *mendax* ('mendacious'), and the participle *ficta* (from which English 'fiction' derives) are used more or less synonymously here. True, both phrases serve to slight Ovid's work, in the wake of the pressures on the exiled poet and in congruence with his apologetic stance; yet, what he offers to Augustus in this passage is precisely a fictional contract, sadly not accepted by the emperor.

Theoretical Texts from Later Antiquity

In later antiquity, one can find a large number of theoretical prose texts that refer to fiction as *mendacium* and also indicate the terminological proximity between the two concepts in the way already observed in Ovid. Fronto, a leading Roman orator of the second century AD, wrote a *Eulogy of Smoke and Dust* in the manner of earlier Greek 'paradoxical encomia,' the paradox referring to the mock-heroic: seemingly unworthy objects such as flies, a bald head, or precisely smoke and dust are praised. In an accompanying letter, Fronto reflects on the compositional principles of this genre. Among the elements that provide pleasure in such eulogies, he also mentions *mendacia* (3):

> Tales of Gods or men must be brought in where appropriate; so, too, pertinent verses and proverbs that are applicable, and ingenious fictions [*conficta mendacia*], provided that the fiction [*mendacium*] is helped out by some witty reasoning.

The fictional contract by which Fronto's *mendacium* is framed is obvious enough. Note also the phrase *conficta mendacia*, "fictitious lies," by which he combines the terms of fiction and lying, perhaps to tilt the ambivalent *mendacium* in the direction of fiction.

Macrobius, at around 400 AD, is known, among other things, as the author of a commentary on Cicero's *Somnium Scipionis*. The *Somnium* is a dream vision about the cosmos, modeled on the myth of Er at the end of Plato's *Republic*. It follows from its visionary nature that it is an invented story in its own right, and as Macrobius tells us, Plato (and potentially Cicero, too) faced criticism because of their use of fiction, seemingly unbecoming in a philosopher. This provokes Macrobius to provide a defence of fiction in philosophical contexts (1.2.6–11). He first identifies a branch of fiction that only entertains and quickly dismisses it as irrelevant. His real interest lies in fiction that also teaches, a category that he further subdivides into narratives that – to abbreviate with modern vocabulary – a) avowedly invent both subject and plot, such as the genre of the fable; or b) pretend to relate a factual subject, such as the visions, but employ fictional elements in the plot. For our purposes, only the passing remark on the fable matters (1.2.9; my translation): "In some stories both the subject is fictitiously [*ex ficto*] arranged and the sequence of narration itself [referring to plot and perhaps also techniques of fictional discourse such as mindreading] is mendaciously [*per mendacia*] connected, just as Aesop's fables which are well-known because of the elegance of their fiction [*fictio*]." Again, 'fiction' and 'lie' appear to be almost synonyms. Moreover, we can see from this example that Greek *pseûdos*, could be translated with *mendacium* in Latin even when used to describe the fictional nature of fables (see above).

The most rewarding passage, however, seems to me to be one that displays an explicit and contrasting definition of the ideas of 'lie' and 'fiction.' It is contained in Augustine's *Soliloquies* (late fourth century AD), a work in which Augustine undertakes a Cartesian quest for self-certitude. The second book opens with a discussion of falsehood, deception and lies. Augustine (or rather his personified Reason, with whom he converses) here distinguishes between 'deceiving' [*fallere*, *fallax*] and 'lying' [*mentiri*, *mendax*] (2.16; translation by G. Watson):

> 'Lying' is to be found in the case of those who lie [the tautology is in the original: *illud autem, quod mendax voco, a mentientibus fit*]. They [the liars] differ from the deceptive in this, that all deceptive creatures have a desire to deceive, but not everyone who lies wishes to deceive. For mimes and comedies and many poems are full of lies, but they are there from a wish to give pleasure rather than to deceive (and indeed nearly everyone who tells a joke tells a lie). But that man is properly called deceptive or deceiving whose business it is to deceive.

If we exchanged the terms of deceiving in this passage with terms of lying, and the terms of lying with terms of fiction, we would arrive at the basic modern definitions of 'lie' and 'fiction' as deceptive / non-deceptive inventions.

But, perplexingly for us, Augustine chooses to define fiction as a non-deceptive lie.[6]

3. *Accounts*

How can we account for this paradoxical use of lexemes of lying to express a concept of fiction? My answer is threefold. It concerns lexical semantics and natural language polysemy (3.1), similar usage in other languages and epochs (3.2), and the author-centered model of fiction in antiquity (3.3).

3.1. Lexical Semantics and Natural Language Polysemy

An obvious answer is, of course, that Greek *pseûdos* and Latin *mendacium* do not exactly mean 'lie,' just as no word in any language can be *exactly* translated into another language. Although the standard definition of these ancient terms remains 'lie,' they seem to be, at least in certain contexts, more tolerant towards a reading that focuses on telling non-factual things without the intent of deceiving. In my selection of passages above, quite a few translators have felt the need to translate *pseûdos* and *mendacium* as 'fiction.' Moreover, although it is correct that antiquity did not develop a technical term for 'fiction' (e.g. Gill 1993, 51: "there is no attempt to find innovative vocabulary"), it would be wrong to conclude from this that natural language words like *pseûdos* and Latin *mendacium* could not partially make up for this lack of a proper term. Alongside other choices such as *mýthos* or *fabula*, Graeco-Roman vocabulary was perfectly able to cover the basic notion of our 'fiction.'

The larger question, to be asked in the fields of the philosophy of language and cognition, is to what extent language determines our thinking and our ability to form concepts. Many scholars (e.g. Gill 1993; Hose 1996) seem tacitly to adopt a version of the Sapir-Whorf-hypothesis according to which language radically determines cognition. Along these lines, the lack of a proper word for 'fiction' in Greek and Latin would be sufficient proof of a lack of a concept of fiction. But my passages above should have provided ample evidence to the contrary. In any case, strong deterministic approaches have meanwhile been largely discredited in the philosophy of language and cognition (Margolis/Laurence 2019, 4.3 'Linguistic determinism and linguistic relativity').

---

6 Some readers may remember Augustine for different terms and concepts of lying, as laid out in his later works *De mendacio* and *Contra mendacium*. This is simply due to the evolving nature of his thought about the subject. For a succinct and recent survey see e.g. Hermanowicz 2018 (on *Soliloquies* 710–711).

3.2. Similar Usage in Other Languages and Epochs

My second consideration points to the fact that Greek and Latin are not freak outliers in an otherwise clear-cut restriction of terms of the meaning of terms of lying to deceiving and deception. Take the example of French *mensonge* (sharing the same root as Latin *mendacium*) in older French. In his historical dictionary of the French language, Rey writes that, "continuing the ancient confusion between 'lie' and 'imagination,' it [*mensonge*] had been applied to fiction in art" (2010, s.v. *mensonge*), a usage dated to the High Middle Ages (*c.*1120). The grande dame of the French seventeenth-century novel, Madeleine de Scudéry, famously accounted for her writing as the 'art of the lie' ("l'art du mensonge"; Penzkofer 1998, title). By using this phrase, she did, of course, not describe her novels as literal lies but as fictions that do not have any intention to deceiving and display a neutralized truth-value. Her choice of words in defending fiction was also motivated by her taking the offensive against critics who actually maintained that fiction was lying. Keeping this in mind, one could analyze Scudéry's use of *mensonge* virtually as if it had been put in quotation marks: she does not speak about the 'art of the lie' (meaning 'lie') but about the 'art of the "lie"' (meaning 'fiction'). Her 'lie' is to be interpreted differently from the traditional concept of the lie. A similar signification of a 'lie' in quotation marks may also be assumed to apply for a number of ancient passages. One might think, for example, of Horace saying that 'Homer "lies"' rather than 'Homer lies' and the whole phrase immediately loses much of its perplexity.

Although the English lexeme *lie* and related Germanic words seem in general more resistant to notions of 'fiction,' the *Oxford English Dictionary* (Draft Addition 1997, s.v. *lie, n.1*; compare s.v. *lie, v.2*) lists an interesting case in point which concerns contemporary African-American English: "In weakened or non-pejorative sense: an anecdote, tale, 'tall story'. *lie and story* n. gossip. Originally and chiefly Black English." Observing this usage, the historian of Blues music, Paul Oliver, writes in 1960: "When there is nothing else to do he joins his fellows to tell 'lies,'" not to deceive anyone but to entertain them with at least partially fictional stories. Compare explicitly on this point Daniel J. Crowely, who reports in a book about Bahamian folklore of 1966: "The narrators themselves refer to a tale as 'a wonderful lie', but they mean to indicate a work of the imagination rather than an untruth."[7]

Finally, one may also point out a certain penchant in modern scholarship for the oxymoronic phrase 'true lies' when describing 'fiction,' particularly when stressing aspects of its 'realness' (which may be no more than an abstract sense of 'relevance'). The titles of Amago's 2006 book *True Lies: Narrative Self-Con-*

[7] All my examples here can be found under the *OLD* entry.

sciousness in the Contemporary Spanish Novel, Cullhed/Rydholm's 2014 edited volume *True Lies Worldwide: Fictionality in Global Contexts*), and Velle's article *Telling True Lies: Metanarration, Intertextuality and (Un)Reliability in Holberg's* Iter Subterraneum (2016) provide three obvious examples.

3.3. The Author-centered Model of Fiction in Antiquity

Today, we are used to practices of fiction in which real-life authors are marginalized in favor of textual, fictitious narrators. We mostly read privately, silently, and without an image of an author in our heads. We tend to accept that the narrative voice speaking to us belongs to the text rather than the outside world. As far as the theory of fiction is concerned, the 'narratological' separation of author and narrator is often seen as the essential, defining characteristic of fiction (e.g. Zipfel 2001, 115–122). Narratologists have asked themselves how it is logically (or perhaps we should say: ontologically) possible for an author to report a story that has not actually happened, how s/he can claim things that are not in fact true. The word *lie* is not necessarily used in these contexts of (onto)logical reference, but it is easy to see how the question could be simplified to: 'How can an author tell non-facts without lying?' The standard answer is that the author does not really claim to report the story himself but puts it in the mouth of an invented narrator. The fictitious narrator, then, is the origin of all fiction. Being a witness to the narrated events, i.e. existing on the same ontological[8] level as the story, the narrator can report it without any suspicion of lying. The narrator may still choose to lie to her/his narratees about particular elements of the story, but that is different from the fundamental, formal, 'ontological lie' of the real-world author telling of things that do not in fact exist.

Antiquity did not know narrators. Both literary practices (oral, performative, face-to-face settings and concepts) and literary theory (mainly poetics and rhetoric) were centered on the author (e.g. Tilg 2019). Famously, for instance, Plato argues in the *Republic* (3.392c–398b) that all literary utterances can be ascribed to either the author or his characters – with the latter being impersonated by the author. Under these conditions, a 'narratological' sidestepping of the 'ontological lie' as described above was not an option. Any element of fiction would have been traced back to the author. Leaving out of account the special and comparatively rare cases in which it was truly believed that an author was just the medium of some higher inspiration (e.g. by the Muses),

[8] The *ontological* level must not be equated with the diegetic level (Genette's *niveau narratif*) or the narrator's relationship to the story (Genette's *personne*). Even an extradiegetic-heterodiegetic narrator is part of the (fictional) ontological continuum uniting storyworld and narrator.

it was his voice that was heard throughout a given work, and it was he who ultimately had to take responsibility for any form of non-factual statement. My contention, and hence my third answer, is that even when it was clear that the non-factual statement was non-deceptive fiction, the vocabulary of lying suggested itself to mark the ontological gap between a factual author and his non-factual (or in the case of fantastic fiction even impossible) inventions in the work. In other words, a working fictional pact could still be referred to as a 'lie' when focusing on the authorial act of inventing.

Take, for comparison, the case of a modern theory of fictional communication that does not operate with a narrator model but attributes all utterances to the author: Searle (1975; and with him later 'pretense' theories of fiction) argues that authors of fictional works do not make 'real,' 'sincere,' 'serious' assertions but 'pretend' to produce them 'as if' they were real, sincere, and serious. Readers, however, do not have difficulty in decoding these pretenses as fiction because larger conventions of a fictional pact are invoked (325–326). Note the vocabulary used by Searle, which is in need of explanation just as was the ancient vocabulary of lying – most thesauri of the English language will in fact list *lying* as a synonym of *pretense*. Immediately after introducing the verb *pretend*, Searle hastens to distinguish between a 'good,' fictional form and a 'bad,' deceptive manifestation of pretense (324–325). In a similar manner, I think, we should be ready to distinguish between the 'good' and the 'bad' lying in the literature of antiquity and accept the concept of fiction inherent in the 'good lying'.

As an afterthought and as a perspective for further research one could also ask how my three answers ((a) polysemy; (b) cross-cultural similarity; (c) author-centered narration), and in particular b) and c), are related to one another. It strikes me that antiquity, the medieval and early modern periods, and contemporary, typically oral black storytelling all foreground authors (speakers) rather than narrators (and this is at least partially also true for the modern titles using the phrase 'true lies'). Perhaps c), then, is the decisive factor throughout history and cultures. The semantics of respective terms of lying would in this case just be a function of our larger approaches to fiction.

Works Cited

Alain, Rey (2010) *Dictionnaire Historique de la Langue Française*. Paris: Le Robert.

Amago, Samuel (2006) *True Lies: Narrative Self-Consciousness in the Contemporary Spanish Novel*. Lewisburg: Bucknell Univ. Press.

Augustine (1990) *Soliloquies and Immortality of the Soul*. Trans. G. Watson. Warminster: Aris & Philips.

Cullhed, Anders, and Lena Rydholm (2014) Ed. *True Lies Worldwide: Fictionality in Global Contexts*. Berlin: De Gruyter.

Feddern, Stefan (2018) *Der antike Fiktionalitätsdiskurs*. Berlin: De Gruyter.

Fronto (1919) *Correspondence*. Trans. C. R. Haines. Loeb Classical Library, 112. Cambridge, MA: Harvard Univ. Press.

Gill, Christopher (1993) "Plato on Falsehood – not Fiction." *Lies and Fiction in the Ancient World*. Ed. Christopher Gill and Peter Wiseman. Exeter: Univ. of Exeter Press. 38–87.

Hermanowicz, Erika T. (2018) "Augustine on Lying." *Speculum* 93: 699–727.

Hesiod (2006) *Theogony, Works and Days, Testimonia*. Trans. Glenn W. Most. Loeb Classical Library, 57. Cambridge, MA: Harvard Univ. Press.

Homer (1995) *Odyssey, Books 13–24*. Trans. A. T. Murray and George E. Dimock. Loeb Classical Library, 104. Cambridge, MA: Cambridge Univ. Press.

Horace (1926) *Satires, Epistles, and Ars Poetica*. Trans. H. Rushton Fairclough. Loeb Classical Library, 194. Cambridge, MA: Harvard Univ. Press.

Hose, Martin (1996) "Fiktionalität und Lüge: Über einen Unterschied zwischen römischer und griechischer Terminologie." *Poetica* 28: 257–274.

Kennedy, George (2003) Trans. *Progymnasmata: Greek Textbooks of Prose Compositions and Rhetoric*. Leiden: Brill.

Lucian (1913) *Phalaris. Hippias or The Bath. Dionysus. Heracles. Amber or The Swans. The Fly. Nigrinus. Demonax. The Hall. My Native Land. Octogenarians. A True Story. Slander. The Consonants at Law. The Carousal (Symposium) or The Lapiths*. Trans. A. M. Harmon. Loeb Classical Library, 14. Cambridge, MA: Cambridge Univ. Press.

Maier, Emar (2019) "Lying and Fiction." *The Oxford Handbook of Lying*. Ed. Jörg Meibauer. Oxford: Oxford Univ. Press. 303–314.

Margolis, Eric, and Stephen Laurence (2019) "Concepts." *The Stanford Encyclopedia of Philosophy (Summer 2019 Edition)*. Ed. Edward N. Zalta Web. 1 Dec. 2020. <https://plato.stanford.edu/archives/sum2019/entries/ concepts/>.

Mecke, Jochen (2015) "Du musst dran glauben: Von der Literatur der Lüge zur Lüge der Literatur." *Diegesis* 4: 18–48.

Meibauer, Jörg (2015) "Konzepte des Lügens." *Zeitschrift für Sprachwissenschaft* 34: 175–212.

Meibauer, Jörg (2019) Ed. *The Oxford Handbook of Lying*. Oxford: Oxford Univ. Press.

Mesturini, Anna Maria (2018) *Ψεῦδος [Pseûdos]: I 'colori' della finzione*. Genoa: Erredi Grafiche Editoriali.

Ovid (1977) *Heroides, Amores*. Trans. Grant Showerman and G. P. Goold. Loeb Classical Library, 41. Cambridge, MA: Harvard Univ. Press.

Ovid (1988) *Tristia, Ex Ponto*. Trans. Arthur Leslie Wheeler and G. P. Goold. Loeb Classical Library, 151. Cambridge, MA: Harvard Univ. Press.

Ovid (1989) *Fasti*. Trans. James George Frazer and G. P. Goold. Loeb Classical Library, 253. Cambridge, MA: Harvard Univ. Press.

Penzkofer, Gerhard (1998) *'L'art du mensonge': Erzählen als barocke Lügenkunst in den Romanen von Mademoiselle de Scudéry*. Tubingen: Narr.

Plautus (2012) *The Little Carthaginian, Pseudolus, The Rope*. Trans. Wolfgang de Melo. Loeb Classical Library, 260. Cambridge, MA: Harvard Univ. Press.

Plutarch (1927) *Moralia*. Trans. Frank Cole Babbitt, vol. 1. Loeb Classical Library, 424. Cambridge, MA: Cambridge Univ. Press.

Rösler, Wolfgang (1980) "Die Entdeckung der Fiktionalität in der Antike." *Poetica* 12: 283–319.

Rösler, Wolfgang (2014) "Fiktionalität in der Antike." *Fiktionalität: Ein interdisziplinäres Handbuch*. Ed. Tobias Klauk and Tilmann Köppe. Berlin: De Gruyter. 363–384.

Searle, John R. (1975) "The Logical Status of Fictional Discourse." *New Literary History* 6.2 (*On Narrative and Narratives*): 319–332.

Stroh, Wilfried (1976). "Hesiods lügende Musen." *Studien zum antiken Epos*. Ed. Herwig Görgemanns and Ernst August Schmidt. Meisenheim on the Glan: Hain. 85–112.

Tilg, Stefan (2019). "Autor und Erzähler – Antike." *Handbuch Historische Narratologie*. Ed. Eva von Contzen and Stefan Tilg. Stuttgart: Metzler. 69–81.

Velle, Thomas (2016). "Telling True Lies: Metanarration, Intertextuality and (Un)Reliability in Holberg's *Iter Subterraneum*." *European Journal of Scandinavian Studies* 46: 215–233.

Walton, Kendall L. (1993) *Mimesis as Make-Believe: On the Foundations of the Representational Arts*. Cambridge, MA: Harvard Univ. Press.

Zipfel, Frank (2001) *Fiktion, Fiktivität, Fiktionalität: Analysen zur Fiktion in der Literatur und zum Fiktionsbegriff in der Literaturwissenschaft*. Berlin: Schmid.

'Feigning Properly': Fiction, Lying, and Moral Philosophy in the Writings of William Baldwin

Ingo Berensmeyer

This paper is going to take a fresh look at the extant writings of William Baldwin (died in or before 1563), especially his tale *Beware the Cat* (1552, printed 1570), in the context of Protestant debates about the legitimacy and acceptability of fiction in early modern England. While previous readings of Baldwin have highlighted religious aspects or innovative modes of narration in his texts, this paper relates Baldwin's work to early modern debates about casuistry and conscience and the usefulness, or otherwise, of imaginative literature. How does Baldwin (who also wrote a popular *Treatise of Moral Philosophy* as well as major parts of *A Mirror for Magistrates*) engage with debates about equivocation and lying, and which literary forms and traditions does he employ in order to present human interiority, moral deliberation, and social conformity or deviance? The paper will attempt to reevaluate Baldwin's writings as part of a larger reassessment of the relationship between concepts and practices of lying and fiction-making in English literature.

> Lying is a sycknes of the soule, which can not be cured, but by shame or reason.
> William Baldwin, *A Treatise of Morall Phylosophie* 1547 (sig. O1^{v})

1. *Introduction*

Fiction is a dangerous beast, and fiction-making an activity fraught with peril, both for its makers and its readers – especially so in the early modern period, as different views of the world, different "ways of worldmaking" (Goodman 1978) vie with each other for supremacy in the epistemological and moral twilight zone between dominant, residual, and emergent forms of thought and norms of behavior. Here, fiction can on the one hand be praised to the skies, as Sir Philip Sidney famously does in his *Apology* or *Defence of Poetry*, as a delightful game and a morally useful pursuit, "lightgiver to ignorance" (1973, 74). On the other hand, "all that fained is, as leasings, tales, and lies" (Spenser 2013, 2.9.51) can be condemned as a useless addition to the real world – or, worse, a pernicious distortion of truth, not much better or perhaps even worse than outright lying. In any case, fiction is usually framed in moral terms and said to require a certain amount of intelligence to tell it apart from other ways of being economical with the truth, like equivocation or other mendacious verbal behavior such as mental reservation, much discussed by early modern Catholic casuists as well as Protestant reformers.[1]

Similar to today's fears of 'fake news,' 'alternative facts' or 'post-truth' (cf. Davis 2017), fueled by social media, the early age of print brought about what Adrian Johns (1998, 423) called a "culture of discredit surrounding printed books." This phrase can be taken both in the sense that an abundance of print made it harder to sift the wheat from the chaff or to tell reliable from unreliable information, and in the sense that excessive users of this new medium – print readers – would experience negative effects on their physical and mental health (380–382).[2] In England, the rapid social and cultural transformations of the Reformation added to the anxiety of the elites in connection with printed texts. Could fictions be combined with print in such a way as to ensure that they would be used for a moral purpose, not to mislead individuals or to spread further confusion among communities of believers torn between conformity and damnation? In this respect, the writings of William Baldwin – most notably *Beware the Cat* – provide a good case study. They constantly probe the limits of truth, lies, and fiction, and thus explore the possibilities and constraints of the literary imagination in early modern print culture. While readings of Baldwin tend to highlight religious aspects or innovative modes of narration, this paper relates him to early modern debates about the legitimacy of fiction. How does Baldwin engage with debates about equivocation and lying, and which literary forms and traditions does he employ in order to present human interiority, moral deliberation, and social conformity or deviance?

2. *William Baldwin and English Reformation Print Culture*

As an important representative of evangelical reform at the court of Edward VI, Baldwin is a crucial figure of mid-sixteenth century English literature. He is best known as the author of a *Treatise of Moral Philosophy* (1547); as a major contributor to, and compiler of, the *Mirror for Magistrates* (1559, 1563); and as the author of *Beware the Cat* (written 1553, printed 1570), a decidedly odd text that combines experimental narrative features with anti-Catholic propaganda and satire. Among his claims to fame is the fact that he wrote the first

[1] As the Canon of Toledo explains in Cervantes' *Don Quijote* (book 1, chapter 47), "lying fictions must be wedded to the intelligence of those who read them" ("Hanse de casar las fábulas mentirosas con el entendimiento de los que las leyeren") (Cervantes 1987, 1: 906–907). The theological discussion about lying in the early modern period is summed up in Sommerville 1988, 159–184. For a more detailed historical account, see Denery (2015). For a theoretical perspective on early modern ways of worldmaking, see Mahler (2019).

[2] On anxieties in connection with the spread of printed texts, see McKitterick (2003).

English sonnet ever to be printed.[3] Starting out in London as a corrector in the printing-house of Edward Whitchurch in 1547, William Baldwin apparently had a talent for finding saleable products in the emerging print market. His *Treatise of Morall Phylosophie* (1547), a collection of "sayinges of the wyse" (title page) frequently reprinted until the mid-seventeenth century, is geared towards a popular audience keen on self-education, combining classical learning with Christian moral teaching. His verse translation of the Song of Songs, *The Canticles or Balades of Salomon* (1549), is a highly original and unusual reinterpretation that presents the Song of Songs not as an erotic text but "as a young person's guide to evangelical Christianity" (Pincombe 2010, 9) tailored to suit the eleven-year-old Edward VI as its dedicatee (Flinker 2000, 31–65).

These Protestant humanist pursuits are augmented by a polemic pamphlet, *Wonderfull newes of the death of Paule the .iii.* (probably 1552), Baldwin's translation from a Latin text, authorship of which has been attributed either to the Lutheran reformer Matthias Flacius or the Italian anti-papalist Pier Paolo Vergerio.[4] The satire *Beware the Cat* followed in 1553 but could not be printed after the death of Edward VI. It was during the Marian regime that Baldwin redacted the collaborative poetic project of *A Mirror for Magistrates,* an influential collection of *de casibus* tragedies in the tradition of Boccaccio and Lydgate.[5] After a first edition of 1554 was apparently suppressed, the book was printed soon after the accession of Elizabeth in 1559. Seven more editions followed until 1610. Baldwin's funeral elegy on Edward VI was printed in 1560, and it is now deemed likely that *Beware the Cat* was also first printed in a no longer extant edition in 1561 (Ko 2009, 33–34). A few more works of contested authorship have been attributed to Baldwin, including the narrative prose text *The Image of Idlenesse* (1556), a very early epistolary narrative that – if it could be more firmly attributed to him – would serve to demonstrate his literary versatility even more (Flachmann 1990). He gave up his career in literature for one in the church, but probably died of the plague in 1563 (King 2004).

3. *Truth's Handmaiden: Baldwin's Defense of Fiction*

It is not known why Baldwin gave up writing and publishing, but it was probably not because of religious scruples about the acceptability of fiction. Frowned upon by many as mere 'toys' – idle or even sinful pursuits –, imaginative writing or 'poetry' (in Sidney's more encompassing sense of the word) was con-

[3] The dedicatory poem to Christopher Langton's *Treatise of Phisick* (London, 1547). The sonnet follows the structure devised by the Earl of Surrey, whom Baldwin admired; see Lucas (2016, 25).

[4] See Overell & Lucas (2010, 180–196), who make a case for Vergerio.

[5] According to King 1982, 360, *The Mirror for Magistrates* is "the major conduit that channeled medieval notions of *de casibus* tragedy into the Elizabethan age."

troversial among Protestant intellectuals. Baldwin's increasing acceptance and enjoyment of fiction – Pincombe refers to his "relaxed and interested attitude towards fiction-making" (2010, 16) – begins already with his early invocation of Saint Augustine, in the *Treatise of Morall Phylosophie,* who famously defended Plato and other Greek philosophers as beneficial for Christian readers, who should be allowed to make better use of ancient wisdom than the ancients themselves:

> So in the doctrine of the Gentyles are not only contayned supersticious and fayned rites [...] but also much good learnyng, mete for to serue the truthe, wyth some moste profytable preceptes of good maners, wherein are founde some truthe, howe to worshyp the eternal and onely God. etc. (Baldwin 1547, sig. $A_1 5^{r-v}$)

Of course, philosophy is not the same as literary fiction, but it stands in a similarly contested position to the word of God as revealed in the scriptures. Here, Baldwin justifies this 'other' of scriptural knowledge as "an handmayden to perswade suche thynges as Scripture doeth commaunde" (1547, sig. $A_1 5^v$). Moral reasoning, inherited from the classics, serves as an additional persuader for the faithful to obey God's laws – which themselves were only gradually and with some difficulty becoming available to be read by lay communities in the vernacular in the form of print.

The didactic impulse of Baldwin's text is clearly part of a missionary 'print evangelism' in the early years of the Protestant boy-king Edward VI. One of the kinds of teaching, Baldwin explains in the *Treatise,* is "by Parables, Examples and Semblables. Wherin by esye and familier truthes, harder thinges and more out of vse are declared, that by the one the other maye be better perceyued and borne in mynd." He invokes Christ as an example of this kind of teaching, but also Aesop: "alludyng and bryngyng vnreasonable thinges, to teache and instructe men, in graue and wayghtye matters" (1547, sig. $A_2 6^r$). Here, Baldwin indeed appears to anticipate the groundline of Sidney's more famous later defense of "things not affirmatively but allegorically and figuratively written [...], us[ing] the narration but as an imaginative ground-plot of a profitable invention" (Sidney 1973, 103). Almost forty years before Sidney, Baldwin opens up a door for fiction in allowing the "vnreasonable" to serve reason itself.[6] Returning to the topic at the outset of book 3, "Of prouerbes and adages," he explains that philosophers of all ages have tried to "entice" people to "delyte" in wisdom through a variety of literary forms: "they deuysed to set out wyse-

6 On the debate about fiction in the early modern period, see Nelson (1973). The debate is neatly summed up by King (1982, 365): "During the Renaissance, license to invent fictions is associated with dialog, comic drama, Lucianic satire, allegory, and beast fable. It was the early Christian identification of truth with canonical scriptures and fiction with lying fables that led to the disguising of apocryphal tales and pseudepigraphous works as documented Christian 'history' rather than freely invented fiction. It might be argued that so long as one relates spiritual 'truth,' no fiction can lie."

dom in sondry kyndes of wrytyng, that euery man myght fynde wherin to delyte, and so to be caught in his owne pleasure" (1547, sig. M7[r]). Anticipating Sidney's (and other Elizabethan writers') key argument for the usefulness of fiction, he argues that plain precepts "lacke [...] the grace of delyte" that is offered by sententiae and other narrative or poetic forms (1547, sig. M7[r]). In his justification of translating philosophers' adages into English verse, he advocates "wytty" and "pleasant" writing that is more easily "retayne[d] [...] in memory" (1547, sig. M7[v]–M8[r]) than dry precepts.

Such literary ornamentation may be acceptable, as in Baldwin's verse translation of the Song of Songs, intended to make its allegorical teachings more memorable. But what about purely fictional stories that have no basis in classical tradition, nor in history, nor in any other verifiable facts? And what about the permissibility, or otherwise, of spreading lies in a good cause? According to one of the precepts – attributed to Socrates – that are collected in his treatise, "He ought not to lye that taketh vppon hym to teach other" (1547, sig. O1[v]). But the problem arises precisely in his translation of *Wonderfull newes*, a polemic that mixes verifiable truths about the life of Pope Paul III (1486–1549) with scurrilous slanders about his sex life. Carrying the word 'wonderful' on the title page, an early modern indicator of fictionality, the text offers an intriguing blend of fact, fiction, and lies. Michael Pincombe has analyzed how this text combines the "evangelical" with the "sensational," advertising with the word 'wonderful' "the pleasure it affords its readers as a piece of rather outrageous fiction" (2010, 7). In his classic study of *English Reformation Literature*, John King already pointed out that the "grotesque sexual images" that illustrate the "false wisdom and spiritual fornication of the Roman church" in *Wonderfull newes* are the flip side of the erotic imagery that Baldwin uses in his translation of the Song of Songs as "a dark metaphor for divine wisdom and love as it is embodied in the true, reformed church" (1982, 372). In both cases, then, we have fictions not as lies, not as the opposite of truth but as its allegorical index – we have a story that enables the recognition of (a) truth, like the parables Baldwin includes in his *Treatise of Morall Phylosophie.* "All this," Baldwin writes of the author of *Wonderfull newes*, "he fayneth properly, but lyeth not I am afrayed" (1552, sig. A2[r]).

With this brief remark, we enter the widespread and varied early modern discussion, among Catholic casuists and Protestant reformers, of lying, equivocation, mental reservation, and "the limits of permissible ambiguity" (Sommerville 1988, 170). When Baldwin says he is "afrayed" of his author telling the naked truth, this may seem like a signal of irony or prurience, especially to modern ears. But it probably needs to be seen, above all, as a defensive move. In the mid-sixteenth century, the discussion of the permissibility of lying was still confined to academic circles, "buried in indigestible Latin tomes" (Sommerville 1988, 177) by obscure theologians. But it was revived in the light of popular –

and populist – outrage around the turn of the seventeenth century after the trials of the Jesuits Robert Southwell (1595) and Henry Garnet (1606). Baldwin's writings of the early 1550s at least indirectly promote the use of falsehoods for the good cause of a Protestant regime. I do not think his assertion that his author "lyeth not" carries a sort of mental reservation, as supplied a few decades later by Sidney (because "he nothing affirms");[7] on the contrary, I surmise it to be more likely an assertion of belief in the author's truthfulness, necessary in a climate in which Augustine's prohibition of lying still held sway. According to Augustine, lying was always wrong, no matter the cause, and absolutely forbidden by God.[8] "When we forsake the truth, we forsake God," as the English Reformer Hugh Latimer preached in 1552, encouraging parents to administer physical punishment to their children for 'making a lie' (Latimer 1844, 501, 503; cf. Sommerville 1988, 182).[9]

The vivid depiction of the Pope's reception into hell, and the enumeration of his sins and crimes, as outlined in *Wonderfull newes*, are not to be regarded as outright lies, then, even if they contain 'wonderful' or incredible propositions that are probably false and that neither the text's author nor its translator take to be statements of actual literal fact. They are – as we would probably say today – 'alternative facts,' or rather depictions of a higher (or more useful) truth that 'lies' (in both senses of the word) beyond mere factual correctness. They are 'facts' that have been dressed to impress. The author "fayneth properly" (Baldwin 1552, sig. A2^{r}) but he does not lie. Such 'properly feigned' narratives are intended to make the truth – paradoxically – more credible through rhetorical techniques of embellishment and colorful *descriptio.*[10] Like Christ's parables or Aesop's fables, these illustrative stories aim to persuade readers, to lead them to an affective realization of (spiritual) truth by means of fiction. This truth is conceived not as the opposite of falsehood in general, but as the opposite of a false system of beliefs about the world, such as is supposedly delivered in the teachings of the Roman church:

> And to thentent that all Englishe men myghte thanke God the more for his aboundant mercy, in deliuering them through knowlege of his truth from the tiranny of so

---

7 Sidney (1973, 102): "The poet is the least liar, and, though he would, as a poet can scarcely be a liar. [...] Now, for the poet, he nothing affirms, and therefore never lieth. [...] The poet never maketh any circles around your imagination, to conjure you to believe for true what he writes."

8 Examples are provided in Sommerville (1988, 182–183): Roger Hutchinson, Hugh Latimer, William Perkins, Richard Baxter.

9 See Sommerville (1988, 183) for more relaxed attitudes to lying in some Lutherans, such as Friedrich Balduin and William Tyndale (and Luther himself), who aver that some deceptions can be charitable and that, while lying is always wrong, a deception is not a lie unless intended to harm one's neighbor.

10 See Pincombe (2010, 17) on the rhetorical techniques of *descriptio* and *evidentia* as forms of "vividly detailed description" that produce "a credible picture of the scene," based on Quintilian's *Institutio oratoria* 4.2.122–124.

> corrupt and stinking an heade [i.e. the Pope], and the better loue and obeye our souer-aygne lord and kyng, theyr head by God appoynted, I haue (good Reader) according to my poore cunnyng, Englished Esquillus Epistle, that al they maye see therein the Popes moste detestable, mischeuous, and deuillishe doctrine, lyfe and dedes : that suche as yet for lacke of knowlege fauour hym, maye throughe credyting this, detest and abhore hym, or at lestewyse his vices, whiche are vnseparably ioyned vnto the Popedome. (Baldwin 1552, sig. $A2^v$–$A3^r$)[11]

As in his *Treatise*, fiction for Baldwin is the 'handmaiden' of truth:

> It is wonderfull (good Reader) to see the sundry diuersities of wittes what meanes they inuente to declare and publishe suche thynges as they thinke necessary to be knowen, some vnder the colour of fayned histories, some vnder the persons of specheles beastes, and some vnder the shadow of dreames and visions, of which thou haste here a notable and wurthy example. (Baldwin 1552, sig. $A1^v$)

This programmatic statement points forward both to *The Mirror for Magistrates*, which makes good use of the device of the dream vision, as well as the rhetorical 'feigning' and narrative embellishment of historical facts. It also anticipates the central conceit of *Beware the Cat*, which is in large part a story told "vnder the persons of specheles beastes."[12]

Fiction, for Baldwin, is defensible when it serves the purposes of learning and the promulgation of truth. Pagan philosophy, even though crucially misguided in a Protestant perspective, may still contain at least "some truthe" (Baldwin 1547, sig. A_1 5^{r-v}). In the form of parables and fables, even the "vnreasonable" (sig. A_2 6^r) may serve reason because illustrative stories are more memorable than dry theoretical precepts. In this, Baldwin anticipates Sidney and other defenders of imaginative writing in the sixteenth century. We have also seen that he endorses outright lying for the sake of a higher truth, though without fully acknowledging this endorsement (and in fact covering it up as a form of 'proper' feigning or fiction-making). In a good cause, not only ambiguity but factual errors and feigned exaggerations may be permitted to persuade the public of the rightness of particular beliefs and the falseness of others.

4. *Dream Visions:* The Mirror for Magistrates

The Mirror for Magistrates is a collection of *de casibus* tragedies in continuation of Lydgate's *Fall of Princes*, with an exclusive focus on English history from Richard II to Edward IV. It is notable in this connection for its multiple authorship, with Baldwin as the central organizing writer and compiler, and for the obviously fictional story, included in the book, of how this group of

11 'Esquillus' is the alleged author of the pamphlet that Baldwin translates as *Wonderfull newes*. On its actual author, see fn. 4 above.

12 On the *Mirror for Magistrates*, see Hadfield (1994, 81–107); Lucas (2009); Archer & Hadfield (2016).

seven additional "learned men" set about composing nineteen verse tragedies and reciting them to Baldwin in a single day. Baldwin as listener and reporter takes the place of 'Bochas' (Boccaccio, the author of Lydgate's model, *De casibus virorum illustrium*), to whom the ghosts of dead princes address their complaints in Lydgate's book; the other writers "tooke vpon themselues euery man for his parte to be sundrye personages, and in theyr behalfes to bewayle vnto me theyr greuous chaunces, heuy destinies, and wofull misfortunes" (Baldwin 1559, sig. A1^{v}). The sheer scale of the project makes this scenario not merely unlikely but impossible – "a charming but impudent fiction of authorship" (Pincombe 2011, 185). According to Pincombe, Baldwin's role in this endeavor was distinct from that of his collaborators. He was the printer or printer's amanuensis, ordered by his employer to manage this project. His lower social status, compared to his fellow poets, set him apart as well. Overall, the prose links between the tragedies tend to downplay questions of historical accuracy, careful not to offend the nobility "by getting the facts wrong about their ancestors," and instead emphasize the moral didacticism of the tragedies (Pincombe 2011, 195).[13]

The second preface and the prose links create an elaborate and lively fiction of the process of composition, making the reader privy to acts of literary creation that usually remain hidden in early modern print culture.[14] But they also display some amount of rhetorical playfulness (cf. Richards 2016, 73). While the poems are often rather dull, the prose interludes make for some entertaining reading, as when Baldwin falls asleep during the poets' discussions and has a dream vision of the murdered Richard, duke of York:

> Whyle he was deuising thereon, and every man seking farder notes, I looked on the Cronicles, and fynding styl fyelde vpon fyelde, and manye noble men slayne, I purposed to haue ouerpassed all, for I was so wearye that I waxed drowsye, and began in dede to slumber: but my imaginacion styll prosecutyng this ragicall [sic] matter, brought me suche a fantasy. me thought there stode before vs, a tall mans body full of fresshe woundes, but lackyng a head, holdyng by the hande a goodlye childe, whose brest was so wounded that his hearte myght be seen, his louely face and eyes disfigured with dropping teares, his heare through horrour standyng vpryght, his mercy cravyng handes all to bemangled, and all his body embuied with his own bloud. And whan through the gastfulnes of this pyteous spectacle, I waxed afeard, and turned awaye my face, me thought there came a shrekyng voyce out of the weasande pipe of the headles bodye, saying as foloweth. (Baldwin 1559, fol. xlviii^{r-v})

13 In this reading, the lack of a "*grand récit* of providential history" in the *Mirror* is deliberate (197); Baldwin's employer, the evangelical printer Edward Whitchurch, went into exile in 1553, and his print shop was taken over by John Wayland, a Roman Catholic (191). This and the Marian regime change provide a plausible explanation for the text's carefulness in political and religious matters.

14 This also links the *Mirror for Magistrates* to *Beware the Cat*, which pretends that the text it presents is actually not quite ready for print publication. Both also share their conversational setting with the Platonic dialog. See Stenner (2015, 339).

This vivid passage is introduced by a manicule, a typographical index, for emphasis. Not only this episode, but the entire *Mirror* is, as Jennifer Richards explains, an example of the rhetorical trope of 'eidolopoeia,' "when a dedde manne talketh" (Richards 2016, 82, citing Rainolde 1563, sig. N1^{v}). Dead men are not wont to tell tales, but here they obviously do – "vnder the shadow of dreames and visions" – even, in one case, a "headles duke speak[ing] thorow his necke" (Baldwin 1559, fol. lxii^{r}). This is yet another literary fiction employed by Baldwin to elicit an affective response in the reader. The question raised by Richards (2016, 84) whether this actually supports or subverts the moral purpose of this collection of cautionary tales remains relevant: for instance, the confession of crimes from the mouth of Richard II is also likely to elicit sympathy for him.[15] Furthermore, though Richard II is a historical figure, he appears here in a self-consciously fictional, imagined speech situation. Whereas in the medieval tradition of the ghost complaint, the ghosts are considered to be real, not fictional (see Geller 1999, 158–159), here, even in the dream vision that Baldwin claims to have, the ghosts are not real apparitions but "a fantasy" (1559, fol. xlviii^{r}). They are imagined to speak in an 'as if' scenario, their 'ghosts' channeled by the literary imagination of Baldwin and his collaborators. In modern terms, they use the "rigid designators" of historical proper names (Kripke 1980, 48–49) to attach remarkable stories and moral messages to them. Here, again, we see Baldwin at work using fictional invention for a morally beneficial purpose.

5. *The Cultural Work of 'Fixion' in the Mid-Sixteenth Century: The Case of* Beware the Cat

We have seen Baldwin justify imaginative writing giving a voice to dead men and also to "specheles beastes." The mention of "specheles beastes" in the preface to *Wonderfull newes* refers back to Aesop (as well as Chaucer and possibly John Skelton), but also forward to his own *Beware the Cat,* probably written a year later, in 1553. This text, presented in the prefatory poem to the 1584 printing, "T.K. to the Reader" as a "fixion" (sig. A2^{r}, l. 20), has been described with some hyperbole as "the first English novel" (Ringler 1979, Ringler & Flachmann 1988). Its use of fiction, I argue, is not an aberration from Baldwin's earlier literary pursuits but their logical continuation. Baldwin had defended Aesop's fables as carriers of truth in his *Treatise of Morall Phylosophie,* as Sidney would do in his *Defence*: "I think none so simple would say that Aesop lied in the tales of his beasts; for who thinks that Aesop wrote it for actually true were well worthy to have his name chronicled among the beasts he writeth

[15] The word "affeccion" is Baldwin's in the *Myrroure* (Baldwin 1559, fol. xix^{r}).

of" (Sidney 1973, 103). Its use of the beast-fable trope of speaking animals, its nested narratives and multiple framing devices, as well as its use of unreliable narration, may well make *Beware the Cat* seem like a weird surreal tale, a pioneer of avant-garde narrative techniques; it also fits perfectly with Baldwin's defense, throughout his work as a writer and translator, of imaginative writing for the sake of championing religious and moral truth.

Even though this text is quite well known and has often been discussed, it may be worthwhile to give a brief outline of its structure. The 'argument' sets this story at the court of Edward VI in the early 1550s, when a group of men gathered around George Ferrers, master of the king's pastimes from 1551 to 1553 (who later collaborated with Baldwin on the *Mirror for Magistrates*), engage in a controversy about "whether Birds and beasts had reason" (Baldwin 1584, sig. A4^{r}).[16] Master Streamer, a "Diuine" (1584, sig. A4^{r}), argues that they have and that he knows from his own experience that animals can communicate. He begins to tell his story: one night, when lodging in a house in Aldersgate attached to the London Wall and next to a printing-house, he hears a group of cats making a racket, and a similar discussion about the abilities of animals ensues. A servant then tells the story of a Staffordshireman who was addressed by a cat in a forest; another man shares the story of an Irish soldier who was strangled by a cat in revenge for killing the cat-leader Grimalkin. We learn that cats can speak, eat an entire sheep, even kill a soldier. The lodgers debate how animals transmit and receive news from other countries (answer: by traveling on human ships). There follows an extended discussion of witchcraft, shapeshifting, and lycanthropy, including some much-noted anti-Catholic remarks about transubstantiation (sig. B5^{r}). Similar to witches who transform themselves into cats and are believed to be ordinary cats, adherents of the old faith believed the Pope to be "but a man [...] whereas indeed he was a very incarnated deuil" (sig. B8^{r}) – a topic close to Baldwin's heart, as attested by the *Wonderfull newes* pamphlet discussed above.

At night in his room, listening to the caterwauling cats on the roof – who are attracted by the human remains of executed traitors displayed on the gate – Streamer finds no rest and resolves to cook up a magic potion described by Albertus Magnus[17] in order to be able to understand the language of animals.

16 I have used the EEBO facsimile of the British Library copy (which lacks the title page extant in the fragment of the 1570 printing, STC 1244), to avoid some of the problematic implications of a modernized text.

17 As Betteridge (2013, 148–149) notes, *The Boke of secretes of Albertus Magnus, of the vertues of Herbes, stones and certaine beasts* (London, 1525) indeed contains a spell – "If thou wilte understande the voices of brydes" – that is similar, if far less elaborate, to the one used by Streamer in *Beware the Cat.* According to King (1982, 392), the *Boke of secretes* was "laughed at as entertaining fiction," an indication of the fact that Streamer is being ridiculed and that *Beware the Cat* is a satirical attack on superstition and false beliefs, "an indirect defense of human rationality" (398).

After having assembled the ingredients with some difficulty and followed the complicated recipe, he is suddenly able to understand cats' speech: "me thought I heard one cry with a loud voice, what *Isegrim*" (sig. C7^{v}). The next night, trying to listen to the cats, he is overwhelmed by the excessive sensitivity of his hearing and shocked when a crow falls through the chimney down on his head, insulting him rudely. He is finally able to follow the cats' conversation the next night. Their meeting is in fact a kind of trial, in which the cat Mouse-slayer defends herself against the accusation of having broken the cats' law of promiscuity. In her defense, she tells of a time when she was living with an elderly couple who were reluctant to relinquish the old faith. She witnessed the sick old woman give in to her confessor to allow him to celebrate mass for her, after which the woman was actually cured of her blindness. (This raises the other cats' doubt that the priest might have brought on the blindness by means of sorcery in order to be able to 'cure' her.) Mouseslayer proceeds to tell how she then lived with a widow who owned a boarding house and was a secret worshipper of the Virgin Mary. The widow worked as a pimp and a dealer of stolen goods, turning young men to a life of crime. Once one of her boarders fell in love with the wife of a merchant, but the woman refused his advances. The widow then invited the woman for dinner and showed her a letter that a young man had purportedly written to the widow's daughter (a married woman) with whom he had fallen in love. The letter was supposedly written on his deathbed after he had starved himself for three days and had asked for a last visit from the widow's daughter. The woman was deeply moved by the letter because it reminded her of her own situation, having jilted the boarder. The bawd then went on to tell her that shortly after the young man's death, her daughter's husband also died suddenly, and that the daughter had since changed into a cat, crying all the time – the bawd had given Mouseslayer mustard to eat to make her cry. The moral of this story, the bawd told the woman, was that "all exstremities are vices," including "to be to [sic] extream in honesty, chastety or any other kinde of vertue" (sig. G3^{v}). As a result of this tale, the woman then agreed to a tryst with the young man at the bawd's house.[18] Mouseslayer, however, intent on taking revenge for having been forced to eat mustard, slips a mouse under the bawd's dresses and then scratches her badly. Afterwards, she lives with the younger woman for a year, who keeps believing Mouseslayer to be the bawd's daughter changed into a cat.

In the subsequent episode, one of the young men in the household 'shoes' the cat's paws in walnut shells attached with pitch; at night, Mouseslayer struts about in the attic, and the noise she makes with her nutshell shoes wakes up the family, who think that the devil himself is upstairs. In one of the story's most farcical high points, two priests are called to exorcize the devil but are

[18] As Betteridge (2013, 153–154) notes, this story is "'borrowed' […] from William Caxton's *Fables of Aesop* (1483), where there is a lengthy version of it."

so scared by the cat that they tumble downstairs, one of them landing with "his face [...] vpon a boyes bare arse, which belike was fallen hedlong vnder him." This priest, we learn, "was so astonished: then when the boy (which for feare beshit him self) had al to rayed his face, he neither felt nor smelt it nor remooued from him" (sig. G6v). The other priest gets burned by his own candle. The cat's plight is recognized and the pitch removed with hot water. Finally, Mouseslayer reports how she ended the affair between the married woman and her lover by helping the husband discover the lover hiding behind a curtain with his trousers down.

After she has finished telling her story, the other cats praise Mouseslayer, saying they will all attend the court of their new ruler Camoloch at "Catnes" (i.e. Caithness) (sig. G8v). Master Streamer goes to bed and has a good night's rest. Next morning, in the garden, he overhears another cats' conversation which fills him in on the earlier story of Mouseslayer's life that he had been missing, briefly summing up her many discoveries of her respective masters' various follies and deceits. After dinner, having eaten "common meat" (sig. H1v), Streamer again loses his ability to understand cats' speech. This ends his narrative; he is promised money from George Ferrers to allow him to travel to Caithness. At that, everybody goes to sleep.

The book closes with an exhortation and a hymn. The exhortation takes up the argument, in the first person of "G. B." (Gulielmus Baldwin), lending the authority of personal acquaintance with Streamer and his interlocutors to what must otherwise appear as "meruelous," "wonderful and strange" (sig. H2v). The story's fictionality is thus embedded in a credible scenario, lending it the authority of oral testimony – a kind of authority that is satirized in the story itself with its nested structure of multiple narratives. It is of course impossible to tell how many early readers believed these stories to be accurate or factually true, how many had doubts, and how many had sufficient literary experience to enjoy it as a tall tale reminiscent of the *fabliau*. But there is one contemporary document to prove that at least one of its early readers took it seriously and even felt called upon to defend the (probably fictional) Gregory Streamer against the insults implied in *Beware the Cat*. A broadside, probably published soon after *Beware the Cat*'s first printing and titled *A short Answere to the boke called: Beware the Cat* (1561, STC 664.5), vehemently denies Streamer's authorship of the story: "The veri truith is so, that Stremer made not that, / Nor no such false fabels: fell ever from his pen, / Nor from his hart or mouth: as knoe mani honest men" (ll. 6–8).[19] Obviously, this writer had great difficulty in

[19] While a Gregory Streamer can be found in the Register of the University of Oxford between 1529 and 1533, nothing else is known about him (Ringler & Flachmann 1988, 58); his first name only occurs in the hymn at the end of *Beware the Cat*, allegedly composed by Streamer himself – unless we assume, with Robert Maslen (1999, 25, note 16), that Streamer is also the author behind the love letter signed "G.S." that is used to 'convert' the woman to adultery.

accepting the moral purpose of Baldwin's fiction-making, repeatedly rejecting the 'truths' of his book as lies: "Every thing almost: in that book is as tru, / As that at Midsomer: in London it doth snu" (ll. 15–16). He calls Baldwin a madman, in so many words, and *Beware the Cat* a "Bagagical boke" (l. 30), eager to protect Streamer from Baldwin's slanderous lies: "You hurt a harmeles man: which no such tales did tel, / As ye were disposed: loude lyes on him to make" (ll. 32–33). This writer's moral goal is clear: "[...] that the truith shuld be knowen / And that the falsite: shuld quite be ouerthrowen" (ll. 56–57).

Yet again, falsehood in the mode of fiction has a serious role to play even in this bawdy story about cats and humans. Looking more closely, one finds that the role of cats in this narrative are quite complex – they do not merely serve as vehicles of anti-Catholic propaganda (see also Boehrer 2010, 110–130). Cats in *Beware the Cat* are not the devil in disguise, but discoverers of secret sins – such as still celebrating mass in secret or having extra-marital affairs. While the laws of cat society are in direct opposition to those of the human social world – where extra-marital sex is strictly forbidden, whereas cats have to accept all comers –, the cats reveal to Streamer the full scope of human depravity. The response to discovery, in all of these cases, is shame. The moral of the story, spelled out in the exhortation, is "to take heed of wickednes, and eschue secret sins and priuy mischevuous counsels; lest (to their shame) all the world at length doo knowe thereof" (sig. H2ᵛ). Anyone whose solution to the prevalence of feline espionage was to rid themselves of their cat would therefore be automatically suspect of naughty activities. As in *The Mirror for Magistrates*, "vices are punished," and "worldly prosperitie" is shown to be "frayle and vnstable" (Baldwin 1559, title page). The exhortation moreover asserts that God, angels, and the devil likewise see and hear everything; "all sinne and wickednes" will *also* be punished by "euerlasting torment" (Baldwin 1584, sig. H3ʳ). Yet shame and physical punishment in *this* world appear to be more terrifying, and thus more socially effective, than the rather distant prospect of eternal damnation in the next.[20] It is no surprise, then, that the word "shame" and its cognates (shameful, shameless) occur fifteen times in the text, the word "hell" only once.

In its narrative technique of nested stories and in its satirical bent, *Beware the Cat* is indebted to the genre of the animal fable, to Chaucer's *House of Fame*, which is mentioned in the text (Baldwin 1584, sig. D1ʳ), or to *The Historye of Reynart the Foxe*, first printed by Caxton in 1481 (which also includes judicial combat before a court of beasts). It also echoes the humanist tradition, especially Erasmus's *Moriae Encomium* (1511), translated into English as *Praise of Folie* (1549) by Baldwin's friend Thomas Chaloner (one of the contributors to the *Mirror for Magistrates*), as well as More's *Utopia*, first published in English

[20] A similar argument is made by Latimer in his sermons: although liars will of course be punished, ultimately, by God, it is safer to punish them in the here and now. Cf. Sommerville (1988, 182–183).

in 1551 – possibly the very year in which Streamer tells his story to the group assembled at court.[21] In its printed form, *Beware the Cat* carries numerous marginal glosses that summarize and comment on the narrative, frequently in a moralistic vein, though the glosses ultimately fail to establish "a single reliable perspective" on the text (Griffiths 2014, 132). The question is how far the satire reaches and whether this moral form is also being parodied – which would throw the moral of the exhortation into question. Or, which seems more likely, were the moralizing glosses meant to be entertaining but nonetheless serious in intent, for all their obvious humor? The cats' stories, after all, are intended to produce laughter – at one point Streamer laughs along with the cats – but still culminate in a serious moral exhortation (defined by the OED as "earnestly admonishing or urging to what is deemed laudable conduct").

Beware the Cat thus enshrines its morality in a series of nested cat narratives, told at several removes from the initial narrator (the persona of 'G. B.'), gradually accumulating a case-by-case argument, as Mouseslayer the cat herself does when she defends herself in front of the court of cats who have accused her of breaking the cats' law of indiscriminate fornication. Unlike curiosity, casuistry here does not kill the cat but keeps her alive and well. Storytelling itself comes to serve the immediate rhetorical purpose of self-defense in the cats' court of law, and the larger homiletic purpose of illustrating human virtues and vices. Baldwin thus uses the "fixion" (1584, sig. A2^r), i.e. fiction, of cats as secret observers of people's sins, crimes and misdemeanors for a serious moral purpose. His "crossing back and forth between the fictional space and the actual world" (Bonahue 1994, 298) is not mere playfulness but a crucial part of the text's homiletic strategy. Unlike some previous readers, I do not think that Streamer's oration, rambling and unreliable as it may be, undermines the "moral interpretation provided in the Exhortation by G.B." (Bonahue 1994, 292) and in many of the marginal glosses. The laughter that the satire generates among the interlocutors in the text, and intends to stimulate in its readers, is a form of public shaming of secret sins and irrational superstitions, sanctioning moral trespasses and encouraging behavior that conforms to Protestant norms of religious and social life. Even when the glosses "maintain[ ] a straight face" vis à vis the grossest moments of physical comedy in Streamer's narrative, these do not counteract but support the moral agenda of Baldwin's satirical intentions. The relationship between the glosses and the main text may be another source of satirical humor, but I would argue that it is not as "clearly unstable" as some readers have made it out to be (Bonahue 1994, 296).[22] As Jane Griffiths

---

21 See Betteridge (2013, 142) and Maslen (2009, 305) on *Beware the Cat*'s parallels to Erasmus and More.

22 On Baldwin's glosses as a response "to academic commentary, but also to a tradition of vernacular writing on the subject of literary authority [...] as well as to evolving paratextual conventions in printed texts," see Griffiths (2014, 123–133).

argues, Baldwin's glosses have an educational function despite his "diversionary tactics": "they educate his readers in good, self-reliant, interpretative practice by demonstrating that the reliability of the printed word is not to be taken for granted" (Griffiths 2014, 128).

In both *The Mirror for Magistrates* and *Beware the Cat*, 'fixion' is firmly embedded in real-life settings intended to lend credibility and authority to the "maruelous," "wounderfull and incredible matters" (Baldwin 1570, title page) it contains. Fantastic it may be, but its object is very much the real world of the mid-sixteenth century with its struggle for coherence amid the turmoil of conflicting belief systems. Read in the context of Baldwin's other literary pursuits, *Beware the Cat* is decidedly less odd than it might otherwise appear. It is a moralistic satire written in the humanist spirit encapsulated in the Horatian precept of combining entertainment with usefulness – "to teach and delight" (Sidney 1973, 80), but above all to teach – as the Spouse (God's church) begs Christ at the end of Baldwin's *Canticles of Salomon* (1549, sig. n2^{v}):

> And whan that I suche secretes shall vnfolde
> As darkly hyd, the scriptures do contayne,
> That in the hartes of all they maye take holde,
> And to thy truth all vnbeleuers gayne[.]

Fiction is here, in other words, to be understood in the mode of allegory, or the "darke conceit" of Spenser's *Faerie Queene* (2013, 714), or, with St. Augustine, a "fiction related to a certain signification" that is then "not a lie but in some way a figure of truth" (qtd. in Nelson 1973, 14). In Baldwin's intention, moral satire may have been the principal goal of *Beware the Cat*, aligning it with the reasons he adduced elsewhere to justify the cultural work of fiction in Reformation England; but it is the realistic vividness of Mouseslayer's narrative that gives pleasure, turning it into a forerunner of novelistic realism.

6. *Conclusions*

Popular as *Beware the Cat* may have been in the Elizabethan era, it is doubtful that many readers would have enjoyed it for the 'right' reasons. What Baldwin was doing in *Beware the Cat*, ultimately, was to try to adapt for a wider audience, in English, the jokiness of humanist models as current in the work of Erasmus and More, who had published their witty entertainments in Latin and thus for a learned elite. It is unlikely that *Beware the Cat* gained many unbelievers to Christ's truth. However, this may have been precisely his intention.

Baldwin's literary trajectory offers an exemplary case study of the concept and legitimacy, or acceptability, of imaginative fiction in the early modern period. In this paper, I have argued that Baldwin introduces falsehoods and lies as permissible parts of narratives when these narratives serve a higher moral and educational purpose. *Beware the Cat,* which has long been regarded as a precursor of the modern novel in English, is no exception but a continuation of Baldwin's literary and popular philosophical program.

As the (strangely literal-minded) printed response to *Beware the Cat* demonstrates, Baldwin's game of mixing truth, falsehoods, and lies into a heady cocktail of fiction, so forward-looking in its narrative innovations, clearly was not to everyone's taste. His works and what little we know about his early readers also remind us that the distinction of fiction from falsehood and lies was a matter of great debate and controversy in the Renaissance. Francis Bacon, in *The Advancement of Learning* (1605), writes that "Euents of true Historie, haue not that Magnitude, which satisfieth the minde of Man; Poesie faineth Acts and Euents Greater and more Heroicall" (sig. Ee2^{r}). An eloquent early reader responded to this quite fiercely, noting in the margin of his copy of Bacon's book that "it is madnes to seeke satisfaction in falsehood. [...] This, I say, is not onely madnes but wickednes. And therefore if poesie have no better end: poets had better be idle then ill occupied, & Plato did well to shut his citie gates against them" (qtd. in Sherman 2008, 13). If such documents help us recognize the controversial status of Bacon's or Sidney's attempts to 'defend' literary fiction in the early modern period, they also make us aware of the extent to which Baldwin's unsettling and experimental mixture of fact and fiction would have constituted a provocation for its first readers.

Works Cited

A short Answere to the boke called: Beware the Cat. [c. 1561] London: n. p., STC 664.5. EEBO facsimile of Society of Antiquaries Library copy.

Archer, Harriet, and Andrew Hadfield (2016) Ed. *A Mirror for Magistrates in Context: Literature, History, and Politics in Early Modern England.* Cambridge: Cambridge Univ. Press.

Bacon, Francis (1605) *The Twoo Bookes of Francis Bacon. Of the proficiencie and aduancement of Learning, diuine and humane.* London: Henry Tomes, STC 1164. EEBO facsimile of Cambridge Univ. Library copy.

Baldwin, William (1547) *A treatise of Morall Phylosophie, contaynyng the sayinges of the wyse. Gathered and Englyshed by Wyliam Baldwyn.* London: Edward Whitchurch, STC 1253. EEBO facsimile of British Library copy.

Baldwin, William (1549) *The Canticles or Balades of Salomon, phraselyke declared in Englysh Metres.* London: Edward Whitchurch, STC 2768. EEBO facsimile of British Library copy.

Baldwin, William (1552) *Wonderfull newes of the death of Paule the .iii.* London: Thomas Gaultier, STC 10532. EEBO facsimile of Bodleian library copy.

Baldwin, William (1559) *A Myrroure for Magistrates.* London: Thomas Marshe, STC 1247. EEBO facsimile of Huntington Library copy.

Baldwin, William (1570) *A maruelous hystory intitulede, Beware the Cat. Conteynyng Diuerse Wounderfull and Incredible Matters, Etc.* London: William Gryffith, STC 1244. EEBO facsimile of British Library copy.

Baldwin, William (1584) [*A maruelous Hystory intitulede, Beware the Cat*]. London: Edward Allde, STC 1245. EEBO facsimile of British Library copy.

Baldwin, William (1988) *Beware the Cat: The First English Novel.* Ed. William A. Ringler Jr. and Michael Flachmann. San Marino, CA: Huntington Library.

Betteridge, Thomas (2013) "William Baldwin's *Beware the Cat* and Other Foolish Writing." *The Oxford Handbook of English Prose 1500–1640.* Ed. Andrew Hadfield. Oxford: Oxford Univ. Press. 139–155.

Boehrer, Bruce Thomas (2010) *Animal Characters: Non-Human Beings in Early Modern Literature.* Philadelphia: Pennsylvania Univ. Press.

Bonahue, Edward T., Jr (1994) "'I know the place and the persons': The Play of Textual Frames in Baldwin's *Beware the Cat.*" *Studies in Philology* 91.3: 283–300.

Cervantes Saavedra, Miguel de (1987) *El ingenioso hidalgo Don Quijote de la Mancha*. Ed. Vicente Gaos. 3 vols. Madrid: Gredos.

Davis, Evan (2017) *Post-Truth: Why We Have Reached Peak Bullshit and What We Can Do About It.* London: Little, Brown.

Denery, Dallas G., II (2015) *The Devil Wins: A History of Lying from the Garden of Eden to the Enlightenment.* Princeton, NJ: Princeton Univ. Press.

Flachmann, Michael (1990) "The First English Epistolary Novel: *The Image of Idleness* (1555). Text, Introduction, and Notes." *Studies in Philology* 87: 1–74.

Flinker, Noam (2000) *The Song of Songs in English Renaissance Literature: Kisses of their Mouths.* Cambridge: D. S. Brewer.

Geller, Sherri (1999) "What History Really Teaches: Historical Pyrrhonism in William Baldwin's *A Mirror for Magistrates.*" *Opening the Borders: Inclusivity in Early Modern Studies.* Ed. Peter C. Herman. Newark, DE: Delaware Univ. Press; London: Associated Univ. Presses. 150–184.

Goodman, Nelson (1978) *Ways of Worldmaking.* Indianapolis: Hackett.

Griffiths, Jane (2014) *Diverting Authorities: Experimental Glossing Practices in Manuscript and Print.* Oxford: Oxford Univ. Press.

Hadfield, Andrew (1994) *Literature, Politics and National Identity: Reformation to Renaissance*. Cambridge: Cambridge Univ. Press.

Johns, Adrian (1998) *The Nature of the Book. Print and Knowledge in the Making.* Chicago: Chicago Univ. Press.

King, John N. (1982) *English Reformation Literature: The Tudor Origins of the Protestant Tradition.* Princeton, NJ: Princeton Univ. Press.

King, John N. (2004) "Baldwin, William (*d.* in or before 1563)." *Oxford Dictionary of National Biography,* Oxford Univ. Press, online ed.

Ko, Trudy (2009) "Backdating the First Edition of William Baldwin's *Beware the Cat* Nine Years." *Notes and Queries* 56.1: 33–34.

Kripke, Saul (1980) *Naming and Necessity.* Cambridge, MA: Harvard Univ. Press.

Latimer, Hugh (1844) *Sermons.* Ed. George Elwes Corrie. Cambridge: Cambridge Univ. Press.

Lucas, Scott C. (2009) *A Mirror for Magistrates and the Politics of the English Reformation.* Amherst, MA: Massachusetts Univ. Press.

Lucas, Scott C. (2016) "A Renaissance Man and his 'Medieval' Text: William Baldwin and *A Mirror for Magistrates,* 1547–1563." A Mirror for Magistrates *in Context: Literature, History, and Politics in Early Modern England.* Ed. Harriet Archer and Andrew Hadfield. Cambridge: Cambridge Univ. Press. 17–34.

Mahler, Andreas (2019) "New Ways of Worldmaking: English Renaissance Literature as 'Early Modern.'" *Handbook of English Renaissance Literature.* Ed. Ingo Berensmeyer. Berlin: De Gruyter. 66–88.

Maslen, Robert (1999) "'The Cat Got Your Tongue': Pseudo-Translation, Conversion, and Control in William Baldwin's 'Beware the Cat.'" *Translation and Literature* 8.1: 3–27.

Maslen, Robert (2009) "William Baldwin and the Tudor Imagination." *The Oxford Handbook of Tudor Literature.* Ed. Mike Pincombe and Cathy Shrank. Oxford: Oxford Univ. Press. 291–306.

McKitterick, David (2003) *Print, Manuscript, and the Search for Order, 1450–1830.* Cambridge: Cambridge Univ. Press.

Nelson, William (1973) *Fact or Fiction: The Dilemma of the Renaissance Storyteller.* Cambridge, MA: Harvard Univ. Press.

Overell, Anne, and Scott C. Lucas (2010) "Whose Wonderful News? Italian Satire and William Baldwin's *Wonderfull Newes of the Death of Paule the III.*" *Renaissance Studies* 26.2: 180–196.

Pincombe, Michael (2010) "Truth, Lies, and Fiction in William Baldwin's *Wonderfull News of the Death of Paul III.*" *Reformation* 15: 3–22.

Pincombe, Mike (2011) "William Baldwin and *A Mirror for Magistrates.*" *Renaissance Studies* 27.2: 183–198.

Rainolde, Richard (1563) *A booke called the Foundacion of Rhetorike.* London: John Kingston, STC 29825a.5. EEBO facsimile of Bodleian Library copy.

Richards, Jennifer (2016) "Reading and Listening to William Baldwin." A Mirror for Magistrates *in Context: Literature, History, and Politics in Early Modern England*. Ed. Harriet Archer and Andrew Hadfield. Cambridge: Cambridge Univ. Press. 71–88.

Ringler, William A., Jr. (1979) "*Beware the Cat* and the Beginnings of English Fiction." *Novel: A Forum on Fiction* 12: 113–126.

Ringler, William A., Jr., and Michael Flachmann (1988) Ed. *Beware the Cat: The First English Novel.* By William Baldwin. San Marino, CA: Huntington Library.

Sherman, William H. (2008) *Used Books: Marking Readers in Renaissance England.* Philadelphia: Pennsylvania Univ. Press.

Sidney, Sir Philip (1973) "A Defence of Poetry." *Miscellaneous Prose of Sir Philip Sidney.* Ed. Katherine Duncan-Jones and Jan van Dorsten. Oxford: Clarendon Press. 73–121.

Sommerville, Johann P. (1988) "The 'New Art of Lying': Equivocation, Mental Reservation, and Casuistry." *Conscience and Casuistry in Early Modern Europe.* Ed. Edmund Leites. Cambridge: Cambridge Univ. Press. 159–184.

Spenser, Edmund (2013) *The Faerie Queene.* Ed. A. C. Hamilton. Rev. 2nd ed. London: Routledge.

Stenner, Rachel (2015) "The Act of Penning in William Baldwin's *Beware the Cat.*" *Renaissance Studies* 30.3: 334–349.

Dissimulation and Lack of Trust: A Central Problem in Politics and Inter-Confessional Relations at the Turn of the Seventeenth Century

Ronald G. Asch

1. *Preliminaries*

In October 1608 Bishop Melchior Klesl, the most important councilor of Archduke Mathias – who also held the title of King of Hungary – wrote a memorandum for the Archduke, addressing the difficult question of toleration granted to heretics. Was it legitimate to make such concessions to Protestants or had such compromises to be considered an unforgivable sin? Klesl who later rose to the position of cardinal and played a central role in imperial politics during the years 1612–1618 when Mathias ruled Germany as Emperor came to the conclusion that it might be permissible "to let the weeds [heresy] grow, if we cannot eradicate them without provoking greater damage." However, such concessions were possible only by way of "connivieren und dissimulieren" (by conniving in fudged compromises and by dissimulating one's own opinions) (Angermeier 1993, 261).[1] Klesl further explained that to tolerate religious opinions and practices which were heretical was, strictly speaking, tantamount to betraying Christ. Those who tolerated heresy crucified Christ a second time. However, God was no tyrant, and expected no ruler to achieve the impossible. When heresy was so strongly entrenched that a victory against such movements was impossible to achieve, it was therefore permissible to 'dissimulate.' (Hammer-Purgstall 1847/51, vol. II, 134–135)

Dissimulation was a central issue in the debates of the early seventeenth century. The term did not necessarily imply that one lied, rather it denoted the decision to conceal one's innermost thoughts and convictions, a way of being 'economical with the truth.' Only by such means became negotiations involving politicians representing the opposing confessional camps of the period possible at all. That at least was Klesl's opinion and many contemporaries would have agreed with him (Asch 2020, 317).

Dissimulation could play a decisive role in multiple contexts. On the one hand dissimulation could be a means of achieving some kind of political and

[1] Klesl wrote that it could under certain circumstances be permissible "das Unkraut wachßen [zu] laßen, weil wüers ohne Schaden nit außreütten khünnen." (Hammer-Purgstall 1847/51, vol. II, 137).

religious compromise in the face of theological convictions – held by potential negotiating partners – which were completely incompatible. At the end, the resulting agreements might be mere rhetorical formulas, fudged compromises, but such fudges could still avoid armed conflict for the time being. On the other hand, dissimulation could be a means for the individual subject or believer to escape the enormous pressure to demonstrate conformity with the prevailing religious orthodoxy which both secular and ecclesiastical authorities exercised. To conceal one's real thoughts seemed to be necessary to retain, secretly, a minimum of intellectual freedom.[2] Dissimulation and outright deceit, however, served even more far-reaching purposes, and were discussed in more wide-ranging contexts. They were part of a theory of politics guided by the idea of reason of state and of the courtier's art as taught by many manuals and practiced at royal and princely courts throughout Europe.

2. *Tacitus, Lipsius and the Necessity of Dissimulation*

How different concepts of dissimulation overlapped and interacted is revealed in the writings of Justus Lipsius who was one of the authors most widely read and debated by courtiers, politicians and officeholders, both Protestant and Catholic, at the end of the sixteenth century. His biography is typical of a scholar who hesitated for a long time to take sides in the religious and political conflicts of his age. Trying to keep his distance from events in his native Netherlands, he first taught at the Lutheran university of Jena, but later moved to Leiden in the Dutch republic, a Calvinist university. Later still in 1590, he converted to Catholicism and obtained a professorship for Latin literature and language in Louvain in the Southern Netherlands. He died in the Spanish Netherlands in 1606.[3] While still a young man, he published to wide acclaim the works of the Roman historian Tacitus (1574) (Lipsius 1574).

Tacitism in the late sixteenth century constituted a powerful counter-movement to the humanism of the high renaissance, which was inspired by Cicero and Livius (Tuck 1993, 31–64). Both the orator Cicero and the historian Livius provided their readers with a clear perception of the world as being divided between the forces of light and darkness, good and evil. Moreover, Cicero was perceived as a strong defender of the ancient ideal of republican liberty.[4] By contrast, the world which Tacitus presented to his readers was far more ambivalent and darker. There were precious few heroes to be found in his works, and if there were heroes, they were more often than not heroes facing

2 See Cavaillé (2002), in particular 348–351 regarding Accetto's *Della dissimulazione onesta* (published in 1641, that is later than most of the writings considered here).

3 See Oestreich (1989) and Sierhuis (2013) for Lipsius and Neo-Stoicism.

4 This is strongly emphasized by Skinner (2002).

defeat. Most of the statesmen, politicians and emperors that Tacitus depicted acted in a deep moral twilight. Tacitus wrote about the murderous intrigues which were every-day occurrences at the court of Roman emperors, for example during Tiberius' rule and the ascendancy of his favorite Sejanus. It was not too difficult to see in such stories a badly concealed criticism of monarchical rule as such. At the same time, Tacitus left his readers in no doubt that republican liberty had forever vanished. Those who wanted to survive in the new post-republican world had to learn the art of concealing their real thoughts, the art of dissimulation.

However, for the ruler himself absolute self-control was equally important in the world of Tacitean politics, a ruler could hardly survive without being a consummate actor. He would have to continually deceive those who tried to find out what he really thought and what he intended to do. The classical example of a ruler who had mastered this art to perfection was Tiberius in the portrait presented to his readers by Tacitus. For the same reasons that the old republican elite, the members of the senate, could never be assumed to be really loyal, the *princeps* could not afford to be sincere: this would have been a dangerous luxury. Thus the Roman *princeps* could become a model for kings and princes in the age of confessional war and conflict when political assassination and even regicide had become a means of settling scores and advancing one's own interests and were condoned and even approved of by militant religious zealots (Morford 1993). Tacitus' works were read as a manual of advice for princes which provided them with the principles of statecraft. We find such an interpretation already in the writings of the Italian historian Francesco Guicciardini (1483–1540) (Gajda 2009, 256). At the same time, readers of the late sixteenth century appreciated Tacitus as a writer who could teach subjects how to survive under the rule of princes that were unpredictable if not tyrannical in their behavior.

This may have been a misreading of Tacitus' real intentions, from a historical point of view, but it remained nevertheless an influential approach. The attraction of Tacitus' works as a source for a sophisticated and reasoned philosophy of statecraft may to some extent have been due to the possibility that by speaking and writing about Tacitus one could implicitly and secretly discuss the dangerous teachings of another, more modern author, Machiavelli. Because Machiavelli was seen as a truly diabolical and anti-Christian writer, one was well advised not to betray too much familiarity with the lessons he had tried to teach in *Il Principe*, whereas the sophisticated humanism of Tacitism was largely seen as unobjectionable.[5]

[5] For Machiavelli see Meyer/Zwierlein (2010). For Tacitus influence in Italy for example in the case of Botero or Scipione Ammirato see Compatato/Quaglioni (2007), in particular 80–81 for Tiberius as the model of the prudent ruler.

Lipsius' most important work of political theory the *Politicorum sive civilis doctrinae libri sex* published in 1589 in Leiden was heavily influenced by Tacitus. The *Politica* were essentially a manual of statecraft which to a great extent consisted of quotations from classical authors such as Tacitus. The other Roman author who shaped Lipsius' thought was of course Seneca, the Stoic philosopher. What Tacitus and Seneca had in common was the climate of moral ambiguity which dominated the age they lived in. In his own works the historian Tacitus – born roughly two generations after Seneca – had extensively dealt with the period of history during which Seneca lived, the age of Nero. According to Tacitus, under the rule of men like Nero there was no longer any room for the traditional virtues of the Roman citizen, such as patriotism and probity. The only place where moral ideals could be realized was the individual's private life. At the end of the sixteenth century, many scholars and intellectuals saw their own age in a similar light, not least of all Lipsius. In his book *De Constantia [...] in publicis malis* (1584) ['On Constancy in Times of Public Disasters] Lipsius recommended an attitude of complete equanimity even in extreme situations, for example when one's country faced ruin and destruction and this fate could no longer be averted (Schmidt 2007, 99–103; see also Neumann 1998, 166–169). According to Lipsius, the wise man could find happiness and moral integrity only in himself by exercising self-restraint and by mastering his passions. That was what Lipsius, following Seneca, taught his readers, Lipsius' neo-stoicism was an attempt to construct an ethical system which would survive the collapse of the political order and remain stable in the throes of confessional conflicts; these circumstances made it difficult to appeal to widely accepted religious values and norms because every theological truth was opposed by contradictory opinions. In its search for stability and peace neo-stoicism provided a solution to problems which many contemporaries felt to be their own (Braun 2011).

In Lipsius' works one encounters a predominant moral relativism. Lipsius was prepared to justify otherwise questionable positions and actions in the name of reason of state or because they provided a survival strategy for individuals in a hostile environment (Lindberg 2011, 81). In Lipsius' work, history was meant to act as *magistra* vitae. Presented as a collection of quotations and as the fruit of centuries of historical experience, the *Politica* often concealed the author's own positions and loyalties, as Jan Waszink notes: "referring to the opinion of others is used as a way to pre-include doubts and possible objections" (Waszink 2004, 110; see also Gajda 2016, 290). Lipsius taught his readers that in order to survive in the world of politics, it was absolutely necessary to hide one's own thoughts and intentions, and this held true for the prince as much as for the subjects. At bottom, the prince could trust his courtiers just as little as the courtiers could trust one another. Lipsius was aware of the fact that the prince – as he presented him – cut a lonely figure, and that his isolation posed a moral problem; yet, a ruler who wanted to survive in a world dominated by treason, could not hope to escape the melancholia of power – a problem that Lipsius, as opposed to Machiavelli, was very much aware of and considered in great detail.[6]

Following the principle that everything had to be subordinated to the logic of *raison d'état* officially established religion for Lipsius primarily served political purposes. The church was part and parcel of a power structure designed to give stability to political authority. Ideally, a state was to be supported and sustained by a uniform religious orientation and a unitary ecclesiastical system. If such homogeneity could not be obtained, toleration could be granted to religious minorities to avoid a civil war, but this was clearly a second-best solution. Theologians and other writers critical of Lipsius saw in such teachings a proof of Lipsius' personal religious indifference, since they transformed individual piety into a mere manifestation of an overarching 'religio civilis' or 'theologia politica.' As a matter of fact, Lipsius like the famous printer Plantin who published his works in Antwerp, may have been a member of a secret spiritual community, the *familia charitatis*. In public, however, he went along with the religious requirements of the relevant political authorities so as not to get into trouble for holding views deemed to be unorthodox or even heretical.[7] For Lipsius it could be imperative for political reasons – and not for religious ones – to impose a unitary form of belief on all subjects. At the same time, he tried to minimize the influence of religion in politics. Personally, he sympathized with a kind of individual liberty of conscience in religious matters. Personal belief was to manifest itself entirely in the private sphere of the believer, if not in absolute secret, as was the case for the internalized convictions held by the members of the *familia charitatis*. Conversely, he accepted the necessity of submitting oneself in public to the form of religion established by the government and by the existing political authorities (Waszink 2004, 86–87).

In many ways Lipsius thus prepared the ground for an attitude to religion and the church which Hugo Grotius later advocated, a 'religio prudentum' (the religion of the wise); at least this was the conviction of those who rejected this kind of confessional ambivalence and ambiguity. Such a *religio prudentum* implied that, while being guided by principles of political expediency, one could choose one's own position from a number of competing religious options, following one's individual tastes and predilections (Mulsow 2003, 146). Such an attitude could easily be combined with a tendency to dissimulate one's real convictions in public, and in real life even required a certain amount of dissimulation if one did not want to run foul of the secular magistrate and church authorities. By advocating discretion and dissimulation in religious

---

6 This is an argument made by Snyder (2009), 124–129.

7 See Mulsow (2003), 144–145, for Lipsius' critics and the controversy regarding a possible *religio politica*. For Lipsius' debate with the Dutch scholar Dirck Volkertszoon Coornhert on religious toleration see Waszink (2004), 115–117.

matters, Lipsius followed a general tendency prevalent during his lifetime. The late sixteenth and the early seventeenth century can justly be seen as a period in which the art of dissimulation and of hiding one's real convictions and feelings was perfected to a degree hitherto unknown. True enough, to be economical with the truth had always been the rule rather than the exception in politics, as it remains today, but what was new in our period was the extent to which dissimulation became a subject of systematic reflection, but also the context which defined its place both in court politics and in confessional conflicts.

For the very reason that in the Renaissance sincerity became an important ethical ideal, the tensions between such an ideal and men's and women's actual behavior became more visible. Whether as a courtier, believer or ruler, the individual often assumed social roles and the norms inherent in them, which he or she found to be out of step with their real selves. Therefore, one's real self had to be protected and preserved by means of systematic dissimulation (Martin 2204, 52–44, 119–122).[8] We clearly see this tendency in the manuals for aspiring courtiers published at the turn of the seventeenth century. Lorenzo Ducci's *Ars aulica* for example, published in 1601, was heavily influenced by Tacitus. Tiberius was presented by Ducci as the very model of the absolute monarch and his favorite Sejanus as the perfect courtier.

However, in the courtly world analyzed by Ducci mistrust becomes the dominant problem. This could not be otherwise as both prince and courtier try to conceal their thoughts and intentions. The courtier's success and survival depend on his ability to look behind the ruler's mask, to see through the façade of polite phrases and affability, while his own intentions and the objectives he pursues remain a deep secret to every observer. But could the courtier really hope to read the prince's character and to second-guess his actions? He had to rely on the deficiencies that inevitably adhered to any attempt to play a role in conflict with one's self. In moments of crisis, under pressure, the real inclinations, proclivities and desires of a person would inevitably become impossible to conceal completely, and this was true for the ruling prince as much as for everybody else, or as Ducci put it (in the words of his English translator Edward Blount):

> But dissimulation, wherewith nature is not invested, but over-shadowed cannot be of that force, but that some beame or raie of the true and naturalle inclination at one time or other will pierce and passe the same. [...] Because the arte of dissembling groweth of a forced and contrary habit unto nature, it cannot be, but many times of his proper force withdrawing it self from so heavy a yoake it will worke actions quite contrary to those of dissimulation." (Blount 1607: 105–106)

However, on no account should the courtier let the prince suspect that he had seen through him and no longer accepted his performance at face value, other-

[8] See Johnson (2011, 59–104). See also Hinz (1992) and Zagorin (1990), as well as Eliav-Feldon/Herzig (2015) and Sommerville (1988).

wise he would fall out of favor (Blount 1607, 113–114). Only the ruler himself enjoys the privilege to state publicly that he has seen through somebody's disguise and pretense. The courtier must play the loyal and gullible servant, while trying at the same time by a show of sincerity and by well-placed but seemingly harmless remarks to provoke the prince to reveal his real thoughts in conversation with his servants and companions at court. However, the prince is well aware of such conversational strategies, so that all real communication at court risks becoming impossible because no word spoken by any of the participants can be taken at face value (Hinz 1992, 377–385 and Snyder 2009, 90–97).[9]

3. *Lack of Trust as a Problem in Inter-Confessional Relations*

The problem which manifested itself so prominently at court – that social interaction was undermined by mutual mistrust – could, however, be seen as a more general one. Political communication on a much wider scale was potentially rendered futile by a lack of trust, in particular in all matters regarding religion and the conflict between the confessional churches.[10] If all attempts before 1618 to achieve a lasting peace settlement were in the end condemned to end in failure both in the Holy Roman Empire and in Europe at large, this was to no small extent due to the fact that each side suspected its opponents of being insincere in their public support for peaceful solutions. Essentially one saw one's antagonists as inherently incapable of harboring peaceful intentions. Thus Protestants regularly accused Catholics of following the principle *haereticis fides non servanda est* ['one need not honor one's promises in dealing with heretics'], which meant that treaties signed with heretics were *eo ipso* null and void, regardless of the oaths one had sworn to observe such agreements. As a matter of fact, few Catholic theologians openly supported such radical positions, but Protestants nevertheless remained suspicious (Ziegler 2017b, 186–195).[11] And indeed there were prominent voices among Catholics who held it to be a grave mistake that concessions to Protestants had been made since the 1550s, a mistake which in their view should be rectified at the earliest possible opportunity. So Protestant suspicions were not entirely unfounded.

Kaspar Schoppe (1576–1649), a well-known scholar and author of numerous tracts, played a prominent role among the Catholic authors who took a revisionist stance with regard to the Peace of Augsburg (1555) and concerning agreements with Protestants in general. In 1619 he published a treatise called

9 See also Asch (2007a).

10 For lack of trust as a specific quality of the prevailing atmosphere in the late 16th century – a reaction to widespread hypocrisy and dissimulation – see Bouwsma (2000, 117), who remarks: "by the later sixteenth century condemnations of hypocrisy reached a crescendo."

11 See Ziegler (2017a), and Brendle (2009).

Classicum belli sacri, that summed up earlier publications which had already criticized all concessions granted to heretics. His *Classicum belli,* probably written some years before 1619, was published just in time to supply the Catholic side with arguments in their war against their Protestant enemies that had broken out in 1618. Even Schoppe did not want to dismantle entirely the Peace of 1555 despite the fact that Ferdinand I in his opinion had been blackmailed by the Protestant princes to grant concessions which he should never have made. But even given the – regrettable – validity of the peace arrangements of 1555, any attempt to construct a right to freedom of conscience on the basis of this treaty – as some Protestant legal experts indeed tried to do – in Schoppe's view had to be rejected completely. The same held good for the claim that Protestant princes were entitled to confiscate ecclesiastical property which had still been in Catholic hands in 1552 (the year when the provisional agreement was signed on which the Peace of Augsburg was based). If Protestants tried to pursue such policies they had to be stopped at all costs, if need be by force of arms.

The concessions made between 1530 and 1555 by the Emperor Charles V and his brother Ferdinand for Schoppe were in themselves highly problematic. They had only been granted, due to the influence of councilors with a questionable political pedigree, like Nicolas Perrenot de Granvelle (1484–1550), chancellor of Charles V. Such dubious 'pseudopolitici' had tried to paper over the conflict between theological truth and heresy for solely political reasons. However, as Schoppe saw it, since a major war between Catholics and Protestants had become inevitable anyway, the time had now come to revise such concessions and to reclaim Catholic rights and possessions lost decades ago (Schoppe 1619).[12] Little wonder that such statements confirmed Protestants in their view that hard-line Catholics only looked for a pretext to suspend and cancel the liberties and privileges they enjoyed thanks to the Peace of Augsburg.

Schoppe was by no means the first Catholic author who had questioned the validity of the concessions made in 1555. Thus already in 1596, Andreas Erstenberger in his *Autonomia* published that year had developed a similar line of argument. Erstenberger, who belonged to the staff of the Imperial Aulic Council (Reichshofrat) in Prague – one of the two highest law courts in the Empire –, severely criticized the so-called *Freistellung* (i.e. the liberty of ecclesiastical princes and dignitaries to choose their confessional allegiance freely) which Protestants claimed for prince bishops who decided to become Protestants and subsequently refused to abandon their position as rulers of ecclesiastical principalities. Provided they succeeded in such a move, this would have transformed many prince bishoprics into hereditary secular dominions. For men like Erstenberger this presented a worst-case scenario which within a

[12] See Jaitner (2004), in particular 63–65.

few years would have led to the complete collapse of the Catholic position in the Empire. However, Erstenberger also rejected with equal fervor the freedom of conscience claimed by Protestant nobles living under the rule of Catholic prelates despite the fact that Emperor Ferdinand had assured the Protestants in the 1550s that such claims would be considered favorably by his judges.

In the last resort, Erstenberger articulated serious doubts regarding the mere possibility of creating a legal framework which allowed Protestants and Catholics to live peacefully next to one another. In his eyes, the one true church and her enemies could never coexist peacefully; this would be like a friendship between wolf and sheep and conflict and war were inevitable. Any conceivable modus vivendi between Protestants and Catholics was bound to remain an illusion: "Welches aber doch ein lauttere Gleyßnerey / unnd angenommene falsche Freundtschafft / und allerdings Unbestendig/ dabey auch weder Glück noch Hail ist" ('which is mere window dressing and a supposed false friendship and one which is unstable, nor can it procure us happiness or salvation') (Burgkardus 1602, part II, fol. 211r and 212r).

Erstenberger further undermined the religious peace by arguing that nobody, not even the Emperor, could make concessions which were incompatible with the well-established legal claims of the Roman church: by doing so he would have claimed jurisdiction in matters of canon law, which however could only be exercised by ecclesiastical courts (Burgkardus 1602, part III, fol. 318r). This was a dangerous argument because it not only threatened to invalidate the Peace of Augsburg; it also implied that any future agreements between Catholics and princes and estates that did not subscribe to the tenets of the Roman church were essentially null and void when the rights of the church were adversely affected. Erstenberger admittedly did not himself go that far; he upheld the Peace of Augsburg as such, but only in so far as the treaty was interpreted in a strictly Catholic sense. This position was hardly likely to reassure Protestants to trust Catholics; on the contrary, it fed their concerns that the latter only waited for the right moment to completely revise the existing legal order, if need be by force of arms (Burgkardus 1602, part III, fol. 318vff.).[13]

The underlying problem was that it was indeed difficult for Catholic authors to find theological as opposed to political arguments which allowed them to present concessions made to Protestants as more than temporary expedients justified by mere necessity since ultimately they were incompatible with the tenets of their Catholic faith. As a congruence, this implied that Catholics could only negotiate with their Protestant opponents by setting aside and dissimulating their most fervently held convictions, as Klesl had indeed argued in the memorandum submitted to Archduke Mathias quoted earlier. Many Protestants therefore believed that sooner or later Catholics would appeal to

[13] For the background of these polemics see Gotthard (2004), pp. 590–600 and Gotthard (2007).

what they saw as incontrovertible theological truths – truths that in their eyes would trump all legal arguments – when the right moment had come to revoke their earlier concessions.

In the writings of the time one encounters many examples for such concern among Protestants. One such example is to be found in the notes that Christian II of Anhalt took in 1635 in his diary, admittedly in the midst of the Thirty Years War when the Peace of Augsburg had already broken down. These notes were taken after a long conversation with the imperial confessor, Father Lamormaini (Lämmermann).[14] Anhalt confronted Lamormaini with the old Protestant view that Catholics held treaties with Protestants not to be protected by any sanctity of contract since a promise given to heretics was inherently invalid. Moreover, Catholics, if need be, would use an assassin's knife against their enemies even if these were anointed kings. Lamormaini understandably was not best pleased by these words and rejected such insinuations whole-heartedly and with some outrage:

> Il le desavoua, & dit, qu'on en calomnie les Jesuites, & que Jacques Clement[15] estoit un perfide[,] un Regicida[,] un homicida[,] un meschant & pervers, quj tua le Roy Henrj III de France. [...]. Que la societé humaine, devoit estre reiglée par bonnes loix & Polices, qu'il ne convenoit pas de transgredier. [...] Quod essent bellj sicut et pacis jura, quæ inviolata servanda. (Anhalt, *Tagebücher*, 3/13 Aug. 1635, 8–9)[16]

During the ensuing discussion, which was apparently quite lively, the Jesuit did, however, concede that an oath somebody had sworn which obliged him to act against essential Christian principles and thus immorally or against the fundamental interests of the one true church was ipso facto invalid. This can hardly have reassured Christian II.[17]

But misgivings about the sincerity of protestations of keeping the peace on the part of potential negotiating partners were not by any means absent on the Catholic side of the confessional divide. Catholics became particularly suspicious when Protestant authors tried to paper over theological differences of dogma in the name of irenicism. Even though irenicism was aimed primarily at tensions between Lutherans and Calvinists, Catholic theologians did not

---

14 Christian II was the son of the man who had been instrumental in securing the Bohemian crown for the elector palatine in 1619, Princes Christian I of Anhalt. Christian II had himself fought in the battle of the white Mountain, and had been taken prisoner but was later pardoned by the emperor. For Lamormaini see Bireley (1981).

15 The monk who killed Henry III of France in 1589.

16 Transl.: "He rejected this argument and said that this was a slanderous attack on the Jesuits and that Jacques Clement was a perfidious man, a regicide, a murderer, a perverted brute, who killed King Henry III of France [...,] that human society should be ruled by good laws and political norms which no one should transgress [...and] that there were laws of war, as much as of peace which should be kept inviolate."

17 "Ich hatte ihm aber nicht dieses, sondern ein anders proponirt, das Sie statuiren: Juramentum, contra Ecclesiastjcam utilitatem præstitum, non tenet, darauf gedachte er, es wehre die utilitas animae darmitt gemeinet." (Anhalt, *Tagebücher*, 4/14 Aug. 1635, 11).

hesitate to severely reject all such attempts to play down the importance of central dogmatic points of conflict.[18]

As an example of this attitude one can cite a tract published in 1614 under the title *De pace Germaniae*. The author, Adam Contzen, was one of the leading Jesuit theologians of the early seventeenth century in Germany. His *De pace* was first and foremost a savage attack on the Heidelberg theologian David Pareus and his attempt to build bridges between Lutherans and Calvinists (Pareus himself was a Calvinist) by minimizing the dogmatic differences between the two sides (Sarx 2010). For Contzen, however, who (like many Catholics) saw Lutheranism as the – just about – acceptable face of Protestant heresy but abhorred Calvin and his followers, the theological syncretism which Pareus propagated was deeply subversive: under the pretense of promoting peace and concord Pareus sowed the seeds of future conflict, undermining the stipulations of the Peace of Augsburg which had granted liberty of conscience only to Lutherans not to Calvinists. For Contzen, Pareus' syncretism was full of deceit; he called it "Machiavelli's disciple" (discipula Machiavelli) and "Epicure's daughter" (filia Epicuri). Such tricks of argument were a "plague to humankind" (pestis humanae societatis) and the "death of all real piety" (mors pietatis). As Contzen saw it, Calvinists like Pareus only pretended to seek peace and compromise; in reality they were fanatics who undermined the very foundations of the Holy Roman Empire and who should be expelled from its borders (Contzen 1616, 2, 430, 436–437).[19] So Contzen certainly did not mince his words when it came to reject Protestant attempts to find common ground for a trans-confessional political and theological dialog which would lead to a more enduring peace.

4. *Surviving in Confessional No Man's Land: The Precariousness of Conversion and Mediation*

The debates which were waged in Germany before 1618 regarding the potential insincerity and deviousness of confessional opponents and negotiating partners in fact followed a model which we can discern much earlier in similar debates in France and other countries. It was not just religious opponents who were mistrusted in these countries, but also – and perhaps to an even greater degree – those who desperately tried to broker some kind of modus vivendi between the warring camps. An example which immediately comes to mind here is the man who managed to end the Wars of Religion in France, Henri de Navarre, Henry IV of France. Admittedly the fact that he had changed his confessional allegiance more than once could easily create the impression that he was a

[18] In Christian theology, the term *irenicism* denotes literary efforts to unify Christian denominations dating back to the late sixteenth century (Stupperich, *Irenik*).

[19] See Bireley (1975).

complete cynic who did not take religion seriously at all. It is not therefore surprising that his last conversion in 1593, when he finally became a Catholic, was particularly controversial. Could this change of allegiance and conviction be taken seriously or was it merely a ploy to win the crown?

In this context Henry's suspected dissimulation became a serious issue in the debates about his legitimacy as king. According to the traditional French laws of dynastic inheritance based on the medieval *lex salica*, Henry had the best claim to the crown when in 1589 the last Valois, Henry III, was killed by an assassin. However, in 1589 Henry was a Protestant and had in 1585 been excommunicated by the Pope. Militant Catholics led by the house of Guise-Lorraine and organized in the Holy League insisted that a heretic could never become king in France, whatever his place in the succession to the crown was according to legal principles. However, when Henry converted to Catholicism in 1593, this situation changed, at least in the eyes of royalist Catholics who felt reassured by the fact that the Archbishop of Bourges had lifted the sentence of excommunication against Henry. And indeed two years later in 1595 the Pope himself confirmed this action and declared that Henry IV was now once more a legitimate member of the Roman Church (Wolfe 1993, Love 2001 and Cornette 2010).

Immediately after Henry IV's conversion, a number of tracts and pamphlets were published that called into question the sincerity of this sudden change of religious allegiance. The authors were mostly radical Catholics who continued to hope that an alliance with Spain would be strong enough to exclude the king of Navarre from the succession. Instead, some of them were prepared to accept even a non-French candidate – from Lorraine or Spain – or in extremis even a woman, for example a Spanish infanta, as successor to the crown (Asch 2014, 25–28).[20] Henry's followers were accused of acquiescing in being misled by the king's histrionics which offered them all the outward signs of Catholicism but not the real thing. The famous dialog between the *Courtier and the Peasant* (*Dialogue entre le Maheutre et le Manant*), which was written in about 1593/94, has the royalist nobleman say that for him it was quite sufficient when he saw the king taking part in the mass and behaving in all other respects like a true Catholic. It would be far too intrusive to explore the king's conscience, asking what beliefs he really held. Moreover, he had sworn an oath of allegiance to the king and as a nobleman he was honor bound to be true to his word as a loyal subject (Cromé 1977, 66 and 79). But the Manant, clearly supporting the Holy League, will have none of it. Since an oath sworn to a heretic was automatically null and void: "Un serment fait contre l'honneur de Dieu et de son Eglise n'est d'obligation et se peut dissoudre aisement" (Cromé 1977, 80). Not surprisingly we are here confronted by the old principle: *Haereticis fides non*

[20] See Ruiz Ibañez (1998).

servanda est, which would later trouble Christian II of Anhalt so much in his conversation with the imperial father confessor.[21]

Of course it may seem only logical to doubt the sincerity of Henry IV's conversion. After all, the king had for a long time been the supreme military leader of the Huguenots and even after his conversion he granted important privileges and almost full scale toleration to them. What made matters worse was his warlike foreign policy which was anti-Spanish throughout, and which he pursued by seeking alliances with Protestant princes and powers.[22] So it may have been unavoidable that militant Catholics did not trust their new king. However, for loyal royalists their very lack of trust made such Catholics themselves untrustworthy because they could never become 'good Frenchmen' (or for that matter good French women), that is 'bons Français' and patriots. The Leaguers angrily rejected this accusation. In their opinion the royalist catchword 'je suis bon Français' ('I am a good Frenchman') was just a pretense to justify a war against God and His church. According to Jean Boucher, a prominent ultra-Catholic theologian, the royalists should take care that the notion of 'bon Français' did not become devalued in the same way in which the concept of 'politique'[23] or the idea of belonging to the 'gens d'honneur' (the 'men of honor') had lost their original meaning. As Boucher wrote in the printed version of his *Sermons de la simulée conversion et nullité de la prétendue absolution de Henry de Bourbon* (1594, sermon no. 9, fol. 371v),[24] these terms had become mere bywords for self-serving opportunism. For Boucher allegiance to the Roman church always trumped patriotism. If the Leaguers were accused of being secretly Spaniards in their innermost thoughts and feelings, the 'politiques' were bound to accuse even the Pope if not indeed Christ himself of being pro-Spanish (Boucher 1594, sermon no.9, fol. 385v–386r). And what could be more preposterous than such an accusation?

Boucher's sermons were published after the king's official conversion, but we find a similar attitude among militant Catholics even before 1593. While Henry was still a Protestant he had already tried to win over moderate Catholics by a variety of concessions and promises. One of the most fanatical Catholic authors known under the name of Rossaeus, probably an Englishman exiled to France, was provoked by this policy to exhort his fellow Catholics not to trust the King of Navarre. In fact, he called for an assassin to kill the would-be king of France, just like Henry III. According to Rossaeus, the French Calvinists would

---

21 An oath sworn against God's honor and that of his church is not binding and can easily be nullified.

22 See Pitts (2009) for Henry's biography and Beiderbeck (2006) and Anderson (1999) for his foreign policy.

23 Though originally denoting those who were masters of the art of statecraft, 'politique' became the catchword for those who argued that confessional loyalties were of less importance than political allegiance in the later stages of the civil war.

24 See Racaut (2013).

never abandon their true objective – to exterminate all Catholics. They would consider killing the Catholics as their bounden duty and as morally right, since they saw the Catholic mass as an act of idolatry and those taking part in it as "Canaanites" and "Moabites" (Rossaeus 1592, 717).[25]

Despite these debates, the Holy League in 1594 could not prevent Henry IV's coronation in Chartres as king of France. Nevertheless, the new king throughout his reign kept being confronted by deep mistrust which militant Catholics continued to harbor against him. Their repeated attempts to remove the Bourbon king from the throne by assassinating him had their origin in this culture of suspicion. Eventually these attempts were successful when Ravaillac managed to kill the king in 1610 (Asch 2014, 32)[26] The fate of the first Bourbon king demonstrates that life in a world dominated by suspicion and mistrust was a dangerous one. To suspect Henry IV of insincerity and of playing a role he did not really identify with was of course a reaction which came natural to many Catholics, given Henry's support for Protestantism in the past and his continued friendship with Protestants. Moreover, after the end of the Wars of Religion Henry remained a ruler who tried to mediate between the hostile confessional camps both in France and in Europe. He remained a go-between between those who saw each other as enemies, he was also a man who dared to cross borders others considered as unbreachable. This behavior could easily place him in a religious and political no man's land. His attempt to demonstrate that he was a true Catholic now and his strategic self-fashioning focused on persuading others of this fact were ultimately unsuccessful (Asch 2014, 29–33).

To try to arrive at compromises and solutions acceptable to all sides was a risky business in a world dominated by religious conflict. It was all too easy to charge the mediator who tried to broker some kind of peace with double dealing, to depict him as a kind of double agent if not an outright traitor to his own side who concealed his rather dubious intentions. Henry IV was not the only politician of the early seventeenth century who saw himself confronted by such accusations. The Dutch statesman Oldenvanbarnevelt, advocate and pensionary of the province of Holland ('landsadvocaat'), suffered a similar fate. Oldenvanbarnevelt had been instrumental in bringing about the truce between Spain and the Dutch Republic in 1609, but militant Calvinists suspected him of being a secret supporter of the Spanish crown. Some even depicted him as a new Duke of Alba in sheep's clothing, (Alba in the Netherlands was of

[25] See page 686, where the author comes to the conclusion "principi haeretici etiam iuranti numquam esse credendum." For Rossaeus see also Valérian (2011). Valérian believes that the Benedictine priest William Gifford who became Archbishop of Reims in 1622 some years before his death has to be identified with Rossaeus, whereas other scholars consider William Reynolds an English theologian who died in 1594 in Antwerp as the author.

[26] See also Pitts (2009), 324–329, and Usunáriz (2017).

course the epitome of the Spanish tyrant who had terrorized the Netherlands in the late 1560s and early 1570s). On the instigation of his principal opponent Prince Maurice of Orange, the powerful commander-in-chief and Stadtholder, and during a period of intense religious unrest and political turmoil in 1618, the Advocate was arrested and executed as a traitor in 1619.[27]

Cardinal Klesl, who pursued a kind of 'Kompositionspolitik' (a policy which was meant to contain and decontaminate the festering political conflicts of the period) in the Holy Roman Empire, and who had started his career as a counter-reformation activist (see above) fell equally foul of the zealots within his own camp. Widely mistrusted, in 1618 he was taken prisoner on the orders of Archduke Ferdinand (the future emperor Ferdinand II) and Archduke Maximilian (Grand Master of the Teutonic Order and regent of Tyrol). Both considered Klesl as 'too soft' in his approach to the rebellion in Bohemia which had broken out in the spring of 1618. Trying hard to win the confidence of Protestants while retaining the trust of Catholics, the Cardinal had acquired a reputation for double-dealing, and was in the end mistrusted by both sides (Rainer 1961/62).[28]

5. *A Special Case? Fudged Ecclesiastical Compromises and the Search for Peace in England*

It has already been emphasized that in order to achieve some sort of modus vivendi between hostile confessional movements and churches both sides had to be prepared to show some self-restraint in demonstrating their conviction that they alone knew the correct way to eternal salvation. However, self-restraint was not always easy to distinguish from dissimulation and such dissimulation bred mistrust. We find such mistrust not only in relations between Protestants and Catholics but also within the same confessional church. This was particularly true for England in the late sixteenth and early seventeenth centuries. The entire Elizabethan church settlement of 1558/59 was based on a number of ambiguous compromise solutions regarding the structure of the church, the liturgy and even, though to a lesser degree, the confession of faith, the Thirty Nine Articles.[29]

This ambiguity originated in the very beginning of the English national church, in the Henrician Reformation. Was the Church of England a truly Protestant church, part of the wider community of reformed churches in Europe? Or was it at heart still part of the Catholic church, a national church which just refused to acknowledge the authority of the Bishop of Rome, preferring to

27 See Steen (2015, 63, 143–145); Israel (1995, 447–459); den Tex (1972, vol. II., 646–689).
28 See also Brockmann (2011, 45–48).
29 See Usher (2011); Collinson (2011); Haigh (1993), and Coffey/Lim (2008).

be governed by the king, or alternatively by the king in parliament, as a sort of secular pope? Admittedly, some of the strictly theological ambiguities were sorted out during the reign of Edward VI (1547–1553). The later confession of faith going back to these years, the Elizabethan 39 Articles which were based on the 42 Articles of 1553, was clearly Protestant in character, and influenced in particular by continental reformed theology as articulated by Zwingli, Calvin and other theologians. In practice, however, if we look at popular piety or the way church services were celebrated, the process of confessionalization for a long time remained a work in progress, if indeed this process was ever completed in England. The confessional profile of the Church of England continued to be less than definite, to some extent even beyond the seventeenth century.[30] For many believers the church of England was clearly a reformed church, with close ties to continental Calvinist communities and with a clear mission to fight 'popery' in all its forms. For others, however, the future of the church lay in pursuing a via media between the extremes, between Rome and Geneva, and was neither Popish nor Calvinist in character.

Elizabeth I deliberately pursued a policy which fudged these issues. Clear answers to questions regarding central theological problems were avoided rather than sought. This had, at least initially, the advantage that in the Church of England there continued to be room for secret Catholics who were prepared to accommodate themselves to the new ecclesiastical settlement, so-called "church Papists" (Walsham 1993). On the other hand, more radical Protestants could also for the time being come to terms with the official church, as long as there remained some hope of a 'further reformation.' Such radical Protestants considered the existing liturgy as problematic, as too 'popish,' and had often reservations about the position of bishops dominating church government while at the same time still exercising secular power. Like the church Papists, militant Protestants, often called Puritans, had to dissemble to find their place within the Elizabethan church, but mostly did so in the hope that the future would eventually belong to them (Walsham 2009, 188–226). Yet, such hopes waned near the end of the Elizabethan period. In the 1590s Puritans came under increasing political pressure. Ecclesiastical law courts, in particular the Court of High Commission, tried to force Puritan clergymen to confess that they actually rejected the Elizabethan church settlement – which would then entitle the High Commission to deprive them of their benefices. When they were asked, for example, whether they fully accepted the *Book of Common Prayer* as valid, without any major reservations, they had to incriminate themselves under oath, the so-called *ex officio oath*. In the past it had been enough not to protest too loudly against the official church settlement. When Puritan clergy evaded some of the rules and stipulations of the *Book of Common Prayer,* in

30 See Collinson (1994); Asch (2018).

practice this was often silently overlooked and went mostly unpunished. Such was now no longer the case, or not to the same extent as in the past. In other words, the widespread dissimulation, which for decades had concealed the real conflicts within the Elizabethan church, was no longer so easily tolerated or condoned (Shagan 2004).[31]

On their part, Puritans saw these proceedings as inquisitorial and as being in conflict with English Common Law (which was technically true, since the procedures of the High Commission were based on Roman Law rules unknown in Common Law courts). They compared them to the infamous Spanish inquisition. At the same time, they insisted that the real traitors within the Church of England, the church Papists, should be weeded out and persecuted much more energetically. Puritans were obsessed by the danger a possible Popish 'fifth column' present in church and state. In their view, secret Catholics were far more dangerous than those who openly confessed their Popish faith. Or, as one contemporary comment of the Apocalypse put it:

> And assuredly if the times should turne, (which God forbid) wee should finde the Church-Papist and the politicke conformable Pseudo-Catholicke, more mercilesse and blood-thirstie against us, then the Recusant. Though the best of theme, no doubt at that day, would bee [...] sharper then a thornie hedge, nay even as a woolfe in the evening (Bernard 1617, "Preface to the Justices of the Peace," To the Justices, before sign. B. 4., no pagination)[32]

Such comments show that the religious dissembler, the hypocrite or secret traitor was a figure who could at times provoke more fear and apprehension than the religious opponent who openly demonstrated his hostility.

Confessional compromises which left too much room for dissimulation and insincerity in religious matters were therefore seen as extremely dangerous. Nevertheless, the Church of England continued to leave much room for confessional ambiguity right up to the outbreak of the Civil War. Yet it was this very ambiguity and the many fudged compromises which were part of the official church settlement that created an atmosphere of suspicion and mutual mistrust. In the long run, these undermined the peaceful cohabitation of different communities and movements within the church of England, as Alexandra Walsham has pointed out:

> By creating conditions in which dissimulation and clandestinity could flourish, it [the Elizabethan settlement, RGA] [...] stimulated anxieties which culminated in the conviction that radical constitutional measures and military action had to be taken to prevent English Protestantism from being undermined from within. (Walsham 2009, 300–301)[33]

---

31 See also Collinson (2013).

32 See Asch (2007b), and for anti-Popery in general Alvarez Recio (2011), and Marotti (2005).

33 For the notion of confessional ambiguity see Pietsch/Stollberg-Rilinger (2013).

6. *Conclusion*

Dissimulation, the decision to hide one's own convictions, could take many forms in the religious and political conflicts of the late sixteenth and early seventeenth centuries. On the one hand, we encounter pragmatic politicians, the 'politici,' who deliberately evaded theological controversies, because otherwise any meaningful dialog with the opposing side would have remained impossible. On the other hand, there were also members of religious minorities who – under the threat of persecution – concealed their beliefs and loyalties so that they could still, in secret, practice their religion. The various types of mistrust presented themselves in a number of different forms. The confessional opponent was by definition mistrusted. One assumed that he would, whenever this seemed convenient, ignore all treaties and promises, arguing that one should obey God rather than men and human conventions. While Protestants became particularly suspicious whenever Jesuits were involved on the other side, because they seemed to be the very epitome of cunning and deviousness (Ziegler 2017b, 67–73) Catholics saw Calvinists as particularly dangerous and treacherous.[34] Yet the *politici* who tried to mediate between the opposing sides were equally mistrusted by almost everybody. In the name of peace or patriotism they seemed to call into question the very legitimacy of the frontiers between the hostile confessional groups, frontiers which had been laboriously constructed by theologians and churchmen ever since the mid-sixteenth century. In an age when the emerging confessional identities were still fragile and precarious in their stability, the mediators and pragmatists seeking compromises could easily appear as cynical politicians who were about to fatally weaken if not to destroy these new identities.

This general confessional climate of distrust and suspicion was reinforced by contemporary political theory heavily influenced by Tacitism and the legacy of Machiavelli's writings. Moreover, for the very reason that men and women were under enormous pressure both at court and in the church to show that they respected higher authorities and the rules imposed on them from above while demonstrating complete conformity with the prevailing orthodoxies in word and deed, deception became an increasingly urgent issue. One could, after all, never be sure that outward conformity was more than a mere performance. In reference to the court, but also to wider social relations, a contemporary English tract on friendship came to the conclusion that "[…] flatterie is now so common that almost every illiterate peasant can represent like a looking-glasse what mans quallities and conditions he will" (M.B. (1596, preface, fol. B 1 v.).

This widespread fear that everybody one was dealing with was entirely insincere, a mere flatterer or dissembler, produced a frantic search for real

[34] See Ziegler (2017b, 178–180), regarding Caspar Schoppe.

authenticity and sincerity, often, though not exclusively, fueled by religious or confessional zeal (Martin 1997, 1330–1335). At the end of the day, the prevailing climate of suspicion, and the assumption that wherever one looked one was confronted by hypocrisy and deceit, threatened to render futile all attempts to achieve lasting compromise solutions either in politics or in religious conflicts. From that perspective, one can argue that dissimulation and lack of trust were phenomena that influenced all political and social relations in the late sixteenth and early seventeenth centuries; they were, in fact, a distinctive mark of the age.

Works Cited

Primary Sources

Anhalt, Christian II. von (2013–2020) *Digitale Edition und Kommentierung der Tagebücher des Fürsten Christian II. von Anhalt-Bernburg [1599–1656]*. Ed. Ronald G. Asch, Peter Burschel, Arndt Schreiber, Alexander Zirr, und Andreas Herz. Wolfenbüttel: Herzog August Bibliothek. Web. 16 Nov. 2020. <https://diglib.hab.de/edoc/ed000228/start.htm>.

B., M. [no complete name] (1596) *The Triall of True Friendship*. London: Valentine.

Bernard, Richard (1617) *A Key of Knowledge for the Opening of the Secret Mysteries of St. Johns Mysticall Revelation*. London: Felix Kyngston.

Blount, Edward (1607) Trans. *Ars Aulica, or the Courtiers Art*. [Lorenzo Ducci, *Arte Aulica* (1601)]. London: Melch. Bradwood.

Boucher, Jean (1594) *Sermons de la simulee conversion et nullité de la pretendue absolution de Henry de Bourbon, Prince de Bearn, à S. Denys en France, le Dimanche 25* Juillet, 1593. *[...]. Par Me Jean Boucher docteur en theologie.* Paris: Chaudiere, Nivelle, Thierry.

Burgkardus, Franciscus [pseudonym for Andreas Erstenberger] (1602) *De Autonomia von der Freystellung mehrerley Religion und Glaube,* 3 vols. [1586]. München: Adam Berg.

Chroust, Anton (1909) Ed. *Briefe und Akten zur Geschichte des Dreißigjährigen Krieges in den Zeiten des vorwaltenden Einflusses der Wittelsbacher*, Bd. XI, *Der Reichstag von 1613*, München: Verlag der M. Rieger'schen Universitäts-Buchhandlung (G. Himmer).

Contzen, Adam (1616) *De Pace Germaniae libri duo*. Mainz: Bernard Gualther.

Cromé, François (1977) *Dialogue d'entre le maheustre et le manant*, Ed. Peter M. Ascoli. Genf: Librairie Droz.

Hammer-Purgstall, Josef Freiherr von (1847/1851) *Khlesl's, des Cardinals, Directors des geheimen Cabinetes Kaisers Mathias, Leben*, 4 Bde. Wien: Kaulfuss.

Lipsius, Justus (1998) *De Constantia – von der Standhaftigkeit*, Ed. Florian Neumann. Mainz: Dieterich.

Rossaeus, Guilelmus (1592) *De iusta rei publicae Christianae in reges impios et haereticos authoritate*. Antwerp: Keerbergius.

Schoppe, Caspar (1619) *Casparii Scioppii consilarii regii classicum belli sacri sive Heldus redivivus*. Ticini: Petri Bartholi.

Tacitus, Publius Cornelius (1574) *Historiarum et annalium libri qui exstant [...] Liber de moribus Germanorum*. Iulii Agricolae vita, Ed. Justus Lipsius. Antwerp: Christophorus Plantin.

Secondary Sources

Albrecht, Dieter (1998) *Maximilian I. von Bayern*, 1573–1651. München: Oldenbourg.

Alvarez Recio, Leticia (2011) *Fighting the Antichrist. A Cultural History of Anti-Catholicism in Tudor England*. Brighton: Sussex Academic Press.

Anderson, Alison Deborah (1999) *On the Verge of War. International Relations and the Jülich-Kleve Succession Crises (1609–1614)*. Boston: Humanities Press.

Angermeier, Heinz (1993) "Politik, Religion und Reich bei Kardinal Melchior Khlesl." *Zeitschrift der Savigny-Stiftung für Rechtsgeschichte, Germ. Abt. 110*: 249–330.

Asch, Ronald G. (2007a) "Der Höfling als Heuchler? Unaufrichtigkeit, Konversationsgemeinschaft und Freundschaft am frühneuzeitlichen Hof." *Krumme Touren. Anthropologie kommunikativer Umwege*. Ed. Wolfgang Reinhard. Wien: Böhlau. 183–203.

Asch, Ronald G. (2007b) "The Revelation of the Revelation. Die Bedeutung der Offenbarung des Johannes für das englische politische Denken im späten 16. und frühen 17. Jahrhundert." *Die Bibel als politisches Argument* (*Historische Zeitschrift*, Beiheft 43). Ed. Andreas Pečar and Kai Trampedach. München: Oldenbourg. 315–332.

Asch, Ronald G. (2014) *Sacral Kingship between Disenchantment and Re-enchantment. The French and English Monarchies 1587–1688*. New York: Berghahn.

Asch, Ronald G. (2018) "Die Reformation und die politische Kultur Englands in der Frühen Neuzeit." *Deutschland und die britischen Inseln im Reformationsgeschehen*. Ed. Frank Lothar Kroll, et al. Berlin: Duncker & Humblot. 135–158.

Asch, Ronald G. (2020) *Vor dem großen Krieg. Europa im Zeitalter der spanischen Friedensordnung, 1598–1618*. Darmstadt: Wissenschaftliche Buchgesellschaft.

Beiderbeck, Friedrich (2005) *Zwischen Religionskrieg, Reichskrise und europäischem Hegemoniekampf. Heinrich IV. von Frankreich und die Protestantischen Reichsstände*. Berlin: Berliner Wissenschafts-Verlag.

Bireley, Robert (1975) *Maximilian von Bayern, Adam Contzen S. J. und die Gegenreformation in Deutschland 1624 – 1635*. Göttingen: Vandenhoeck & Ruprecht.

Bireley, Robert (1981) *Religion and Politics in the Age of the Counterreformation. Emperor Ferdinand II, William Lamormaini, S. J. and the Formation of Imperial Policy*. Chapel Hill: North Carolina Univ. Press.

Bouwsma, William J. (2000) *The Waning of the Renaissance 1550–1640.* New Haven: Yale Univ. Press.

Braun, Harald E. (2011) "Justus Lipsius and the Challenges of Historical Exemplarity." *(Un)masking the Realities of Power. Justus Lipsius and the Dynamics of Political Writing in Early Modern Europe*. Ed. Erik de Bom. Leiden: Brill. 135–162.

Brendle, Franz (2009) "Der Religionskrieg und seine Dissimulation. Die 'Verteidigung des wahren Glaubens' im Reich des konfessionellen Zeitalters." *Krieg und Christentum. Religiöse Gewalttheorien in der Kriegserfahrung des Westens*. Ed. Andreas Holzem. Paderborn: Schöningh. 457–470.

Brockmann, Thomas (2011) *Dynastie, Kaiseramt und Konfession. Politik und Ordnungsvorstellungen Ferdinands II. im Dreißigjährigen Krieg*. Paderborn: Schöningh.

Cavaillé, Jean-Pierre (2002) *Dis/simulations. Jules-César Vanini, François La Mothe Le Vayer, Gabriel Naudé, Lous Machon et Torquato Accetto. Religion, Morale et Politique au XVIIe siècle*. Paris: Champion.

Coffey, John, and John C. H. Lim (2008) Ed. *The Cambridge Companion to Puritanism*. Cambridge: Cambridge Univ. Press.

Collinson, Patrick (1994) "The Cohabitation of the Faithful with the Unfaithful." *From Persecution to Toleration. The Glorious Revolution and Religion in England*. Ed. Ole Peter Grell, Jonathan Israel and Nicholas Tyacke. Oxford: Clarendon Press. 51–76.

Collinson, Patrick (2011) "The Politics of Religion and the Religion of Politics in Elizabethan England." *This England. Essays on the English Nation and Commonwealth in the Sixteenth Century*. Ed. Patrick Collinson. Manchester: Manchester Univ. Press. 36–60.

Collinson, Patrick (2013) *Richard Bancroft and Elizabethan Anti-Puritanism*. Cambridge: Cambridge Univ. Press.

Compatato, Vitto Ivo, and Diego Quaglioni (2007) "Italy." *European Political Thought 1450–1700. Religion, Law and Philosophy*. Ed. Glenn Burgess, Simon Hodson and Howell A. Lloyd. New Haven: Yale Univ. Press. 55–101.

Cornette, Joël (2010) *Henri IV à Saint-Denis. De l'Abjuration à la Profanation*, Paris: Belin.

Crouzet, Denis (1998) *La Sagesse et le Malheur. Michel de L'Hospital, Chancelier de France*. Seyssel: Champ Vallon.

den Tex, Jan (1972) *Oldenbarnevelt*. 2 vols. Cambridge: Cambridge Univ. Press.

Eliav-Feldon Miriam, and Tamar Herzig (2015) Ed. *Dissimulation and Deceit in Early Modern Europe*. Basingstoke: Palgrave Macmillan.

Gajda, Alexandra (2009) "Tacitus and Political Thought in Early Modern Europe." *The Cambridge Companion to Tacitus*. Ed. A. J. Woodman. Cambridge: Cambridge Univ. Press. 253–268.

Gajda, Alexandra (2016) "The Gordian Knot of Policy. Statecraft and the Prudent Prince." *The Oxford Handbook of the Age of Shakespeare*. Ed. R. Malcolm Smuts. Oxford: Oxford Univ. Press. 286–305.

Gotthard, Axel (2004) *Der Augsburger Religionsfrieden*. Münster: Aschendorff.

Gotthard, Axel (2007) "'Sey ein durchgeend werkh wider die Evangelische.' Bedrohungsszenarien in lutherischen Ratsstuben." *Konfessioneller Fundamentalismus. Religion als politischer Faktor im europäischen Mächtesystem um 1600*. Ed. Heinz Schilling. München: Oldenbourg. 209–234.

Haigh, Christopher (1993) *English Reformations. Religion, Politics and Society under the Tudors*. Oxford: Clarendon Press.

Hinz, Manfred (1992) *Rhetorische Strategien des Hofmannes. Studien zu den italienischen Hofmannstraktaten des 16. und 17. Jahrhunderts*. Stuttgart: Metzler.

Israel, Jonathan (1995) *The Dutch Republic. Its Rise, Greatness and Fall, 1477–1806*. Oxford: Clarendon Press.

Jaitner, Klaus (2004) "Einleitung." *Kaspar Schoppe, Autobiographische Texte und Briefe, Band I, Philotheca Scioppiana, eine frühneuzeitliche Autobiographie, 1576–1630*. Band 1. Ed. Klaus Jaitner. München: Beck. 1–230.

Johnson, James H. (2011) *Venice Incognito. Masks in the Serene Republic*. Berkeley: California Univ. Press.

Johnston, Rona (2003) "Melchior Khlesl und der konfessionelle Hintergrund der kaiserlichen Politik im Reich nach 1610." *Dimensionen der europäischen Außenpolitik zur Zeit der Wende vom 16. Zum 17. Jahrhundert*. Ed. Friedrich Beiderbeck, et. al. Berlin: Berliner Wissenschafts-Verlag. 199–222.

Kim, Marie Seong-Hak (1997) *Michel de L'Hôpital. The Vision of a Reformist Chancellor During the French Religious Wars*. Kirksville: Truman State Univ. Press.

Lindberg, Bo (2011) "Stoicism in Political Humanism and Natural Law." *(Un)masking the Realities of Power. Justus Lipsius and the Dynamics of Political Writing in Early Modern Europe*. Ed. Erik de Bom. Leiden: Brill. 76–91.

Lloyd, Howell A. (2017) *Jean Bodin, 'This Pre-Eminent Man of France.' An Intellectual Biography*. Oxford: Oxford Univ. Press.

Love, Ronald S. (2001) *Blood and Religion. The Conscience of Henry IV, 1553–1593*. Montreal: McGill-Queen's Univ. Press

Marotti, Arthur F. (2005) *Religious Ideology and Cultural Fantasy. Catholic and anti-Catholic Discourses in Early Modern England*. Notre Dame: Notre Dame Univ. Press.

Martin, John Jeffries (1997) "Inventing Sincerity, Refashioning Prudence. The Discovery of the Individual in Renaissance Europe." *American Historical Review* 102: 1309–1342.

Martin, John Jeffries (2004) *Myths of Renaissance Individualism*. Basingstoke: Palgrave Macmillan.

Meyer, Anette, and Cornel Zwierlein (2010) Ed. *Machiavellismus in Deutschland. Chiffre von Kontingenz, Herrschaft und Empirismus in der Neuzeit*. München: Oldenbourg.

Miernowski, Jan (2002) "'Politique' comme injure dans les pamphlets au temps des guerres de Religion." *De Michel de l'Hospital à l'édit de Nantes. Politique et religion face aux églises*. Ed. Thierry Wanegffelen. Clermont-Ferrand: Presses Université Blasie Pascal. 337–356.

Morford, Mark (1993) "Tacitean Prudentia and the Doctrines of Justus Lipsius." *Tacitus and the Tacitean Tradition*. Ed. T. J. Luce and A. J. Woodman. Princeton: Princeton Univ. Press. 129–151.

Mulsow, Martin (2003) "Mehrfachkonversion, politische Religion und Opportunismus im 17. Jahrhundert – ein Plädoyer für die Indifferentismusforschung." *Interkonfessionalität – Transkonfessionalität – binnenkonfessionelle Pluralität. Neue Forschungen zur Konfessionsthese*. Ed. Kaspar von Greyerz, et al. Gütersloh: Gütersloher Verlagshaus. 132–150.

Oestreich, Gerhard (1989) *Antiker Geist und moderner Staat bei Justus Lipsius (1547–1606) – der Neustoizismus als politische Bewegung*. Ed. Nicolette Mout. Göttingen: Vandenhoeck & Ruprecht.

Pietsch, Andreas, and Barbara Stollberg-Rilinger (2013) Ed. *Konfessionelle Ambiguität. Uneindeutigkeit und Verstellung als religiöse Praxis in der Frühen Neuzeit*. Gütersloh: Gütersloher Verlagshaus.

Pitts, Vincent J. (2009) *Henri IV of France. His Reign and Age*. Baltimore: Johns Hopkins Univ. Press.

Racaut, Luc (2013) "'La boutique de malédiction.' Jean Boucher et l'hypocrisie." *Œuvres & Critiques* 38. 2: 83–94.

Rainer, Johann (1961/62) "Der Prozeß gegen Kardinal Klesl." *Römische Historische Mitteilungen* 5: 35–163.

Ruiz Ibañez, José Javier (1998) "Les choix du roi. Les limites de l'intervention espagnole en France 1592–1598." *La Paix* de Vervins. [1598] Ed. Frédérique Pilleboue and Claudine Vidal. Amiens: Fédération des Sociétés d'Histoire et d'Archéologie de l'Aisne. 139–160.

Sarx, Tobias (2010) "Die Heidelberger Irenik am Vorabend des Dreißigjährigen Krieges." *Union und Liga 1608/09. Konfessionelle Bündnisse im Reich – Weichenstellung zum Religionskrieg?* Ed. Albrecht Ernst and Anton Schindling. Stuttgart: Kohlhammer. 167–196.

Schmidt, Alexander (2007) *Vaterlandsliebe und Religionskonflikt. Politische Diskurse im Alten Reich (1555–1648)*. Leiden: Brill.

Shagan, Ethan H. (2004) "The English Inquisition. Constitutional Conflict and Ecclesiastical Law in the 1590s." *The Historical Journal* 47. 541–565.

Sierhuis, Freya (2013) "Autonomy and Inner Freedom: Lipsius and the Revival of Neostoicism." *Freedom and the Construction of Europe. Free Persons and Free States*. 2 vols. Ed. Martin van Gelderen and Quentin Skinner. Vol. 2. Cambridge: Cambridge Univ. Press. 46–64.

Skinner, Quentin (2002) "Classical Liberty and the Coming of the English Civil War." *Republicanism. A Shared European Heritage*. 2 vols. Ed. Martin van Gelderen and Quentin Skinner. Vol. 2. Cambridge: Cambridge Univ. Press. 9–28.

Snyder, Jon R. (2009) *Dissimulation and the Culture of Secrecy in Modern Europe*. Berkeley: California Univ. Press.

Sommerville, Johann P. (1988) "The New Art of Lying. Equivocation, Mental Reservation and Casuistry." *Conscience and Casuistry in Early Modern Europe*. Ed. E. Leites, et. al. Cambridge: Cambridge Univ. Press. 159–188.

van der Steen, Jasper Andreas (2015) *Memory Wars in the Low Countries, 1566–1700*. Leiden: Leiden Univ. Press.

Stupperich, Robert (n.d.) "Irenik." *Historisches Wörterbuch der Philosophie Online*. N. d. Web. 16 Nov. 2020. <https://www.schwabeonline.ch/schwabe-xaveropp/elibrary/start.xav?start=%2F%2F*%5B%40attr_id%3D%27verw.irenik%27%20and%20%40outline_id%3D%27hwph_verw.irenik%27%5D.>

Tuck, Richard (1993) *Philosophy and Government, 1572–1651*. Cambridge: Cambridge Univ. Press.

Usher, Brett (2011) "New Wine into Old Bottles. The Doctrine and Structure of the Elizabethan Church." *The Elizabethan World*. Ed. Susan Doran and Norman Jones. London: Routledge. 203–221.

Usunáriz, Jesús Maria (2017) "L'assassinat d'Henri IV et les Publicistes Espagnoles du XVIIe siècle." *Régicides en France et en Europe (XVIe–XIXe siècles)*. Ed. Isabelle Pébay-Clottes, et al. Genf: Librairie Droz. 255–280.

Valérian, François (2011) *Un Prêtre Anglais Contre Henri IV. Archéologie d'une Haine Religieuse*. Paris: Éditions L'Harmattan.

Walsham, Alexandra (1993) *Church Papists. Catholicism, Conformity and Confessional Polemic in Early Modern England*. Woodbridge: Boydell Press.

Walsham, Alexandra (2009) *Charitable Hatred. Tolerance and Intolerance in England, 1500–1700*. Manchester: Manchester Univ. Press.

Waszink, Jan (2004) "Introduction." *Justus Lipsius Politica. Six Books of Politics or Political Instruction*. Ed. Jan Waszink. Assen: Van Gorcum. 3–203.

Wolfe, Michael (1993) *The Conversion of Henri IV. Politics, Power and Religious Belief in Early Modern France*. Cambridge: Harvard Univ. Press.

Zagorin, Perez (1990) *Ways of Lying. Dissimulation, Persecution, and Conformity in Early Modern Europe*. Cambridge: Harvard Univ. Press.

Ziegler, Hannes (2017a) "Privy Council Deliberations on Trust. The Holy Roman Empire around 1600." *Trust and Happiness in the History of European Political Thought*. Ed. László Kontler and Mark Somos. Leiden, Boston: Brill. 281–301.

Ziegler, Hannes (2017b) *Trauen und Glauben. Vertrauen in der politischen Kultur des Alten Reiches im Konfessionellen Zeitalter*. Affalterbach: Didymos-Verlag.

Truth, Lies, and the Good Life in Michel de Montaigne, Madeleine de Scudéry, and Several Others

Dallas G. Denery II

1. Montaigne on Truth-Telling and Lies

Never one to take the direct path when he could meander instead, Michel de Montaigne (1533–1592) begins his essay "Of Liars" reflecting on the nature of memory – actually, on the nature of his own memory. It is, he informs us, terrible. He forgets names and promises so often that people accuse him of lacking heart and conscience. But this isn't fair. If he is good at anything, he claims, it is being a friend, and he wishes that people would simply accept his "infirmity, without making it into a sort of malice" so alien to his true nature (Montaigne 1965, 22).

Then again, he adds, lacking a good memory has its advantages. It places a hedge against vain ambition and strengthens one's faculty of judgment. Why bother to engage in negotiations to improve his lot when he knows full well he will have forgotten all his promises within days? And as for his powers of judgment? Unable to recall the opinions of others, he is daily compelled to think for himself. More, he knows many people whose memories are so overloaded with details and circumstances that whenever they tell a story, they quickly lose the thread, wandering off into alleys and avenues that no one cares to visit. Perhaps Montaigne remembers little, but his speech is all the better for it, briefer and more direct (Montaigne 1965, 22–23).

And, as it turns out, more honest.

There is, Montaigne continues, no point in bothering to tell lies if you can't remember them. You will trip yourself up sooner or later, expose yourself and your deceit. People seem to envy the prudent who shape their words to please the powerful, calling the same thing gray now and yellow later. But this praise seems too quickly given. How successful can these lies be if we recognize the prudence at work behind them? Simpler not to lie at all than to entangle oneself and one's reputation in such disreputable behavior. "In truth," Montaigne asserts, "lying is an accursed vice" (Montaigne 1965, 23).

Montaigne draws a distinction between "giving a lie" and "lying." The difference hinges on what the speaker thinks. We "give a lie" when we speak a falsehood but believe it to be true. In other words, we believe we are being honest and forthright even though our words are false. By contrast, we lie when we speak against our conscience, when we state something that we believe is false (Montaigne 1965, 23). This is an important distinction for Montaigne. Although he leaves it implied, as he leaves so much so often implied throughout his essays, his friends and acquaintances must have often thought him a liar – regularly breaking promises, failing to live up to commitments, or misstating past events – simply because he had innocently forgotten them. Montaigne, despite his desire to be forthright and sincere in his dealings with others, may well appear no different than the duplicitous and deceitful, and appearances matter.

We are neither angels nor God able to perceive directly to the truth of things. We are, Montaigne notes in another essay, "Of the Art of Discussion," merely men "and it is a wonder how physical [our] nature is." Our judgments depend upon our senses which "perceive things only by their external accidents," only by their appearances. This applies not only to the natural world, but the civil world as well. We would be foolish to deny the extent to which society and government depend upon appearances – ceremonies, signs and symbols. Consider the case of religion. The reformers tried to construct a religious system "all contemplative and spiritual," stripped of Catholic imagery, ritual, and order. Perhaps this appeals to some people, but not all, and without something solid to look at and hold on to, without "mark, title, and instrument of division and faction," without pope, cardinal, bishop, priest, monk, and layperson, it slips through their fingers, intangible and ungraspable. Though we are more than our bodies, we are never not our bodies (Montaigne 1965, 710).

Montaigne returns to the question of lying and dissimulation repeatedly throughout his book of essays because it allows him to dig ever deeper into the nature of our humanity and existence, into the ever-fluid distinction between inside and outside, appearance and reality, surface and depth, body and soul. He repeatedly asserts the importance of being truthful and honest, even as he wonders what exactly it means to be truthful. "We are men," he writes at one point, "and hold together, only by our word. If we recognized the horror and the gravity of lying, we would persecute it with fire more justly than other crimes" (Montaigne 1965, 23). In "Of Presumption," he asserts that "truth is the first and fundamental part of virtue" and that we serve it well, when we serve it for itself, not because it earns us praise or honor, but simply because we love it (Montaigne 1965, 491).

But serving truth is difficult and being true to ourselves complicated. Those very trappings and rituals, coverings and distinctions of status, so necessary for holding society together, can lead us away from ourselves: "We are nothing but ceremony," he writes in "Of Presumption," "ceremony carries us away, and we leave the substance of things; we hang on to the branches and abandon the trunk and body" (Montaigne 1965, 478–479). We are taught to act ashamed in public of activities we indulge in when alone and we bow respectfully to people we abhor. We hide our thoughts, while saying only what others want to hear. This sort of deception is so common among the French, Montaigne contends in another essay, that it is no longer considered a vice, but merely a "manner of speaking and, perhaps, even a type of virtue." "Men," he writes, "form and fashion themselves for [lying] as if it were an honorable practice, for dissimulation is among the most notable qualities of the century." (Montaigne 1965, 505)

Montaigne is particularly interested in how we form and fashion ourselves and this lends his comments on lying particular significance. In an opening address to his future readers, Montaigne famously explains that he is the subject of his essays, truthfully presented, warts and all. Had he been raised among those more innocent people of the New World who still exist "in the sweet freedom of nature's first laws," he would have gladly portrayed himself wholly naked. Unfortunately, he was born in France, and so the covering begins (Montaigne 1965, 2). He takes up the topic of clothing again in "Of the Custom of Wearing Clothes." He finds it incredible to imagine that God would have created us naked if our nakedness would have made it difficult for us to survive. All creatures, he asserts, "are naturally equipped with sufficient covering to defend themselves against the injury of weather." If we wear clothes, it is merely due to custom and that custom has changed us into the sort of beings who now cannot live without clothing and coverings. We are what we wear and styles change with the season (Montaigne 1965, 167).

He explains this notion of change more fully in one of his best-known essays, "Of Giving the Lie," when he asks, "If no one reads me, have I wasted my time, entertaining myself for so many idle hours with such useful and agreeable thoughts?" The answer, of course, is "No" because the very writing of the book has made him who he is. Here is Montaigne's explanation in full because no paraphrase can do it justice:

> In modeling this figure upon myself, I have had to fashion and compose myself so often to bring myself out, that the model itself has to some extent grown firm and taken shape. Painting myself for others, I have painted my inward self in colors clearer than my original ones. I have no more made my book than my book has made me – a book consubstantial with its author, concerned with my own self, an integral part of my life; not concerned with some third-hand, extraneous purpose like other books. Have I wasted my time by taking stock of myself so continually, so carefully? For those who go over themselves only in their minds and occasionally in speech do not penetrate to essentials in their examination as does a man who makes that his study, his work, and his trade, who binds himself to keep an enduring account, with all his faith, with all his strength. (Montaigne 1965, 504)

> Moulant sur moy cette figure, il m'a fallu si souvent me testonner et composer, pour m'extraire, que le patron s'en est fermy, et aucunement formé soy-mesme. Me peignant pour autruy, je me suis peint en moy, de couleurs plus nettes, que n'estoyent les miennes premieres. Je n'ay pas plus faict mon livre, que mon livre m'a faict. Livre consubstantiel à son autheur: D'une occupation propre: Membre de ma vie: Non d'une occupation et fin, tierce et estrangere, comme tous autres livres. Ay-je perdu mon

> temps, de m'estre rendu compte de moy, si continuellement; si curieusement? Car ceux qui se repassent par fantasie seulement, et par langue, quelque heure, ne s'examinent pas si primement, ny ne se penetrent, comme celuy, qui en fait son estude, son ouvrage, et son mestier: qui s'engage à un registre de durée, de toute sa foy, de toute sa force. (Montaigne 2007, 703–704)

Whatever else we might think about the model in question, it is not static, painted once and captured forever. Descartes would later claim that the truth of the self was the cogito, the thinking thing, a truth once grasped, forever held. Montaigne, instead, describes a process or practice interested more in truthfulness than in truth. As we reflect upon ourselves, we change and so we must now reflect on our changed self. What matters, he observes in "Of Repentance," is the effort we make at being faithful to what we see, the externals, the appearances, even as we realize we can never move beyond them (Montaigne 1965, 610–611; Martin 2013, 960).

This task is difficult to achieve because a million little things constantly distract us from it and lead us away from ourselves. Rules of etiquette and ceremony train us to misrepresent ourselves. Montaigne confesses that "civility and reason" sometimes restrain him from saying what he thinks in public, but he disgorges his thoughts at home, repairing the damage done to his virtue (Montaigne 1965, 504). If truth really is a social bond, the very first such bond is the one that binds us to ourselves; on this all other bonds are secured. This is another reason Montaigne begins his essay "Of Lying" with a discussion of memory. Without a memory to help distance himself from the present, Montaigne is all the more forced to consider himself in the here and now. What matters is frankness. Montaigne is frank about what he sees within himself, while simultaneously aware that every seeing is provisional and limited (Leushuis 2009, 110).

We are always in a process of development and what we do shapes who we are. Our lies transform us no less than our truthfulness. Montaigne suggests this in all sorts of ways. People who counterfeit being sick often become sick, and conversation with weak and disorderly minds acts like a contagion on our own (Montaigne 1965, 704). We can even lie to ourselves. The vainglorious carelessly misjudge themselves and those they love, misrepresenting themselves to themselves and others. It is not so much that we are evil, but inane; not wretched, but worthless. And this means we are always too eager to misrepresent ourselves to ourselves and to others, to lie and dissimulate (Montaigne 1965, 221).

Montaigne's thoughts about lying and truthfulness are inextricably tied up with this skepticism and his belief that the truth of things themselves is forever beyond us. The soul, he notes in "Of Democritus and Heraclitus," "treats a matter not according to itself, but according to herself" (Montaigne 1965, 220). Perhaps things have stable qualities, but we can't know them. We know only what we perceive and the soul shapes what we see as she sees fit. Incapable of moving beyond appearances, the only honest thing for us to do is to accept them, experience them, and examine them. Our situation requires frankness, not cleverness. Cleverness is the quality of those who think there is something beyond appearances, who double them up with dissimulations, talk of universals, and aspirations of glory. To be clever is to be duplicitous, and to be duplicitous is to be a liar (Schreiner 2003, 357–367). The good life is less a truth to be achieved, than a way of existing that allows a person to be whole and wholly at home with their experience.

2. *Thinking About Lying From Augustine to the Scholastics*

Montaigne's conception of truth, lying, and the good life is not everyone's, not least because there is no place for God in it. That lack of God is important. It helps us place Montaigne's ideas in a trajectory of thinking about lying that extends from Augustine (c. 354–430) in the early fifth century to the scholastics of the later Middle Ages, and from there on to the Enlightenment.

The superficial aspects of Augustine's thinking are rather well known. Augustine was among the first to raise the famous example of the killer at the door. Is it acceptable to lie about the whereabouts of an innocent man when unjust persecutors, threatening the man with death, come pounding at your door demanding you tell them where he is? Augustine's answer was an adamant, "No." As far as Augustine is concerned, the Bible speaks as if with one voice when it condemns deceit. Quoting Paul's letter to the Romans, Augustine writes, "Thou hatest all the workers of iniquity; thou wilt destroy all that speak a lie." The prohibition could hardly be clearer, Augustine contends, could hardly be more absolute (Augustine 1952, 171–172).

Never questioning this exceptionless prohibition against lying, Augustine does try to explain it and to explain why God places it at the center of a life of human excellence. He does this most fully in *On the Trinity*. Reflecting on the opening lines of John's gospel, he points out that it imagines the essence of God and the nature of creation as a series of speech acts – "In the beginning was the Word, and the Word was with God and the Word was God," and later, "And the Word became flesh and lived among us, and we have seen his glory, the glory as of a father's only son, full of grace and truth." Reflecting on these lines, Augustine discerns a model for proper speech and proper action. God's creative words are complete and true, the speaker fully and truthfully reflected in its utterance, the Father equal to the Word and both equal to the Word made Flesh. "The beginning of every work is the word," Augustine writes, and just as God made all things through "His only begotten word, so there are no works of man which are not first spoken in the heart." The Word was made flesh, he argues, to serve us as an example of how to live, "that we might have no lie either in the contemplation or in the work of our word" (Augustine 2002, 189). Every lie is a sin because, fundamentally, every sin is a lie, every sin takes the form of a lie in which our words and deeds do not reflect what we really are, beings created in the image of God who is Truth.

Every lie might be a sin, but Augustine recognized that not all lies are equal. In an earlier treatise, "On Lying," he catalogued eight different kinds of lies, ranking them from most to least sinful. The details needn't detain us because the details didn't much detain Augustine. In the final analysis, he argued that we must never risk entering into the moral calculus of weighing our lies against their perceived benefits. In a moment of weakness, we might lie without forethought in order to save a friend's life. Perhaps God will forgive us, perhaps he won't. But we should never lie with the expectation that he will forgive us because we acted with good intentions. For Augustine, lies only incidentally concern the world. Lies are sinful because they sever our relation to God who is Truth. Every lie is, first and foremost, a lie against God. It is God who is the aggrieved party, not the person to whom we lie (Augustine 1952, 165–166).

Although theologians from the twelfth to the fourteenth centuries repeatedly assert their allegiance to Augustine's ideas about lying, their allegiance was relatively superficial. While they unanimously affirm that every lie is a sin, they seem entirely unaware of the trinitarian foundations for Augustine's prohibition. The Dominican theologian Thomas Aquinas (c.1225–1274), for example, repeatedly asserts that every lie is a sin. When we lie, he explains, we misuse language which is supposed to truthfully represent our thoughts. But why is misusing language so bad? Aquinas contends that when we misuse language, when we lie, we offend against the virtue of truth. Significantly, Aquinas links truth with another virtue, justice, which concerns our dealings with others. When we lie, we violate that justice that requires us to render what is due to others, to deal with them fairly and openly (Aquinas 1947, 1662–1663).

There are, in other words, two ways of thinking about our lies: with respect to God and with respect to our fellow men and women. Aquinas' mentor Albert the Great made this clear in his commentary on Aristotle's *Nicomachean Ethics*, when he asks whether it is justifiable for a person to lie in order to save their state. He opts to examine the question from two perspectives, the spiritual and the political. With respect to God, lies are never justified. No finite temporal advantage can outweigh the infinite and enduring good of the soul's salvation. Considered politically, however, Albert admits that the ends might sometimes justify the means and a person might virtuously "lie in words or deeds." He adds that the spiritual must always trump the political, that ultimately every lie is a sin, but for all that, the conversation has clearly shifted from Augustine's earlier absolute prohibition (Albert 1968, 288; Kempshall 1999, 67–73). There are two ways to think about lies, as they relate to God and as they relate to the world.

This line of thinking reaches its culmination around the beginning of the fourteenth century, in the writings of the Franciscan theologian Duns Scotus (c.1266–1308). Scotus asks whether every lie ought to be understood as directly opposing God. In other words, should Albert's spiritual framework for judging lies apply to every lie? Scotus argues that not every lie opposes God who is the first truth: some lies are about secondary truths, about things in the world. This leads Scotus to ask if lies are necessarily, that is, essentially, sinful. While the Ten Commandments prohibit both murder and lying, the story of Isaac and Abraham demonstrates that commandments can be changed and that God could lift the ban against murder. Lying is certainly not so grave a deed as murder, Scotus contends. Accordingly, God could, should He wish, lift the prohibition against lying. If lying is not necessarily sinful, then when is it sinful? (Scotus 1986, 484–488)

Following a line of thought that had been developing among Franciscan writers for much of the century, Scotus suggests that the evil of lying rests in the intentions of the liar. What if our intentions are good? Scotus turns to the story of the Hebrew midwives who lie to Pharaoh in order to save the newborn Jewish babies. He suggests that theirs was a "polite lie," a lie which hurts no one and helps others. God, he argues, would have rewarded their actions because their sin was only venial and committed with the best of intentions. Taking this sort of justification one step further, he then asks whether a powerful motive of charity could compel a person to commit a venial sin, compel a person to lie. In other words, are there situations which more or less require us to lie for the sake of being virtuous and charitable? Scotus answers, "Since such an evil is of itself not eternal but temporal, it does not seem that one ought to omit something which of itself is the cause in some way of eternal good" (Scotus 1986, 496–497). Put differently, he can imagine a situation in which lying would not only be forgiven, but would be the right thing to do. Living an excellent life would require living a life that, occasionally at least, requires us to deceive.

Scotus' question moves us to a question of much importance to medieval thinkers – in what sort of world do we live? Do we live in a world so convoluted and perplexing that sometimes circumstances will require us to sin to achieve the good, to sin in order to avoid greater sins? Scotus seems to think so, as does Gratian, the twelfth-century Bolognese canon lawyer who, in his *Decretals*, suggests that when "an inescapable danger compels us to commit one of two evils, we must choose the one that makes us less guilty." (Gratian 1993, 49) For the most part, subsequent legal writers and theologians rejected this position. There is, they maintained, always a guiltless choice. The perplexity we face in such dire circumstances has nothing to do with the world and everything to do with the perplexed individual. What sort of God would have placed us in a world in which we had no choice but to sin, no choice but to disobey him? There are always sinless options, and if we are perplexed that simply means we are too muddle-headed to discern the proper action (Dougherty 2011, 22–25; but not always, see Corran 2018).

3. *Lying and Dissimulation in the Court*

Too often histories of lying leave the medieval story here, with theologians repeating that every lie is a sin, no matter the circumstances, no matter our intentions. As a result, medieval culture serves as a perfect foil for the rise of Renaissance realpolitik and the hubbub of an emerging modern world busily shedding itself of the spiritual idealism of a simpler time. But history is never that simple and this story only works if we assume that theologians spoke for everyone, that the opinions of scholastic writers were the opinions of people who never read such luminaries as Thomas Aquinas or Duns Scotus. If theologians imagined a world in which there were always sinless, if not easy, options, the members of Europe's ecclesiastical and royal courts thought differently.

As early as the eleventh century, the Benedictine monk and future cardinal Peter Damian (c.1007–1072/3) already perceived that the structure of courtly society necessarily transformed men into liars. Success in court requires pleasing your superiors and getting the best of your peers, and this requires one to lie and dissimulate. A cleric, Damian suggests, must be loose with his money and even looser with his tongue. He must "smother his lord with affable words" and "delight him with fawning flattery" (Damian 1988, 300). It would become a lament repeated across the centuries. In the twelfth century, John of Salisbury (c.1115/20–1180), who, from his bureaucratic post at Canterbury Cathedral, knew that most famous of medieval clerics, Thomas Beckett (c. 1119/20–1170), devoted his greatest book to laying bare the illusions of the court and the endless deceptions of his fellow courtiers. In the *Policraticus*, John writes:

> The most dangerous situation ... that men of eminence have to face, lies in the fact that the enticements of fawning fortune blind their eyes to truth. The world heaps upon them its wealth and pleasures and thereby kindles and fosters a craving for self-indulgence. The soul, deceived by allurements of many kinds, proving false to its own inner light, by a sort of self-betrayal goes astray as the result of its desires amid the deceptions of the outer world. (John of Salisbury 1938, 11)

Perhaps God made the world and, though it is a fallen one, it is still good; but man made the court, and there is nothing good about it, nothing true about it.

Writing some 200 years after John of Salisbury had warned the man of eminence of the dangerous allure of the court, Christine de Pizan (c. 1364–1430) offered a similar warning to princesses and noble women. In *The Treasure of the City of Ladies*, Christine imagines the princess waking in her comfortable bed, in her richly appointed room, surrounded by servants, closets filled with clothes and jewels. Members of the court tell her what they believe she wants to hear. They flatter her and disparage her enemies. If she is not careful, she will believe these lies, believe she is owed what she has and deserves still more. She will overstep her limits and with that step, trip and fall. If the situation of the courtier is dangerous and fraught with treachery, the situation of the princess is so much the more harrowing. Often a stranger at court, married to the lord, yet an outsider, the subject of gossip and jealousy, she has only herself and her good reputation to rely upon. She must actively work to protect herself from her enemies and the envious, from their deceits and carefully worded promises, from their lies. *The Treasure* is a handbook to teach the princess how to accomplish these difficult tasks (Christine de Pizan 2003).

Unlike the theologians, who offer their ethical dictums from the abstract perspective that philosophical inquiry grants, confident in the universal applicability of their moral principles, both John and Christine imagine their ethics to be deeply context-bound. The consequence of this shift in perspective as it concerns lying is clear in both works. Though both writers rehearse the standard prohibition against lying, both simultaneously undercut it. John repeatedly attacks the deceptions of flatterers and condemns all manner of lies, but he admits to lying when it serves his purposes. In an earlier work, he contends that "that deception is good which effects benefits, and by which joys, life, and salvation are looked after" (John of Salisbury 1987, 175). Christine is no different, asserting at one moment that the princess must hate all lies, and later advising her when and how to lie to others in the court, offering counsel concerning the importance of what she refers to as "just hypocrisy" (Christine de Pizan 2003, 48). Christine states explicitly that this behavior is not only useful in the world, but pleasing to God.

For both John and Christine – indeed, for most of the courtly tradition which would wind its way through the Renaissance and Enlightenment, before finally petering out in the nineteenth century – the perplexities of the court upset whatever certainties the theologians had imagined resided in moral absolutes. John is the rare medieval thinker to admit to a sort of skepticism. We are human – finite, flawed, and fallible. We must be cautious, hesitant to accept as true much of what we see and be happy with probability instead of certainty. In our daily dealings with the world, we must give up the demonstrative logic of the philosophers in exchange for, first, dialectical logic, which deals with the probable, and, second, rhetoric, which examines the specific circumstances in which we must decide how to act. The court is a convoluted and deceptive place, and we can find ourselves in situations in which moral standards are in conflict with one another. Imagine a courtier asks the princess whether her husband is having an affair. He is and the princess knows it. The princess confronts a moment of moral perplexity as she weighs competing and opposed moral demands – the duty not to lie against the duty to protect her husband

and to protect her own position so that she can continue to carry out her functions as princess (Christine de Pizan 2003, 38, 55). Christine and John imagine something like a rhetorical ethics. Just as Cicero proposed that the orator must fit his speech to the moment, to the crowd, to the facts at hand, and to the desired end, so must the courtier fit his words and deeds, so must the princess (Nederman 1988). Sometimes we must lie and that is not a vice, but part and parcel of living the good life in the hothouse of the court.

These ideas about lying and excellence, already developed in medieval courtly literature, would flourish throughout the Renaissance, in the writings of Machiavelli, Castiglione, della Casa, and many others. They would be translated from Italian into every European language, summarized, parodied, and copied. Success at court, success in society, requires that we say what people want to hear and act as they expect us to behave. In his 1547 parody of social etiquette, *The Philosopher of the Court*, Philibert de Vienne (fl. 1542–1548) informed his readers, "The gentleman courtier is not subject to himself; if it is necessary to laugh he laughs, if it is necessary to grieve, he cries, if it is necessary to eat, he eats, and if it is necessary to fast he fasts" (Philibert 1990, 81–87). The line between sheer toadying and utter self-abasement to social requirements becomes vanishingly thin. Reflecting on this predicament, the Englishman Nathaniel Waker explained that we must learn how "to demean ourselves acceptably" before our superiors, without appearing willing "to lick the very spittle from under their feet" (Waker 1681, 7). While many authors still condemned lying, their advice made clear how important it was to hide our thoughts and to present ourselves as society expects, not as we are.

Both John and Christine had advocated deceit as a means of fending off the dangers of the court. Sixteenth- and seventeenth-century writers were certainly aware of the dangers of courtly life, but something else seems to animate their recommendations for duplicity. Stefano Guazzo (1530–1593), who served as a diplomat for the Gonzagas, Mantua's ruling family, makes this clear in his 1574 treatise, *Civil Conversation*: "The world is full of and subsists by flattery, which is more in fashion than peeked beards and large ruff," he writes. "You see how all persons for the sake of peace, and to avoid contention, and that they may appear agreeable in company, comport themselves in the best manner they can to other men's talk and behavior" (Guazzo 1738, 62). Lies, dissimulation, and hypocrisy grease the wheels of civil society. Montaigne, following a long tradition, had argued that the truth held human society together. If our word could not be trusted, then all was lost. Many of his early modern contemporaries had come to see things differently. Flattery smoothed the rough edges of our civil engagements. Lies and flattery no longer merely protected us from the dangers of the court; they made social life possible.

Towards the end of the seventeenth century and into the eighteenth, the Jansenist theologian Pierre Nicole (c.1625–1695) and the philosopher Bernard

Mandeville (c.1670–1733), especially in *The Fable of the Bees*, would explore the productive power of self-love and self-interest, suggesting that they, along with the deceits they engendered, were the hidden hand behind social harmony and economic flourishing.[1] Nicole contended that a society composed of individuals acting solely in the name of self-love would appear no different from a society of virtuous individuals. If the difference between the two mattered from the religious point of view, it had no bearing at all from the perspective of the day-to-day business of getting on with life (Nicole 1696, 78–112; Keohane 1980, 293–303; Herdt 2008, 248–261).

But could we ever even know our own motives, could we know to which society we belong? Echoing Montaigne, Nicole admitted that a person could martyr themselves out of self-love and be none the wiser for it. For his part, Mandeville suggested Nicole's society of virtuous individuals was a pipe dream. Our every action is selfish from start to finish, he claimed, but if we were to let other people know our intentions, they would never give us what we want. That is why we clothe our selfish desires in garments of charity and virtue, knowing that fooling others is the best way to satisfy our own desires. In the end, Mandeville concludes, we even deceive ourselves as we come to believe the lie that charity, not greed, motivates our actions (Mandeville 1924; Dickey 1990, 387–431; Herdt 2008, 272–275).

4. *Two Visions of Truth-Telling and the Good Life: Montaigne and Madeleine de Scudéry*

What of human excellence and virtue in a society in which facades and appearances proliferate and the truth – of others, of ourselves – forever recedes from view? Montaigne offers one response, a sort of immersion in the moment, in transient experience, a mindful absorption in appearances and a frank recognition that we will never penetrate beyond them. This returns us to his distinction between giving the lie and lying. Montaigne offers an ethics which accepts giving the lie, at least in the sense that we can never really know the truth of things or of ourselves. The best we can do is try to be truthful, to express faithfully who we think we are even as we change so much in the telling that our words forever miss their mark. No doubt this results in much of Montaigne's continuing appeal – the command that we be our best possible selves in the face of our failure to ever be the best, representing a sort of nobility in failure.

In so far as Montaigne holds lying to be noxious and destructive of social relations, his analysis falls in line with a long tradition that believed that truth

[1] On the notion of the hidden hand and interest in self-organizing systems, see, Jonathan Sheehan and Dror Waxman, Invisible Hands: Self-Organization and the Eighteenth Century (Chicago: The University of Chicago Press, 2015).

is the bond that holds us together. Both Pierre Nicole and Bernard Mandeville suspected this was not the case at all. Lying has real social utility, even though it is a vice. Madeleine de Scudéry (c.1607–1701), who was among the most popular writers of the seventeenth century, questioned whether lying was a vice at all. In 1680, she published *Conversations on Various Subjects*, based on the premise that good conversation "is the greatest pleasure of well-bred people, the most ordinary way to introduce, not only politeness to the world, but also the purest morals and the love of glory and virtue" (Scudéry 1680, 1). Rather than locate social cohesion in the binding truth of our words, Scudéry locates it in the activity of conversation itself, in the successful flow of pleasing words that carry the listeners along, each with the other, in a harmonious setting.

Unlike Nicole and Mandeville, who stress the productive power of self-love, Scudéry seems to condemn it. Conversation grinds to a halt in annoyance, rancor, and dispute when participants who seek to win every argument dominate the proceedings, or when they speak too much about themselves or their favorite topics. We must endeavor to keep our conversations moving along, saying what needs to be said and refraining from things that might bring talk to a standstill. We must practice the art of complaisance "which yields without weakness, praises without flattery ... without affectation and baseness, and renders society agreeable, and life easier and more diverting" (Scudéry 1680, 279). This means that at times we will go along with conversations that might bore us, concealing our true feelings for the sake of others. But we must do this so skillfully that people will think our participation utterly sincere, our words the spontaneous expression of hidden thoughts.

Montaigne gives up on truth even as he attempts to find solace in truthfulness: he may give the lie, but he will never lie. In *Conversations on Diverse Subjects*, Scudéry seems happy enough to renounce truth and truthfulness altogether, never seeking anything beyond the smooth progression of external appearances and rituals. In a conversation entitled, "On the Knowledge of Ourselves and Others" one of her characters claims that in order "to pass one's life sweetly, it is necessary to remain on the surface of things, for should one penetrate any deeper, a person may find that those same pleasures are bitter." We can never know what another really thinks, whether their apparent sincerity is a sign of their real affection for us or a mask hiding dark designs. Worse, we can never really know ourselves. We love ourselves so much that as we try to deceive others, we end up deceiving ourselves. Scudéry imagines it as a problem in perspective: we cannot know others because we are too far from them, we cannot know ourselves because we are too close (Scudéry 1680, 71–72).

Conversation becomes an end in itself, less important for its content than for its performance. Picking up on language from earlier courtly writers, such as the Italian Stefano Guazzo, Scudéry locates social coherence, not in truth, but in simple civility: "[Civility]," another of her characters explains, "is necessary to the society of all mankind, it promotes all pleasures, maintains friendship, and without it we should be ever in a state of war and irritated" (Scudéry 1680, 264). It is also utterly superficial, fit for the secluded world of the salon, an idyll for the rich and the aristocratic elite. But then again, Montaigne's response to the world's deceptive appearances was also to seek a seclusion that his position and wealth made possible. And again, he found solace in conversation, first with his friend La Boétie (c.1530–1563), and then, after his friend's death, in the memories of those conversations that spilled across the pages of his essays (Magnien 2016, 99–116).

Both Montaigne and Scudéry are interested in the question of human happiness, of what it means to lead a good life, and both are keenly aware that the answer to that question depends on our relationship to truth and lies. Both recognize the near insurmountable difficulty of recognizing the truth, of discerning dishonesty, and that we need to reconcile ourselves to constant uncertainty about ourselves and about others. And yet, their respective solution to the challenge differs immensely, as, perhaps, we should expect from two writers whose works appeared nearly a century apart, the one a man, the other a woman. Montaigne remains content with appearances, as he converses with himself, attending to his every specificity and particularity, as he changes from moment to moment, forever unsure whether or not he is giving the lie. For her part, Scudéry instrumentalizes and then doubles down on appearances, multiplying them for the sake of social harmony. Lies are useful and, given that they are inescapable, we might as well use them.

Both writers take for granted that deception and uncertainty are part and parcel of human existence and in this they are representative of their age. Augustine may well have contended that every lie was a sin against God and a violation of our very nature as beings created in His image, but over the centuries writers had slowly stopped worrying about God when they worried about lies. Instead, they worried about this world, and this world seemed unworkable without lies. Traditionalists might claim that, were lying acceptable, the bonds of society would break, but experience taught writers like Scudéry and Mandeville that this was far from the case. In the Gospel of John, Jesus famously describes the devil as the father of lies, the prince of this world. The devil's lie severed our links to Paradise, forever marring God's creation with illness and vice, deception and death. As the seventeenth century moved into the eighteenth, it proved difficult for many people to imagine a world that was not full of lying and deceit, and maybe that wasn't such a terrible thing after all.

Works Cited

Albert the Great (1955) *Super Ethica.* Ed. Ephrem Filthaut. Münster: Aschendorff.

Aquinas, Thomas (1947) *Summa of Theology*. Trans. Fathers of the English Dominican Province. New York City: Benziger Brothers.

Augustine (1952) "Against Lying." *Treatises on Various Subjects*. Ed. Roy J. Deferrari. Trans. Harold B. Jaffee. Washington, DC: Catholic Univ. Press. 112–175.

Augustine (2002) *On the Trinity*. Ed. Gareth B. Matthews. Trans. Stephen McKenna. Cambridge: Cambridge Univ. Press.

Christine de Pizan (2003) *The Treasure of the City of Ladies*. Trans. Sarah Lawson. London: Penguin Books.

Corran, Emily (2018) *Lying and Perjury in Medieval Practical Thought: A Study in the History of Casuistry*. Cambridge: Cambridge Univ. Press.

Damian, Peter (1988) *Die Briefe des Petrus Damiani*, vol. 2, *NR. 41–90*. Ed. Kurt Reindel. Munich: Monumenta Germaniae Historica.

Dickey, Laurence (1990) "Pride, Hypocrisy and Civility in Mandeville's Social and Historical Theory." *Critical Review* 4.3 (Summer): 387–431.

Dougherty, M.V. (2011) *Moral Dilemmas in Medieval Thought from Gratian to Thomas Aquinas*. Cambridge: Cambridge Univ. Press.

Guazzo, Stefano (1738) *The Art of Conversation*. London: J. Brett.

Herdt, Jennifer (2008) *Putting on Virtue: The Legacy of the Splendid Vices.* Chicago: Chicago Univ. Press.

John of Salisbury (1938) *Frivolities of the Courtiers and Footprints of the Philosophers: Being a Translation of the First, Second, and Third Books and Selections from the Seventh and Eights Books of the Policraticus of John of Salisbury*. Trans. Joseph B. Pike. Minneapolis: Minnesota Univ. Press.

John of Salisbury (1987) *Entheticus Maior and Minor.* 3 vols. Ed. Jan van Laarhoven. Leiden: E.J. Brill.

Kempshall, M.S. (1999) *The Common Good in Late Medieval Political Thought.* Oxford: Oxford Univ. Press.

Keohane, Nannerl O. (1980) *Philosophy and the State in France: The Renaissance to the Enlightenment*. Princeton: Princeton Univ. Press.

Leushuis, Reinier (2009) "Montaigne *Parrhesiastes*: Foucault's Fearless Speech and Truth-Telling in the Essays." *Montaigne After Theory, Theory After Montaigne*. Ed. Virginia Kreuse. Seattle: Washington Univ. Press. 100–121.

Mandeville, Bernard (1924) *The Fable of the Bees: Or, Private Vices, Publick Benefits*. 2 vols. Oxford: Clarendon Press.

Mangien, Michel (2016) "La Boétie and Montaigne." *The Oxford Handbook on Montaigne*. Ed. Philippe Desan. Oxford: Oxford Univ. Press. 99–116.

Martin, John Jeffries (2013) "The Confessions of Montaigne." *Religions* 3: 950–63.

Montaigne, Michel de (1965) *The Complete Essays of Montaigne*. Translated by Donald M. Frame. Stanford: Stanford Univ. Press.

Montaigne, Michel de (2007) *Les Essais*. Ed. Jean Balsamo et al. Paris: Gallimard.

Nederman, Cary (1988) "Nature, Sin and the Origins of Society: The Ciceronian Tradition in Medieval Political Thought." *Journal of the History of Ideas* 49.1 (January–March): 3–26.

Nicole, Pierre (1696) "Of Charity and Self-Love." *Moral Essays, Contain'd in Several Treatises on Many Important Duties…Done into English by a Person of Quality*. Vol. 3. London: Sam Manship.

Philibert de Vienne (1990) *Le Philosophe de court*. Ed. Pauline M. Smith. Geneva: Librairie Droz.

Schreiner, Susan (2003) "Appearances and Reality in Luther, Montaigne, and Shakespeare." *The Journal of Religion* 83.3: 345–380.

Scotus, John Duns (1986) *Duns Scotus on the Will and Morality*. Ed. and trans. Allan B. Wolter. Washington, D.C.: Catholic Univ. Press.

Scudéry, Madeleine de (1680) *Conversations sur divers sujets*. Vol. 1. Paris: Thomas Amaulry.

Waker, Nathaniel (1681) *The Refin'd Courtier or, A Correction of Several Indecencies crept in Civil Conversation: Written Originally in Italian by John Casa, from thence in Latin by Nathan Chytroeus, and from both by way of Paraphrase, made in English by N.W.* London: Matthew Gillflower.

"Born with a Lie in My Mouth": Counterfeit and Counterfactuality in It-Narratives

Vid Stevanović

1. *Introduction*

In a central passage of Charles Gildon's *The Golden Spy*, a narrating voice claims that "Gold wou'd not lye" (Gildon 1709, 175). What makes this short proposition remarkable is that the narrator uttering these words is no narrator in any traditional sense of the word: the voice that speaks is that of a gold coin. *The Golden Spy* is a collection of different stories told by a variety of European coins to a human frame-narrator, who only appears as a device of narrative cohesion that links the different episodes together. With this peculiar layout, Charles Gildon's text – published in 1709 – heralds the emergence of a unique genre of tales in which non-human entities assume the position of first-person narrators.

Until fairly recently, this genre seemed to have fallen out of the canon of English literature and therefore needs at least a short introduction. Object-narratives, also called *it-narratives* or novels of circulation, constitute a genre of texts that rose to prominence in the eighteenth century (Bellamy 2007; Blackwell 2007). In these texts, the objects – mostly commodities – relate the stories of their circulation through human societies: coins, coats, and wigs fashion their own biographies. Since they are largely the products of lesser-known writers and trace their origins to *roman-à-clef* satires that depended heavily on historical context, it is perhaps not all too surprising that they have attracted limited interest up until the last decade. In recent years, an increasing appreciation of popular literatures, the publication of a critical anthology of the genre (Blackwell 2012a), and an interest in non-human agencies in literature have all served to rekindle critical interest in these texts.

Much of this recent interest in the genre can be attributed to the conflicting narrative constellation it employs. On the one hand, these object-narrations are characterized by a high degree of experientiality and a 'natural' narrative configuration (see Fludernik 1996, 13), i.e. an autodiegesis that emulates naturally-occurring forms of storytelling. On the other hand, the emphasis that the stories put on the position of their storytellers as fundamentally alien to human society, thereby consciously taking advantage of opportunities for defamiliarization,[1] has made them prime objects for the study of "unnatural narratives" (Alber et al. 2010). My thesis is that this subgenre of it-narratives, in which coins and bank notes serve as narrators, radicalizes tendencies that are latent in the idea of a a narrating object. That is to say, they accentuate the epistemological and ontological implications of such non-human speech.

2. *'Money Talks' – From Metaphor to Counterfactuality*

When we encounter the trope of *prosopopoeia* giving voice to coins and bank notes, it seems at first that what we are witnessing is the literalization of a metaphor: *money talks*. Yet the case is more ambivalent: instead of conceptualizing object-narration as the literalization of a metaphor, I propose to follow the distinction between metaphor and counterfactuality as it is drawn in pragmatic linguistics.

In *Truth, Metaphor and Counterfactual Meaning*, Mark G. Lee undertakes to differentiate these two terms. He associates metaphor with the direct equation of vehicle and tenor (source and target domain), in the sense that the two domains are directly fused, assuming the form of a true statement without mediation. Metaphor thus creates a space in which the propositional content of its expression is treated as literally true (Lee 2010, 126). This is not quite the case with object-narrators. When the first gold coin in English literature begins to tell its story in *The Golden Spy*, a human frame-narrator is confounded by the sounds of a slight whisper coming from the direction of his purse. To his surprise, he discovers a couple of gold coins endowed with the gift of speech. In the following nights, they emulate the structure of the *Decamerone*, as they each tell the stories of their circulation through human societies. Similar structural layouts, featuring a human frame-narrator, are found in many other money narratives. Until the end of the eighteenth century, it-narratives frequently rely on this kind of mediation to make plausible the idea of non-human narration.[2]

Following Lee, such a setup can be understood to reflect the structure of the counterfactual. The counterfactual is divided into an antecedent and a consequent, the antecedent being the proposition that opens up the space in which the consequent holds true. In this case, the antecedent is the assumption that 'money can talk,' and the consequent is that 'it does not lie.' By evoking the sentence structure of a conditional, in claiming that "Gold wou'd not lye," the

[1] The conflicting relationship between defamiliarization and empathy has been explored in Bernaerts et al. 2015, 82–83.

[2] Oftentimes, the it-narrators appear at moments in which the narrative reliability of the human frame-narrators is questioned –for instance when they are shown to be the products of dreams etc.

gold coin in Gildon's story testifies to the emergence of such a counterfactual space.[3] We can understand this quite literally by completing the phrase: 'if gold could speak, it would not lie.' From the standpoint of classical logic, the consequent is always trivially true if the antecedent is false.[4] Yet, as Lee observes, this does not apply to pragmatic language use. In practice, counterfactuals are either accepted or dismissed, based on the contenability[5] of their propositions, i.e. the verification of prepositions that do not contradict the antecedent (Lee 2010, 125, 127-128; Goodman 1947, 137): "certain counterfactuals are treated as reasonable if they can be verified by showing that if the antecedent was indeed true, then the consequent would follow" (Lee 135). Thus, much like a metaphor, a counterfactual need only be internally consistent, but not true with respect to any outside knowledge. But unlike conventionalized metaphor, counterfactual space is characterized by a fundamental openness that calls for an internal verification of the consequent.

In order to understand the validation of the truth-value of this counterfactual, one has to return to the historical situation that produced these texts. It-narratives saw their heyday between early colonialism and the rise of the British Empire in the late eighteenth century and thus also between pre-capitalist modes of production and the social transformations that paved the way for the first industrial revolution. These socio-economic developments coincided with an epistemological transformation: empiricism established itself as the dominant method of knowledge production. While previously – in natural philosophy – epistemic authority rested on the human ability to reason, to induce and deduce conclusions, it was gradually replaced by the strategy of the falsification of a hypothesis through experiment. These experiments increasingly began to rely on witnesses that were not subject to the sensory faults that humans are prone to: science began to rely on instruments. Such objects came to embody the fantasy of a non-human access to an outside reality – a way of knowing that is not always already potentially distorted through the prism of human subjectivity. Bruno Latour sketches this epistemological shift that was taking place in the experimental laboratories of the seventeenth and eighteenth centuries:

> [T]he scientists declare that they themselves are not speaking; rather, facts speak for themselves. These mute entities are thus capable of speaking, writing, signifying within the artificial chamber of the laboratory [...]. Little groups of gentlemen take testimony from natural forces and they testify to each other that they are not betraying but translating the silent behaviour of objects. (Latour 2012, 29)

---

3 The use of a modal verb in this claim points to the subjunctive mood that characterizes the protasis of a counterfactual (OED, s.v. counterfactual, adj.).

4 The antecedent is false by definition, else one could not speak of a counterfactual statement.

5 "The *contenability* problem [...] is the problem of finding the correct set of relevant true statements which do not contradict the antecedent but support the entailment of the consequent" (Lee 125).

In the laboratory, a strange sort of ventriloquism is at work. The scientist's role is conceived as that of a passive vessel that gives voice to the non-human agency of the object, whose 'speech' alone is the guarantor of scientific authority.

This setup involves a double proxy: the 'facts' can reach language only through two agents of translation. The mute non-human agents, that is, the scientific instruments, register 'facts' in what Latour calls their "[...] showing, signing, writing and scribbling" (2012, 23), and this 'speech' of the instruments is then translated into scientific discourse by the scientists. Speech is imagined as a procedure of grafting: scientists speak, but they speak with the voice of another. Their speech consists in giving voice to otherwise mute objects. It is an instrumental speech; one that itself gives birth to the facts that can talk back to the scientific community.

I argue that it-narrators transpose this position of instrumental testimony to the realm of literature, insofar as the money or other objects in question effectively relate to the human subject as objects outside of human subjectivity, as material things. As such, these objects are ready to serve as mediators through which a privileged epistemology can be achieved, catering to the fantasy of unperceived perception conceptualized as that of a "pure empiricism" (Benedict 2001, 94). Thus, when the human frame-narrator at the end of *The Golden Spy* reassures the reader that there is "[...] no intelligence as [a Gold coin] can give" (Gildon 1709, 304), he actively invokes the context of contemporary scientific discourses. The gold coins draw on their status as non-human things in order to guarantee an epistemological surplus-reliability. The gold coins thus stand in opposition not only to the morally and intellectually fallible human narrators, but also to the numerous liars, fraudsters, and conmen that populate the story and whose scheming constitutes the subject-matter of it-narratives.

As the genre proliferates around the middle of the eighteenth century, *The Golden Spy* is succeeded by a profusion of narratives in which pieces of money tell the stories of their circulation. These money narrators range from the domestic farthings, shillings, pounds, and guineas to various foreign pieces of silver and gold. What unites them is their emphasis on narrative reliability. One exemplary tale from this period, published in 1782, is *The Adventures of a Rupee*, in which a piece of gold tells its life story, starting from the moment it is discovered by peasants in the Tibetan mountains. Near the end of its narrative, the rupee once again stresses its trustworthiness, which is proffered as the reason for ending the narrative:

> Gentle reader, this shall be the last chapter of my adventures, for I would not [...] tell any thing that is not absolutely true, though by acting otherwise, I might imitate many grave historians, and celebrated biographers. [...] I spent my hours in separating truth from the ashes of time. Our eyes can penetrate with the same ease the shade of antiquity, and the prejudice that surrounds the modern day. (Scott 2012, 70)

Here, the it-narrator dissociates itself explicitly from its human counterparts, the "grave historians, and celebrated biographers." Unlike them, it will only speak truth, paradoxically claiming reliability by narrowing down the scope of its observations: this humbled-down scope of direct witnessing is the very thing that sustains its claim to reliability. The content for which the gold coin claims this truthfulness consists in its various adventures triggered by the quick succession of its owners, which lead to the coin's journey from India into Europe, from the hands of the Sultan of Mysore to those of the King of England.

To reduce the rupee to a mere device for rendering plausible the formal interlinking of these adventures, as proposed by some critics (e.g. Link 1980, 79), misses the importance that *The Adventures of a Rupee* and other it-narratives place on the material specifics of its narrators. As in other it-narratives, the specific materiality of the object in question is reflected in the narrative dynamics of its story – the way in which an object is made use of in human society determines the scope of its narration.

3. *Thing, Commodity, Money:* The Adventures of a Rupee

At the very beginning of *The Adventures of a Rupee*, the eponymous object starts out as something that is utterly foreign to human society. Consider one of its first sentences, in which the piece of gold gives an account of its early days:

> The sun saw me in the mountains of Thibet an ignoble lump of earth. I was then undistinguished from the clods that surrounded me by the splendour of my appearance, or the ductility of my substance; but I contained within myself the principles of my future form, and certain parts of the rays of light remaining in the cavities of my body, by degrees I assumed colour and the qualities which I had not before. [...] I remained many centuries, ignorant of the world or its inhabitants. (Scott 2012, 34)

At the beginning of its story, the it-narrator's ontological status is that of a thing, something that is not the object of use, but of perception: it is *zuhanden*, "present-at-hand," in the Heideggerian sense (Heidegger 1967, 25–26; Harman 2010, 18–19). As it is still utterly "[...] ignorant of the world or its inhabitants," it is not perceived by human subjectivity, but only by another non-human observer, the sun. Similarly, it is not human labor that realizes the potentiality of the rupee's form, but the agency of natural phenomena, the "rays of light." The coin is a thing at the margins of the human world: a thing not of signifiers and subjects and societies, but of matter and form, of color and light. The rupee of Helenus Scott does not start out as an object embedded in the daily commerce of human life, but as something that is no longer or not yet useful to humanity (Heidegger 1967, 73; Unverzagt 2013, 21–25).

However, the piece of gold does not remain in this state for long: it is discovered and dug out by two friends, who realize that the piece of metal they have found is gold. Immediately, a brawl ensues over the question of who has the more substantial claim to it, and the winner takes home the valuable metal. The it-narrator can incite this kind of desire in its discoverers because, in its relation to them, it is no longer a thing. As soon as they categorize it as gold, it starts to represent value, more precisely, two types of value.

First, it carries a set of physical characteristics (malleability, ductility, resistance to corrosion, etc.) that make it a useful resource for human labor. Its propensity to being useful to someone gives shape to what in classical and Marxist political economy is called the use-value of a commodity. But use-value only defines the relationship of the commodity to the subject that puts it to use. It is a necessary condition for its commodity-being. However, as the story progresses, the peasant who managed to secure the gold will precisely not use it for any of its positive qualities as an object, nor will any of its successive owners. Instead, it is used as a repository of value and a means of exchange. In order for it to function as such a repository, it must be the carrier of a second type of value, namely a certain amount of exchange-value: it must be exchangeable for other commodities at a certain rate. Exchange-value, then, is not a specific quality, but a quantitative relationship.

Only eight years before the publication of *The Adventures of a Rupee*, this insight stands out as one of the first tenets of what was to become the science of political economy. In *An Inquiry into the Nature and Causes of the Wealth of Nations* (1776), Adam Smith writes:

> The word VALUE, it is to be observed, has two different meanings, and sometimes expresses the utility of some particular object, and sometimes the power of purchasing other goods which the possession of that object conveys. The one may be called 'value in use;' the other, 'value in exchange.' (Smith 2008, 32)

Whereas use-values are defined positively, exchange values are inherently negative. They are differential relations in the sense that value manifests itself only as "the power of purchasing other goods." The sufficient condition of commodification is fulfilled only when the object steps into a relationship with other commodities.

At this point, a parallax effect is at work. From the perspective of use-value, the coins' usefulness to someone is the basic condition of their mobility as commodities. But in a society that produces for exchange, such as the emergent capitalism of eighteenth-century Britain, this logical primacy of use-value is subverted. From the perspective of exchange-value, use-values must appear merely as the "[...] material depositories of exchange value" (Marx 1977, 27). In order for this value to be realized, its use-value must be suspended as it changes owners. Thus, in the scene of the rupee's discovery by the peasants, an ontological transition is taking place: what was formerly a thing becomes a commodity. In this process it acquires the use-value and exchange-value that provide the necessary and sufficient conditions for its mobility.

This first split between use-value and exchange-value results in the rupee recognizing itself as an object not only of use, but also of value. A formerly self-identical object is now split into two halves. Yet its metamorphosis does not stop here. Soon after the victorious peasant brings the narrator home, he melts it down and turns it into the eponymous rupee. During this process, the rupee suffers another loss of identity. Unlike the split between use-value and exchange-value, this metamorphosis is described in detail:

> I am dragged from my subterraneous abode – They apply the strongest force of fire to my body, till part of my substance assumes a liquid state – I am next poured into a mould, which gave me the roundness and character I still retain. After I had undergone these changes, they called me a RUPEE. (Scott 2012, 35)

In this procedure, the material body is literally torn apart and transformed. The fragmentation effected by the use of dashes and the immediacy evoked by the present tense lend a dramatic force to the process of melting. The transformation is finalized by the shape that is given to the metal and the denomination that is stamped on it: a split is produced between the signifier of value – the rupee – and the material carrier on which this signifier is inscribed – the piece of gold.

The rupee thereby re-enacts a primal scene in the historical development of money. The first types of money emerge where one particular commodity begins to assume the function of a general equivalent of exchange. In this status of a general equivalent, that commodity takes on the function of expressing the relations between the values of all other commodities. In this process, "[...] [t]he money commodity [...] acquires a formal use-value, originating in its special social function; the point being that one commodity now has its use-value determined to be only its exchangeability" (Mehrotra 1991, 74). For the commodity that has thus become a general equivalent of all other commodities, its use-value collapses into its exchange-value. It is useful for what it can be exchanged for.

However, in its elemental form, money is commodity money, i.e. a commodity that assumes the status of a general equivalent, while retaining its use-value *qua* commodity. It serves as a means of exchange, but it can at any time be withdrawn from circulation and used as a commodity (Selgin 2015, 93). The golden rupee thus takes on the function of money, but its status lies in between that of a commodity and representative money. By being melted down to form a coin, the piece of metal acquires the representative function of the denomination that is stamped on it, but since the denomination refers to its own weight in gold, it still retains a use-value that is not identical with its exchange-value. Historically, this function of commodity money was taken on by gold. Marx's aphorism, that "[...] although gold and silver are not by Nature money, money is by Nature gold and silver" (Marx 1977, 62), testifies to the contingent nature of this historical connection. Certain material properties mean that these metals are better suited to take on the function of general equivalent, but there is no historic determinism at work. Nevertheless, the association of these metals – particularly of gold – with money carries considerable weight and extends to the point that gold becomes synonymous with money. In *The Adventures of a Rupee*, this historic connection is cemented by means of a retrograde teleology, since the designation of 'rupee' is applied to the piece of gold from the first page of the narrative, before it is cast into a coin.

As an instance of commodity money, the rupee *is* value. Regardless of the fact that the Marxist tradition determines the value of a commodity as the result of the socially necessary labor time invested in its production, and neoclassical economic theory conceptualizes value as the effect of a marginal increase in utility, the spontaneous ideology of value is that of an *intrinsic* value. In using the metal as a repository of value, its owners act *as if* it was the naturally-occurring form of value (see Marx 1977, 52).[6] Thus, although the rupee is a sign split into signifier and signified by virtue of the signifier of value, it still carries with it the fantasy of intrinsic value. The narrator testifies to the social reality of this identity of substance and value when it has recourse to the language of myth: "[...] whatever appellation you give to the God of Gold, it is certain that it is I whom the Persians formerly worshipped, and whom all the nations of the earth at present adore" (Scott 2012, 36). The materiality of the coin is thus extrapolated into mythical proportions. The narrative authority that the rupee qua narrator claims through this self-identity is twofold. First, it is acquired by virtue of its being a non-human entity, a thing that is not prone to the sensory deceptions and subjective distortions that a human narrator would be likely to suffer. Secondly, its narration is authoritative because it is valuable as a signifier in a symbolic order in which it is firmly tied to a signified value or a signifier of value. It circulates as the representation of value while simultaneously being treated as the embodiment of this value. Having become money, the narrating object functions not only as an instrument of epistemology, but also as an instrument of exchange.

The rupee's progression through different modes of being that are sketched above is the motor of its narrative progression. Only by enticing specific desires is the circulation of the coin guaranteed. By telling the story of its gradual inclusion in human systems of exchange, the rupee dramatizes a progression from thing to sign. But while this progression implies a movement of abstraction, the text counters it by insisting on the materially embedded ideology of intrinsic

6 This spontaneous ideology is materially embedded in the sense that it is not dependent on the individual's consciousness, but on the performance of the act of exchange itself. For this phenomenon, for which Alfred Sohn-Rethel coined the term "Realabstraktion," real abstraction, see Sohn-Rethel 1975, 188.

value. What does this then mean for the reliability of such a narrator? From the perspective of semiotics, the golden rupee undergoes a twofold operation. First, a split is introduced into a formerly self-identical thing, dividing it into a signifier and a material to embody that signifier. In a second step, this signifier then refers to the value that one rupee represents. For this, however, it needs to point to this material carrier itself as its referent. As the ideology of commodity money holds that value resides in precious metals, the purity of the coin's material becomes the embodiment of value to which the (standardized) coin refers. In terms of semiotics, the contenability of the counterfactual claim is materially validated: this signifier of value "wou'd not lye."

4. *Coin and Counterfeit:* The Adventures of a Bad Shilling in the Kingdom of Ireland

This claim holds true for the rupee, and it recurs in the strong claims to veracity that are assumed by other object-narrators. However, there is a subtype of it-narratives that undermines this referentiality in a very radical manner. Consider, for example, another tale told by a coin: *The Adventures of a Bad Shilling in the Kingdom of Ireland,* published in instalments from 1805 to 1806. At first, the account that this "Bad Shilling" gives of itself is fairly similar to that of the rupee. Originally belonging to a pagan statue, this piece of pure silver is rediscovered by an unsuspecting peasant. Like the rupee, it tells its story as it experiences a quick succession of owners and is finally cast into a coin. However, this is where the two stories start to diverge. The silver ends up in the hands of a criminal and is forged into the eponymous "Bad Shilling." In this process, the supposedly pure silver is melted down – adulterated with base metals – and cast into the form of a silver shilling. Similar to the previous example, the coining process in which the false shilling is forged is described in meticulous detail and rather dramatic language:

> He [the counterfeiter] had stamps cut resembling the marks of the most opulent dealers in Dublin, and with several of these he made weighty and grievous impressions on me and my fellows. The greatest torment in my formation was yet to come. Over one of the large furnaces in the manufactory was placed a plate of Iron, until it was red hot. On this a number of us were arranged in order. There we remained until we were almost in a state of fusion. We were then precipitated into aquafortis. [...] The sudden immersion into this potent liquid drew to our exterior the far greater part of the silver contained in each, and gave us that appearance, which passed us on a deceived public for sterling. ("Bad Shilling," 154–155)

The silver is adulterated and fashioned to resemble a one-shilling piece in a way that allows it to pass for legal tender. In the process of its discovery and minting, the piece of silver undergoes the same conceptual splits that the rupee suffered. But – in contrast to its golden counterpart – this results in a double break of the integrity of the narrator: first the purity of the silver ingot is lost, it is mixed with "copper, tin etc" ("Bad Shilling," 155), and subsequently this mixture is treated in such a way that a split between the pure silver and its adulterants is achieved. Whereas, as an it-narrator, the silver had formerly laid claims to authority either via its self-identity as a material, or its status as a signifier inseparably bound to a signified of value, this material integrity is now lost. What does this mean for the contenability, that is, the verification of the presupposition that do not contradict the antecedent of a talking coin? A subject that is thus split, one would assume, should have forfeited its reliability together with its material identity. Yet the bad shilling continues to circulate and to relate events with the same narrative authority, *as if* it still retained its privileged position.

Derrida has described this counterintuitive behavior of counterfeit money in *Donner le temps 1: La fausse monnaie* (1991). In this essayistic text, Derrida takes up the phenomenon of counterfeit money as a philosophical problem. He finds his cues in "La fausse monnaie," a short story by Baudelaire, in which a *flâneur* gives a counterfeit coin to a beggar. While the text is usually read for its elaboration of the uniquely Derridean concept of the gift, focusing on the problem of the counterfeit proves worthwhile. One of Derrida's central insights concerns the ontology of the counterfeit: "[c]ounterfeit money is never, *as such*, counterfeit money. As soon as it is what it is, recognized *as such*, it ceases to act as and to be worth counterfeit money" (Derrida 1992, 87). The false coin only becomes counterfeit at the moment it is discovered as such, but then no longer has any exchange-value.

Insofar as it serves as an instrument of exchange, we have seen that the coin's use-value is only realized in its exchange-value. Since its use-value *is* its exchange-value, it realizes its use-value as long as it is able to circulate, by affirming its practical status as legal tender. In circulation, it behaves *as if* its signifier (the denomination) corresponded to its signified (the value of the weight of its material). Thus, as long as it circulates, it effectually functions as money, in that it is perfectly capable of fulfilling the purpose of an instrument of exchange. Only at the moment of its discovery does it turn into counterfeit. It follows that even after being adulterated, the coin can resume its circulation as a shilling. It passes for currency. Thus, as in the case of the rupee, the potential use-value of the silver qua commodity is never retrieved, and hence the shilling cannot be distinguished from 'real' money. The question remains what status the speech of such a narrator might have, whose problematic referentiality is embodied materially, but whose circulation (and functioning) as a signifier of value seems unaffected by this. Melted down and cast into the counterfeit, the coin receives the epithet "BAD" ("Bad Shilling," 155), but the moral implication of this designation leaves the narrator's epistemological integrity intact. As long as it passes for currency, the narrator circulates with the same narrative authority as before. Only its discovery as counterfeit puts an end to this reliability and the narration as a whole: the story ends abruptly as the coin's fake denomination is detected and it is nailed to a shop-counter. Its epistemic authority is thus vouched for by its ongoing circulation that in turn hinges on its supposed authority as legal tender.

5. *Representative Money:* The Adventures of a One-Pound Bank Note

A last subgroup of money narratives can shed light on what is implicit in this apparent paradox. *The Adventures of a One-Pound Bank Note*, published in 1819, is a narrative that is emblematic of a conceptual progression in the history of money. At the beginning of the narrative, the bank note recounts the story of its 'birth' in the characteristic mock-autobiographical fashion of the genre:

> It has been the custom, and still is, with historians to precede their narrations by an account of themselves; and, before they enter upon the main facts and events which professedly engaged them to take up the pen, to give the reader a sketch of their 'birth, parentage, and education.' Some have gone as far back as to touch upon certain particulars relating to them before they were born. The example of one of our countrymen of no mean rank in the republic of letters, might be pleaded as a precedent for this *embrio-biography*, which at first sight seems a little out of the regular course of grave, or, more properly, *stern* history. Indeed, whatever an author should say of transactions concerning himself before he was born, can be but on an imperfect authority, a mere 'gossip's tale;' and what judges in these matters would pronounce hearsay evidence only. ("Bank Note," 231; original emphasis)

These first words of the bank note toy with the idea of relating circumstances that happened before its 'birth.' The passage is ripe with rather direct allusions to such a tale: the "grave, or more properly, *stern* history" that the bank note sets out to tell refers to the same narrative endeavor that we are familiar with in *Tristram Shandy*. But the rebuttal of this idea is not without consequence here: it connects directly to the object-narrator's aspiration to "pure empiricism" (Benedict 2001, 94). It does not draw epistemic authority from the fantasy of an authorial and transcendent meta-perspective, but from its very embeddedness in the here and now as a material object. From such a perspective, it has to dismiss both the "gossip's tale" and "hearsay evidence" as unreliable. But even though it first dwells on its narrative authority in a fashion that is typical of the genre, it is quick to revoke this claim:

> The greater part of the world, however, is not altogether unacquainted with my very *conception;* nor would it be otherwise than vain and idle in me to conceal from the rest of it that I was the offspring of *interest* rather than of *desire*. My parents have been accused of *illicit connections* [...]. Besides, I have of myself a great weight of suspicion to stand under, without undertaking to justify the actions of those who were the authors

> of my existence. [...] Without consulting the horoscope, I soon discovered that an evil planet ruled my destiny; and that I had been born (shocking to tell) with *a lie*, not with a silver spoon in my mouth. ("Bank Note," 231; original emphasis)

This passage stands in stark contrast to the ways the golden rupee and the bad shilling started their autobiographies. The affective dimension of "desire" that draws human subjects to the precious metals in the preceding examples is here plotted against the much more abstract "interest." Whereas natural forces shaped the silver and gold bodies of these narrators, the bank note is a product of human intentionality, something that is always already a signifier in a system of human commerce: its "parents" are quite literally its "authors." This carries crucial implications for the narrator's reliability. The narrator cannot mobilize the fantasy of surplus reliability through an existence outside of human affairs. Instead, the bank note's fundamental entanglement in the deceitful human world is called out in the "illicit connections" that these "authors" are accused of. Finally, should not the bank note's admitting of being born with a "lie [...] in [its] mouth" lead us to suspect the bank note of being as 'bad' as the earlier eponymous shilling? Yet one wonders: this time it is not a counterfeit coin that we are listening to, but legal tender. There seems to exist a problematic tension between legality and illegitimacy.

This tension is fleshed out in more detail once we consider that the "evil planet" alluded to conventionally referred to Saturn.[7] In the course of its cultural history, Saturn has acquired conflicting connotations. The evil planet is at the same time the god of the bucolic golden age; it is the symbol of both liberation and of potential social disintegration. These conflicting tendencies are conjoined in Saturn in his role of the god of wealth, accounting and money. His temple housed the Roman treasury, thereby associating the god with a long history of anxiety about the societal impact of commerce (Garstad 2002, 961–963). The bank note combines this evocation of an ambiguous patron deity with the insight that it was born with a lie in its mouth, i.e. that at its very heart it is a tool for deceit. Hence, even though the note is issued as legal tender, its ability to realize its use-value and serve as an instrument of exchange seems anything but certain. The bank note laments this lot time and again:

> [...] I found myself subjected to daily insinuations and humiliations; and though my *tender condition* might be supposed a protection against any direct violence, yet it did not prevent my discerning the many contemptuous allusions at my *connections*. These were generally veiled under an insidious or ambiguous kind of compliment; such as that 'I was *a thing full of promise* – pity I could not inspire confidence equal to that promise', for then I might live for ever: with various other artfully dissembled phrases of that nature. ("Bank Note," 232; original emphasis)

[7] This association goes back at least to Ptolemy's discussion of Saturn's character in the *Tetrabiblos* (Ptolemy 1822 [2nd century], Book IV, Ch. 9).

The skepticism with which the bank note is met in public, the "insinuations" and "humiliations" point to a situation in which the ability of the bank note to realize its use-value is under constant threat. By virtue of its denomination, it is "full of promise" but it is uncertain whether this promise can be kept, whether it can be *cashed in*. Since the bank note is not considered to possess value on the basis of its material body, its value is guaranteed by a third position, that of language. Its denomination *promises* that it can be exchanged for the equivalent value in commodity money at the Bank of England. As its body is stamped with language, its circulation becomes dependent on its successfully referring to a third position. Value is now the value of the Other.

Faced with this semiotic structure of a representative money economy, Jean-Joseph Goux proposes a homology between economic and linguistic systems of exchange.[8] Following his argument, we can see how at the semiotic level "[...] the relationship between language and being begins to be problematic" (Goux 1994, 17):

> Just as in the economic sphere there arises the question of convertibility, that is, the existence or not of a deposit serving to back the tokens in circulation, likewise in the domain of signification the truth value of language will become a crucial concern. (17)

In light of such suspicion, the bank note is under a constant injunction to prove its referentiality. For doing so, it refers to its institutional connection to the state, its birth in the "largest edifice in the chief city of Europe" ("Bank Note," 232), i.e. the Bank of England. This location is contrasted with the "subterraneous dwelling in Mutton-lane" (232), where one of its rivals, a private promissory note, is supposed to have been written. The "marks of finery by Nurse Newland" (232), that is the signature of Abraham Newland, the chief cashier of the Bank of England, are called upon to add further authority and suggest a more substantial claim than could be guaranteed by any private person.

In the early nineteenth century, at a time when different representations of value competed for public confidence, the bank note is working hard at solidifying its position as a general equivalent of value. Claiming this position in the decades around 1800 when bank notes appear as it-narrators is no trivial task: in the history of money, this time marks a transitional period in which different contenders for the function of the instrument of exchange compete against each other as well as against established signifiers of value. Different types of merchant tokens that are valid only for certain goods or only in certain areas, promissory notes issued by merchants and later traded amongst them, and of course the first type of 'official'[9] paper-money, issued directly by the

[8] See also the use of money-signifiers as example in Ferdinand de Saussure's *Course in General Linguistics* (Saussure 1959, 118).

[9] The official character of the bank note, as contrasted with the promissory note, is guaranteed by the institution. It is a bond, but a bond with a standardized denomination and

Bank of England, all circulate as signifiers of value (Poovey 2008, 46–51). What unites them is that they cannot claim the same unmistakable referentiality as commodity money. The "apology" ("Bank Note," 231) that the bank note offers thus links with historical anxieties about the legitimacy of paper money.

In contrast to coins made of precious metals, paper money embodied – quite ostensibly – the effectual divorce of value from material. The "weight of suspicion" (231) that the bank note stands under is its very lack of weight in valuable material. Unlike the bad shilling, which is turned into the embodiment of a lie when its valuable silver is adulterated with base metals and stamped with a false denomination, the bank note acknowledges its problematic referentiality from the start. After all, it is born with a lie in its mouth: its corporeality can only lay claim to a mere surface, a sheet of paper that carries inscriptions of value, but not to the intrinsic narrative authority of a thing made of a precious metal, for example a "silver spoon." As it cannot connect to this authority of intrinsic value that gold or silver mobilize, the bank note has to rest its claims on mere words. In the inscription of monetary value, language and economy are inseparably fused: functioning as the guarantors of meaning, words have to be taken at face value and credited with the trust that they can indeed be converted into what they claim.

Yet, as the bank note itself hints at, this story is told at a moment in time in which many people refused to accept bank notes (Poovey 2008, 44–45), effectively treating them as counterfeit money. The spontaneous ideology of intrinsic value invests trust in the mute material of gold and silver, but not in the potentially deceitful words inscribed on paper. This seemingly naïve conflation of (bad) counterfeit and (good) paper money soon touches upon a more ambiguous problematic. The etymology of the word *counterfeit* serves to shed light on this relationship. Around 1800 the word *counterfeit* lent itself to more ample semantics, although it has lost these meanings by now. In addition to referring to a false object or person, it was also used in the sense of designating a picture or an image (OED, s.v. counterfeit, n. and adj.). Though still current in the work of Edgar Allan Poe, this particular meaning is nowadays almost forgotten in English, but survives in the German word *Konterfei*, designating 'someone's likeness.' The counterfeit thus connects representation to deceit, as the deceiving surface image of the counterfeit introduces the very possibility of representing that which is not. Hence, representative money is pre-structured by the narratives of counterfeit money, as they exemplify the arbitrariness of the link between signifier and signified. Much as the Christian tradition figures the Fall of Man as the birth of the lie (Denery 2015, 5), the transition from commodity money to paper money appears as a fall into representation. The original sin is the sin of representation that allows for representing not only

no interest, which is not issued by a private person, but by a bank that *de facto* holds the status of a central bank.

what is, but also what is not, thus forever forfeiting the fantasy of a pre-lapsarian identity between *les mots et les choses*.

6. *Counterfeit and Counter-Fact*

From this perspective, paper money is the logical extension of the principle of representation that is figured in the counterfeit, which must appear as the internal exception to the rule of intrinsic value. The material body of money is reduced to the surface needed for the language of value to imprint itself. It is useful for buying what it can be exchanged for, but it 'passes' only to the extent that it is believed to be able to pass even further. In terms of semiotics, paper money is the generalization of the exception that was the counterfeit. Its functioning depends on conventionalization.

At this point, the money-narrators' preoccupation with their own validity intersects with their claim to veracity. It is money that "wou'd not lye," and yet was "born with a [...] lie in [its] mouth." Faced with the subversive power of representative and counterfeit money, we have to return once again to etymology: one can trace the roots of both, counter-fact and counterfeit, to the same word, the old French *contrefait*: to make or produce in opposition to [something] (OED, s.v. counterfeit, n. and adj.) This is more than a mere play on words: both lexemes share a structural homology. Like the counterfeit coin, the counterfactual story rests on a constitutive antecedent. That is to say, a minimal suspension of disbelief guarantees the realization of the consequent. As the 'contenability' of their presuppositions (i.e. those statements that do not contradict their antecedent) is validated, coin and story are deemed passable.

By representing what is not, counterfeit acquires a radical dimension in subverting the social link that is constituted by the general equivalent. As the ambiguous role of the patron-deity of money suggests, counterfeit can be a tool both for personal liberation and social disintegration. In this sense, counterfeit and the term *counterfactual* both refer to the potential subversion of an established system. As counterfeit money threatens the functioning of money, by giving rise to a general suspicion as to the validity of signifiers of value, counterfactuals subvert an ontological order trough representing that which cannot be. Both lay bare the contingent character of a given symbolic order.

Finally, one can understand the problem of representative money as the problem of the peculiar narrative constellation of it-narratives. We have seen that in early money narratives the text is fitted with a frame-narrator who sets forth an apology for the un-natural fact of a speaking object, as in the case of the coin in *The Golden Spy*. This 'lie' is the antecedent to a counterfactual: by accepting the coin, by allowing the money-narrator into circulation, the coin's owners validate its presupposition. As the genre develops, this strategy of naturalization through a frame-narrator withers away,[10] with more texts featuring a direct narration by an autodiegetic object. In the development of the genre, the counterfactual antecedent is conventionalized whilst the truth-check on its presuppositions grows obsolete: the counterfactual structure gives way to that of a conventionalized metaphor. The assumption of an object-narrator is treated as literally true for the space of the narration and meta-reflexive narratives such as the one above disappear, while it-narratives slowly merge with early Victorian children's literature (Bellamy 2007, 131–133). As the ontological problem of representative money translates into the poetological problem of counterfactual literature, the content of the money-narrator's stories *works through* the constitutive problem of its form. In the course of the last decades of the eighteenth century, the 'unnatural' concept of the object-narrator is thus naturalized (Alber 2011, 50). The conventionalization of the non-natural narrative of an autodiegetic object at the turn of the century thus follows the historical conventionalization of non-natural paper money as a reliable signifier of value. In the center of this process stands a deceitful coin that is re-staging the drama of its counterfactual paradox.

Works Cited

"Adventures of a Bad Shilling in the Kingdom of Ireland" (2012 [1805-1806]). *British It-narratives, 1750–1830. Volume 1: Money*. Ed. Liz Bellamy. London: Pickering & Chatto. 135–161.

"The Adventures of a One-Pound Bank Note" (2012 [1819]). *British It-Narratives 1750–1830. Volume 1: Money*. Ed. Liz Bellamy. London: Pickering & Chatto. 229–239.

Alber, Jan, Jan Iversen, Henrik Skov Nielsen, and Brian Richardson (2010) "Unnatural Narratives, Unnatural Narratology: Beyond Mimetic Models." *Narrative* 18.2: 113–136.

Alber, Jan (2011) "The Diachronic Development of Unnaturalness: A New View on Genre." *Unnatural Narratives, Unnatural Narratology*. Ed. Jan Alber and Rüdiger Heinze. Berlin et al.: De Gruyter. 41–76.

Bellamy, Liz (2007) "It-narrators and Circulation: Defining a Subgenre." *The Secret Life of Things: Animals, Objects, and It-Narratives in Eighteenth-Century England*. Ed. Mark Blackwell. Lewisburg, PA: Bucknell Univ. Press.

Bellamy, Liz (2012) Ed. *British It-Narratives, 1750–1830. Volume 1: Money*. London: Pickering & Chatto.

[10] Viktor Link, although he aims at a larger analysis of non-human narrators, agrees that the disappearance of the framing-apparatus occurs at a rather late stage in the development of the genre (Link 1980, 58).

Benedict, Barbara M. (2001) *Curiosity: A Cultural History of Early Modern Inquiry*. Chicago: Chicago Univ. Press.

Bernaerts, Lars, Marco Caracciolo, Luc Herman, and Bart Vervaeck (2015) "The Storied Lives of Non-Human Narrators." *Narrative* 22.1: 68–93.

Blackwell, Mark (2007) Ed. *The Secret Life of Things: Animals, Objects and It-Narratives in Eighteenth-Century England*. Lewisburg, PA: Bucknell Univ. Press.

Blackwell, Mark (2012a) Ed. *British It-Narratives, 1750-1830*. 4 vols. London: Pickering & Chatto.

Blackwell, Mark (2012b) Ed. *British It-Narratives, 1750-1830. Volume 4: Toys, Trifles and Portable Furniture*. London: Pickering & Chatto.

Denery, Dallas G.II (2015) *The Devil Wins: A History of Lying from the Garden of Eden to the Enlightenment*. Woodstock: Princeton Univ. Press.

Derrida, Jacques (1991) *Donner le temps 1: La fausse monnaie*. Paris: Galilée.

Derrida, Jacques (1992) *Given Time I: Counterfeit Money* [1991]. Trans. Peggy Kamuf. Chicago: Chicago Univ. Press.

Fludernik, Monika (1996) *Towards a 'Natural' Narratology*. London and New York: Routledge.

Garstad, Benjamin (2002) "Saturn, the First Coins, and the Meaning of ab ipso in Tertullian's 'Apologeticum' 10,8." *Latomus* 61: 961–963.

Gildon, Charles (1709) *The Golden Spy*. London: Woodward and Morphew.

Goodman, Nelson (1947) "The Problem of Counterfactual Conditional Sentences." *Journal of Philosophy* 44: 113–128.

Goux, Jean-Joseph (1994) *The Coiners of Language*. Trans. Jennifer Curtiss Gage. Norman, OK: Oklahoma Univ. Press.

Harman, Graham (2010) "Technology, Objects and Things in Heidegger." *Cambridge Journal of Economics* 34.1: 17–25.

Heidegger, Martin (1967) *Sein und Zeit* [1927]. Tubingen: Max Niemayer.

Hoey, Allen (1988) "The Name on the Coin: Metaphor, Metonymy, and Money." *Diacritics* 18.2: 26–37.

Keenleyside, Heather (2012) Ed. *British It-Narratives, 1750-1830. Volume 2: Animals*. London: Pickering & Chatto.

Latour, Bruno (2012) *We Have Never Been Modern* [1993]. Trans. Catherine Porter. Cambridge, MA: Harvard Univ. Press.

Lee, Mark (2010) "Truth, Metaphor and Counterfactual Meaning." *Tropical Truth(s): The Epistemology of Metaphor and Other Tropes*. Ed. Armin Burkhardt and Brigitte Nerlich. New York: De Gruyter. 123–136.

Link, Viktor (1980) *Die Tradition der außermenschlichen Erzählperspektive in der englischen und amerikanischen Literatur*. Heidelberg: Carl Winter.

Lupton, Christina (2012) Ed. *British It-Narratives, 1750-1830. Volume 3: Clothes and Transportation*. London: Pickering & Chatto.

Marx, Karl (1977) *Capital: A Critique of Political Economy* [1867]. Moscow: Progress Publishers.

Mehrotra, Santosh (1991) "On the Social Specifications of Use-Value in Marx's Capital." *Social Scientist* 19.8-9: 72–77.

Oxford English Dictionary Online (2020). Oxford Univ. Press. Web. 21 Jan. 2020.

Poovey, Mary (2008) *Genres of the Credit Economy: Mediating Value in Eighteenth- and Nineteenth-Century Britain*. Chicago and London: Chicago Univ. Press.

Ptolemy, Claudius (1822) *Tetrabiblos* [2nd century]. Trans. J.M. Ashmand. London: David and Dickson.

Saussure, Ferdinand de (1959) *Course in General Linguistics* [1916]. Ed. Charles Bally and Albert Sechehaye. Trans. Wade Baskin. New York: McGraw.

Scott, Helenus (2012). "The Adventures of a Rupee" [1782]. *British It-Narratives, 1750–1830.* Volume 1. Ed. Liz Bellamy. London: Pickering & Chatto. 27–73.

Selgin, George (2015) "Synthetic Commodity Money." *Journal of Financial Stability* 17: 92–99.

Sohn-Rethel, Alfred (1975) "Die Formcharaktere der zweiten Natur." *Das Unvermögen der Realität: Beiträge zu einer anderen materialistischen Ästhetik*. Ed. Gisela Dischner et al. Berlin: Verlag Klaus Wagenbach. 185–207.

Smith, Adam (2008) *An Inquiry into the Nature and Causes of the Wealth of Nations* [1776]. Volume 1. Ed. Edwin Cannan. Chicago: Chicago Univ. Press.

Unverzagt, Christian (2013) *Heidegger und das Sein der Dinge*. Norderstedt: Books on Demand.

"A Shocking Deception": Legal Fictions and Lying in *The Woman in White* and *No Name*

Katrin Althans

Fiction is the lie through which we tell the truth.
Albert Camus

1. *Introduction*

The fiction of Wilkie Collins is a playground on which the uneasy relationship of truth, lies, and fiction with reference to both law and literature is clearly being negotiated. As Lyn Pykett writes, much of Collins's work is "organized around legal issues, such as wills, inheritance laws, property rights, and marriage laws" (2005, 130). By including legal issues in his plots, Collins in his literary fiction draws attention to contemporary anxieties and takes a stand in current debates surrounding those issues. His major emphasis is on ongoing legal reform concerning marriage and female property rights. Lyn Pykett has demonstrated how Collins responds "to the debates around the Divorce and Matrimonial Causes Act of 1857 and the defeated Married Women's Property Bill of 1856" in his *The Woman in White* and *No Name.* She also points to the various Royal Commissions inquiring into the state of marriage laws between 1865 and 1868 in *Man and Wife* (2005, 134). However, Collins's fiction additionally concerns the level of legal concepts. One such legal concept in which the law's problematic treatment of fact, fiction, lying, and truth becomes apparent is that of legal fictions. By carefully mapping out the mechanics of legal fictions in his literary fictions, Wilkie Collins narratively explores the connections between truth and lying, its disowned sibling, in law. Thus in his critique of the law, he exposes the law's insistence on truth and its self-perception as factual discourse and also adds to our contemporary understanding of the nature of legal fictions.

As all the concepts I will be examining fail to have universally accepted definitions and instead are subject to intense debate among scholars, it is necessary to first extract the basic ideas which inform the notions of lying, truth, and fiction in law and literature before fleshing out my contentions with reference to the representation of falsehoods in Collins's *The Woman in White* and *No Name*. Let me therefore first turn to dissecting the complicated case of lying, truth, and fiction in the law.

2. Considerations of Truth and Lying in Law

Lying is conspicuously absent from law dictionaries. While *The Philosophy of Law: An Encyclopedia* has an entry on "Truth," there is no corresponding entry for "Lies" or "Lying." Instead, lying is dealt with in the entry on "Error, Deceit, and Illusion" (Niggli 1999, 265); and even there it is not mentioned explicitly. Rather, the author prefers to paraphrase the element of lying inherent in the legal concepts of error, deceit, and illusion by describing them as "forms of deviance from or misrepresentation of truth" (265). Again, references to truth predominate. Accordingly, no legal definition of lying is provided except for its relation to truth – which itself is defined as "an ideal that consists in the warranted assertibility of a thesis or a set of theses" (Kramer 1999, 873). Likewise, when discussing lying as a necessary element of white-collar offenses, Stuart P. Green is concerned with the *structural nature* of lying, but again defines lying against the background of a purported truth value of statements: "the term lying refers to (intentional) deception that (1) comes in the form of a verifiable assertion, and (2) is literally false. By verifiable assertion, I refer to a statement that has a determinable truth value (ie is either true or false [...])" (2006, 77). In his later contribution to the *Oxford Handbook of Lying*, Green briefly repeats his earlier definition of lying and then goes on to consider it as one of the elements of a number of criminal offenses such as perjury or fraud (2019, 483). As Frank Schäfer in his chapter on unlawful and lawful lies in this collection shows, the same holds true for German law. Lying, it seems, is the black sheep of the legal family, mentioned only as a necessary element of criminal offenses and as a distortion of law's pet concept truth. This tradition is already evident in William Blackstone, who in his *Commentaries on the Laws of England* defines lying as "a criminal violation of truth," but also as "derogatory from sound morality" (1830, vol. 4, 41–2). Lying, he reasons, is therefore only relevant for the law and thus "liable to the temporal punishment of human tribunals" when "it carries with it some public inconvenience," whereas "private vices [i.e., lying without public inconveniences] are subject to the vengeance of eternal justice" (42). Inversely, Bernard Williams asks about truth "whether it can be more than relative or subjective" and links it to a "reflex against deceptiveness" (2002, 1). The relation of truth and lying thus seems to be one of mutual dependence.

There are, of course, numerous philosophical approaches to truth and lying (cf. Glanzberg 2018; Mahon 2016), but this is not the proper place to consider them in detail. What I am interested in instead is the relation between truth, lying, and fiction in the law and the ways in which it is questioned in literary representations of legal fictions in Wilkie Collins's novels *The Woman in White* and *No Name*. In order to properly assess this relation, together with its literary representation, it is nevertheless necessary to look at the different types of truth in law and at lying as "a subset of deception" (Green 2006, 77) to determine how this affects the understanding of legal fictions.

As Robert S. Summers states, many scholars from disciplines outside the law believe that the most important task of trial court proceedings (1999, 497) consists in finding "the truth," i.e., to bring to light the events as they happened at a given moment in time. After all, the idea of truth looms large in sworn testimony when witnesses are sworn in to tell "the truth, the whole truth, and nothing but the truth" (Oaths Act 1978, s. 6, ss. 1[1]). However, Summers clarifies that it is necessary to distinguish between what he calls "substantive truth" and "formal legal truth" (1999, 498). Whereas the first refers to a factual truth (based on the assumption that there exists a determinable truth which in a trial can be reconstructed through witness reports and other evidence), the second refers to "whatever is found as fact by the legal fact-finder (judge or lay jurors or both), whether it accords with substantive truth or not" (Summers 1999, 498). Accordingly, "formal legal truth may [...] fail to coincide with substantive truth" (1999, 499). Summers here references Hans Kelsen, who characterizes legal facts as facts which are created through legal decisions "even if in the sphere of nature the fact has not occurred" (1944, 218). Kelsen goes on to argue that such a legal fact only has significance in the legal sphere since it is detached from reality (1944, 218). If we take Kelsen's reasoning to apply to Summers's thoughts on truth, we find that in the law we are concerned with a particular kind of truth which retains meaning only within the limits of the legal sphere. Accordingly, if lying is still characterized by its relation to truth within that sphere, there might be a specific form of legal lying, i.e., of lying with relevance in the legal world alone.

However, when we turn to Green's condition of a lie being "literally false," with which he refers to the "literal meaning" of a sentence (2006, 77), we are confronted with a situation in which the law disrupts its own logical reasoning and establishes a reference to external reality. Green does not take into account the slipperiness of the term *literal* and bases his argument on the assumption that there exists "a determinable truth value" (2006, 77), thus turning a blind eye to discussions about the nature of truth both inside and outside the law. In his discussion of the rules on perjury and their history in Common Law jurisdictions he again comes back to the requirement of "literal falsity" and explains the extent to which this criminal offense brings the outside world into the courtroom as a point of reference against which the falsity of a statement is to be measured (2006, 135–136). This leaves us with two levels which are intertwined: one concerning the philosophical concepts of truth and lying in law and a second one examining truth and lying in actual legal practice. Whereas, in the first context, both truth and lying are defined relationally as its

[1] Abbreviation s. for section and ss. for sub-section.

other's other, in the second context they need a point of reference outside the legal world to determine their existence.

Even though Kelsen defines his legal facts as facts "to which the law attaches certain consequences" (1944, 218) and despite the fact that Summers elaborates on which factors outside of the courtroom impact on the difference between legal and substantive truth (1999, 499–500), *in their arguments* they both emphasize that the law is a closed system: legal facts and legal truth only have consequences within the sphere of the law. Neither Kelsen nor Green takes the argument a step further. They do not consider the repercussions of legal facts and legal truth in the world outside legal philosophy. Here I am venturing on unsafe ground since an uncritical synthesis of legal philosophy and legal practice is lacking on several levels. Nevertheless, I plan to explore the connection between these two areas rather than uphold this divide. The concept of legal fictions offers some help here. They are themselves positioned at the intersection of legal philosophy and practice – and bring us one step closer to literary fictions.

3. *Legal Fictions in* The Woman in White

In both *The Woman in White* and *No Name*, Wilkie Collins conflates the legal and the extra-legal world by fictionalizing the legal fiction of *filius* (and *filiae*?) *nullius* in the form of Sir Percival Glyde (in *The Woman in White*) as well as of Norah and Magdalen Vanstone (in *No Name*). Together with other variations on the topic of legitimacy, illegitimacy, and identity, Collins through the fictional representations of legal concepts in his novels sheds light on the fraught relationship of truth, lying, and fiction in the law.

Collins is one of a number of novelists who have contributed to the "controversy" concerning legal fictions which took place in the first decades of the Victorian age (Stone 1985, 125). Much of this controversy was sparked by Jeremy Bentham's criticism of legal fictions: "in English law, *fiction* is a *syphilis*, which runs in every vein, and carries into every part of the system the principle of rottenness" (1843, vol. 5, 92). In this critique, he placed himself in opposition to William Blackstone, whose position was shared by John Austin and Sir Henry Maine, the other two important legal voices in the debate at that time (Harmon 1990, 9). First and foremost, this debate was primarily concerned with the question if legal fictions have a rightful place in English law at all (3); whereas "[t]he structure of the fiction," as writes Pierre J. J. Olivier, "has received scant attention" (1975, 32). Bentham's characterization of a "fiction (in law)" as "a wilful falsehood" is noteworthy in that he literally contrasts legal fictions with the notion of "truth" (1843, vol. 5, 13). His take on legal fictions may thus well be summed up as a "condemnation of legal fictions as falsehood and lies" (Stolzenberg 1999, 230). Likewise, about 40 years later, Maine rejected the idea of legal fictions as something "merely fraudulent" (1861, 27) and instead proposed to understand a legal fiction as "any assumption which conceals, or affects to conceal, the fact that a rule of law has undergone alteration" (26).

Both standpoints have influenced later works on legal fictions. Many legal scholars today agree that at the heart of legal fictions lies a falsehood which may initiate unpredictable consequences (Stern 2017, 313–314). It is, writes Frederick Schauer, an "intentional untruth in the law" and as such "seems an especially odd thing for an institution allegedly committed to truth-finding" (2015, 114). Again, the emphasis is on truth in the law and, like lying, the legal fiction is characterized in relation to this truth, as an "untruth." At the same time, legal fictions hover uneasily between truth and lying or rather seem to exist altogether outside of this matrix. As Lon Fuller famously states: "a fiction [...] is neither a truthful statement, nor a lie [...]" (1930, 366). A legal fiction is not a truthful statement, as the degree of its inadequacy to reality "is outstanding or unusual" (1930, 370): Minorca obviously is not "at London, in the parish of St. Mary le Bow, in the ward of Cheap," as the legal fiction used in Mostyn v Fabrigas has it ((1774) 1 Cowp 161, 164). To be considered a lie, on the other hand, the legal fiction lacks the element of deception: "a fiction is distinguished from a lie by the fact that it is not intended to deceive" (Fuller 1930, 367). Rather, it is described in terms of Vaihinger's *As if*, i.e., in the sense of "bewusstfalscher [sic] Annahmen" (1922, 20), "consciously false assumptions" (Vaihinger 1935, xlvi): the falsity of the legal fiction is known and "it is used with a complete consciousness of its falsity" (Fuller 1930, 370).

This famous definition, however, does not reflect the multifariousness of the concept, nor does it take into account the structural difficulties it involves. This has only recently been pointed out by Maksymilian Del Mar and William Twining in their *Legal Fictions in Theory and Practice*. They make a point of not wanting to "impose any one example or function, or indeed definition [of legal fictions] on the contributors" (Del Mar 2015a, xx). Accordingly, the definitions used in that volume range from classical ideas of legal fictions as falsehoods to approaches which discuss them as "true legal propositions" (Lind 2015, 84) or in terms of "absence [...] or [...] presence of proof" (Del Mar 2015b, 226). Furthermore, Del Mar and Twining draw attention to the fact that there is a difference in considering legal fictions *in theory*, i.e., in terms of understanding the nature and structure of legal fictions, or *in practice*, i.e., the ways in which legal fictions are used by legal practitioners (Del Mar 2015a, x). This echoes Kelsen's argument in his critique of Vaihinger: "Deutlich zu scheiden von den rechtstheoretischen Fiktionen sind die sogenannten 'fictiones juris', sind die Fiktionen der Rechts*praxis*, das ist: des *Gesetzgebers* und *Rechtsanwenders*" (Kelsen 1919, 638); "What needs to be clearly distinguished from the fictions of legal theory are the so-called 'fictiones juris,' the fictions of legal *practice*, i.e.

of the *legislator* and of the *application of the law*" (Kelsen 2015, 9). Kelsen is also keen to emphasize the fact that legal theory makes no claims concerning a "Naturwirklichkeit," an "actual reality," and that thus legal fictions of legal theory, such as the concept of the legal person, are always fictitious with regard to a legal reality only and have no bearings outside of that reality (1919, 634; 2015, 6). Although there are contradictions inherent in legal fictions, Kelsen writes, they merely contradict the legal world. It is only if legal theory claims to have factual reality as its "Erkenntnisgegenstand" ("object of cognition") that those legal fictions also contradict factual reality (1919, 633–634; 2015, 5–6).

As Kelsen shows, the use, nature, and definition of legal fictions are complex and hard to navigate. Any attempt at unraveling the many strands of scholarship concerning legal fictions, both historical and contemporary, would require more space than available here, which is why I will need to focus on one particular aspect only. I, therefore, resist the impulse to establish a working, much less stable, definition with which the legal fictions described in *The Woman in White* and *No Name* can be analyzed. Collins's treatment of legal fictions in his work, I argue, is neither a mere criticism of them nor is it an inventory of the theories of legal fictions proposed by jurists in the eighteenth and nineteenth centuries. Instead, I suggest reading the ways in which the legal status of illegitimate children is presented in the two novels and how this questions legal assumptions about truth, lying, and fictions as another means of approaching the nature of legal fictions.

"A bastard," writes Blackstone, "is one that is not only begotten, but born, out of lawful matrimony" (1830, vol. 1, 455). Under English law until 1926, when the Legitimacy Act was passed, a subsequent marriage of the parents did not legitimize children born out of wedlock unlike in civil law jurisdictions and canon law (Baker 2011, 490). Blackstone emphasizes that one of the main reasons for this rule is "the desire of procreating lawful *heirs*" (1830, vol. 1, 455). Despite the Legitimacy Act, the doctrine of *filius nullius*, of a bastard being considered the son of nobody, still applies to peerages (Baker 2011, 490). Therefore, even though an illegitimately born son can now be legitimated through his parents' subsequent marriage, he can never be heir to a title. In *The Woman in White*, it is Sir Percival Glyde whose illegitimacy is at the heart of an intricate web of deception and lying, and the secrecy surrounding this fact is one of the driving forces of the plot. Legally speaking, Sir Glyde was born an illegitimate child and this, as Walter Hartright correctly notes, "would deprive him [...] of the name, the rank, the estate, the whole social existence that he had usurped" (Collins 2003, 510). The usurpation Hartright refers to is Glyde's claim to the hereditary title of "the rank of baronet," and the linked "property in Hampshire" (Collins 2003, 77). He achieves this deception by inserting a faked marriage entry, that of his parents, into the register of Old Welmingham Church in order to legitimate his birth. These multiple acts of lying and deception performed by Sir Percival Glyde can be shown to have an impact on the understanding of the general structure of legal fictions. In order to explain the ways in which the nature of legal fictions may be explained through the lies Glyde tells it is, however, necessary to go into more detail and to read Collins's text through the eyes of the law.

Sir Glyde's criminal actions are numerous. First, there is the instance of the forged entry in the marriage register itself and, second, his taking possession of the estate as the heir of Blackwater Park. The legal consequences of the first action are accurately described by Walter Hartright when he states that this "might, in past years, have hanged him [Glyde] – might even now transport him for life" (Collins 2003, 510). It seems that tampering with entries in marriage registers was regarded as particularly harmful in a peaceful society relying on strict rules of succession; the Marriage Act of 1753 expressly made such tempering a felony without benefit of clergy, i.e., it carried an automatic death penalty (s. XVI). The Forgery Act of 1830, while still considering "inserting any false Entry in any Register of Baptism, Marriages, or Burials" a felony, reduced the punishment to the then-common transportation "beyond the Seas" or even only imprisonment, "at the Discretion of the Court" (s. XX). Forgery itself has been defined by Blackstone as "the fraudulent making or alteration of a writing to the prejudice of another man's rights" and included among the offenses against private property (1830, vol. 4, 247).

This is important on two counts: on the one hand, the inclusion of forgery among other property-related offenses, when applied to the world of *The Woman in White* suggests a connection between property and identity or legitimacy which is upset by the forgery. On the other hand, the insistence on the "making or alteration of a writing" highlights that it is the authenticity of the document alone that is in question and not the authenticity of the claim itself. In the context of *The Woman in White*, the first observation, that of a connection between property and identity, is related to the medieval legal logic of "treating status as akin to property" (Baker 2011, 471) and explains why there are efforts to ensure the legitimacy of heirs to hereditary titles. Once this carefully constructed system of equivalence is disturbed, as it is by the fake entry of his parents' marriage in the official church register as inserted by Glyde, the principles underlying English society seem to be at risk. As Sara Malton convincingly argues, Glyde, through his forgery, "enacts a violation of genealogy," "a violation of cultural memory," and his "falsehood [...] has debased [...] the annals of English history, the baronetcy, and the rightful heir to the Glyde name" (2014, 42–43).

The second observation, that the forgery affects only the authenticity of the document, adds another facet to the understanding of the falsification of documents. Sir Percival's act of forgery does not constitute a lie about his legitimacy, but only falsifies the register. It can thus be described as a palimpsestic act in that it overwrites the material register, but it is not figuratively palimpsestic, as it does not overwrite Glyde's identity as an illegitimate son. Though the false entry deceives people as to the legitimate birth of Sir Percival Glyde, it does so only because the forgery creates the (false) instrument with which the deception is accomplished. Malton is right when she points out that there is a "conceptual alignment of bastardy and forgery in Victorian narratives" and that forgery and illegitimate children both "threatened established systems of authority" (2014, 7). As she argues, nineteenth-century novels often focus on "the fraudulent foundation – the lie" and "the lack of authenticity" (2014, 12). However, she fails to consider the relations between illegitimacy, forgery, and the legal fiction of *filius nullius*, the legal concept haunting the bastard.

At this point, the linguistic structure of the Common Law rules as written down by Blackstone make it necessary to revisit Kelsen's critique of Vaihinger: Kelsen meticulously explains why Vaihinger's elaborations on the phrase "as if" as used in statutes do not concern legal fictions, but rather "Pseudofiktionen des Gesetzgebers," "pseudo-fictions of the legislator" (1919, 630; 2015, 3). The use of "as if" in Art. 347 of the German Commercial Code (Vaihinger's example), according to Kelsen, does not equate an extra-legal fact with another extra-legal fact, but only stipulates that the same legal consequences apply to both (1919, 639; 2015, 10): "Die Sprachform des 'Als ob'," Kelsen argues, "ist somit gar nicht wesentlich, sie kann durch das 'Ebenso wie' ersetzt werden" (1919, 639); "The grammatical form of the 'As-If' thus is not in any way essential, it can be replaced by a mere 'just as'" (Kelsen 2015, 10). Kelsen concludes that if the phrase *as if* is used in statutes, the two things related one to the other by these means are by no means the equivalent in the world outside the law, but are equated for legal purposes only: "Daß sie 'rechtlich' gleich seien, bedeutet nichts anderes, als daß bei natürlicher *Verschiedenheit* des Tatbestandes die *gleiche* Rechtsfolge eintritt" (1919, 640); "That they are 'legally' the same simply means that despite a natural *difference* in fact the *same* legal consequence is supposed to follow" (Kelsen 2015, 10). The use of *as if*, writes Kelsen, is only an efficient means to allow two different facts or situations to be subsumed under the same wording of the law (1919, 640; 2015, 10). For English Common Law, by contrast, Blackstone avoids an *as-if*-construction. He summarizes the consequences of being a bastard as "he can inherit nothing, being looked upon as the son of nobody [...]" and as having his "primary settlement [...] in the parish where born, for he hath no father" (1830, vol. 1, 459). Blackstone further reasons that "[t]he incapacity of a bastard consists principally in this, that he cannot be heir to anyone, neither can he have heirs, but of his own body; for, being *nullius filius*, he is therefore of kin to nobody, and has no ancestor from whom any inheritable blood can be derived" (1830, vol. 1, 459). Blackstone here describes a reality which the phrase "as if" is lacking and thereby establishes a fact in a reality outside of the legal world: a *filius nullius* is not only treated *as if* he was nobody's son, he *is* nobody's son. Taking Blackstone's text at grammatical face value, one could consider the legal fiction a lie (the illegitimate son is not nobody's son), but the emphasis Blackstone puts on the bastard's incapacity to inherit (property and title, even parish) complicates matters. The legal fiction of *filius nullius* as defined by Blackstone seems to foreground the *legal consequences* attached to the status of a "bastard." Thus he again seems to implicitly create a contradiction within the legal world only, without making a statement about the extra-legal world: even though not being entitled to inherit has real-world effects on the "bastard," the question of succession itself is an entirely legal one. This, then, would make the legal fiction not a lie, but a statement which creates legal truth, and only after the legal truth has been determined does it lead to real-world consequences.

In *The Woman in White*, the story of Sir Percival's illegitimacy and the forged entry into the marriage register at Old Welmingham not only plays out at the intersection of illegitimacy and forgery but also on the narrative level. The secret of Glyde's illegitimacy is embedded in narratives which consist of witness statements. The first reference to Sir Percival's parents is a story written down (and possibly edited) by Walter Hartright. It was told to him by Marian Halcombe, who "could only speak on these topics from hearsay; but she was reasonably certain of the truth of what little she had to tell" (2003, 456). Due to its having been twice re-told, thus constituting double hearsay, this first story (in which Sir Percival's mother is said to have been married to his father, Sir Felix Glyde) calls into question the reliability of the details presented in the novel as being true. The second instance in which information on the Glydes' family history is given consists of the marriage register of Welmingham Parish Church and its copy in Mr Wansborough's office in Knowlesbury. However, the authenticity of both original and copy can only be determined through the narration of Walter Hartright; he is the only character who gets to see both books. Finally, the corrected version of the story of Sir Percival's parents, and thus of his illegitimate birth, is presented through the letter that Mrs Catherick sent to Walter Hartright. Yet he is an autodiegetic narrator who keeps undermining his own reliability by again and again protesting the authenticity of his account (cf., for instance, Collins 2003, 9, 525) – a feature listed by Nünning as typical of unreliable narrators (1998, 28). Later he even admits to having edited parts of the story (cf., for instance, Collins 2003, 414, 543). Hartright's insistence on having copied the letter, the origin of which is itself in question, "exactly, word for word" (Collins 2003, 528) is therefore hardly proof of the story's authenticity. The fact that Mrs Catherick has been introduced as a fallen woman of low moral standards (2003, 467–470) also raises suspicion as to the veracity of the letter's content, although her alleged moral failures are outlined by hearsay only (it is, in fact, Hartright who spreads the rumor which he has received from Mrs Clements).

What is interesting about all these pieces of information relating to the Glyde family presented in the novel is the fact that the only authentic and genuine piece of evidence is the birth certificate which Sir Percival produces: "the certificate of his birth was easily got – he was born abroad, and the certificate was there in due form" (Collins 2003, 530). This certificate is mentioned in Mrs Catherick's letter to Walter Hartright, in which she has set down "what [she] heard from him [Sir Percival]" (Collins 2003, 530). Despite the reader hearing about it through double hearsay, there is, for once, little doubt about the authenticity of the certificate. We learn that it has been obtained from the proper foreign authorities. Curiously, it is the only certificate in the novel which is not used under false pretenses, asserting facts which do not pertain to the real world (as are, for instance, the death certificate of Lady Glyde or the marriage register). Hence, the only aspect of Sir Percival's identity which is confirmed as genuine is that of his being the (natural) son of his parents, Sir Felix Glyde and Cecilia Jane Elster. Although, strictly speaking, the name of his mother on the birth certificate as well as Sir Percival's surname are not their own. This circumstance, in turn, helps one to understand the nature of the legal fiction of *filius nullius* in particular and of legal fictions in general: in *The Woman in White*, the bastard is indeed the *son* of Sir Felix Glyde, but not the *heir* (of title or even name). The legal fiction of *filius nullius* is thus understood as creating exclusively legal consequences and not as constituting a lie in the extra-legal world. Another look at Blackstone supports this view. Blackstone explicitly mentions "the ties of nature" as opposed to "any civil purposes." Whereas in the legal world a bastard is the son of nobody, in the extra-legal world a man may still not "marry his bastard sister or daughter" even though they are not legally related (1830, vol. 1, 458). Blackstone thus acknowledges a conceptual difference of bastardy in the legal sense as compared to the natural world.

There also is the question of Sir Percival's taking possession of the estate as heir to the baronetcy and to Blackwater Park. In Mrs Catherick's account of what Glyde told her, she says that "he came to England at once, and took possession of the property. There was no one to suspect him, and no one to say him nay. [...] He had no difficulty, so far – he took possession, as a matter of course" (Collins 2003, 530). James E. Mahon explains that, in philosophy, lying involves "that a person make a statement" (statement condition), which "requires the use of language" (2016, 3). "According to the statement condition," Mahon continues, "it is not possible to lie by omitting to make a statement" (2016, 4). Deception, on the other hand, does not require a statement to be made, thus it is possible to deceive by, for instance, pretense (Mahon 2016, 41). Following this reasoning, Glyde, by conveying the impression of being the legitimate son of Sir Felix Glyde, succeeded in deceiving the people at Blackwater Park, but he did not do so by lying. Neither did he lie to the rightful heir of the estate, who "was a distant relation, who had no idea of ever getting it, and who was away at sea when his [Sir Percival's] father died" (Collins 2003, 530). Interestingly, throughout the text, the forged marriage entry and Glyde's usurpation of the position of baronet are treated as separate issues; in fact, the only instance in the text in which a "certificate of his parents' marriage" (which is itself only a document based on the forged entry) is mentioned occurs in connection with a reference to the obstacle imposed by the law to "borrow money on the property" (Collins 2003, 530).

In the legal world of the nineteenth century, Glyde's actions would have been considered *false pretense*: "there might be a sufficient false pretence [...] by the acts and conduct of the party, without any verbal representations of a false and fraudulent nature" (Russell 1843, vol. 2, 293). As such, false pretense is penalized under statutory law (Larceny Act 1827, s. 53). It is, however, distinguished from lying, i.e. cheating "by a mere false affirmation, or bare lie," which is not an indictable offense at Common Law, nor is it found in statutes (Russell 1843, vol. 2, 282). Thus lying (outside perjury), unlike false pretense, is of no legal relevance in and of itself (cf. also Blackstone's considerations on lying, 1830, vol. 4, 41–2). However, Sir Percival is in fact also impersonating another, viz. the rightful heir to the Glyde title and estate, and as Russell writes "falsely personating another [...] is so nearly allied to forgery, and so often blended with it, that these offences have been [...] made felonies alike" (1843, vol. 2, 540). In the legal context, Sir Percival's actions are thus much more closely aligned with what is at the center of the *filius nullius* motif: the forged entry in the marriage register. There is, therefore, a telling difference between the world of the law and the diegetic world of the novel, and this reflects on the nature of legal fictions and their falsity. Once again the novel distinguishes the relevance of legal fictions within the legal realm from that in the extra-legal world of the plot.

The way in which the legal fiction of *filius nullius* is described in *The Woman in White* thus contributes to the discussion of the nature of legal fictions in the law. Another example concerns the way the legal fiction of coverture is dissected in the novel. In its structure and consequences, this issue is closely related to the concept of *filius nullius*. Blackstone writes that "by marriage, the husband and wife are one person in law: that is, the very being or legal existence of the woman is suspended during the marriage, or at least is incorporated and consolidated into that of the husband"; she is "a *feme-covert* [sic]" (1830, vol. 1, 442). Although Blackstone again does not use an "as if" construction but refers to husband and wife as indeed being "one person," he immediately qualifies this identification by restricting it to the law and the "legal existence of the woman." Even more explicitly than in his writings about illegitimate children, Blackstone here asserts that a wife's status of *feme covert* only matters in the legal context but has no bearings on the extra-legal world when he lists a number of legal duties and obligations derived from the legal fiction of unity of person. However, this legal unity of person encroaches upon the identity of women in similar ways as do the rules of *filius nullius* in the case of male illegitimate children. We are therefore justified in taking a closer look at the question of female identity under coverture in *The Woman in White*. As Lenora Ledwon writes, "the law of coverture becomes the novel's metonym for the loss of female identity" (1993, 10), a loss which mirrors the loss of identity visited upon bastard children in the form of *filius nullius*.

As a result of her marriage to Sir Percival Glyde, Laura Fairlie in many ways loses her identity (as Laura Fairlie), and this can be read as a critique of the legal status of married women. First, as her half-sister Marian quite precisely observes, her marriage "*transformed* Miss Fairlie into Lady Glyde" (Collins 2003, 191, emphasis mine). Laura has not only lost her name, but it has been replaced by that of her husband. Through coverture, her legal identity has been subsumed under that of her husband. This loss of legal identity has often been referred to as a "symbolic 'civil death'" (Ledwon 1993, 107). Although the symbolic use of the term needs to be distinguished from the actual legal concept of civil death as the loss of civil rights, in the context of *The Woman in White* it allows for an interesting reading of Laura's situation. Having first been subsumed under the identity of her husband, Sir Percival Glyde, Laura's identity is then completely stripped from her when she is taken to the lunatic asylum under the name of Anne Catherick, whereas her identity as "Laura, Lady Glyde" (Collins 2003, 405) has been suppressed and is dead and buried. The symbolic *civil* death of marriage has been converted into the lie of an *actual* death. In fact, the engraving on the tombstone which documents Laura's death for all the world to see is the only instance which is referred to in the text as a lie, even repeatedly so (Collins 2003, 445, 549, 591). Analogously, Walter Hartright in his pursuits to re-establish Laura's identity declares that he is "serving [...] the cause of truth" (Collins 2003, 591). However, the identity he seeks to restore is not that of Laura *Fairlie*, i.e. Laura in the image of her maiden name, but that of Laura *Hartright*, since, after the death of Sir Percival, she married Walter and is now his legal wife. Eventually, Laura is duly reinstated as the niece of Frederick Fairlie (Collins 2003, 618–619) and, most importantly, the son she has with Walter Hartright legitimately succeeds his great-uncle as "*the Heir of Limmeridge*" (Collins 2003, 627).

Does the representation of coverture in *The Woman in White* then culminate in a lie in the extra-legal world? As the text makes clear, it is the engraving on the tombstone Walter calls a lie, and it is only "in the eye [...] of the law" that Laura is "socially, morally, legally – dead" (Collins 2003, 413). Thus, the lies which are manifested in "the narratives of death certificate and tombstone" are what keep Laura legally dead (MacDonagh & Smith 1996, 278–279). What we have here, then, is not a legal fiction which is the origin of a lie in the outside world; rather, we are confronted with a lie which (unlawfully) has legal consequences – Laura is dead for the world and the law not because of a legal fiction, but because of an extra-legal document, i.e. the tombstone. Even though the legal fiction of unity of person has been taken to its extreme by being symbolized as a kind of death, this has only ever been a *legal* death as far as Laura is concerned, never real death in the world outside the law. Therefore, the representation of coverture in *The Woman in White* supports my argument that the text scrutinizes the nature and structure of legal fictions, drawing a sharp line between the legal and extra-legal world and carefully tracing the consequences and effects of legal fictions back to their origins, which are rooted in both truth and lying.

At the same time, the complexity of the textual evidence on legal fictions also serves as a critique of the concept of legal fictions in more general terms and ties in with the overarching criticism of the law in Collins's texts. After all, when the epitome of *filius nullius*, Sir Percival Glyde, dies a horrible death in the flames (Collins 2003, 515–518), his identity remains unstable even in death, for the police are not able to conclusively identify his body (which is burned beyond recognition) and need to rely on circumstantial evidence (Collins 2003, 522). Moreover, the prototypical unity of person in the novel, that of Count Fosco and his wife, is described as lethal (Collins 2003, 215–216) and can thus be read as a thinly disguised critique of the legal fiction of the *feme covert*. Let us now turn to Collins's *No Name*. As we will see, whereas in *The Woman in White* the focus is on the *structure* of legal fictions, *No Name* can be read as a universal critique of the concept of legal fictions. It does so in its representation of illegitimate daughters and by linking the artificiality of legal fictions to that of literary fictions.

4. *Legal Fictions in* No Name

Simon Stern considers a defining feature of legal fictions that they are explicit in "displaying their artifice in a way that other doctrines do not" (2017, 314). In parallel, Sundeep Bisla when analyzing the domestic beginning of *No Name* presents it as a means "to disclose [...] the artifice at its [domestic novel's] basis" (2010, 2). Collins, he argues, in *No Name* reveals "the artifice inherent in its [domestic novel's] models, the upstanding Victorian and pre-Victorian citizenry and society" (2010, 2). Similarly, Stern points out that "the more ostentatious doctrines [i.e., legal fictions] call attention to the creative operations that pervade the legal realm but that usually pass unnoticed" (Stern 2017, 315). There is, then, a striking resemblance on a structural level between legal fictions and the text of *No Name*, and this is echoed in the ways in which the fiction of *filius nullius* is represented in the novel.

After their father's death in a train accident, Norah and Magdalen Vanstone are left "Nobody's Children" (Collins 2004, 109). Their mother and (legitimate) sibling have died in childbirth. Since their parents were not married at the time of their births and English Common Law until 1926 did not legitimate children "by a marriage *ex post facto*" (Blackstone 1830, vol. 1, 455), they no longer have the status of legal heirs. Their case thus is similar to that of Sir Percival Glyde, and yet different: they are women and as such to a certain degree exempt from the legal consequences attached to the status of *filius nullius*. Having argued for the view that the legal fiction of *filius nullius* does not make any assertion concerning the actual biological status of father and child but only about the legal right to inherit, I will not treat Norah and Magdalen Vanstone as full *filiae nullius*, for, as Michael Neill concludes, "[...] legal bastardy [...] was almost automatically imagined as a male condition" (1993, 275). The legal status of females as illegitimate only mattered in terms of the question of who had to provide for them (compare Blackstone's "ties of nature" (1830, vol. 1, 458)). The question of legitimacy, in fact, is of no importance for female bastards, because they, in a system of strict male primogeniture, can inherit neither title nor estate. However, legitimate daughters could inherit "their *reasonable* parts," i.e., their share of one-third of the goods, if the father died intestate (Blackstone 1830, vol. 2, 492). In *No Name*, the inheritance of money is a very complex affair. With his recent marriage to his daughters' mother, Mr Vanstone's initial will has been rendered void and the legal order of succession now applies, which leaves Norah and Magdalen "helpless at their uncle's mercy" (Collins 2004, 108–109). The mercy he shows them, then, reflects the attitude the Common Law shows illegitimate children: he distinguishes between "a place in the world to which they are not entitled" as opposed to "their proper position," one which "becomes their birth" (Collins 2004, 123). Apart from their titular loss of their father's name, the daughters are also left destitute thanks to the legal fiction of *filius nullius*. This cruel situation created by the law is commented on by the narrator, who refers to the uncle's language in the letter as "atrocious sentences" (Collins 2004, 124). Mr Pendril, the lawyer, is even more explicit: "I think it a disgrace to the nation" (Collins 2004, 110).

When we turn to the structure of legal fictions in relation to truth, lying, and deception, which is laid bare in the text of *The Woman in White*, we can see that in *No Name* a less sophisticated approach prevails. In its critique of the law, the novel connects the legal fiction of *filius nullius*, together with that of the unity of person, to various forms of lying and deception in general, but it ignores the subtleties which *The Woman in White* reveals: "Any conspiracy, any deception, is justified to my conscience by the vile law which has left us [Norah and Magdalen] helpless," says Magdalen (Collins 2004, 275). As she later confesses, her "wickedness [...] has made Nobody's Child Somebody's Wife" (Collins 2004, 484). Through lying and deceiving, she re-claims her family name as her own. Her marriage to her cousin, however, does not restore her maiden name but instead imposes the name of her husband upon her, which is only coincidentally that of her parents. Thus Magdalen by no means becomes entitled to what would have been rightfully hers had she been legitimate. It is the legal unity of person framework which tricks her into believing she has legitimated herself as Magdalen Vanstone.

Due to its failure to go into the details of truth, lying, and deception as far as legal fictions are concerned, *No Name* is much more explicit in its general criticism of the Common Law. The meta-critical qualities of *No Name* and its critique of its genre (which Bisla reads as challenging the constraints of the domestic novel) and of legal fictions (which Stern reads as highlighting the creative tendencies of the law) are all the more apparent when reading the legal fictions in the novel as a comment on both the law and domesticity. By unashamedly emphasizing the cruelty of the law without losing itself in details, *No Name* draws attention to the failures of legal fictions as well as of Victorian society.

5. Conclusion

"Collins's interest in the dilemma of namelessness," writes Mark Ford in his introduction to *No Name*, "is part of his life-long preoccupation with the means by which a social identity is constructed, and, equally, how it may be borrowed, invented, dismantled or buried" (Collins 2004, ix). At the same time, Collins is also interested in the ways in which the law, particularly by means of legal fictions, creates a legal identity. The ways in which both social and legal identity are depicted in *The Woman in White* and *No Name* disclose their common origin in practices of lying and deception and their relationship to issues of truth.

In the texts, the identity of both illegitimate and legitimate children is at stake and constantly questioned, and so is the legitimation of legal fictions. In both *The Woman in White* and *No Name* Collins challenges the nature as well as the structural complexity of legal fictions, demonstrating their uneasy relationship with truth, lying, and deception. The attention paid to jurisprudential details in these works as well as more general criticism of legal fictions thus allow us to read both texts as comments on the law which help the reader to understand its mechanics.

Works Cited

(1774) 1 Cowp 161. [Mostyn v Fabrigas]

Baker, John H. (2011) *An Introduction to English Legal History*. 4th ed. Oxford: Oxford Univ. Press.

Bentham, Jeremy (1838–1843) *The Works of Jeremy Bentham*. Ed. John Bowring. 11 vols. Edinburgh: William Tait.

Bisla, Sundeep (2010) "Over-Doing Things with Words in 1862: Pretense and Plain Truth in Wilkie Collins's *No Name*." *Victorian Literature and Culture* 38.1: 1–19.

Blackstone, William (1830) *Commentaries on the Laws of England* [1765–1769]. 17th ed. 4 vols. London.

Collins, Wilkie (2004) *No Name* [1862]. Ed. Mark Ford. Penguin Classics. London: Penguin.

Collins, Wilkie (2003) *The Woman in White* [1860]. Ed. Matthew Sweet. Penguin Classics. London: Penguin.

Del Mar, Maksymilian (2015a) "Introducing Fictions: Examples, Functions, Definitions and Evaluations." *Legal Fictions in Theory and Practice*. Ed. Maksymilian Del Mar and William Twining. Cham: Springer International Publishing. ix–xxix.

Del Mar, Maksymilian (2015b) "Legal Fictions and Legal Change in the Common Law Tradition." *Legal Fictions in Theory and Practice*. Ed. Maksymilian Del Mar and William Twining. Cham: Springer International Publishing. 225–253.

Forgery Act 1830. 11 Geo. 4 & 1 Will. 4 c 66.

Forgery and Counterfeiting Act 1980. 1981 c 45.

Fuller, Jon (1930) "Legal Fictions 1/3." *Illinois Law Review* 25.4: 363–399.

Glanzberg, Michael (2018) "Truth." *The Stanford Encyclopedia of Philosophy*. Ed. Edward N. Zalta. <https://plato.stanford.edu/archives/fall2018/entries/truth/>.

Green, Stuart P. (2006) *Lying, Cheating, and Stealing: A Moral Theory of White-Collar Crime*. Oxford: Oxford Univ. Press.

Green, Stuart P. (2019) "Lying and the Law." *The Oxford Handbook of Lying*. Ed. Jörg Meibauer. Oxford: Oxford Univ. Press. 483–494.

Harmon, Louise (1990) "Falling off the Vine: Legal Fictions and the Doctrine of Substituted Judgement." *The Yale Law Review* 100.1: 1–71.

Kelsen, Hans (1919) "Zur Theorie der juristischen Fiktionen: Mit besonderer Berücksichtigung von Vaihingers Philosophie des Als Ob." *Annalen der Philosophie* 1: 630–658.

Kelsen, Hans (1944) "The Principle of Sovereign Equality of States as a Basis for International Organization." *The Yale Law Journal* 53.2: 207–220.

Kelsen, Hans (2015) "On the Theory of Juridic Fictions: With Special Consideration of Vaihinger's Philosophy of the As-If" [1919]. Trans. Christoph Kletzer. *Legal Fictions in Theory and Practice*. Ed. Maksymilian Del Mar and William Twining. Cham: Springer International Publishing. 3–22.

Kramer, Matthew H. (1999) "Truth." *The Philosophy of Law: An Encyclopedia*. Ed. Christopher B. Gray. 2 vols. Garland Reference Library of the Humanities. New York: Garland. 873–874.

Larceny Act 1827. 7 & 8 Geo. 4 c. 29.

Ledwon, Lenora (1993) "Legal Fictions: Constructions of the Female Legal Subject in Nineteenth-Century Law and Literature." Diss. U of Notre Dame.

Lind, Douglas (2015) "The Pragmatic Value of Legal Fictions." *Legal Fictions in Theory and Practice*. Ed. Maksymilian Del Mar and William Twining. Cham: Springer International Publishing. 83–109.

MacDonagh, Gwendolyn, and Jonathan Smith (1996) "'Fill up all the gaps': Narrative and Illegitimacy in *The Woman in White*." *The Journal of Narrative Technique* 26.3: 274–291.

Mahon, James E. (2016) "The Definition of Lying and Deception." *The Stanford Encyclopedia of Philosophy*. Ed. Edward N. Zalta. <https://plato.stanford.edu/archives/win2016/entries/lying-definition>.

Maine, Henry Sumner (1861) *Ancient Law: Its Connection with the Early History of Society, and its Relation to Modern Ideas*. London: John Murray.

Malton, Sara (2014) *Forgery in Nineteenth-Century Literature and Culture: Fictions of Finance from Dickens to Wilde*. Basingstoke: Palgrave Macmillan.

Marriage Act 1753. 26 Geo. II c. 33.

Neill, Michael (1993) "'In Everything Illegitimate': Imagining the Bastard in Renaissance Drama." *The Yearbook of English Studies* 23: 270–292.

Niggli, Marcel A. (1999) "Error, Deceit, and Illusion." *The Philosophy of Law: An Encyclopedia*. Ed. Christopher B. Gray. 2 vols. Garland Reference Library of the Humanities. New York: Garland. 265–266.

Nünning, Ansgar (1998) "*Unreliable Narration* zur Einführung: Grundzüge einer kognitiv-narratologischen Theorie und Analyse unglaubwürdigen Erzählens." *Unreliable Narration: Studien zur Theorie und Praxis unglaubwürdigen Erzählens in der englischsprachigen Erzählliteratur*. Ed. Ansgar Nünning. Trier: WVT. 3–39.

Oaths Act 1978.

Olivier, Pierre J. J. (1975) *Legal Fictions in Practice and Legal Science*. Rotterdam: Rotterdam Univ. Press.

Pykett, Lyn (2005) *Wilkie Collins*. Oxford World's Classics. Authors in Context. Oxford: Oxford Univ. Press.

Russell, William O. (1843) *A Treatise on Crimes and Misdemeanors*. 2 vols. 3rd ed. London: Saunders and Benning.

Schauer, Frederick (2015) "Legal Fictions Revisited." *Legal Fictions in Theory and Practice*. Ed. Maksymilian Del Mar and William Twining. Cham: Springer International Publishing. 113–129.

Stern, Simon (2017) "Legal and Literary Fictions." *New Directions in Law and Literature*. Ed. Elizabeth S. Anker and Bernadette Meyler. New York: Oxford Univ. Press. 313–326.

Stolzenberg, Nomi Maya (1999) "Bentham's Theories of Fiction: A Curious 'Double Language.'" *Cardozo Studies in Law and Literature* 11.2: 223–261.

Stone, Marjorie (1985) "Dickens, Bentham, and the Fictions of the Law: A Victorian Controversy and its Consequences." *Victorian Studies* 29.1: 125–154.

Summers, Robert S. (1999) "Formal Legal Truth and Substantive Truth in Judicial Fact-Finding: Their Justified Divergence in some Particular Cases." *Law and Philosophy* 18: 497–511.

Vaihinger, Hans (1922) *Die Philosophie des Als Ob: System der theoretischen, praktischen und religiösen Fiktionen der Menschheit auf Grund eines idealistischen Positivismus*. 1911. 7th and 8th ed. Leipzig: Felix Meiner.

Vaihinger, Hans (1935) *The Philosophy of 'As if': A System of the Theoretical, Practical and Religious Fictions of Mankind*. Trans. C. K. Ogden. 2nd ed. London: Kegan Paul, Trench, Trubner & Co.

Williams, Bernard (2002) *Truth & Truthfulness: An Essay in Genealogy*. Princeton: Princeton Univ. Press.

III. Contemporary Extensions: Playing with Facts and the Non-Factual

Truth Be Told: The Aesthetics of Lying in Contemporary Theater

Daniel Morgenroth

> "My god, it was so cool! I loved to tell lies when I was a kid – that is, I was not a liar but ... I was fascinated that I could say untrue things but do it convincingly [so] that people would believe me; maybe that explains why I always wanted to be an actress."
> – Robert Lepage, *Polygraph* (in Gale and Deeney 2010, 718)

1. *Introduction*

Lying and performance are both fundamentally creative processes in the literal sense of the word. Both actors and liars make us believe something which is not factually true. In other words, they open up an epistemological space of possibility which dissolves strict factuality.

> Good liars usually display some of the following traits: natural performers, being well-prepared, being original (quick-minded), rapid thinking, being eloquent, good memory, not experiencing fear or guilt [...], good acting. (Vrij 2008, 379–381)

It follows that good liars are frequently good performers and vice versa. This is also at the core of the ancient debate about mimesis and truth in art. The first to voice his antagonism was of course Plato, who wanted to ban theater from his ideal state altogether (2000, 389b–c and 603b). Others have proven themselves fervent proponents of lying, such as Oscar Wilde, who claimed that art imitates life far more than the other way round (2008, 982) and that art's only aim is "the telling of beautiful untrue things" (992). Later, in the twentieth century – long after Nietzsche's deliberations on the frailty of speech as a medium of truth – Federico Fellini, when asked about his art and its relation to life and truth, bluntly stated, "I'm a born liar" (Pettigrew 2003, title). Thus, the relationship of the performing arts to truth and to lying is a complicated and nuanced one. It is highly contingent on historical circumstance and the performance itself. For instance, Plato's fear of delusion through mimesis can certainly be discussed in the context of a proscenium show with actors employing realistic Stanislavski techniques. A Brechtian performance is quite a different matter: here, actors do not seek to convince the audience of any verisimilitude. Today, the once heated debate around the performing arts, truth, and reality has largely been settled due to our post-postmodern understanding of truth as a construct. Nonetheless, the ontological link between liars and actors, who both perform and create deserves some investigation.

While the lexeme *to perform* is used in many and quite varied contexts, such as theater, business, or technology,[1] I refer to the word as denoting an 'as-if situation,' that is, in its theatrical sense; or, as Richard Schechner has it, I deploy it to indicate a situation of "showing-doing" as opposed to one of just "doing" (2006, 28). Such an 'as-if situation' can be defined by an ontological relationship between actor and spectator: one sees "that the performers pretend that the interaction is something other than what it actually is and that the observers are aware of this pretense" (Osipovich 2006, 461). The second aspect in this definition marks the point at which the similarities between liars and performers end: audience members are aware of the pretense of the 'as-if situation,' while someone who is lied to is not and believes in the veracity of the speaker. In other words: in a conversation, a liar and an addressee will generally as a given accept the same factual world surrounding them, while a performance event as a rule "involves an attempt on the part of the participants to create an alternative reality out of their co-presence" (Osipovich 2006, 469). There is then a different economy of trust at work in the two situations. Being lied to is always experienced more or less as a breach of trust and has hurtful consequences (Vrij 2008, 23–24).

In everyday situations of lying and misleading this is perfectly understandable. But how does lying work in the theater, where the audience is aware of a situation of make-believe and is at the same time in a position of dependence and, consequently, in a position of trust (Faulkner 2007, 538)? If one assumes like Osipovich that the audience collaborates with performers to create fictional realities, then trust would not have to be seen as trust in facts shown on stage but rather as trust in the promise of entertainment, education, provocation, etc. within a framework of make-believe. This is what I would call a contract of entertainment between performers and audience, marked by certain rules of behaviour (i.e. silence and clap when appropriate) in exchange for entertainment. Lying disturbs this economy of trust and power. Spectators find themselves in a position in which they are even more powerless than is usually the case in the theater because the performers, unbeknownst to them, will not deliver what they promised they would.

Such deception[2] can be used in numerous ways, it can be a comic device, for instance in Richard Bean's *One Man Two Guvnors* (2011), a reworking of

[1] For a good discussion of the term 'perform' and its various uses see McKenzie (2001, 1–40) or Sheperd & Wallis (2010, 112–115).

[2] I use deception as an umbrella term for both lying and misleading. While lying denotes an active act of untruthfulness (i.e. actively warranting to someone that A while believing that not A), misleading denotes untruth by omission or conversational implicatures (for an in-depth discussion see Williams 2002, 98–100 and Carson 2010, 15–24).

Goldoni's *Servant of Two Masters*, in which an audience member was pulled from the audience and put inside the dramatic action on stage. They had to follow James Cordon's character's directions, were hid from other characters in a wardrobe and under the table, which eventually caught fire, and were finally hosed down with a fire extinguisher by Cordon. The audience roared, presumingly both in shock and laughter, and only later did it emerge that the spectator had been planted. Here, the audience's trust is breached for comic purposes. But it can also be used to complicate notions of performance, fiction and reality. An example of this would be the first scene of Tom Stoppard's *The Real Thing* (1984), which misleads audiences into believing that they are seeing fictional reality when in fact they are seeing a scene of a play inside the fictional world, i.e. characters playing characters. Lying can further be used as a form of activism in works that are located between performance art and entertainment, such as Mike Daisey's *The Agony and Ecstasy of Steve Jobs* (2012), a show on inhumane working conditions at Apple's manufacturing sites in China. The work was sold as non-fiction, but later revealed to have been made up to a substantial degree (Isherwood 2012). Another example are Walid Raad's lecture performances on the history of Lebanon or the international activities of the CIA, in which he mingles fact and fiction with the high earnestness of a scholarly lecture so that audiences believe in their veracity (Lepecki 2006 and 2007). Raad thereby seeks to interrogate our understanding of historical truth and documents. He refers to this mixture of truth and fiction as *aesthetic facts*, pointing out that in artistic production, the criterion of the aesthetic effect is more important than factuality. As will be seen in the performances under scrutiny in this essay, all of them have a similar impetus in that they use deception or blur the lines between fact and fiction, but do so with a clear artistic objective or claim in mind.

Theatrically then, lying can emerge in two ways, first as a *sujet* (from Iago all the way to Algernon Moncrieff), and secondly on the level of mediation, as a breach of the contract of entertainment between performer and spectator. Such a breach might, in its own right, be qualified as an artistic strategy. In a sense, it can be understood as a radical subset of what Jacques Rancière understands as the "distribution of the sensible" (Rancière 2001, 12). Not only are audiences subject to the limitations of the strongly policed 'economy of power' of the theater space that regularly leaves them mostly silent and passive, but that very power economy turns out to be itself mere make-believe when performers consciously betray their audiences.

In the following, I want to consider three performances from, roughly, the past two decades which battle with questions of truth, factuality, and 'fakeness' (although many more could be named). They arguably go beyond the examples above and actively play with audiences' trust and conceptions of theater.

As cultural critic Ralph Keyes stated rather sweepingly in 2004: "I think it's fair to say that honesty is on the ropes. Deception has become commonplace at all levels of contemporary life" (2004, 5). While Keyes does not shy away from exaggeration and is fairly pessimistic in his views, it does seem that around the turn of the millennium, an unease with concepts such as truth and veracity became more pronounced. In the world of Donald Trump and fake news, a widespread sensation of fakeness and distrust in the media has established itself (Schulze 2017, 9–14). The performing arts have in turn taken up issues of fakeness, lying, and veracity and made use of such mechanisms.

2. Quizoola!: *Intimate Theater*

Founded in Sheffield in 1984, Forced Entertainment (FE) has been one of the towering entities of experimental theater in Britain for more than twenty-five years (Green 2013). FE puts the viewer in the center of attention, focusing on individual, unique experiences and personal narratives as opposed to a commodified, uniform product. The appeal to individual perception, narration, and interpretation can be observed in their durational performances. These are shows that typically last six to twenty-four hours. My example here is *Quizoola!* (1996).

First developed at the Institute of Contemporary Arts in London as a forty-five-minute show, it was later expanded into a six-hour version (Yates 2013). It still tours today. The play centers on two actors on a makeshift stage surrounded by a circle of light bulbs on the floor. The spectators sit on chairs around the stage, on the same level as the performers. The two performers take turns asking each other questions, loosely following an ever-expanding catalog of roughly two thousand questions, but they are free to repeat, jump, or make up questions. The audience is at liberty to stay, leave, and come back as they please. The performers wear badly drawn clown make-up, which – along with the light bulbs and a makeshift sign in the background – all give the impression of a performance that is not quite finished, something temporary, premature and provisional. The questions in the performance range from a simple quiz style to the philosophical or intimate:

> Do you have your own bike?
> How old are you going to get?
> Do you like me?
> Do you like yourself?
> What is your most recent memory?
> What is the average snowfall for this time of year?
> What is the average number of lovers for a woman or a man?
> What is the average number of keys people lose?
> Which is the strongest: a steel chain or a fibre rope?

> Who holed up in Gotham City?
> Which is the smallest: a neutron or a proton?
> Which is the worst: a half truth or a partial lie?
> [...]
> Is it true that you're lost and don't know where to turn?
> If you spoke another language would you still be you?
> What happens to the food that we eat?
> How do houses breathe?
> What happens when the soul leaves the body?
> What is Ohms [sic] Law?
> [...]
> How old are you?
> How old are you going to get?
> Do you have your own bike?
> Do you always do as you are told?
> Do you like me?
> Do you love me?
> Why do you like me? Do you like yourself?
> What are trees?
> [...]
> What is your favourite sexual position?
> Do you believe in destiny?
> In your opinion is history created by great men or by the inevitable moments of social forces? (Etchells 1997, 20–21)

A performer who is on stage, improvising and answering questions for hours and hours, will find it difficult to keep up a certain character, persona, or mask. As the actor grows tired, her defences and performance mask will weaken. In other words, as time goes by, audiences can never be sure if the actor is still in character or if she is speaking in her own voice. The audience feels that possibly they are not hearing a character's words but actually seeing an individual who is speaking honestly, answering, or confessing on stage. While this phenomenon must always remain ambiguous, it is evident that a feeling of intimacy, of being close to someone or something 'real' arises: "So your attraction here is to the possibility of a moment of truth, or the possibility of revealing a true self, not truth itself" (Etchells in Heathfield 2004, 95). The concept of question and answer alone seems to hint at the problem of truth and lying. Any answer in the performance can always be a lie, the truth, or anything in between. Audiences can never be sure, and it may very well be that performers skilfully deceive their audience and trick them into believing something real is happening while they are still fully in control. Liz Tomlin contends that all the strategies of earnestness and seemingly genuine personas are nothing but deliberate aesthetic choices, designed to produce the very effect of felt authenticity[3] (2013, 84). Tim Etchells has admitted that audience manipulation

3 For an in-depth discussion of authenticity see Wolfgang Funk's seminal work (2013), for its theatrical use see Schulze (2017).

always plays a role in FE's works (in Heathfield 2004, 96). Thus, there are both moments of conscious audience manipulation, of lying and misleading, and sudden incursions of the real. Spectators are the ones who must decide which stories to believe. Consequently, while frequently used as an artistic strategy, the problem of truth and lying in this kind of performance is only of secondary importance. As Etchells makes clear, what counts is the aesthetic effect:

> Lies and mistakes can tell as much about a person as 'true' answers. Lies can be convincing lies, transparent lies, skilfully sold [sic] lies, incompetent lies. True answers can sound like untruths (Etchells 2013, n.p.).

In short: whether a statement is true or false, whether an actress is genuinely herself or playacting may be a question for epistemology, but not for aesthetics and phenomenology.[4] The effect of the performance is strong and emerges despite, or rather because of, this uncertainty.

Quizoola! is a constant game of truth and lying. It is up to each spectator to judge the veracity of a statement; yet, spectators are left in the dark as to what to believe and what not. The performers frequently do not adopt a fixed character, which a spectator could more easily judge, but rather meander between different characters and personas. After hours and hours of performance, one can never be quite sure how near to truth or to a genuine person one has come. Actors tire, begin to lose concentration, shift in their attitude, and (seemingly) blunder out facts that they did not intend to disclose. The audience keenly observes this process of gradually losing one's stage persona and allowing the real person to shine through. It is worth noting that one is only looking for a 'possibility of a moment of truth,' not truth with a capital 'T.' This fleeting moment is then perceived as authentic. The audience and the performers go on a journey together, battling time and fatigue, looking for moments of possible truth.

As the boundary between person and persona begins to dissolve, the performer herself may enter a state somewhere between performance and real life, on the border between fact and fiction, where exhaustion has taken its toll. Tim Etchells has commented that, after the 24-hour version, he himself was no longer certain of what he had said:

> You know you've been talking for hours and hours without a break, but quite what was said can seriously evade you – a feeling akin to that following long conversations in general, perhaps, especially late night, complex or emotional ones. (Etchells 2013, n.p.)

At this moment, all boundaries between truth and lying are dissolved in a continuum of aesthetic effects between people on stage and people watching,

---

4 Harald Weinrich already pointed out that a lying sentence and a true sentence are structurally and phonetically the same. They differ only in their relation to the factual world (2005, 39).

all of them tired, all of them worn out by the constant urge to judge veracity and aesthetic effect. What we find is a community of people in a room seeking a truth that can never be obtained with certitude.

3. Internal: *The Betrayed Spectator*

Another burgeoning and highly successful field of performance theater which makes use of mechanisms of truth, trust, and betrayal is that of one-on-one performances, i.e., performances that feature only one actor and one spectator. They have been a major force in the performing arts in the first decade of the new millennium (Gardner 2009). It is difficult, if not impossible, to categorize them or give some sort of general description as they are so manifold in terms of both structure and content. A one-on-one can last from one minute to an hour. Usually, these performances are site-specific or site-based and draw on the aesthetics of live art (Zerihan 2009, 3). The only common characteristic is the very fact that these works feature one performer and one spectator. Festivals featuring one-on-one performances have been staged for three consecutive years at Battersea Arts Centre (BAC) in London (BAC 2013, n.p.), and at several events in Australia (Wilson 2012, n.p.), while similar projects are also happening in New York and other cities around the globe (Logan 2010, n.p.).

One of the first theater companies to celebrate wider critical success with one-on-one performances was the Belgium-based performance group Ontroerend Goed, founded in 1994. The group's name roughly translates to "touchingly good, [or] so good it moves you" (Costa 2011, n.p.). At the 2009 festival, their performance *Internal* became "Edinburgh's most discussed show" (Dickson 2009, n.p.). The performance has been characterised as "a mixture of speed-dating and group therapy" (Gardner 2009, n.p.). The format of the show is quite straightforward. Five performers interact with five participants at a time. In the show, each participant is shown to a separate space with one performer where they are

> sitting at a little restaurant table opposite a handsome actor, usually of the opposite sex, who offers a glass of wine, gazes into their eyes, and then begins to make contact, either by asking searching questions about life and love, or by asking if they can hold hands, touch your face, stroke your hair. (McMillan 2009, n.p.)

The performers started a conversation, trying to build trust, always making sure to have the participant narrate as much and as personally as possible about their own life. Questions could become very intimate (e.g., 'Would you kiss me?'). After an approximately twenty-minute session, the performers and participants all came together as a group and each performer talked about the person they had encountered. They explicitly enumerated what they had found out, what they liked, but also the secrets they had been trusted with (e.g., 'What

I don't like about her is that she would have kissed me although she has a boyfriend. She's a cheat'). Obviously, this strategy was perceived as hurtful or even as a form of betrayal by participants who had proffered trust and honesty towards the performers. After this 'group session,' the actors danced with the participants, apologized for disclosing their secrets, and wrote nice letters to the participants, telling them once more about the things they had found positive about them. After the show, the letters were mailed to the participants' home addresses. They were signed with the same names the performers had given during the performance. Whether this name was the actor's true name or that of a stage persona remained an open question.

The entire performance was designed to lure participants into believing that something real was happening, i.e., that they were talking to a real person. Of course, participants must have been conscious of the theatrical situation; but even in an experimental performance, there is always a possibility of meeting a real character rather than a staged version, or is there? This naturally entails the elimination of all factors that normally denote theatricality and make-believe. The abolition of any audience-performer division is the first step in this direction. Performers frequently made physical contact with participants in a sensual, positive, and friendly fashion. This, for many spectators, served as a trigger for mental proximity. The whole setting was, furthermore, designed to emanate a sense of homeliness and comfort, inducing participants to 'let down their guard.' Finally, performers always played (?) or even *were*, to a degree, themselves. They introduced themselves by first name. Never did the impression arise that they were reciting lines from a prefabricated text. As a consequence, a number of participants opened up substantially, and the effect of both the encounter and the betrayal was profound on them: "a girl in my group said she'd cried as a result of what she'd gone through; on the other hand, someone else was enchanted, genuinely touched by the intimacy Internal [sic, no italics] seemed to offer" (Dickson 2009, n.p.).

The promise of an authentic moment and the promise of unbounded intimacy with a stranger was a strong siren call for a number of participants, which they willingly embraced. The performer is a stranger who can be trusted because she is precisely that: a stranger. Just as one would be able to confess one's secrets more easily to a professional who is a stranger (e.g., a priest or a doctor), the performance creates the possibility to finally 'get something off one's chest' or to give in to one's unacknowledged desires in a safe setting. No one must or will ever hear about this. As we have lost the confessor to theological doubt, this role is replaced by a paid performer who creates the illusion of safety and confession, or – as Foucault has it – by the therapist who alleviates our psychological distress (Butler 2008, 161).

But was it really an illusion? Did the performers lie to their audience? In the strict sense, they never told them that they would keep their secrets (which would have been a lie), but their behavior and the setting surely implied confidentiality (which was misleading). Deception here is an artistic measure – but to what purpose? McMillan suggests that the piece should be interpreted with Erving Goffman's dictum of 'the performative self' (1959, 23) in mind. For him, it "makes us think about truth and lies in such encounters. These actors are probably adopting fictional characters; but then how often are any of us completely truthful in presenting ourselves to others" (McMillan 2009, n.p.)? The performers and the participants both present themselves in a certain, maybe a truthful way to the other. The performance thus mimics real life in the performative sense. In other words: to a large degree, it is the participant who makes the performance. Depending on their input and openness, the show can "be moving, devastating, almost life-changing" (McMillan 2009, n.p.) or it can be boring.

Internal creates a space of individual responsibility and tailor-made experience in which the inputs regulate the potential gains. At the same time, *Internal* is a comment on the current state of affairs when it comes to disclosure, personal information, and intimacy. Alexander Devriendt explains that they wanted to show how fast one could build a meaningful relationship with a stranger (Logan 2010, n.p.). The use of betrayal is the artistic measure that exposes pseudo-authenticity and pseudo-intimacy. It is a *caveat* that stresses that meaningful relations cannot be built in minutes. Ever since their first creation, (social) media have exponentially increased the means of making contact with strangers and have frequently been criticized and questioned for shallowness, voyeurism, etc. Thus, the performance is both: a work of art that through its sensuality and physical proximity demonstrates how people long for such non-digital encounters, and, at the same time, a meditation on the difference between mental and physical proximity and our urge for intimacy at a time when we are more connected than ever (digitally) and more separated and alone than ever (physically) (Lanier 2018, 123). As Achille Mbembe has pointed out, the late capitalist subject is dependent on its ability to reconstruct its inner life publicly and offer it on the market like a tradable commodity. *Internal* demonstrates how frail the trust in such mechanisms is.

4. Taking Care of Baby: *Documentary Theater*

The enormous popularity of verbatim theater, documentary drama, and a number of similar hybrid forms of theater in the first decade of the twenty-first century has been widely acknowledged by scholars (Reinelt 2006, 70; Lane 2010, 59; Sierz 2011, 58). The rise of verbatim theater is most often linked to the felt mendacity of politics and of the world at large:

> Verbatim theatre grew in popularity across the millennium thanks to the public's distrust of politicians, journalism and respected organisations such as the BBC and the Metropolitan Police Force, and the rise of celebrity 'real-life' drama via reality TV programmes and talent competitions. Theatre's reputation as a politicised and critical medium for exposing the truth fed a public desire for the 'real' answers to political scandal, providing an alleged clarity that other mediums could not provide. (Lane 2010, 77–78)

Theater was seen as a counter-locus or an antidote to a world that was perceived as mendacious and fake. By bringing documents and actual cases of criminal behavior or political misconduct to the stage, playwrights such as Richard-Norton Taylor and companies such as Recorded Delivery have built themselves sizeable audiences. London's Tricycle Theatre staged dozens of investigative 'tribunal plays' on topics such as the Srebrenica massacre, Tony Blair's joining George Bush in the Iraq war, or racial injustice in the UK (Brittain 2014). The felt fakeness of media and the world at large is here countered with austere courtroom sets, the presentation of actual documents on stage, and an acting style that seeks to imitate, respectively, the 'talking heads' of a documentary film, or actual witnesses in a court room. The result of these strategies, obviously, is nowhere near a neutral objective truth: editing has taken place; the selection of the material involves certain presuppositions in the first place; actors speaking in a different person will of course not be the same as actual witnesses; etc. (Martin 2006, Megson 2009, 197, Schulze 2017, 221–231). A number of formats have dedicated themselves to the problem of objective truth, lying, and authenticity and have sought to complicate these questions on-stage.

For an example case let us look at Dennis Kelly's *Taking Care of Baby* (2007). This play is certainly meta-textual, even meta-theatrical, because it questions what we hold true and what we accept as truth in the theater and other media. It "fooled audiences into thinking that a fictional play about a woman accused of murdering her baby was a real documentary drama" (Edgar 2012, 9). The play starts with a straightforward and very common truth claim that is shown on a screen:

> [t]he following has been taken word for word from interviews and correspondence. Nothing has been added and everything is in the subjects' own words, though some editing has taken place. Names have not been changed. (Kelly 2013, 5)

The play deliberately lies to its audience. It claims to present a discourse of factuality when in truth (no pun intended) it should claim a discourse of fictionality. It lies to the audience with the intention of critiquing its own status and audiences' expectations of truth. One can even say that the play, unbeknownst to the first-time spectator, playfully engages with the conceptions of truth and truth claims. This becomes manifest when the character of Dr. Millard speaks about truth and lying.

DR. MILLARD: Generally speaking. Lying doesn't really work. When you think about it. Whether you're lying to yourself or to another human being, we sort of know the truth. Somewhere. Generally, generally somewhere we know the truth. Not always, but ... (15)

On the most basic level, the figure of a doctor, preferably in a white lab coat, is a signifier for science, neutrality, and trustworthiness. The doctor in Kelly's play holds a course on lying and its impossibility. Later on, the audience will learn that the doctor himself is a liar who made up an illness and was not thorough in his research. The play is almost cheeky in its use of lying right at the beginning. It is as if the play shouted at the unwitting audience, 'Look, I am going to lie to you, and I am telling you about lying right now, but you will not hear it because you will believe my authority!' For instance, the doctor gives an explanation of brain size and lying, involving primates, which sounds credible and scientific. He even returns in a later scene, discussing the prevalence of untruthfulness in society (20). Here again, the play seems to scream its own mendacity at the audience, which however fails to recognise it (Brantley 2013, n.p.).

In a similarly playful and metatextual manner, the author appears as a character in the fictional world, or, in fact, he does not. There are a number of instances where the author is referred to (21, 59–60) or where people in a taped conversation refer to 'us,' instead of 'I' (62), implying that the author is with them. In other words, here absence also creates presence. The author remains elusive and is never present on stage, his presence is repeatedly implied when characters refer to 'Mr Kelly' or when he is heard as a voice offstage on tape recordings (21, 60 f., *passim*). The author becomes something like a divine *hors-texte* figure because he is never physically present but always hovers about, externally validating the discourse. In the text, it is the author's expressed aim to "get at the truth" (66, also 18–19, 21, 65–66): this author believes he can present the one correct and single truth. However, in his presence-absence, the play subverts the idea of one simple truth and ridicules such claims. This is expressed in the second of the three 'movements' in the play, where the play's truth claim is reiterated, but this time in a version riddled with errors:

> The following has been word from taken word for interviews and correspondence. Everything is in the subjects' own words and place, nothing has been added though some has taken editing. All names have been changed (31).

Here, the audience may become suspicious of the truth claim for the first time. The entire play revolves around the single word 'truth.' Characters bring up the topic and discuss the concept so often (21, 27, 45, 46, 4, 65–66, 77) that it is hard to miss the isotopic field. So, possibly, audiences will understand the phrase that "[t]his is about truth," but not in the sense that they had thought it had in the beginning. Over the course of the play, it emerges that *all* characters are lying or not telling the truth. For instance, the MP's story about rescuing her daughter from a highly dangerous drug den is later on retold by the daughter's boyfriend who tells his version of the drug story. In this narrative there are no gangsters nor any danger at all, but just a college party and the presence of a very overprotective mother (Kelly 2013, 86). This intradiegetic example points out to the audience how the same facts, seen through different eyes and narrated accordingly, become two completely different truths – neither of which can claim exclusivity.

Before the play's original staging, there were four prominent cases of infanticide in the UK which likely served as inspiration. The US reviewer of the play even felt he had to inform his readers that the play was all fiction because the story would sound so credible and familiar: "[j]ust to make things clear — because your program will not — there is no real Donna McAuliffe, although you may swear you remember reading about her case" (Brantley 2013, n.p.). Thus, this play, just like documentary theater, presents a hybridization of the real world and a fictitious world on stage; only it does so more cleverly. By employing well-known cases of infanticide as a topic and analog, and by pretending to be a documentary-style play, it puts the audience in a position where they have to decide what to believe on stage or in documentary theater. But the final validation of the performance happens in the audience's mind where they connect and possibly equate the fictive events on stage and the real life stories from outside the theater walls. In the final 'movement' of the play, the whole structure of truth validation collapses. The familiar truth claim on screen has been distorted beyond recognition:

> Te foling has beenlown takhen wormed for wspoord frondrm intews and cughorrevieence. Nothything has been odded and evering is in the subjts' awn wongrds, tho sam editing hoes keplan tace. All nas havece been chaed (87)

Here the play finally reveals its multifarious approaches to truth and lying. Everything was a lie – or was it just fiction?

5. *Beyond Truth and Lying*

Theater has come a long way from Plato's suspicions of imitative poetry up to the anything-goes attitude of a time after postmodernity. Today, it seems we are struggling again with problems of credibility and truth – albeit on another level. Live art has taken up these issues deploying its unique force of bodies in co-presence who are (seemingly) enacting moments of truth in a live moment.

Forced Entertainment's durational works (a technical term for theater performances of a continuous format) highlight the fact that we can never be certain of a truth on stage, but their audiences are given the hope that in a common effort of deciphering reality we might possibly glimpse moments of truth. By means of performance and betrayal, Oentroerend Goed question our trust in other people and how we expose and comport ourselves in digital/non-digital environments. They ask how we as humans of flesh and blood can behave in a world that is ever more removed, digital, and ephemeral in its encounters and relationships. This question becomes more urgent, when we consider that practically anything self-experienced, or any physical encounter, is considered as truthful. However, today we are more and more deprived of such first-hand and direct experiences, and consequently need to re-think what we hold to be true or genuine. In short: how do truth and trust work in the digital age? Much of contemporary critical documentary theater has served to complicate our notion of what we hold true and which facts and presentations of current events we can trust. However, this is a double-edged sword, as uncritical documentary theater can exacerbate feelings of fakeness, of not being told the truth, and of distrust in media and public information. Dennis Kelly's play makes a point that truth is something shifting, personal, and situational, while all the facts may still be the same.

As these examples indicate, the problem of lying and faking versus truth and veracity seems a pressing preoccupation for contemporary society in the global north. The performing arts are taking up these issues and treat them with artistic strategies that often playfully lie and mislead in order to engage audiences in a thought process. The performances themselves, however, are neither mendacious nor true; they all reside in the realm of artistic production, and therefore the question of veracity becomes an aesthetic, not an empirical one. The truth of a show or performance lies in the aesthetic effect it has on its audience. While the play may speak about truth and lying, it is measured against individual perception, not against reality. This is the great opportunity which the performing arts have to offer us: they have a certain immediacy and thus allow us to test out the contemporary problematization of truth in a playful, aesthetic dimension before drawing conclusions regarding the real world.

Works Cited

Performances:

Internal (2009) Oentroerend Goed. Dir. Alexander Devriendt. Edinburgh Fringe Festival.

One Man, Two Guvnors (2011) Dir. Nicholas Hytner. Royal National Theatre, Lyttleton Theatre, London.

Quizoola! (1996) Dir. Tim Etchells. Institute of Contemporary Arts, London.

Taking Care of Baby (2007) Dir. Anthony Clark. Birmingham Repertory Theatre.

Secondary Sources:

BAC (2013) "Battersea Arts Centre Homepage." Web. 16 Nov. 2020.

Brantley, Ben (2013) "A Story to Question, Word for Word." *The New York Times*. 25 Feb. 2014. Web. 16 Nov. 2020.

Brittain, Victoria et al. (2014) Ed. *The Tricycle: Collected Tribunal Plays 1994–2012*. London: Oberon Books.

Butler, Judith (2008) *Undoing Gender*. London, New York: Routledge.

Canton, Ursula (2008) "We May Not Know Reality, but It Still Matters – a Functional Analysis of 'Factual Elements' in the Theatre." *Contemporary Theatre Review* 18.3: 318–327.

Carson, Thomas (2010) *Lying and Deception: Theory and Practice*. Oxford: Oxford Univ. Press.

Costa, Maddy (2011) "Ontroerend Goed: Are You Sitting Uncomfortably?" *The Guardian Online*. 28 March 2013. Web. 16 Nov. 2020.

Dickson, Andrew (2009) "Internal: The Ultimate Test for Edinburgh Audiences?" *Guardian Theatre Blog*. 01 Aug. 2012. Web. 16 Nov. 2020.

Edgar, David (2012) "A Hard Time for British Plays: David Edgar Defends the Vibrancy of British Playwriting." *Hard Times* 91: 7–12.

Etchells, Tim (1997) *Certain Fragments: Contemporary Performance and Forced Entertainment*. London: Routledge.

Etchells, Tim (2013) "An Island, a Prison Cell, a Hotel Bed, a No Man's Land: Some Thoughts About Quizoola24! from Tim Etchells." 17 Sep. 2013. Web. 16 Nov. 2020. <http://notebook.forcedentertainment.com/?p=797http://>.

Faulkner, Paul (2007) "What Is Wrong with Lying?" *Philosophy and Phenomenological Research* 75.3: 535–557.

Funk, Wolfgang (2015) *The Literature of Reconstruction: Authentic Fiction in the New Millenium*. London: Bloomsbury.

Gardner, Lyn (2005) "I Didn't Know Where to Look." *The Guardian*. 15 October 2013. Web. 16 Nov. 2020.

Gardner, Lyn (2009) "How Intimate Theatre Won Our Hearts." *The Guardian*. 01 Aug. 2012. Web. 16 Nov. 2020.

Gale, Maggie B. and John F. Deeney (2010) *The Routledge Drama Anthology and Sourcebook*. London: Routledge.

Goffman, Erving (1959) *The Presentation of the Self in Everyday Life*. New York: Double Day.

Green, Chris (2013) "Forced Entertainment." *Performa Magazine*. 28 March 2013. Web. 16 Nov. 2020. <https://performamagazine.tumblr.com/post/42953624125 /forced-entertainment>.

Heathfield, Adrian (2004) "As If Things Got More Real: A Conversation with Tim Etchells." *Not Even a Game Anymore: The Theatre of Forced Entertainment*. Ed. Judith Helmer and Florian Malzacher. Berlin: Alexander Verlag. 77–99.

Ishwerwood, Charles (2012) "Speaking Less Than Truth to Power." *The New York Times*. Web. 23 March 2012.

Kelly, Dennis (2013) *Taking Care of Baby* [2007]. London: Oberon Books.

Keyes, Ralph (2004) *The Post-Truth Era: Dishonesty and Deception in Contemporary Life*. New York: St. Martin's Press.

Lane, David (2010) *Contemporary British Drama*. Edinburgh: Edinburgh Critical Guides.

Lanier, Jaron (2018) *Zehn Gründe, Warum Du Deine Social Media Accounts Sofort Löschen Musst*. Hamburg: Hoffmann und Campe.

Lepecki, André (2006) "'After All, This Terror Was Not without Reason': Unfiled Notes on the Atlas Group." *The Drama Review: A Journal of Performance Studies* 50.3: 88–99.

Lepecki, André (2007) "In the Mist of the Event: Performance and the Activation of Memory in the Atlas Group Archive." *The Atlas Group (1989–2004): A Project by Walid Raad.* Cologne: Verlag der Buchhandlung Walter König.

Logan, Brian (2010) "For Your Eyes Only: The Latest Theatrical Craze Features a Single Performer with a Single Audience Member." *The Independent*. 15 Oct. 2013. Web. 16 Nov. 2020.

Martin, Carol (2006) "Bodies of Evidence." *The Drama Review: A Journal of Performance Studies* 50.3: 8–15.

McKenzie, Jon (2001) *Perform or Else: From Discipline to Performance*. London: Routledge.

McMillan, Joyce (2009) "Internal." *The Scotsman*. 10 Oct. 2010. Web. 16 Nov. 2020. <http://www.edinburgh-festivals.com/viewshow.aspx?id=1587074>.

Megson, Chris (2009) "*Half the Picture*: 'A Certain Frisson' at the Tricycle Theatre." *Get Real: Documentary Theatre Past and Present*. Ed. Alison Forsyth and Chris Megson. Basingstoke: Palgrave. 195–208.

Osipovich, David (2006) "What Is a Theatrical Performance?" *The Journal of Aesthetics and Art Criticism* 64.4: 461–470.

Pettigrew, Damian (2003) Ed. *I'm a Born Liar: A Fellini Lexicon*. New York: Harry N. Abrams.

Plato (2000) *The Republic*. Trans. Tom Griffith. Cambridge: Cambridge Univ. Press.

Rancière, Jacques (2011) *The Politics of Aesthetics: The Distribution of the Sensible*. London: Continuum.

Reinelt, Janelle (2006) "Toward a Poetics of Theatre and Public Events." *The Drama Review: A Journal of Performance Studies* 50.3: 69–87.

Schechner, Richard (2006) *Performance Studies: An Introduction*. London: Routledge.

Schulze, Daniel (2017) *Authenticity in Contemporary Theatre and Performance: Make It Real*. London: Bloomsbury.

Sheperd, Simon, and Mick Wallis (2010) *Drama/Theatre/Performance* [2004]. The New Critical Idiom. Ed. John Drakakis. London: Routledge.

Sierz, Aleks (2011) *Rewriting the Nation: British Theatre Today*. London: Methuen.

Stoppard, Tom (1984) *The Real Thing*. London: Samuel French.

Tomlin, Liz (2013) *Acts and Apparitions: Discourses on the Real in Performance Practice and Theory, 1990–2010*. Manchester: Manchester Univ. Press.

Vrij, Aldert (2008) *Detecting Lies and Deceit: Pitfalls and Opportunities*. Wiley Series in Psychology of Crime, Policing and Law. Ed. Graham Davies and Ray Bull. Chichester: John Wiley & Sons.

Weinrich, Harald (2005) *The Linguistics of Lying*. Seattle & London: Washington Univ. Press.

Wilde, Oscar (2008) *The Complete Works of Oscar Wilde*. New York: Harper Perennial.

Williams, Bernard A. O. (2002) *Truth & Truthfulness: An Essay in Genealogy*. Princeton and Oxford: Princeton Univ. Press.

Wilson, Laetitia (2012) "The Ups & Downs of One-on-One." *RealTimeArts Magazine*. 15 Oct. 2013. Web. 16 Nov. 2020.

Yates, Daniel B. (2013) "Submit Your Questions for Quizoola!" *Exeunt Magazine*. 28 March 2013. Web. 16 Nov. 2020. <http://exeuntmagazine.com/features/your-questions-for-quizoola/>.

Young, Stuart (2009) "Playing with Documentary Theatre: *Aalst* and *Taking Care of Baby*." *New Theatre Quarterly* 25.1: 72–87.

Zerihan, Rachel (2009) *Live Art Development Agency Study Room Guide on One to One Performance*. Web. 27 August 2021. <https://www.thisisliveart.co.uk/resources/one-to-one-performance-2009/>.

How to Tell a True Migration Story: Authenticity and (Non)Fictionality in Contemporary US-American Migration Narratives

Rüdiger Heinze

1. Based on True Events: Introduction

In a way, the title of this essay is both incomplete and indirect. Most of the essay does, of course, address the titular issues. However, it also addresses the question – and, quite honestly, concern over – how it is possible that various contemporary US-American politicians (chief among them the President of the USA, still incumbent at the time of writing) and political figures and commentators can pronounce virtually countless lies and falsehoods (for the purposes of this essay understood 'simply' as intentional contra-factual assertions) without this communicative behavior having any measurable detrimental or divisive effect whatsoever (by any poll, survey, or interview known to me) on their supporters. Not to be misunderstood: I am not naively and/or nostalgically assuming that there used to be a 'good old time' when politicians (or human beings in general, in fact) did not lie. It would be equally naïve, however, and even downright preposterous, to argue that the quality and quantity of these lies, and with them the political landscape, has not changed – their having a long history notwithstanding. I believe, of course, that the question can be answered, from a number of perspectives and by different academic disciplines.

At first glance, the latter phenomenon might not seem to have anything to do with migration narratives. However, it is the central tenet of this essay that we can only understand the current US-American political landscape by looking at the wider cultural landscape and its history, and, further, that narrative(s), cultural identity, and non(fictionality) play a decisive role. In fact, I am going to argue that underlying and undergirding many of Trump's key statements are foundational US-American cultural narratives – myths such as American Exceptionalism, Manifest Destiny, the American Dream – and that it is the appeal to these myths that makes him and his counterfactual statements appear 'credible' and persuasive to his audience, in other words: authentic. The complementary, titular side of this argument posits that this 'authenticity effect' can, somewhat ironically, also be found in the reception of migration narratives (which themselves are part and parcel of another US-American myth, namely the myth of the 'nation of immigrants' as John F. Kennedy has phrased it), and that its functionality here can help explain its current valence and functionality in politics. In order to make this point, I am going to take what may appear to be a detour by beginning with a curious phenomenon, which, however, is central to my argument.

In reviewing, analyzing and discussing contemporary US-American immigrant fictions, many – in fact, almost all – critics (most of them US-Americans) in one way or another refer to the author's biography. The reference may be tangential or central to the argument, it may explicitly employ the adjective 'autobiographical' or not, but where it is made, it is invariably made as a rhetorical gesture of authentication. It is supposed to indicate that there is an inherent connection between the narrative and the author's life and personal experiences and that therefore the narrative is somehow more 'truthful,' 'credible,' or, in other words, 'authentic.' This connection is rarely, if ever, specified in detail. Usually, critics point to some general parallels between the narrative's protagonists and the author's life in terms of target/source country, migrational experience, and/or family constellation. In other words, the term 'autobiographical' is not used as the adjective of the noun autobiography, but rather as a shortcut for 'contains some facts and/or events similar to those of the author's life.' In their urge to establish what we might call *autobiographicality*, critics sometimes go so far as to completely ignore blatantly divergent aspects such as gender, age, or socio-economic context.[1]

As if to warn against such facile appropriation by critics, many novels and/or short stories about migration even contain forewords by, or interviews with, the authors emphasizing that their narrative is fictional. They concede that, while certainly personal experiences inevitably make their way into one's writing, and while there may be some general similarities (say, number of siblings, country of origin, migrational route), they as authors are not to be trusted and cannot themselves reliably remember what really happened and what did not. More often than not, the authors also admonish that the distinction between fictional and nonfictional should not matter for the relevance of the story. Contemporary writers particularly popular among critics for such 'autobiographical' reception are, for example, Jhumpa Lahiri, Julia Alvarez, Junot Díaz, Ana Castillo, Amy Tan, Angie Cruz, and many more. Indeed, for some of these writers (Lahiri or Alvarez, for example) it is hard to find a review or a critical essay that does not employ the noted kind of authentication. Even the well-known novelist Anne Tyler, an almost prototypical 'WASP,' in various reviews is given the credit of 'authentic' access to the Iranian-American immigrant experience,

[1] They also do not systematically distinguish between factuality and nonfictionality, although the two concepts are obviously not identical, since nonfictionality is first and foremost used as the opposite of fictionality (referring to, say, a nonfictional narrative such as a biography), while factuality is first and foremost used in (predominantly non-literary) discourses distinguishing between fact and non-fact, such as a lie or a (how-ever intentioned) counterfactual assertion.

granted to her novel *Digging to America* because she was married to an Iranian immigrant.

For example, in Jessica Cantiello's otherwise insightful and detailed essay on what she calls 'pseudo-memory' and trauma in Julia Alvarez's novels, she does not consistently distinguish between fiction and pseudo-memory (which is defined as invented memory). Nor does she distinguish between the fictionality of the novel per se and the fictionality of the pseudo-memory within the novel, although their indexical and logical relation to the actual world is substantially different. Cantiello even proposes that "storytelling is a complicated confluence of truth, lies, and memory, and memory is not always to be trusted" (2011, 85); "one cannot assume that any version of the story is in fact the best, the most authentic, or the most real" (2011, 86); in fact, Alvarez's novels are a "conglomeration of pseudo-memories, as the characters' memories and stories from the first book intermingle and contradict each other" (2011, 92) and thus contain "many different voices" (2011, 93) and a "multiplicity of representations" (2011, 94). In short, it would seem that there is no steady ground on which to base the claim that the two novels are autobiographical in the conventional understanding of the term.

Yet the baseline argument for her essay is that Alvarez's two novels are "autobiographical" and that they feature an "alter ego named Yolanda García, whose stories draw from Alvarez's own life" (Cantiello 2011, 83) in order to substantiate her claim. Like many other critics, she refers to Alvarez's abundant nonfiction publications (essays and interviews), in which it is repeatedly stated that she has drawn material for her novels from her own life and family. However, in those same interviews and essays, Alvarez also repeatedly cautions that her memories are 'just stories' and are 'recast' to fit the demands of her fiction and that she has altered, added and subtracted so much that she, herself, cannot any longer tell what is factual and does not see the need to do so.

Another example of this kind of 'authentication' is the reception of Jhumpa Lahiri's fiction. In a recent *New York Times* review of Jhumpa Lahiri's latest book, the collection of short stories *Unaccustomed Earth*, it is claimed that the underlying theme of all stories is "the fact that America is still a place where the rest of the world comes to reinvent itself," and that "the place to which you feel the strongest attachment isn't necessarily the country you're tied to by blood or birth: it's the place that allows you to become yourself. This place . . . may not lie on any map" (Schillinger 2008, n. pag.). This assessment is accompanied by a reference to the biography of Lahiri. She was born in London to Bengali immigrants and raised in Rhode Island and would thus qualify as an example of the children of immigrants frequently portrayed in her stories. The biographical reference is used to authenticate the author's privileged access to the experience of children of immigrants. The fact that there are significant differences between Lahiri and her protagonists (in terms of gender, class, historical and cultural contexts) is hardly ever given any attention. All in all, the review pays little attention to the stories as fictional narratives but rather treats them as if they were slightly embellished social reports based on Lahiri's own life and experiences. This is a pattern that recurs in various critical essays on Lahiri's work; more on this later.

To some degree, the described phenomenon is not entirely surprising, nor is it entirely new. Many early US-American immigration narratives are autobiographies, memoirs, diaries, or compiled letters. They are life writings about becoming American, about assimilation and identity, and they follow the formal traditions of earlier canonical US-American autobiography. These narratives about marked (i.e. minority) cultural practices have a long tradition of being read as slightly embellished, but basically 'authentic'/'true'/nonfictional social reports or ethnographies (more on this below). Accordingly, their authors often were and still are regarded as informants about the life and cultural practices of 'their' cultural formation. Contemporary reception and criticism of narratives about marked cultural practices, including those signposted as fictional, obviously still carry vestiges of this ethnographic tradition: the texts are treated as 'authentic' and thereby implicitly nonfictional representations of the 'cultural identity' of a particular group and/or the author.

It would be easy and tempting to see this purely as a matter of identity politics; of course it is, in part. These are narratives about migration, identity, and culture(s). In the US-American context, it would be hard to imagine that their reception could not invoke identity politics. Feuilleton writers and commentators on both sides of the Atlantic outbid one another in pointing out that and how contemporary US-American culture is all about identity politics. In fact, this claim itself has become an almost unquestioned narrative and myth.[2] And while identity politics certainly play a role in explaining this authentication of fictional migration narratives as 'almost nonfictional,' they are not the whole story.[3]

[2] Put bluntly, in its most radical expressions, identity politics assumes, for example, that only an African American can adequately represent – i.e. speak for – 'the African American experience.' The same would be true for any other racial/ethnic identity/group. Although identity politics arise out of legitimate concerns over representation, discrimination, and appropriation, the inherent problems of such essentialism should be obvious and have been amply pointed out and criticized. The debate reached a high point in the 1980s and 1990s. Winfried Siemerling's and Katrin Schwenk's 1996 collection of essays provides a contemporary overview and debate of this 'pure puralism.' That the debate is not over can be seen in the heated discussion over Cornel West's scathing criticism of both Barack Obama and the writer Ta-Nehisi Coates for not being 'true' African Americans because of their alleged neo-liberalism.

[3] As Nancy Isenberg points out in her recent monograph on "white trash" (2016) in the USA, American politics has been about identity politics for a long time, in various different forms and guises. Also, in light of the immigrant history of the USA and the concurrent debates, it is naïve and counterfactual to think that there was ever a time when a vast majority of (US-)Americans wholeheartedly embraced the notion that they are a

More specifically, I argue that there are several interconnected concepts and discourses at play here, namely authenticity, cultural identity, and fictionality. Without taking them all into account, we cannot understand the obvious penchant by reviewers and critics to authenticate migration narratives as 'authentic'/autobiographical (in the sense explained above) and the wider cultural significance of that penchant. In fact, I will try to show that this phenomenon has wider cultural significance in that it is actually indicative of a much more general and deep-reaching cultural phenomenon – a phenomenon that has variously been labeled 'post-truth' or 'post-factuality.'[4] The terms refer to the puzzling fact that the outright and evident falsehood and counterfactuality of numerous claims and statements – often part of entire conspirative stories such as those underlying the 'birther movement' – made in various public discourses for a significant section of the receiving audience does not appear to have any relevance at all regarding their credibility.[5] On the contrary, such communicative behavior and the attendant invented stories appear to be a sign of authenticity and reliability for their 'believers,' and do not feature as mendacity and inconsistency, as could be expected. Attempts to explain this phenomenon of 'post-factual' communication and narration within the binary logic of true/false or factual/non-factual are doomed because this communicative strategy purposely eschews and circumvents such binary logic and therefore cannot be explained by it. The phenomenon becomes quite clear, however, once one realizes that these claims and stories operate not on the level of (non)factuality but rather on that of 'authenticity,' a kind of 'third term' that supersedes/circumvents factuality by working with, and appealing to, 'felt' truth. In other words, these invented claims and stories are, or construct themselves to be mythic narratives (in the Barthian sense) and/or appeal to widespread cultural myths such as the American Dream or American Exceptionalism, resonating with what people feel is true, regardless of facts. This phenomenon, as I will argue, somewhat ironically and paradoxically connects these invented narratives to fictional narratives about cultural identity.

---

pluralistic society/culture containing many different 'cultures' on an equal footing, or that this, if it were the case, would be a good thing. Samuel Huntington's *Who Are We* (2004) is just one prominent example of what Samuel Ludwig terms "thin pluralism" (2003).

4 For an overview of the current discussion (and its history) of 'post-truth' and 'alternative facts' see Lee McIntyre's monograph *Post-Truth* (2018).

5 During the first presidential campaign of Barack Obama, the so-called 'birther movement' (prominently supported by Donald Trump) claimed that Barack Obama was not a natural-born citizen of the USA, that his birth certificate was forged, and that therefore (as laid out in article II of the US Constitution) he could not become president of the USA. It is part of an entire set of – overwhelmingly right-wing – conspiracy theories about Democrats, African Americans, other minorities, and gender politics.

2. *'Cross my heart and hope to die': Authenticity, Cultural Identity and Fictionality*

Most readers will recognize the intertextual allusion in the title of this essay: in Tim O'Brien's 1990 short story collection about the Vietnam War, *The Things They Carried*, there is a story called "How to Tell a True War Story." It is a metafictional story (or perhaps better: disquisition) about the difference between 'what really happened' in the war (if that is possible to determine at all) and a 'true' war story. For O'Brien, truth has nothing to do with factuality and verifiability. He writes: "You can tell a true war story by the questions you ask. Somebody tells a story, let's say, and afterward you ask, 'Is it true?' and if the answer matters, you've got your answer" (89) – by which he means no, it is not. The answer should not matter. In another story in the same collection ("Good Form"), he distinguishes between story-truth and happening-truth, arguing that "story-truth is truer sometimes than happening-truth" (203), and thus fiction 'more true' to whatever point is being made than nonfiction.[6]

A similar, albeit theoretically undergirded, argument is made by Hanjo Berressem in an essay on Bret Easton Ellis's novel *Lunar Park*. Berressem argues that autobiographical authenticity is constituted via a referential pact ("which promises that the events described in the text can be tested against real-life") and an autobiographical pact (which merges the "identity of author, narrator and protagonist into one identical unit") (2010, 273). Following Berressem's logic, a novel can be "completely true in terms of an authentic expression" and also "completely false in terms of an always already 'inauthentic' representation" (2010, 275). More generally, Richard Walsh (using relevance theory, linguistic pragmatics, and the cooperation principles of Grice for a rhetorical approach to fictionality) argues that "for the purposes of communication [and fictional narratives are acts of communication – R.H.], the propositional criterion of truth is a subordinate consideration to the contextual pragmatic criterion of *relevance*" (2008, 156; my emphasis). This does not imply that the distinction between truth and falsehood is irrelevant or indifferent; but "the truth of an assumption need not depend upon the truth of the encoded form of an utterance, or *its literal meaning*" (2008, 157; my emphasis) and can be contextually recuperated as relevant via various interpretive strategies.

Clearly, none of these arguments are helpful for systematically distinguishing between fiction and nonfiction, factuality and counterfactuality (nor do they necessarily aim to). They do, however, more or less explicitly alert us to two issues: first, the fact that the relevance of some narratives is not exhaustively determined by their identification as fictional or nonfictional, while, secondly

6 In all this, he never explains what he means by 'true' and he also does not reveal to the reader how to actually tell a true war story.

and almost ironically, it is exactly these kinds of narratives (about war, trauma, etc.) that are frequently queried regarding their factuality.[7]

Generally, it seems that certain areas of human experience seem to make special demands on their representation and fictionalization. Again and again, memoirs, autobiographies and other allegedly nonfictional texts about, for instance, abuse, discrimination or, most drastically, genocidal persecution that turn out to be invented kindle severe reactions of censure; the literary scandals are legend. Texts that break the autobiographical pact between author and reader – which many modern and postmodern historiographic metafictional narratives have done with relish in order to point at the narrativity (and thus implied partial fictitiousness) of history – meet with criticism whenever they do not at least announce their 'fictionality.' Narrative theorists that conflate the difference between the fictional and the nonfictional – correctly pointing out that there is no fail-proof single way to determine the difference and that both types of texts share narrative strategies[8] – should, according to Sidonie Smith and Julia Watson, at least acknowledge the problems of this conflation (2008).

Even fictional texts about special experiences such as migration, culture-specific rituals and customs, and so on, are treated with suspicion based on the assumption that such experiences cannot, should not, or must not be fictionalized. When they are, their fictionalization is usually expected to be especially scrupulous and exacting in its depiction of these experiences, though it is seldom clarified just what scrupulous and exacting may mean in this context. Literary texts about cultural practices, among them immigrant fictions, often meet with similar demands, which I would attribute to the ideological baggage of ideas about cultural identity and difference that they are assumed to carry. As Werner Sollors points out, "ethnic writers operated under a system that has been called 'compulsive representation,' for they were often read as informants about the collectivities they were believed to embody" (2002, 390), so that "readers have overemphasized and exaggerated the (frequently exoticized) ethnic particularity of the works" (1986, 11). Put in inverse mode: "Are the respective texts duty-bound to be representational, some prescribed version of the community from which they arise? [...] Does a demographic minority always write minority literature?" (Lee 2012, 114).

---

[7] The suspicion is actually quite old (captivity and slave narratives are regularly questioned regarding their factuality), pervasive (entire genres undermine the distinction between fictional and nonfictional or play with it, e.g. New Journalism or the nonfiction novel), and current (for example, in so-called docu-soaps, scripted reality, embedded journalism in the medium of graphic novels such as by Joe Sacco, and various other formats). And the issue is, obviously, also far from resolved.

[8] The debate over signposts of fictionality – or whether there even are any, intra- or extra-textual – has a long history and has not been settled, nor is it ever likely to. For a comprehensive and topical overview and discussion of the various facets of this debate and the critical faultlines, see Monika Fludernik and Marie-Laure Ryan's Handbook *Narrative Factuality* (2020), especially Frank Zipfel's essay on panfictionality in the collection.

The interconnected assumptions behind these representational expectations are that migrational experiences and the cultural practices of immigrant groups are special and serve to reveal a person's and a group's 'cultural identity;' that all such texts should also be especially 'authentic' in the representation of these experiences; and that even the leeway usually granted to fictional texts is overridden or at least restricted by the demand to 'authentically' represent these special experiences and identities. The conceptually problematic notion of cultural identity and representation underpinning this chain of assumptions is here compounded by the conceptual and definitional challenges of the terms authenticity and fictionality. While fictionality is at least a narratologically differentiated and problematized concept that has been studied in detail and whose problematic aspects have attracted extensive attention[9], the renewed, proliferating and multidisciplinary deployment of authenticity is primarily characterized by a definitional lacuna, which in turn is (paradoxically) inherent in the concept itself. Moreover, it is paradigmatically substituted with synonyms such as sincerity, honesty, purity, or even 'truthiness.'

The problem with, or, perhaps better: challenge of authenticity is that it is a highly flexible, inherently ambiguous, even paradoxical, context-dependent category that has a long and complicated history in a variety of philosophical traditions and academic, but also artistic, disciplines. While it has never been out of use or entirely outside the vista of critical attention (see Charles Taylor's influential *The Ethics of Authenticity* (1991) or, earlier, Lionel Trilling's equally influential *Sincerity and Authenticity* (1972)), it has received renewed attention during the past two decades.

In the introduction to their collection of essays *Funktionen von Wirklichkeit* (2011), Wolfgang Funk and Lucia Krämer describe the basic dilemma:

> One could severely abridge this paradox by summarizing that as an aesthetic, epistemological and ethical category, 'authenticity' by definition necessarily evades any form of unequivocal representation. This proposition is based on the assumption that a constitutive characteristic of authenticity is the immediate and unmediated expression of some kind of unalienable essence or core that derives its aesthetic as well as ethical persuasion exactly from the fact that it can be neither explicated nor instrumentalized. (2011, 8; my – abridged – trans.)

In other words, authenticity is not only semantically dependent on its discursive context (in which its meaning/use may differ significantly – this is true of most categories)[10] but, more importantly and paradoxically, essentially 'empty' because once it is represented, once the ascription of anything as 'authentic'

---

[9] See, for example, Tobias Klauk's and Tilmann Köppe's handbook on fictionality (2014) or Lut Missine's, Ralf Schneider's, and Beatrix Theresa van Dam's *Grundthemen der Literaturwissenschaft: Fiktionalität* (2020).

[10] Peter Schneck writes: "authenticity does not simply 'happen' in, say, a spontaneous act of self-expression; it is created and constructed over time by reference to already established 'authenticities'" (2010, 258).

is explicated, elaborated, and mediated, the authentic ceases to be authentic because the logic of the term demands that it cannot be re-presented, repeated, mediated, imitated, etc. Appropriately, Straub has titled her collection *Paradoxes of Authenticity* (2012). It is fitting, then, that the subtitle of Jacob Golomb's monograph on authenticity (1995) includes the phrase "In Search of." In the entire monograph, there is no substantial definition of the term by Golomb himself, and intentionally so, as he announces early on. At the most, he is willing to concede that authenticity is the "incessant yet indefinite" (1995, 21) process of "freely forming one's self-hood" and requires the "pathos of incessant change" (1995, 12).[11]

Since then, there have been various careful attempts at defining and explaining what authenticity may mean, and how it functions in various different contexts. Most proposals note both the paradoxical quality of the concept and, at the same time, its relevance and the ensuing need to pay critical attention to it; apart from this, they share three further insights.

For one, wherever critics write primarily about persons and their communities (and not about objects or artefacts), they agree that authenticity "has the quality of being somehow connected with, and expressive of, the core of the actor's personality. It brings into play the actor's uniquely personal, as opposed to culturally or socially shared, identity" (Ferrara 1998, 5). It describes "a person who acts in a way that we think of as faithful to herself and her principles" (Varga 2012, 2)[12] cultivating his/her 'true self' (Guignon 2004, ix; Coupland 2014, 19).

Second, there is agreement that authenticity is neither 'one thing' but rather comprises a cluster of attributes, nor static but rather relational and processual. Varga distinguishes between nominal and expressive authenticity (for artworks and artefacts; 2012, 1); Guignon distinguishes between the traditions of self-possession (self, personal) and self-loss (social, communal) (2004, 6–7); and Lacoste et al. write in the introduction to their collection of essays that authenticity may be attributional (eye of the beholder) or interactional (2014, 2), and that it is, most importantly, negotiable (2014, 8). In their essay on "Kinds of Authenticity" (2016), Newman and Smith similarly identify the root of the problem of authenticity as a concept. Taking their cue from Denis Dutton, they point out that authenticity is a "dimension word," i.e. "a word whose specific meaning is uncertain until one knows which dimension of authenticity is being discussed" (2016, 610). But even when the dimension is known, the meaning often remains vague and elusive. They go on to identify different uses

11 Appropriately, Haselstein et al. have titled their collection *The Pathos of Authenticity* (2010).

12 Notice the use of 'we.' Without saying it here, Varga hints at the importance of the social community an individual is imbedded in and its potential as a source of conflict. Coupland expressly argues that the concept usually surfaces at the "interface between personal and social identities" (2014, 19).

of authenticity but argue that all these superficially different versions actually converge into four fundamental kinds of authenticity judgments along two dimensions: "type of entity" and "source of information" (2016, 613). Of particular importance for my argument are categorical and value authenticity because they a) are dependent on our expectations and thus highly subjective and b) "pertain to agents and in particular, moral agents" (2016, 613), specifically the extent to which "someone's behavior embodies the values of a particular *culture*" (2016, 613, my emphasis). Finally, Handler and Saxton, two anthropologists writing about living history, argue that an authentic experience which makes individuals feel truly themselves needs narrative coherence, that it needs to be emplotted and constituted as a story (1988, 243). This aspect will play a key role in the second part of my argument.

Third, and lastly, there is not one critic who does not emphasize that despite its paradoxical nature, authenticity is important both because it clearly matters to people and communities since "there is obviously something clearly right about the ideal of authenticity" (Guignon 2004, ix; see also Coupland 2014, 19), and because it may actually be understood as a heuristic and epistemic device, a "tool that can be used for critical inquiry" (Straub 2012, 12).[13]

It should be obvious, then, that any binary approach (authentic/inauthentic & fictional/nonfictional) to literary texts about the migrational experiences or specific cultural practices is bound to be reductive and problematic. There is no definitive authority to determine just what counts as authentic and what does not; more importantly, this kind of authenticity implies a static and homogeneous notion of culture and cultural identity behind cultural practices, and thus a notion of literary texts as mainly mimetic and static representations of 'real' and 'true' experiences and a 'real' or 'true' 'identity.' If we treat literary texts about cultural practices as a kind of social report about a special real-world experience, the status of such texts as fictional constructions is of secondary importance. No wonder, then, that 'authenticity' is often found in the context of the critical discourses I am talking about above: if 'autobiographical' is a soft version of 'nonfictional,' and if 'nonfictional' is 'truthful' and therefore authentic, then autobiographical implies authentic.

Perhaps the best-known examples of this kind of logic are the notorious debates between Frank Chin and Maxine Hong Kingston, and between Leslie Marmon Silko and Louise Erdrich. In both debates, one writer accused another of being inauthentic and betraying/selling out their culture. In the so-called pen war, Chin accused Kingston of faking Asian American traditions and cultures in her *Woman Warrior*, especially because she was mixing (fictional) Chinese myths and her own (nonfictional) memoir, while Kingston insisted on artistic freedom and the impossibility and fallacy of authentic representation, and in

[13] It is, for example, irreplaceable for anthropologists and ethnographers, or for art historians.

turn accused Chin of sexism. Likewise, Silko accused Erdrich of inauthentic hybridizing of Native American storytelling traditions, thereby providing an inauthentic representation of the respective tribal cultures. This is especially ironic since Silko herself has been criticized for 'selling out' Native American culture by the writer Paula Gunn Allen. Both debates are symptomatic of the tensions between postmodernism and multiculturalism and of the question of how 'best' to 'authentically' represent cultural identity, if that is deemed possible at all.

The issue is compounded by the specific history of the USA, in which, from its inception, narratives of national identity, immigration, and cultural identity have intersected in complex and often contradictory ways, occasionally overshadowing or even supplanting other narratives, most importantly class. The current phenomenon of post-factual narration cannot be understood without this historical context. As a nation the USA was founded in opposition to Britain by an already diverse group of immigrants/colonials, who established this state on a new continent, with a new landscape and ecosphere, with a new political organization, new laws, social life, institutions, and infrastructure; it then became an ever-changing (demographically, but also geographically) nation of immigrants. The USA has from the very beginning intensely debated the question of its national and cultural identity; much more so, and much more explicitly so, than most other nations. That debate has never stopped. Since immigration is one of the key components and myths of the USA, past and present, immigration per se is necessarily at the heart of any debate about the nation's identity, thereby unavoidably turning US-American immigrant literature into one central arena for that debate. As a result, immigrant fiction is never 'just' about the immigrant experience of a particular person or group; it is always, implicitly or explicitly, about the alleged cultural identity of the USA, or, in other words, about 'becoming American.' This is one reason why so many immigrant fictions are *Bildungsromane* or coming-of-age narratives, almost regardless of the protagonist's biological age.

However, this presents us with another problem. 'Culture' and 'cultural identity,' despite the "hefty workout" (Appiah 2005, 114) these terms have been getting, are almost impossible to define. Often enough, 'culture' serves merely as an umbrella term either for all human activity ('an entire way of life') of a given community, for the sum of its artistic productions, or for those remaining practices once political, economic or social ones have been subtracted. In discussions of 'mainstream' culture, immigration, integration, race, and ethnicity, the term 'culture' is often accompanied by some metaphorical correlative equally undefinable and over- and underdetermined, such as the melting pot, mosaic, pizza pie, or salad bowl. At the worst, "culture and even religion can become essentialized to the point that they can serve as a functional equivalent of biological racism – culture, put another way, can do the work of race, when peoples or ways of life are seen as unchangeable as pigmentation" (Foner 2005, 217). In the context of a critique of hybridity, Floya Anthias argues that belonging and personal and collective identity "do not depend solely on cultural practices or beliefs" (2001, 622), that the notion of culture as "a core element of identity and belonging" (2001, 620) eschews various other factors such as gender and class, and that "cultural resources are only one of a set of resources used by ethnic groups" (2001, 629).

In addition, as Walter Benn Michaels cautions, focusing exclusively on identity and difference comes at another price:

> Questions about what it means to be yellow or what it means to be American are questions about who we are rather than about how much (or little) we own, and while such questions have always played a significant role in American literature, they have [...] come to play an absolutely central role both in the literature and the literary criticism of the last thirty years. (2011, 1017)

This, however, is a problem because social and economic injustice have taken a back seat when in actuality, issues of race and economics are intricately connected, as intersectional theory has convincingly shown. In his book *The Trouble With Diversity* (2006), Michaels claims that the USA has learned to love difference and that "[i]nstead of trying to treat people as if their race didn't matter, we would not only recognize but celebrate racial identity.[...] [W]e love race – we love identity – because we don't love class" (2006, 5–6). In fact, he argues, "the focus on identity functions not just to distract people from the increase in inequality but to legitimate it" (2011, 1027). Such legitimation is gratifying (2011, 2023) because an economic issue is represented as a cultural one, which is much easier to contain; after all, it is what makes America America (2011, 1023). The myth of the USA as a nation of immigrants and cultural diversity (a myth often accompanied by the – contrafactual – myth that this diversity has always been welcomed and celebrated) has, in other words, made it difficult to address issues of social and economic injustice and inequality – exactly at a time when such inequality and injustice have increased, the recent economic boom notwithstanding. Whenever such issues are addressed, they are, somewhat unsurprisingly, cloaked in the mantle of national and cultural identity.[14]

---

[14] As Winfried Fluck has argued together with Welf Werner (2003), one reason why the USA is traditionally less troubled about sharp socio-economic differences is that differences as a result of gender or race are unfair because they are genotypic (one cannot be blamed for one's gender or race), while class differences can be overcome (one can be blamed for 'laziness'). Fluck (2002) has also argued that in the course of the second half of the twentieth century, economic matters and class membership have receded behind the focus on an 'expressive individualism.'

3. *'The Real Thing'? Jhumpa Lahiri's* The Namesake

Lahiri is one of the best-known writers of immigrant fiction at this time. Her very first collection of short stories won the Pulitzer Prize for fiction; since then, she has written several novels, another collection of short stories, and various essays. Like almost all immigrant novels, *The Namesake* (2003) is about different kinds of immigrants, different kinds of migration experiences, and all kinds of experiences. Somewhat predictably, reviews and criticism focus largely on cultural identity and diaspora, authenticating the novel's quality and plausibility as a fiction of immigration with references to Lahiri's biography, thereby in turn ignoring the complexities and facets of the novel and, ironically, downplaying its fictionality. This pattern repeats itself with regard to Lahiri's other fiction.

The novel is about a Bengali couple, Ashoke and Ashima Ganguli, who, after an arranged marriage in India, move to the US because the husband has been offered a doctoral position at MIT. He later becomes a professor of engineering. Once in the USA, they have a son and a daughter, and it quickly becomes clear that the family is going to stay. Most of the novel traces the life of the son, Gogol, from birth to adulthood. The novel gets its title from the fact that the husband had been in a serious train accident in India and had taken away from it a deep gratefulness to his favorite writer Gogol, a volume of whose collected stories saved his life by accidentally drawing the attention of the rescue team. Because they have, for reasons of tradition, not yet decided on a name for their firstborn when he is delivered and are waiting for a letter from the grandmother with the name, but have to, for bureaucratic reasons, decide on a name on the spot, the father chooses Gogol as a temporary solution. As it turns out, the letter never arrives, the grandmother dies, and thus the name sticks, despite the fact that Gogol is later given another, 'official' name. The major part of the narrative traces Gogol's life in episodes covering his education (from kindergarten, school, college, and university to the first years of his professional life as an architect), his family life (his relationship to mother and father and his sister Sonia, his visits to the extended family in India, his father's sudden death, his mother's impending departure from the USA), important rituals (for example regarding his first food (the rice ceremony/annaprasan) and food in general, family and/or religious celebrations such as Deepavali, Puja, or Christmas –which they celebrate for the sake of the children –, mourning, marriage), and his love life (from his first kiss, his first and second relationship, to his marriage and divorce).

Clearly, the novel is both a coming-of-age narrative and a migrational narrative that frames issues of identity via the overarching theme of naming and names, specifically Gogol's. One could, as a result, also summarize the story in terms of Gogol's names and his changing attitude towards them. Initially, he does not have a name, or rather: his intended name is suspended in mid-air and will forever be both implicitly present and lost. He is then given a provisional name under the assumption that his 'real name' will arrive later. When it does not, the name Gogol sticks as 'pet name' and as the name on all legal documents. Later, his parents decide on Nikhil – meaning 'encompassing all' – as his 'good name' (i.e. 'public' name) before he enters kindergarten. However, Gogol wants to remain Gogol. It is only when he grows up and discovers that his name is odd and unique that he begins to loathe it. From then on, whenever he has the chance to be with people who do not know him, he gives Nikhil as his 'real' name; at the first legal opportunity, he officially changes his name to Nikhil. This is the name with which he enters college and makes new friends, girlfriends, etc. Only later does his father tell him about the real reason for his first name. For most of Gogol's adulthood (the narrator always calls him Gogol), he remains Nikhil, but continues to feel awkward about his other name, keeping it a secret from most people. Finally, at the very end of the novel, he begins to read the short story *The Overcoat* that was so dear to his father.

The Namesake is a typical immigration narrative in that we have immigrants whose pre-departure time, transition, arrival, and consecutive acculturation are depicted in detail. Some space is granted to cultural practices, to mostly minor initial cultural 'clashes' with the surrounding culture, and to the adapting, adopting, and hybridizing of cultural practices over time. It is also typical in that it is a fairly ordinary family story and a story of, ultimately and for most characters, relative success. The historical context of the revolutionary 1965 immigration act is present insofar as it makes the premise of the entire story possible/realistic, but it remains in the background and is never addressed, much less reflected upon, in detail. In general, there is very little explicit self-reflection on cultural identity and difference, minority and mainstream culture, the Indian 'diasporic' community in the US, and so on (there is much more of that in Lahiri's short stories in *Interpreter of Maladies* (1999) and *Unaccustomed Earth* (2008)). Most of the self-reflection on identity is framed by the issue of Gogol's name. Even this reticence and reservation, however, are typical of one tradition of immigrant fiction, namely the one in which the immigrant experience and the ensuing acculturation are depicted in a matter-of-fact, even unobtrusive manner, or framed via another theme. Its investment, I would argue, is in the immigrant as American, and the American as a human, capturing a pertinent trend in much critical theory.

There are, obviously, many more complications in the novel, but even these are, at a closer look, typical of most immigrant fiction in that most immigrant fiction is about much more than 'simply' immigration. First of all, the immigrant experience itself is complicated. Even Gogol's mother and father have quite different migrational experiences because he works, she does not, he is first to migrate to the US, she comes second, he chooses to migrate, she simply follows him. More significantly, the bulk of the narrative is not about the immigrant parents, but about their son, who, being born in the US, is, of course, a US citizen. He has no first-hand migration experience except visiting his parents' homeland one summer; a homeland to which he has no ties other than his parents. The diasporic community that is so often portrayed in Lahiri's other stories is of little importance to him. Only once does his cultural background matter significantly: when he marries a Bengali woman and the marriage is performed in a traditional ritual (incidentally, they both feel they marry in spite of their parents' expectations, not because of them). But then, that marriage fails because his wife falls in love with a Russian immigrant. More importantly, while cultural affiliations, practices, and experiences of difference do matter, they matter differently and to different degrees to different characters. What is more, so do gender, sex, class, and education. First of all, Gogol's sister has no problems, at least none are mentioned. Much of the novel is about Gogol's love life and education, for which his odd name matters, but not so much his alleged 'Indianness.' The ambivalent feelings Gogol has for his 'WASP' girlfriend and her and her family's lifestyle (both distance and envy) have at their core not only differences in culture, but also in class and habitus (despite the fact that his parents are well-off). In other words, the novel depicts all kinds of different experiences, most of which have to do with coming-of-age. And in this regard, Gogol is not so different. One could, of course, take the issue of names and naming as a metaphor strictly of cultural identity; but that would ignore the many different situations in which the name plays a role and the many facets of Gogol's identification process – a process, by the way, which is not finished at the end. Fittingly, the narrative is written in present tense, which produces the impression of things happening 'right now,' of presence and continuous, gradual disclosure, emphasizing the process of life and becoming, whatever that may be.

In the end, it is, ironically, the beginning of Gogol's life that points us to the key theme of the novel: the 'original,' intended name is lost forever in transit, and no one will ever know it. If we wait for that name, that 'true' 'identity' and unambiguous signifier, to arrive, we may as well wait forever. Its journey, just like that of every immigrant and, in fact, every human being, is never over and knows no certain destination until it is, literally, over.

Little of this irony, complexity, and multifariousness makes it into the critical reception of Lahiri's work so far. I have already alluded to the typical response patterns in reviews; many of the longer critical essays on *The Namesake* repeat these patterns. There are a number of essays on hybridity and migration, inheritance, identity and alienation, or cultural practices and dilemma – and of course, all of these aspects matter, but they are not the only ones to matter. In addition, many of the essays work with vaguely or entirely undefined notions of 'cultural identity,' usually opposing India and the USA, and usually locating the protagonist Gogol – as a child of immigrants – 'in-between' or 'beyond'.

Similar to the work on Alvarez, the majority of the critical assessments are accompanied by a reference to Lahiri's biography, who was born in London to Bengali immigrants and raised in Rhode Island; her writing and her characters are labeled 'autobiographical' or 'semi-autobiographical'. Again, the biographical reference appears to authenticate the author's privileged access to the experience of 'South Asian American' children of immigrants. None of the essays that engage in this authentication care to elaborate what exactly is meant by 'autobiographical,' much less what difference it might possibly make that the author is female and the protagonist male.

4. *Making America Great Again: Lies, Felt Truth, and the American Dream*

As the transition to the second part of my argument might seem slightly jarring, let me briefly, and, for the clarity of the argument, somewhat pointedly summarize my key points so far:

1.US-American migration narratives are an important part of discourses of US-American (im)migration in general. These, in turn, touch upon fundamental questions/issues of US-American cultural and national identity, including the (factually mostly correct) mythical narrative of the USA as a nation of immigrants, and, by extension, the (factually incorrect) mythical narrative of everyone, including immigrants, having the equal opportunity to pursue their own 'happiness' and prosperity, i.e. the American Dream.

2.As a consequence, US-American migration narratives have a special status as they are seen to deal with a special, prototypical US-American experience. As a further consequence, they are often received, reviewed, and criticized with a particular, often monofocal, eye on whether they 'adequately', i.e. authentically, represent that special experience (what Varga or Dutton might term 'expressive authenticity'). One key attribute of this authenticity appears to be whether these narratives are as close to 'the real life/experience' as possible, i.e. 'almost nonfictional'. One prominent token, in turn, of this 'isomorphism' (as Handler and Saxton would call it) appears to be the author's own biographical background. Put bluntly: Only someone who has lived the experience can tell about it – which happens to be a central tenet of identity politics.

A recent study of the US-American Right by sociologist Arlie Russell Hochschild (2016) elucidates this conjunction of authenticity, identity, fictionality, and economics in an apparently completely different and unrelated context. Taking as her corpus numerous extensive interviews with citizens who self-identify as 'right,' she 'extracted' and then abstracted a 'deep story' about what is going on in the USA today. She then 'fed back' this story to her interview partners in a feedback loop to see whether they agreed with it; all of them did, with some minor revisions. That deep story, it turns out, is about the amorphous 'American Dream' and its perceived failure. What is crucial for my argument is not only the actual content of the story; it is, predictably, mostly about economic disillusionment and frustration over 'others' who work less hard (read: minorities, immigrants, 'special interest groups' etc.) seemingly being given an unfair advantage, and thus a vindication of Bannon's strategy of focusing on economics and nationalism.[15] Equally important is that the interviewees believe that the myth used to be 'true' and has been corrupted, or, in other words, that America used to be great and can become great again – with the right person at the head of the nation. It is, essentially, a quasi-religious narrative of birth (innocence), fall (corruption), and salvation (redemption). Of course, this narrative needs a savior.

Lastly, Hochschild emphasizes that "[a] deep story is a *feels-as-if* story – it's the story feelings tell, in the language of symbols. It removes judgment. It removes fact. It tells us how things feel" (2016, 135; original emphasis). It is important to note that, as Hochschild points out, we all have a deep story. Even though the actual term is not used, we could just as well say that a deep story is a story that feels 'authentic' without much regard for factuality – a deep story is, in fact, a myth. It becomes more important that certain narratives (e.g. the American Dream and its corruption) present what is considered – either by the majority or by other members of the respective group – an 'authentic' rendering of a particular experience or feeling (e.g. the feeling of being forgotten by politicians in far-away Washington, D.C., while perceived out-groups – here minorities, special-interest groups etc. – are privileged and preferred).

In other words, the 'readers' of Trump's 'story' (Make America Great Again so that everyone can fulfill their very own American Dream) believe that story to be authentic, i.e. 'true,' i.e. nonfictional, regardless of its evidential contrafactuality. This myth is so entrenched in US-American cultural history and identity formation (so much a 'deep story') that the countless lies with which Trump 'garnishes' it, do not matter. On the contrary, Trump himself is seen as the embodiment of that myth, so that he, too, his person and identity, become 'authentic.'

Let me briefly return to the conjunction of authenticity and identity in the reception of immigrant fictions to highlight the similarities of the two phenomena: the reception is characterized by the feeling that a piece of fiction

[15] In an interview with Robert Kuttner, Steve Bannon, figurehead of the US-American Right, former head of the right-wing news network Breitbart News, and former chief strategist of the Trump administration, explains the key element of his political strategy: "The Democrats, the longer they talk about identity politics, I got 'em. I want them to talk about racism every day. If the left is focused on race and identity, and we go with economic nationalism, we can crush the Democrats" (2017, n.p.).

(though not just any fiction, but fiction about a 'special experience' that is part of the mythical narrative of the USA as a nation of immigrants) is actually, to an unspecified degree, a piece of nonfiction, without the facts having to match. This 'feeling' is necessarily based on a 'match of authenticity' between the narrative and the audience's expectations regarding this narrative (in other words: categorical and value authenticity; see above). The key difference between these two phenomena is that while Trump makes every effort to appear as an authentic storyteller to his audience so that his narrative 'feels true,' many writers of fiction (if we are to believe their public statements) stress that the relevance of their stories does not depend on their status as either fictional or nonfictional.

Clearly, I do not think that the existence of this similarity between the two phenomena is a coincidence. Many immigrant fictions are, among many other things, narratives about what it means to be/become 'American;' they participate (whether they want to or not) in the negotiation of a national identity. In other words, they do the work of 'myth,' in particular the myth that the USA is a nation of immigrants (which is, of course, factually correct, but factuality is not the primary aspect of myth). If we now look at the content of Hochschild's deep story, we find that, ironically, it is also about what it means to be American, only that it focuses on another aspect of that identity and myth; namely, the myth that hard work, self-sufficiency, and initiative pay off; if not for you, then for your children. Crucially, the initial playing field in this story is level for all players. Note that both narratives – the one about cultural identity and the one about the American dream – are about identity, though not exclusively the same identity politics of 'smaller' (i.e. non-national) aggregate 'cultural groups;' they are also both about socioeconomics. Many immigrant fictions also are about hard work, self-sufficiency, and initiative (and ultimately success stories). However, as I have argued, the latter aspect is often overlooked in the reception of immigrant fictions, which are usually taken to be about cultural identity, and only that.

In light of all this, it becomes easier to explain, among other things, why Donald Trump appeals to many US-Americans over and beyond older, rural, white, male Republicans (what some commentators call the white identity of mainstream USA) despite the fact that some of his comments could be expected to alienate large voter groups (women, second-generation immigrants, etc.). Conventional 'identity logic' simply does not fully explain his success. Rather, he finds favor across a diverse spectrum of the US-American public among those disappointed with the national mythic promises of the American Dream – just like Barack Obama, by the way.[16] Since few of the participants

16 Another, somewhat less important, but nonetheless fundamental factor of Trump's appeal is his language. I would argue that it is a misunderstanding to assume that Donald Trump appeals to large voter groups across a wide spectrum *despite* his often vulgar, racist, and sexist language, but that, rather, it is *because* of this language that many peo-

in this myth-inflected discourse (be they politicians or writers of fiction) have questioned the myth per se (other than, for example, Bernie Sanders), it is almost 'convenient' (for lack of a better word) that the socioeconomic paradoxes and problems can be 'hidden' behind debates about cultural/national identity.

It also becomes easier to explain why it is pointless to falsify a counterfactual statement (i.e. a lie) that is part of a deep story, or a narrative that is perceived as authentic, simply with contrary facts and factuality. Authenticity circumvents any binary concept of fact and non-fact, fictionality and nonfictionality – in some contexts, appearing authentic is much more important than adhering to facts.[17]

5. *Conclusions*

'Felt truth' and authenticity may be highly amorphous, ephemeral, negotiable, and dynamic, and thus challenging to come to grips with for scholars, but they constitute an important element of the production and reception of certain narratives and may command the belief of significant parts of the political constituency. This needs to be taken into account when analyzing why and how cultural narratives, myths, and deep stories take hold and are being perpetuated, and to what effect. Similarly, 'forgetful' or monofocal critical reception may appear as an unavoidable but negligible professional deformation, when in fact it is, I believe, a tell-tale sign of wider discursive practices that have very real and, literally, powerful consequences.[18] Depending on one's disciplinary bent, the eminent power of narrative(s) may be re-assuring (or perhaps self-evident), but, depending on the context, it can also be devastating. Lastly, I would like to point out just how ironic and mind-bogglingly paradoxical it is that we can

ple find him authentic. As Charles Guignon explains, "genuine authenticity comes to be seen as a matter of giving uninhibited expression to these tendencies [cruelty, hostility, aggression], and this means rejecting the sorts of 'making nice' and common courtesy of so-called 'polite society'" (2008, 281). Coupland similarly argues that language may express authenticity in various ways, among them personal authenticity and authentic cultural/group membership (2014, 21). By using the language he does, Trump signals and affirms his membership in the group that constitutes his supporters, even though that group actually might not have seen itself as an 'in-group' before the 2016 elections.

17 Ironically, a close look at the migration narratives that are so often upheld as textual strongholds and paragons of authenticity and cultural identity shows that, nine times out of ten, they cleverly undermine such reductive appropriation. Unfortunately, that irony is often lost.

18 These practices also are, by the way, context- and domain-sensitive. In other words, there may be similarities and parallels between populism, identitarian movements, and debates about 'post-factuality' in the USA and Europe, but we should not conflate them. On the contrary, there are important differences, not least of all in the specific cultural narratives, myths, and deep stories that 'work' in one context, but not another. Ignoring these differences will lead to gross misunderstandings and even dangerous simplifications.

diagnose a return of and penchant for the 'real,' but that it comes in the form of a concept – authenticity – that inherently obviates the very possibility of determining that 'real.' It would almost be funny if the consequences were not so dire.

Works Cited

Alvarez, Julia (1991) *How the García Girls Lost Their Accents*. New York: Plume.

Alvarez, Julia (1997) *¡Yo!* New York: Plume.

Anthias, Floya (2001) "New Hybridities, Old Concepts: the Limits of 'Culture'." *Ethnic and Racial Studies* 24. 4: 619–641.

Appiah, Kwame Anthony 2005) *The Ethics of Identity*. Princeton: Princeton Univ. Press.

Berressem, Hanjo (2010) "'Father, don't you see I'm writing?' Authenticity, Pathos, and Eigenvalue in Bret Easton Ellis's *Lunar Park*." *The Pathos of Authenticity*. Ed. Ulla Haselstein et al. Heidelberg: Universitätsverlag Winter. 271–290.

Cantiello, Jessica Wells (2011) "'That Story About the Gun': Pseudo-Memory in Julia Alvarez's Autobiographical Novels." *MELUS* 36. 1: 83–108.

Coupland, Nikolas (2014) "Language, Society and Authenticity: Themes and Perspectives." *Indexing Authenticity. Sociolinguistic Perspectives*. Ed. Véronique Lacoste et al. Berlin: De Gruyter. 14-40.

Ferrara, Allessandro (1998) *Reflective Authenticity. Rethinking the Project of Modernity*. New York: Routledge.

Fluck, Winfried (2002) "The Humanities in the Age of Expressive Individualism and Cultural Radicalism." *The Future of American Studies*. Ed. Donald E. Pease and Robyn Wiegman. Durham: Duke Univ. Press. 211–230.

Fluck, Winfried, and Welf Werner (2003) Ed. *Wie viel Ungleichheit verträgt die Demokratie? Armut und Reichtum in den USA*. Frankfurt a.M.: Campus.

Fludernik, Monika, and Marie-Laure Ryan (2020) Ed. *Narrative Factuality: A Handbook*. Revisionen 6. Berlin: De Gruyter.

Foner, Nancy (2005) *In a New Land: a Comparative View of Immigration*. New York: New York Univ. Press.

Funk, Wolfgang, and Lucia Krämer (2011) Ed. *Fiktionen von Wirklichkeit: Authentizität zwischen Materialität und Konstruktion*. Bielefeld: Transcript.

Golomb, Jacob (1995) *In Search of Authenticity. From Kierkegaard to Camus*. New York: Routledge.

Guignon, Charles (2004) *On Being Authentic*. New York: Routledge.

Guignon, Charles (2008) "Authenticity." *Philosophy Compass* 3.2: 277–290.

Handler, Richard, and William Saxton (1988) "Dyssimulation: Reflexivity, Narrative, and the Quest for Authenticity in 'Living History'." *Cultural Anthropology* 3.3: 242-260.

Haselstein, Ulla, Andrew Gross, and Maryann Snyder-Körber (2010) Ed. *The Pathos of Authenticity*. Heidelberg: Universitätsverlag Winter.

Hochschild, Arlie Russell (2016) *Strangers in Their Own Land*. New York and London: The New Press.

Huntington, Samuel (2004) *Who Are We?* London: Free Press.

Isenberg, Nancy (2016) *White Trash. The 400-Year Untold History of Class in America*. London: Atlantic Books.

Kingston, Maxine Hong (1976) *The Woman Warrior. Memoirs of a Girlhood Among Ghosts*. London: Alfred A. Knopf.

Klauk, Tobias, and Tillmann Köppe (2014) *Fiktionalität. Ein interdisziplinäres Handbuch*. Revisionen 4. Berlin: De Gruyter.

Kuttner, Robert (2017) "Steve Bannon, Unrepentant." *The American Prospect* 16 Aug. 2017. Web. 10 Oct. 2020.

Lacoste, Véronique, Jakob Leimgruber, and Thiemo Breyer (2014) Ed. *Indexing Authenticity - Sociolinguistic Perspectives*. Berlin: De Gruyter.

Lahiri, Jhumpa (1999) *The Interpreter of Maladies*. Boston: Houghton Mifflin.

Lahiri, Jhumpa (2003) *The Namesake*. London: Harper Perennial.

Lahiri, Jhumpa (2008) *Unaccustomed Earth*. New York: Knopf.

Lee, A. Robert (2012) "Multiethnicities: Latino/a and Asian American Fiction." *American Fiction After 1945*. Ed. John N. Duvall. Cambridge: Cambridge Univ. Press. 114–128.

Ludwig, Samuel (2003) "Thin Pluralism: Some Observations on American Multiculturalism." *Theories of American Culture – Theories of American Studies*. Ed. Winfried Fluck and Thomas Claviez. *REAL: Yearbook of Research in English and American Literature* 19: 225–245.

McIntyre, Lee (2018) *Post-Truth*. Cambridge, MA: MIT Press.

Michaels, Walter Benn (2006) *The Trouble with Diversity*. New York: Holt.

Michaels, Walter Benn (2011) "Model Minorities and the Minority Model – the Neoliberal Novel." *The Cambridge History of the American Novel*. Ed. Leonard Cassuto, Clare Virginia Eby, and Benjamin Reiss. Cambridge: Cambridge Univ. Press. 1016–1030.

Missine, Lut, Ralf Schneider, and Beatrix Theresa van Dam (2020) Ed. *Grundthemen der Literaturwissenschaft: Fiktionalität*. Berlin: De Gruyter.

Newman, George, and Rosanna Smith (2016) "Kinds of Authenticity." *Philosophy Compass* 11. 10: 609–618.

O'Brien, Tim (1990) *The Things They Carried*. New York: Penguin Books.

Rossinow, Doug (1998) *The Politics of Authenticity. Liberalism, Christianity, and the New Left in America.* New York: Columbia Univ. Press.

Schillinger, Liesl (2008) "American Children." Review of *Unaccustomed Earth*, by Jhumpa Lahiri. *New York Times* 6 Apr. 2008: N. pag. Web. 10 Oct. 2020.

Schneck, Peter (2010) "Fake Lives, Real Literature: JT Leroy and the Hustle for Authenticity." *The Pathos of Authenticity*. Ed. Ulla Haselstein et al. Heidelberg: Universitätsverlag Winter. 253–270.

Siemerling, Winfried, and Katrin Schwenk (1996) Ed. *Cultural Difference and the Literary Text. Pluralism and the Limits of Authenticity in North American Literatures.* Iowa City: Iowa Univ. Press.

Smith, Sidonie, and Julia Watson (2008) "The Trouble with Autobiography: Cautionary Notes for Narrative Theorists." *A Companion to Narrative Theory*. Ed. James Phelan and Peter J. Rabinowitz. Malden: Blackwell. 356–371.

Sollors, Werner (1986) *Beyond Ethnicity: Consent and Descent in American Culture*. Oxford: Oxford Univ. Press.

Sollors, Werner (2002) "Ethnic Modernism." *The Cambridge History of American Literature. Volume Six: Prose Writing, 1910–1950*. Ed. Sacvan Bercovitch. Cambridge: Cambridge Univ. Press. 355–556.

Straub, Julia (2012) *Paradoxes of Authenticity. Studies on a Critical Concept.* Bielefeld: Transcript.

Taylor, Charles (1991) *The Ethics of Authenticity*. Cambridge, MA: Harvard Univ. Press.

Trilling, Lionel (1972) *Sincerity and Authenticity*. Cambridge, MA: Harvard Univ. Press.

Varga, Somogy (2012) *Authenticity as an Ethical Ideal.* New York: Routledge.

Walsh, Richard (2008) "The Pragmatics of Narrative Fictionality." *A Companion to Narrative Theory*. Ed. James Phelan and Peter J. Rabinowitz. Oxford: Blackwell Publishing. 150–164.

This Narrator Nothing Affirms, Therefore He Lies? Truth-speaking and Discursive Power in Teju Cole's *Open City*

Martin Riedelsheimer and Eva Ries

1. *Introduction*

The discussion about whether or not fiction is capable of producing lies is more than two millennia old. This debate has been carried out with a view to the morality of literature (and art as a whole) on the one hand, and to the ontological status of the storyworld on the other. One part of the problem remains that "[t]here is no universally accepted definition of lying" (Mahon 2016; see 2008, 211) and that philosophical approaches to truth are likewise contested. Historically, there have been two tendencies: either to look for 'higher truths' in fiction (see Lamarque 2014, viii), or, conversely, to accuse writers of fiction of producing lies. Against the Platonic accusation that all fiction is just a lie, with which, as Peter Lamarque sums up the argument, poets "seduce a gullible audience into thinking they speak with real authority" (2014, 124), Philip Sidney has famously held that the poet "nothing affirms, and therefore never lieth" (2012, 1068). Indeed, if we accept James Mahon's general definitions, by which lying is the production of a "believed-false statement [...] with the intention that the other person believe that statement to be true," while deception is "to intentionally cause to have a false belief that is known or believed to be false" (2016), then a writer of fiction can hardly be accused of lying, since authors of fiction do not usually claim that they report the 'truth' and only seldom attempt to hoodwink their readers into believing such a thing. What is more, modern literary studies mostly refrain from guessing the poet's or author's intentions that are central to such acts as lying and deceiving.

Nevertheless, readers may get the impression that some fictional texts are deceptive or that they are confronted with outright 'lies' within the narrative discourse. Such cases have mostly been discussed with regard to a narrator, rather than the author, engaging in an act of lying or deception and have been classified as unreliable narration. In unreliable narration, generally speaking, the 'lie' (if such a thing may pass within the realm of the fictional) is the narrator's, who 'affirms' occurrences that do not seem to be supported by the overall narrative, whose 'truth' they deviate from. However, this does not fully take into account the narrator's privileged discursive position – after all, the narrator is the one who produces the 'truths' of the narrative in the first place – that might allow a narrator to withhold information *without* necessarily deceiving the reader or lying to them outright.

This theoretical problem is put to the test in Teju Cole's 2011 novel *Open City*, which showcases a form of narrative performance that resorts to silence to disavow truth-speaking without uttering demonstrable falsehoods. Not only does Cole's novel prominently question the norms that determine truth and falsehood in our everyday and political discourses, it also negotiates the connection between truth and (discursive) power as discussed by Michel Foucault (see below in section 2). The novel approaches the topic of truthfulness through its autodiegetic narrator Julius, who plays the double role of uncovering truth by giving a voice to oppressed discourses while simultaneously engaging in such oppression in his own narration. The ensuing tension between the narrator's resistance to discourses of power and his perpetuation of such discourses is instrumental in highlighting a paradox ingrained in the notion of truthfulness if seen through a Foucauldian lens. On the one hand, truth for Foucault depends directly on discursive power. This can be considered a relativist understanding of truth. On the other hand, in his late work Foucault admits to the necessity of truthfulness as a value that manifests itself for example in the practice of *parrēsia*, i.e. truth-speaking (on which see below). Cole's narrator juxtaposes these two notions of truthfulness, when, faced with an accusation of rape, he simply remains silent on the issue and so denies the reader any insight into the events. By rendering the facts of the case inaccessible in this way, the narrative marks its own opacity and directs readers' attention to the mechanisms of discursive power inherent in Julius's narration and, in a wider sense, in any instance of the production of truth. This power, as the novel also shows, somewhat paradoxically can only be countered by acts of truth-speaking.

The novel then highlights a central conundrum or paradox in our relationship towards the truth: while objectivity forms a necessary ideal in any production of truth, this ideal can neither be obtained by subjects nor would a truth that has not been subjectivized be of any use since it lacks a relationship to the subject. Thus, although fiction as a consequence of its ontological status cannot 'lie,' Cole's *Open City* shows that it can still emerge as an arena in which claims to truthfulness and the mechanisms of discourse production that generate what is perceived as the truth are scrutinized. Literature, therefore, can function as a means of critique that participates in or even initiates a never to be finished search for the truth.

2. *Foucault on Truth and Truthfulness*

The tension between truthfulness as a value and truth as a mere construct features prominently in the work of Michel Foucault, who has characterized his entire philosophical project as a "history of truth" (Foucault 1992, 11). While in his earlier writings Foucault emphasizes the constructed character of truth and its alignment with power, in his late work on the concept of *parrēsia* he stresses the importance of truthfulness as a value. According to Foucault (1980, 133), truth is "to be understood as a system of ordered procedures for the production, regulation, distribution, circulation and operation of statements." It is, therefore, as Michael Ruoff (2018, 262; our translation) argues, "the product of a discourse whose aim it is to justify certain modes as well as rules of behaviour," and thus truth remains tightly linked to power itself. For Foucault (1991, 79), "the production of truth [...] mean[s] [...] the establishment of domains in which the practice of true and false can be made at once ordered and pertinent." Notions of truth might thus, historically speaking, range from the judgment of God to more modern-day concepts of proof, involving professional specialization and subjects competent to speak the truth in a certain area. The latter thus necessarily includes norms according to which statements can be falsified or judged to be lies.

In his later work, Foucault assigns a much more positive value to the significance of truthfulness in political contexts as well as in processes of self-subjectification. The problem he was implicitly addressing in those texts can be located in the problematic conclusions that might be drawn from a constructivist approach towards truth with regard to any kind of morality: in short, the assumption that truth might be a mere construct might also foster ethical relativism.[1] In his late writings on the history of sexuality Foucault points out that his focus on the techniques of the self in Roman and Greek culture uncovers concepts of subjectivity that deviate from the Cartesian tradition, demonstrating that a different form of subjectivity is possible, namely one that re-grants a certain kind of autonomy to the subject after its death (Foucault 1992, 6–9). The practice of *parrēsia*, or truth-speaking, plays a vital role in these techniques of the self (Foucault 2019, 19).

'Speaking the truth' can occur on different levels: the political level, on which an individual stands up either to tyranny or to the *demos* in democratic societies; and the personal level, on which *parrēsia* is used as a means in techniques of self-formation in which the truth about an individual is told to this individual by one of his or her friends, or in which the individual questions him- or herself about his or her relation to the truth (Foucault 2019, 15). In both cases the individual puts him- or herself in a relation to the truth and therefore participates in what Foucault terms 'games of truth.' What is

[1] As Thomas Flynn observes, the charge of ethical relativism was not unique to Foucault's brand of poststructuralist thought: "Foucault was facing an issue that many have regarded as the Achilles' heel of Marxism and structuralism alike: the moral implications of their theories of history and society. Do they lead to a sterile amoralism, rendering inconsistent any viable moral theory?" (Flynn 1987, 225).

striking in Foucault's account of *parrēsia* is that the different variants of *parrēsia* amount to a somewhat double-edged concept: whereas the subject can directly influence the games of truth, it is also subject to the truth of others. Therefore, while the individual has a certain degree of autonomy in partaking in these games of truth, this autonomy is limited by the discourses of others and by an ideal of objectivity that is reflected in the juxtaposition of different perspectives. Thus, a precarious balance is created between subjectivity and objectivity in productions of truth. According to this conception, truth cannot be found out or discovered but is created in an active process that is never quite finished. While Foucault then does not produce any such thing as a definition of what truth *actually* is (Flynn 1987, 227), in his writings on subjectivity and truth he clearly assigns a value to the concept of truthfulness. The alternatives to the traditional Cartesian conceptions of subjectivity which he proposes involve truthfulness as an ethos[2] on several levels.[3] The notion of an absolute truth in discourse is thus discarded and replaced by truthfulness as ethos (Gros 2019, xvii), a concept that becomes a central value in Foucault's late writings. This makes for a somewhat ambivalent stance towards truth from the perspective of Foucault's oeuvre as a whole. Overall, while for Foucault truth is necessarily historically variable and can never be absolute, truthfulness remains a central value in processes of self-subjectification that re-introduce a partial autonomy of the subject – *parrēsia* thus is a technique of the self that allows an individual to enter into a relationship with the truth by challenging discourses of truth production.

3. *Being Truthful – Counter-discursive Productions of Truth in* Open City

In *Open City* these different notions of truth, i.e. the denial of any kind of absolute truth as well as the concept of *parrēsia* and truthfulness, are negotiated in the autodiegetic narrator Julius, a Nigerian psychiatrist living in New York City. While he associates himself with objectivity and frames himself as a subject qualified to speak the truth, these claims are repeatedly undercut in his own narrative discourse and ultimately challenged entirely when, at the end of

2 Ethos is understood by Foucault as 'habit' (Waldow 2013, 53) and does not necessarily include any interaction with the other – which is central to most other approaches towards ethics – but rather refers to any kind of coherent political attitude that an individual might develop.

3 The positive evaluation of different kinds of *parrēsia* becomes particularly evident from the fact that for Foucault the whole practice of critical philosophy is rooted in the various manifestations of *parrēsia* that he describes in his lectures on this topic (Foucault 2019, 224; Gros 2019, xix).

the novel, he is confronted with an act of *parrēsia* that must altogether question the narrative's truth production.

Julius is assigned a position as a competent subject speaking the truth within the discourse of his profession of clinical psychiatry. In his free time, he strolls aimlessly through the city, observing its inhabitants as well as talking to them. In a typical flâneur's manner he walks back "into a vanished time," as Walter Benjamin (1999, 416) puts it, uncovering both the hidden parts of the city's history and the hidden traumata of its inhabitants.[4] In this, Julius''s strolls mirror his practice of psychiatry, transferring his expertise in speaking the truth in this particular field to the streets of the city. Moreover, Julius performs several other norms that function as markers for speaking the truth in the twenty-first century, such as aiming at an ideal of objectivity as well as giving very detailed historical information on the sites he visits.[5] In this, his tone is mostly neutral and distanced, projecting disinterested observation (see Steckenbiller 2018, 5), and his detailed descriptions cause a temporal stretching in his narrative that suggests precision. His reporting creates the impression that Julius's main interest lies in an acute representation of facts. As Rebecca Clark puts it, "The sweeping range of knowledge – or at least abundance of factoids – that Julius recalls at a moment's notice as he aimlessly wanders the city seems to mimic a bird's-eye view, a privileged perspective that can pan out to see, read, and map the whole, from a subject position of disinterested omniscience (or at least omni-vision)" (2018, 186). Within the logic of the fictional world, Julius thus seems to engage in, or at least mimic, factual speech.[6]

An example that shows several of these markers of truth is when during one of his walks Julius comes across a bookstore, in which he looks for a book written by one of his patients:

> At around ten, I entered a bookshop, [...], and as I went in I remembered a book I had wanted to look at for a long time: a book of historical biography by one of my patients. I found it quickly – *The Monster of New Amsterdam* – and settled in among the quieter stacks to read it. V., an assistant professor at New York University and a member of the Delaware tribe, had based the book on her doctoral dissertation at Columbia. It was the first comprehensive study of Cornelis Van Tienhoven. Van Tienhoven had been notorious as a seventeenth-century *schout* of New Amsterdam [...]. He had arrived in 1633, as a secretary for the Dutch East India Company, but as he climbed up the social ladder, he became known for his many brutal acts, notable among them a raid he led to murder Canarsie Indians on Long Island, after which he had brought back the victims' heads on pikes. [...] V's book made for grim reading. It was full of violent

4 See e.g. also Miller (2015, 199): "Julius [...] is preoccupied with New York's past. At times he looks at New York as if he were an archaeologist."

5 Especially his rigorously objective collecting of data is marked in the novel: "Everything and everyone that Julius encounters seems to be leveled out into information" (Clark 2018, 194).

6 See also Gabriele Rippl (2018, 279) and Pieter Vermeulen (2015, 97), who both emphasize the resemblance between Julius's associations and entries on *Wikipedia*.

> events, and in the endnotes were reprinted the relevant seventeenth-century records. (Cole 2011, 25–26)

Julius's narration here displays several norms necessary for the production of truth. First, the information on Van Tienhoven is very detailed, includes exact dates, and relates back to historical facts. Second, since this information seems to be drawn directly from an academic book, it is bolstered with the authority of academia as proof of the truthfulness of the information given by the narrator. This is then again emphasized when Julius explicitly refers to the sources at the end of the book, highlighting a common academic practice of truth production. Moreover, as Julius chances upon the bookshop during one of his strolls, this shows how his practice of flânerie is tightly linked to his work, i.e. to a realm in which he actually is in the position of a subject competent to speak the truth. It is only because V. is his patient that Julius is led to include the narration of the hidden collective trauma of the Canarsie Indians in his narrative of New York.

In several complementary scenes, Julius either encounters sites in the city that trigger him to uncover lesser-known parts of the city's history or meets people who tell him stories of individual as well as collective trauma. Those traumata then run counter to what might be considered white discourses of power. The stories that Julius reveals mostly belong to ethnic minorities, whose narratives of trauma form counter-discourses to white hegemonic discourses about New York. In juxtaposing the received truths of the majority with conflicting voices from the margins, this narrative practice already implies the constructed character of any notion of an absolute truth (Hartwiger 2016, 5). Thus, there is no single absolute truth about the city that determines its identity, but the city's identity is constantly re-created throughout the text. Julius's narration, therefore, aligns with the first part of a Foucauldian notion of truth in that it rejects absolute truth and accepts that the construction of truth is always linked to the workings of power. At the same time, it performs and even emphasizes the ideal of objectivity by checking hegemonic discourses with more marginalized voices.

4. Truth and Unreliability – Julius's Relativism and Underreporting

Nevertheless, the novel does not stop at simply producing a post-colonial counter-discourse to the implicit hegemonic discourse of power. Instead, it shows Julius adopting precisely the problematic stance towards ethics that might follow from constructivist notions of truth and that Foucault was accused of supporting. This becomes clearest in a passage in which Julius discloses his personal beliefs and self-image 20 pages before the end of the novel. In this scene Julius commits to his own brand of ethical relativism[7] and even extends this self-image to his potential readership:

> Each person must, on some level, take himself as the calibration point for normalcy, must assume that the room of his own mind is not, cannot be, entirely opaque to him. Perhaps this is what we mean by sanity: that, whatever our self-admitted eccentricities might be, we are not the villains of our own stories. In fact, it is quite the contrary: we play, and only play, the hero, and in the swirl of other people's stories, insofar as those stories concern us at all, we are never less than heroic. [...] We have the ability to do both good and evil, and more often than not, we choose the good. When we don't, neither we nor our imagined audience is troubled, because we are able to articulate ourselves to ourselves, and because we have, through our other decisions, merited their sympathy. (Cole 2011, 243)

Hence, according to Julius, not only can every individual judge for themselves whether they perceive their own actions to qualify as 'good' or 'evil,' but the option of anyone identifying themselves as 'evil' is excluded entirely. The problematic conclusion from Julius's views would seem to be that: no matter how bad an action might be, it will not register as negative in one's image of oneself, because "we are able to articulate ourselves to ourselves" and can, therefore, justify any action to ourselves. Julius thus uncovers his own purely relativist stance towards the truth – since the truth about the identity of the individual remains entirely subjective – and combines it with a relativist stance towards ethics – since according to his point of view we can always reinterpret our own actions as justified.

Such an apparent relativization of truth as an absolute concept, and possibly even the implicit rejection of searching for any truth as a value, can also be found elsewhere in Julius's narration, including at the level of the narrative discourse itself. One example where extratextual historical facticity is abandoned occurs when Julius narrates his encounter with Pierre, a Haitian shoeshiner he meets in the underground part of Penn Station. In rendering the conversation he has with the shoeshiner, Julius almost entirely surrenders the narrative voice to Pierre's first-person narrative, which is presented in free direct speech for the most part (Cole 2011, 71–74). Pierre claims that he left Haiti together with his employer, a Mr. Bérard, "when things got bad there" (Cole 2011, 71–72) due to what he calls "the terror of Boukman" (2011, 72). This places Pierre's life in the context of the Haitian revolution of 1791, in which Dutty Boukman was a leader of the slaves who fought for their freedom. The same temporal frame is corroborated when Pierre claims that after Mr. Bérard's death, in New York, he bought freedom for himself and his sister (Cole 2011, 73). As the rest of Julius's narrative is set in the twenty-first century, this would make Pierre over

[7] See also Li (2018, 67), who refers to Julius as "committing [an] ethical lapse as he is in many ways 'isolated from all loyalties.'"

200 years old, a clear deviation from the realism and historical factuality the novel seems to pursue up to that point.

Taken by itself, this break with factuality is difficult to assess, particularly since it is not Julius himself who seems to deviate from the truth. By surrendering the narrative voice to the shoeshiner, Julius assumes the role of a neutral narrative medium, a task he fulfills by rendering Pierre's narration without any notable intrusion – and above all without any evaluation, conforming with the ideal of disinterested objectivity he seems to pursue elsewhere. Even when Pierre violates the norms of what is possible within the conventions of realism, and thus departs from any historical factuality, Julius still seems to be within the parameters of the truthful as far as his own narrative is concerned: after all, he listens to and records the shoeshiner's story in the same way he does when it comes to his patients or to other characters he meets on his walks through the city. Yet although he proves to be a precise commentator on historical facts elsewhere, he either does not recognize the obvious contradictions in the shoeshiner's account or willfully ignores them, thus leaving open the question whether the narrator's evaluation of events can be trusted at all. In this way, the novel points out how common norms of truth only form part of an overall construction of truth that does not ensure that the speaker who obeys these norms actually speaks the truth.

This opens up a discrepancy between the way in which truthfulness is constructed at the story level and at the discourse level of the narrative. To be precise, it raises the question of the narrator's (i.e. Julius's) responsibility for the truthfulness of his narrative. Does the narrative voice, which is part of the narration's discourse, have to check the truthfulness of the story it renders? As the narrator in this case does not provide any comment on what he reports (i.e. on Pierre's story), but only seems to record it faithfully, the 'lie,' if it may be so termed, is Pierre's. However, while Julius in this case does not produce a false statement himself, his lack of any comment on Pierre's story nevertheless tears open a gap in the narrative that may be perceived as deceitful by the reader. As a consequence of this evaluative gap, a 'gapped truth' – one where it is entirely unclear who has violated the norm of truthfulness at this point –, is created in the narrative of *Open City*, which then points towards the difficulty of rendering truth in narrative, or, following (early) Foucault, to the way in which discursive mechanisms are essential in the construction of what is considered to be true.

A similarly gapped version of the truth, albeit at a much more personal level for the narrator, occurs towards the end of the novel. On his walks through the city, Julius meets Moji, the sister of one of his school friends from Nigeria. They keep loose contact until Moji invites him to a party, where she confronts Julius and tells him that when they were both teenagers he had raped her (Cole 2011, 244). While this sudden revelation certainly casts doubt on Julius's moral evaluation, it is in particular his response that seems problematic with regard to the status of truth in the novel. For the narrator remains silent on the issue and does not only exclude Moji, but also the reader from any insight into his reaction to this accusation – a behavior that distinctly echoes the shoeshiner episode. Instead, he leaves the party and goes home, upon which the chapter, the novel's penultimate, ends. The last chapter is set in autumn, leaving a conspicuous temporal gap of several months to the night of the party, which takes place in May (Cole 2011, 232), and never returning to the rape. On the one hand, this lack of any direct reaction on Julius's part does not seem to constitute an outright case of lying. Rather, Julius seems to have taken to heart Sidney's (2012, 1068) claim that lying depends on an affirmation of facts and therefore avoids the lie by not speaking on the matter at all and thus not 'affirming' anything. On the other hand, there is something about this narrative non-engagement that rings entirely false. There is a cleavage between Julius's actions as a character who makes uncovering hidden trauma his business and his stance as a narrator who remains silent on and so engages in repressive discourse. Again, an evaluative gap opens up in Julius's narrative, only this time the gap concerns a rather more personal story than the vaguely political narrative of Pierre the shoeshiner.

Essentially, this cleavage is the result of a clash between what James Phelan (2005, 12) has described as the "character functions" and the "telling functions" of an autodiegetic narrator, a clash which results in the highlighting of the narrator's "synthetic function" as a touchstone for truth-speaking, or for the way in which essential truths may become difficult to access due to the distribution of discursive power. The telling functions are distinguished into the "narrator function," which refers to the narrator acting as a "reporter, interpreter, and evaluator of the narrated for the narratee," and the "disclosure function," which comprises the communication between narrator and readers in which a narrator may for example unwittingly reveal information beyond what is actually said to the narratee (Phelan 2005, 12). With regard to both functions, Julius's silence on the matter leaves a gap that is difficult to fill.

The reporting, interpreting, or evaluating that the narratee is offered by Julius is minimal, reluctant, and gapped. While Moji's accusation is presented by the narrator, the rhetorical construction of the narrative gives the impression that this reporting happens only reluctantly. Thus, Julius mentions his unwillingness to go to the party in the first place (Cole 2011, 231) and the chronology of his accounts of the party is oddly shuffled, with a lengthy description of his leaving the party and walking home inserted before the confrontation with Moji is reported, as if the narrator's intention were to defer or avoid this reporting. Further, the way in which the accusation itself is subtly framed in Julius's reporting suggests that only a minimal account of Moji's claims is presented. Julius renders Moji's allegation in indirect speech and in a strongly summarized version – the "probably six or seven minutes" (Cole 2011, 244) she spends presenting her version of events are condensed to just about one page of text and so reduced to a minimum –, both of which means that the victim's voice is broken in the prism of the voice of the accused who wields the narrator's control of the narrative. Crucially, Julius's account only reverts to allowing Moji direct speech[8] when she turns to the present and accuses him: "You'll say nothing, she said. I know you'll say nothing. I'm just another woman whose story of sexual abuse will not be believed" (Cole 2011, 245).

Moji indeed correctly anticipates what happens next: during and after reporting the confrontation with Moji at the party, Julius says nothing about either the truth or falsity of Moji's claim that he had "forced [himself] on her" (Cole 2011, 244) or about his reactions, both cognitive and emotional, to such an accusation. This means there is no overt evaluating or interpreting of Moji's claim on offer. Julius's only evaluative statements do not pertain to the veracity of the accusation, but to the way in which Moji presents it and possibly to her own conviction of its truth, since he admits that "[s]he had said it as if, with all of her being, she were certain of its accuracy" (Cole 2011, 244). Overall, in this case, the evaluating and interpreting functions of the narrator seem even more strongly curbed than the reporting function, and the narrator functions are reduced to a bare minimum.

There is then little in Julius's narration that allows either the narratee or the reader to make an informed decision on what truly happened and to what extent Julius is guilty, which makes Julius's narrative at this point an extreme case of what Phelan (2005, 52) calls "underreporting," a type of narration that "occurs when the narrator tells us less than he or she knows." What exactly is it, though, that Julius must know but does not tell? First, his emotional reaction to the severe accusation he is confronted with is missing entirely. The reduction of all narrator functions to a minimum means that Julius's disclosure function is likewise reduced: there is little to be inferred from Julius's silence beyond a general sense of discomfort with the situation that is expressed in his reluctance to present the events – unless, that is, one were to infer an admission of guilt from Julius's silence on the matter. Second, it is above all the facts of the case that are drowned out by the narrator's silence. Julius does not give any indication of whether he remembers the night of the alleged rape at all and of course does not comment on the veracity of Moji's claims either.[9] Al-

8 As Clark (2018, 193) as well as Pieter Vermeulen (2013, 48) point out, throughout the novel Julius directly incorporates other characters' speech in his own narration without separating the discourses of other characters from his own by means of quotation marks.

9 While Julius earlier, when he encounters Moji for the first time in New York, remembers going to a party at the house of Moji's brother as a teenager and Moji later says that the rape took place at such a party, he does not mention anything about the party except that it was "a wild one, with lots of drinking" (Cole 2011, 157). Importantly, the narrator again uses his discursive power to present the narrative discourse in such a way as to

though Phelan (2005, 52) stresses that "[n]ot all underreporting [...] constitutes unreliability," but only the omission of "salient" (2005, 52n) information that cannot be expected to be inferred by the narratee or reader, Julius may still be considered unreliable by these standards, as the ellipsis in his narrative cannot be filled with any certainty. However, this kind of unreliability does not make the narrator a liar, since there clearly is a difference between 'not speaking' and 'not speaking the truth.' Julius's refusal to 'affirm' anything in connection with Moji's accusation simply creates a narrative gap that proves impossible for the reader to fill and deprives readers of any yardstick by which to measure the narrator's deviation from the truth.

Nevertheless, Julius's act of 'not affirming' may still be seen as deceptive, or intentionally misleading, because it clashes with what Phelan (2005, 12) calls the mimetic character function, that is, with the novel's naturalistic depiction of Julius as a real person. Here it seems altogether unbelievable, or out of character, that Julius should show no response whatsoever to Moji's accusation, even though Moji directly challenges him to "say something now" (Cole 2011, 245). In remaining silent, Julius pushes the ideal of a disinterested objectivity to the limit, pretending to act as a non-involved reporter of the accusation against him. The implicit denial of his own investedness that this behavior suggests thus indeed appears to be an act of "torturous deception" (Cole 2011, 244). For a human being (and by extension for a realistically conceptualized character) it seems impossible not to react to claims that must rattle their entire social existence: the mimetic illusion of a life-like narrator is clearly broken here.

As a consequence, the *function* of this lack of a reaction is thrown into sharp relief. Due to the flaunting of mimetic conventions in the character of the narrator at this point, readers are likely to become aware that there is something 'strange' about this narrator's story. This is also what Phelan (2005, 13, see 28, 20) suggests when he argues that violations of a narrator's mimetic character function highlight their "synthetic functions," i.e. the narrator's wider textual functions as an "artificial construct[]" within the narrative. That is precisely what happens here: the realization that the narrator acts 'oddly' by not disclosing everything there might be to disclose raises a number of questions that are relevant to the way narrative and notions of truthfulness are interwoven. When Julius is accused of rape, the readers are encouraged to make a decision on whether or not to believe the accusation.[10] As it were, this puts them into the position of a judge or jury at trial, poring over the textual evidence of Julius's

separate the only morsels of information pertaining to the rape from the moment of Moji's accusation.

10 This is not to say that all readers will necessarily respond to the text in the same way or that their decision on whether or not to believe the accusation will be uniform. However, in following Phelan's rhetorical approach to narrative, we also accept his premise that some readings offer themselves more readily than others, while nevertheless no reading can be considered definitive (see Phelan 2005, 18–19). In the case of *Open City*,

innocence or guilt, a task that – as in many real-world rape trials – is made difficult or perhaps even impossible by the silence of the accused.[11] As the accused here is the narrator of the entire story whose task it is to make the diegesis available to readers in the first place, his silence also must mean the end of the narration, or at least of this particular strand, which then continues to linger in the reader's mind, but is not picked up again over the few remaining pages of the novel. In the end, Julius's underreporting and his clearly voiced relativist stance have the potential to alert readers to the problem of truth and lying in *Open City* and in fiction in general.

5. "Areas of Opacity" – Narrative and Power

Indeed, Julius's silence can be said to touch on almost existential questions of narrative. It would appear that the most prominent synthetic function of this narrative gap is to highlight the problems of the notion of truth in narrative. As Julius observes with regard to his own profession as a psychiatrist:

> As physicians [...] we depend, to a much greater degree than is the case with nonmental conditions, on what the patient tells us. But what are we to do when the lens through which the symptoms are viewed is often, itself, symptomatic: the mind is opaque to itself, and it's hard to tell where, precisely, these areas of opacity are. (Cole 2011, 238)

This is equally true for readers of narrative. Peter Lamarque (2014) has called this the "opacity of narrative," a concept that seems to be echoed here. For Lamarque, the opacity of a narrative ensues because the mode of its presentation is intricately linked to its contents:

> Rather than supposing that narrative descriptions are a window through which an independently existing (fictional) world is observed, with the implication that the very same world might be presented (and thus observed) in other ways, from different perspectives, we must accept that there is no such transparent glass – only an opaque glass, painted, as it were, with figures seen not *through* it but *in* it. (Lamarque 2014, 3; original emphasis)

It is then the narrative perspective itself that constitutes an integral part of the narrative (Lamarque 2014, 11). The lens, be it that of the narrator of a (fictional) narrative or that of the narrator of a personal story of illness, as would be the case with Julius's patients, in this sense is indeed symptomatic of what it depicts.

---

the lack of any response to the accusation seems to put the question of whether or not to believe Julius back to the reader very urgently.

[11] This raises the question whether a character narrator who appears as a realistically drawn human being must adhere to stricter standards of 'unmasking the self' than could be expected of a real person – after all, in practically all democratic legal systems the accused has the right to remain silent and not to comment on any accusations.

In a similar vein, the Foucauldian notion of truth might be considered one of opacity: any access to truth is only possible through the prism of power, which means that truth is opaque in as far as it rests in and on discourses of power.

In *Open City*, this is thematized precisely through the narrative gaps and through the way in which the narrator frames these omissions. It is typical of first-person narration that the narrator who reports the events also frames them as a character involved in them – the events thus reported become inseparable from the narrator's perspective and mode of presentation. While this is the case in any narrative, Julius's personal investment in Moji's story must make the mechanisms of the narrator's framing more transparent. Immediately after musing on the relative nature of normalcy and on how "we are not the villains of our own stories," he introduces readers to Moji's accusation:

> And so, what does it mean when, in someone else's version [of a story], I am the villain? I am only too familiar with bad stories – badly imagined, or badly told – because I hear them frequently from patients. I know the tells of those who blame others, those who are unable to see that they themselves, and not the others, are the common thread in all their bad relationships. There are characteristic tics that reveal the essential falsehood of such narratives. But what Moji had said to me that morning [...] had nothing in common with such stories. She had said it as if, with all of her being, she were certain of its accuracy. (Cole 2011, 243–244)

Although he overtly acknowledges Moji's claim to truthfulness, by distancing her story from the 'bad stories' of his patients – where notably Julius does not seem to distinguish between 'badly imagined' and 'badly told' – he expresses his doubt in a subtle manner, finally relegating her story to the fictional realm of the 'as if.' What is more, Julius goes on to wield his discursive power as a narrator in rendering Moji's accusation in a summarized, "clinical" (Clark 2018, 196) version, initially in indirect speech. As a consequence, he regulates the way in which her claim is presented and implicitly sets the benchmark for any evaluation of it as true or false, or, in this case, relegates it to the status of the undecidably opaque and possibly made up. This marks a stark contrast to the way in which he gives voice to suffering elsewhere in the novel – in particular to the way in which he almost entirely surrenders his narrative voice to the Haitian shoeshiner. As opposed to Pierre's, Moji's voice is only presented in direct discourse briefly, at the end of the passage. Hence the initial full brunt of her accusation is defused in the detachedness of indirect speech. What Julius's presentation of Moji's story makes clear, then, is that all along – not just after admitting to a relativist stance towards truth – as a narrator he has been covertly in control of what passes as truth in his narrative. It is therefore the inevitable opacity of *any* narrative that is exposed in the manner in which Julius presents Moji's accusation.[12]

[12] See also Miller (2015, 203), who claims that in this passage Julius "is talking about his profession but he is also talking about himself."

The point of the narrative here is that an absolute notion of truth and violent discursive power are just as much entangled as violence and a radically relativist stance towards truth. In other words, an absolute subjectivization of discourses of truth is equally violent as their absolute objectivization.[13] Moreover, objectivity can never be obtained by a singular voice that would only ever veil its own subjectivity by claiming to be entirely objective. Quite on the contrary, objectivity can best be achieved by the polyphony of voices that is implied by the juxtaposition of Julius's narrative with Moji's accusation (although this accusation still forms part of Julius's narrative or his discourse of power). Paradoxically, Julius's subjectivity is exposed by his apparent insistence on a disinterested objectivity. This seeming objectivity clashes with the fact that he, like any subject, inevitably must have a subjective perspective on the issue because he is personally involved in it. It is through Moji's account of the rape that the subjectivity of Julius's entire narrative is unmasked. After all, this is a narrative which – as much as it might aim at an ideal of objectivity – is still based on processes of selection and subjective framing. Nevertheless, the way in which his narrative seems to emphasize objectivity becomes marked precisely when he is faced with Moji's personal accusation because this confrontation foregrounds Julius's function as a character – a life-like representation of a human being – and thus underscores the limitations that follow from every human being's singular perspective. Moreover, objectivity is linked with Julius's relativist stance towards the truth as well as towards morality, which becomes clear in his introduction to Moji's story. Paradoxically, then, the fact that through his ostentatious objectivity Julius entirely glosses over his own subjectivity only uncovers precisely his subjective framing of Moji's story, and what serves as a marker of truth throughout most parts of the story now emphasizes the suspiciousness of his account. Ultimately, Julius's attempt at strict disinterested objectivity seems to blur any access to truth to the same extent as any radically subjective take on the truth might do.

6. *Narration as* parrēsia – *The Truthfulness of Critique in* Open City

What remains is the question of whether an alternative to these two opposing ends of the spectrum – the relativist stance towards truth and the absolute notion of truth – can be found. Foucault suggests such an alternative in the orientation towards truthfulness in what he describes as techniques of the self. This orientation is exemplified in the practice of *parrēsia*, which occurs in *Open City* on several levels. Moji's accusation against the narrator qualifies as an act

---

[13] See also Katherine Hallemeier (2014, 241f), who argues that Julius's "frequent incorporation of others' stories into [his] own can be read as admirably worldly, problematically passive, or both."

of *parrēsia* both on a personal and on a political level. It constitutes an act of personal *parrēsia* because Moji tells Julius the truth about himself and thus might contribute to his formation of self by means of the techniques of the self – if only Julius were interested in any such practice. This personal *parrēsia*, "[t]he *parrēsia* of a friend, [...] prevents the care of the self from succumbing to the flightiness and expediency of egotism" (Gros 2019, xvii). It is therefore usually employed in order to keep the subject from taking him- or herself as "the calibration point for normalcy" (Cole 2011, 243) and does not allow for an entirely subjective construction of identity.

Yet, Moji's narrative just as well qualifies as an act of political *parrēsia*, since she is well aware of the political position that she puts herself in by accusing Julius of rape. Political *parrēsia* often faces an imminent threat of death to the subject speaking the truth: either the truth-speaker's actual death or their death as a speaking subject due to being silenced by the discourse of power (Foucault 2019, 43). Thus, Moji is fully aware of Julius's discursive power to remain silent and that her own victimized position is one that "will not be believed" (Cole 2011, 245). This means that she knows that by speaking her truth she deprives herself of her own subject position, i.e. she is aware of the fact that she risks her death as a speaking subject. Moreover, the scene creates an analogy to the relationship between hegemonic discourses and counter-discourses that Julius expressed throughout the story. Moji's accusation now puts him into the position of being faced with a counter-discourse to the (narrative) discourse of power that he has been producing as the autodiegetic narrator of the story all along. While Julius quite openly announces that his discourse constitutes an act of performance that among other things serves his own construction of identity – "we play, and only play, the hero" (Cole 2011, 243) –, Moji's narration then forms a counter-discourse, created by her own *parrēsiastic* act, to Julius's narrative of the heroic subject. This act forms an example of truth-speaking in which the subject puts herself into a relation with the truth and where the presence of her subjectivity thus unmasks the impossibility of the objectivity of the discourse of power.

Whether Moji's *parrēsia* actually becomes such a counter-discourse or whether it is canceled out and not believed, then depends on the reader and their evaluation of her narration. Readers who, in Foucault's sense, set themselves in a relationship towards the truth and therefore take the possibility into account that Julius might be an unreliable narrator would – in a retrospective reassessment of the narrative (see Clark 2018, 183) – start to examine the story for factual evidence and might discover Julius's particular art of 'framing' his story and using his discursive power for his own means. Moji's act of *parrēsia* therefore can start an analysis of the workings of power within the discourse of the narrative text itself on behalf of the reader. In other words: the work that the reader might end up doing is basically the work of critique as suggested by Michel Foucault:

> The critical ontology of ourselves must be considered not, certainly, as a theory, a doctrine, nor even as a permanent body of knowledge that is accumulating; it must be conceived as an attitude, an ethos, a philosophical life in which the critique of what we are is at one and the same time the historical analysis of the limits imposed on us and an experiment with the possibility of going beyond them *[de leur franchissement possible]*. (Foucault 2000, 319)

Here, the philosophy Foucault envisions focuses on the uncovering of discourses and the workings of power that structure our systems of knowledge. Simultaneously such a philosophy should reflect on the ways by which we may escape the limits that those systems impose.

Similarly, in *Open City*, the reader's investigation of Julius as a possibly unreliable narrator unmasks the workings of power in the novel and at the same time makes visible the limits of knowledge and truth within the narrative. Those limits can be found in the opacity of narrative itself, which is powerfully represented not only by the narrative gaps that Julius creates and that can never satisfactorily be filled by the readers but also by his subtle framing of everything he recounts throughout the text. Even more, this opacity of narrative in general, which represents the limits of what can be known by individuals, is illustrative of the workings of discursive power itself. Hence, the novel problematizes our norms of truth production by pointing out the limits of the ideal of objectivization while emphasizing the participation of power in any subjectivization of discourse. This function ties in with what Foucault, referring to the philosophical performances of the Cynics, describes as philosophical *parrēsia* and which, according to him, constitutes the root of "the critical tradition of philosophy in our society" (Foucault 2019, 224).[14] As the various examples that Foucault names prove, the Cynics' performances in no way included only truthful speech, although the questions that they brought up might indeed be considered 'truthful' in the sense that they critiqued existing social norms. This is also the case with the narrator's unreliability in *Open City*: the novel uses the narrator's performance of untruthfulness to inquire into the very notion of truth and its interrelation with discursive power. *Open City*

[14] For the Cynics, philosophy becomes a way of life and is to be understood as a "visible performance of truth" (Schmid 2000, 276). The questioning of norms is directly translated into the individual life and thus forms a 'style of existence.' While the probably most famous example of Diogenes living in a barrel reduces life to its bare needs and so questions societal norms of what could be considered a necessity in life, Foucault also mentions examples that are strikingly reminiscent of contemporary political performance art, as e.g. an instance in which Diogenes presents a horse with a laurel wreath during the Olympics for a fight it won against another horse and hence problematizes the norms according to which athletes are rewarded a price after winning a competition (Foucault 2019, 171–2).

also demonstrates how this interrelation can be problematized through acts of *parrēsiastic* narration. Similar to the Cynics' performances, the narrative that "nothing affirms," because it is fictional, might then not lie, but rather speak a truth by means of being untruthful.

Works Cited

Benjamin, Walter (1999) *The Arcades Project.* Trans. Howard Eiland and Kevin McLaughlin. Cambridge, MA: Belknap.

Clark, Rebecca (2018) "'Visible Only in Speech': Peripatetic Parasitism, or, Becoming Bedbugs in *Open City.*" *Narrative* 26.2: 181–200.

Cole, Teju (2011) *Open City*. London: Faber and Faber.

Flynn, Thomas (1987) "Foucault as Parrhesiast: His Last Course at the Collège de France (1984)." *Philosophy & Social Criticism* 12.2-3: 213–229.

Foucault, Michel (1980) "Truth and Power." *Power/Knowledge: Selected Interviews and Other Writings 1972–1977.* Ed. Colin Gordon. Trans. Colin Gordon, Leo Marshall, John Mepham, and Kate Soper. New York: Pantheon. 109–133.

Foucault, Michel (1991) "Questions of Method." *The Foucault Effect: Studies in Governmentality with two Lectures by and an Interview with Michel Foucault.* Ed. Graham Burchell, Colin Gordon and Peter Miller. Chicago: Chicago Univ. Press. 73–86.

Foucault, Michel (1992) *The Use of Pleasure: The History of Sexuality.* Vol. 2. Trans. Robert Hurley. London: Penguin.

Foucault, Michel (2000) *Ethics: Subjectivity and Truth.* Ed. Paul Rabinow. Trans. Robert Hurley et al. London: Penguin.

Foucault, Michel (2019) *Discourse and Truth & Parrēsia*. Ed. Henri-Paul Fruchaud and Daniele Lorenzini. Trans. Nancy Luxon. Chicago: Chicago Univ. Press.

Gros, Frédéric (2019) "Introduction." In: Foucault (2019) *Discourse and Truth & Parrēsia.* Ed. Henri-Paul Fruchaud and Daniele Lorenzini. Trans. Nancy Luxon. Chicago: Chicago Univ. Press. xiii-xx.

Hallemeier, Katherine (2014) "Literary Cosmopolitanisms in Teju Cole's *Every Day is for the Thief* and *Open City.*" *Ariel: A Review of International English Literature* 44.2–3: 239–250.

Hartwiger, Alexander Greer (2016) "The Postcolonial Flâneur: *Open City* and the Urban Palimpsest." *Postcolonial Text* 11.1: 1–17.

Lamarque, Peter (2014) *The Opacity of Narrative.* Lanham: Rowman & Littlefield.

Li, Stephanie (2018) *Pan-African American Literature: Signifyin(g) Immigrants in the Twenty-First Century.* New Brunswick: Rutgers.

Mahon, James Edwin (2008) "Two Definitions of Lying." *International Journal of Applied Philosophy* 22.2: 211–230.

Mahon, James Edwin (2016) "The Definition of Lying and Deception." *The Stanford Encyclopedia of Philosophy.* Ed. Edward N. Zalta. https://plato.stanford.edu/archives/win2016/entries/lying-definition/ (accessed 31/01/2020).

Miller, Stephen (2015) *Walking New York: Reflections of American Writers from Walt Whitman to Teju Cole.* New York: Fordham.

Phelan, James (2005) *Living to Tell About It: A Rhetoric and Ethics of Character Narration*. Ithaca: Cornell Univ. Press.

Rippl, Gabriele (2018) "The Cultural Work of Ekphrasis in Contemporary Anglophone Transcultural Novels." *Poetics Today* 39.2: 265–285.

Ruoff, Michael (2018) *Foucault-Lexikon: Entwicklung, Kernbegriffe, Zusammenhänge.* 4th ed. Paderborn: Fink.

Schmid, Wilhelm (2000) *Auf der Suche nach einer neuen Lebenskunst: Die Frage nach dem Grund und die Neubegründng der Ethik bei Foucault.* Frankfurt/Main: Suhrkamp.

Sidney, Philip (2012) *The Defense of Poesy. The Norton Anthology of English Literature*. Ed. Stephen Greenblatt et al. 9th ed. Vol. B. New York: Norton. 1044–1083.

Steckenbiller, Christiane (2018) "Diasporic Ways of Knowing: Teju Cole's *Open City.*" *New Directions in Diaspora Studies: Cultural and Literary Approaches*. Ed. Sarah Ilott, Ana Cristina Mendes and Lucinda Newns. London: Rowman & Littlefield. 71–85.

Vermeulen, Pieter (2013) "Flights of Memory: Teju Cole's *Open City* and the Limits of Aesthetic Cosmopolitanism." *Journal of Modern Literature* 37.1: 40–57.

Vermeulen, Pieter (2015) *Contemporary Literature and the End of the Novel: Creature, Affect, Form.* Basingstoke: Palgrave Macmillan.

Waldow, Stephanie (2013) *Schreiben als Begegnung mit dem Anderen: Zum Verhältnis von Ethik und Narration in philosophischen und literarischen Texten der Gegenwart.* Munich: Fink.

Ambiguous Counter-Discourses. Documentary Literature and the Perpetrator

Tom Vanassche

1. *Introduction: The Perpetrator's Unreliability*

Descriptions of Nazi crimes which are proffered by the National Socialists themselves are suspect, even more so when they are provided with decades of hindsight. The reasons for this are twofold. *First*, any autobiographical description is characterized by the "inherent narrative distance between the narrator as narrator and the narrator as protagonist" (Riggan 1981, 24); it is also influenced by "subjective and therefore humanly fallible elements: the narrator's memory, selective processes, and attitudes in the telling of the story" (Riggan 20–21). Moreover, social psychology shows that the reconstruction and retelling of personal memories about a particular time period are influenced by representations of the same era in various media (Welzer et al. 2015, esp. 105–128), warping personal memory. *Second*, apart from these inaccuracies (which arise without malice or treacherous intent), perpetrators have many reasons to lie, whether in blatant fashion or through omission. There is a strong temptation for them to lie, nor only when they are defendants (cf. Friedlander 1995, 263, 270; Hipp 2020), but also when they try to reinstate themselves in society.

Although the accounts of 'old Nazis' are therefore to be met with due suspicion, it is clear that many readers and interlocutors have allowed themselves to be fooled – suffice it to point to the largely affirmative readings of the wartime memoirs of various Wehrmacht generals complicit in the Shoah.[1] This has had important implications for early historiography on the 'Third Reich,' which was, in Nicolas Berg's words, marked by a "Nähe zwischen Historiker und Täter" ('closeness between historian and perpetrator'; Berg 2003, 588; transl. mine) – and not only in Germany, as his example of Gitta Sereny's uncritically

[1] The popularity of these generals in post-war (West) Germany caused Alexander Kluge to anonymize them when quoting them in his 1960s documentary prose. Gunther Martens (2014, 34) summarizes Kluge's retrospective explanation in *Chronik der Gefühle* (2000): "this was necessary at the time, because these names [...] still had a very familiar, even heroic ring which was liable to detract from the ambition to analyse the organisational structure of the catastrophe." Although Kluge's 'catastrophe' refers to the German defeat at Stalingrad, it equally pertains to the complicity of the Wehrmacht in the Shoah – the Sixth Army, annihilated at Stalingrad, had supported the SS *Einsatzgruppen* in the Ukraine.

empathic attitude towards Albert Speer demonstrates.[2] These examples demonstrate the potential of such accounts to seduce audiences keen to find 'good Germans' or even 'good Nazis.' If the narrator is unreliable, then so may be the reader who does not detect the unreliability. Indeed, the "archetypical first-person narrative situation," of which autobiographical narrative is a prime example, is not only marked by the narrator's fallibility, but also by the "auditor's assimilation, comprehension, and retention of what he hears, in conjunction with his own human reactions to the storyteller as an individual" (Riggan 1981, 20–21). Here, a strong case can be made for the application of these observations beyond literary fiction.

In *Opa war kein Nazi* ('Grandpa was not a Nazi'), Welzer, Moller, and Tschugnall demonstrate how German families tend to develop a sanitized narrative about their parents' and grandparents' lives during the so-called 'Third Reich' and the Second World War, an account in which these people were not engaged in (war) crimes nor – in whatever capacity – in the persecution of the Jews. Families tend to 'protect' parents and grandparents, who lived through the Nazi dictatorship as adults. It is precisely *because* they largely acknowledge National Socialism as an unacceptable ideology responsible for unspeakable suffering that they try to uphold a positive family identity in which there is no place for National Socialist thought or National Socialist crimes. Their family narrative is a construct in which the family is not contaminated by the evil of National Socialism. If one were to take these stories at face value and extend their implications, there would have existed in Germany a National Socialist dictatorship without any National Socialists. But the truly interesting element is that this happens even in families where the (grand)parents acknowledge their complicity in war crimes: the descendants decide – consciously or subconsciously – to ignore any evidence that challenges their positive family identity (Welzer et al. 2015, 11).

These examples demonstrate, then, the (unavoidable) unreliability of the perpetrator and the (potential) unreliability of listeners or readers, especially those emotionally close to a perpetrator. They also demonstrate that the relations between both strands of unreliability are diverse. Yet it seems that both strands are strategic: the unreliable perpetrator wishes to whitewash his own guilt and manipulate commemoration, while the 'unreliable reader' or listener may have their own (conscious or subconscious) reasons for reinterpreting history.[3] The

2 Berg (2003, 589) refers to Sereny's *Albert Speer. His battle with truth* (1995) and mentions both similarly sympathetic (Golo Mann, Robert Kempner) *and* critical (Eric Goldhagen, Matthias Schmidt) voices on Speer's attempts at becoming his own historiographer.

3 It is obvious that, as soon as the children or grandchildren of (potential) perpetrators recount the latter's activities, attitudes, and experiences, they become unreliable narrators, too. But the unreliability must be sought not in the inaccuracies of memory (or not primarily there) but rather in the interpretation of their (grand)parents' narratives preceding their own re-narration.

questions underlying this essay are the following: how does literary fiction react to this phenomenon? And does the concept of lying advance our understanding of narrative unreliability? These questions will be addressed through a discussion of two critical aesthetic responses to the perpetrator's unreliability. I will briefly look at the perhaps more common format – the Nazi as unreliable narrator – before turning to the ambivalences found in documentary fiction, notably in Dieter Schlesak's *Capesius, der Auschwitzapotheker* (2006).

2. *Narrative Unreliability as Aesthetic Response: Perpetrator Fiction*

When fiction gives a voice to war criminals, it tends to distance itself from them through unreliable narration – either clearly or in a subtly implicit manner. The 'old Nazi,' certainly the National Socialist mass murderer, can easily be added to Riggan's list of picaros, madmen, naifs, and clowns as a first-person narrator whose reliability is fraught from the very outset "simply by the unacceptability of that philosophy in terms of normal moral standards or of basic common sense and human decency" (Riggan 1981, 36).[4] Riggan subscribes largely to a rhetorical approach to narrative unreliability, emphasizing (like Wayne Booth) the discrepancy between the implied author and the narrator, and more precisely, between their respective norms (cf. Booth 1983, 158–159). Moreover, from this perspective, the reader is presumed to be a non-Nazi or even anti-Nazi, and this perspective does not address the fact that readers with Nazi sympathies would not assume from the outset that the Nazi perpetrator is morally corrupt. The cognitive approach to unreliability, by contrast, does not consider the implied author as the significant element in exposing unreliability but instead frames narrative unreliability as the discrepancy between the narrator's "worldview, [...] moral standard, values, or beliefs" and that of the reader (Hansen 2007, 227; cf. Nünning 1998, esp. 20, 23–26; Nünning 1999, esp. 58–59, 62–64, 73).[5] Indeed, Riggan's use of terms such as "unacceptability," "normal moral standards," "basic common sense," and "human decency' are normative, and his identification of unreliable narrators indicates a discrepancy between his own moral framework and that of the narrator. In other words,

[4] If we immediately suspect the Nazi narrator to be unreliable (which I merely posit and which certainly does not hold true for every individual reader), it is due to what Per Krogh Hansen has labelled "intertextual unreliability" (Hansen 2007, 242). As Hansen notes, this unreliability is not rooted in the text (though the narrator's unreliability is often demonstrable and not merely instinctively plausible) but is due to the reader's horizon of expectations – because we have learned (the hard way, one might add) to distrust Nazi narrators in fiction or in non-fiction (let alone in real life).

[5] Riggan's (1981, 36) "community of implied author and reader" echoes Wayne Booth's "secret communion of the author and reader behind the narrator's back" (Booth 1983, 300; cf. Riggan 1981, 35).

the cognitive approach explains Riggan's attribution of unreliability not to an invisible implied author but rather to Riggan as a reader, who assumes that his moral framework corresponds with that of the author.[6]

The question, then, is: what implications might a cognitive approach have for the unreliability of Nazi narratives? If unreliability lies in the eye of the beholder, if the norms and values at the core of that attribution vary diachronically and culturally (which is doubtlessly true), are we not hinting at a vulgarized understanding of Hannah Arendt's thesis of the banality of evil?[7] This is precisely what is at stake in Jonathan Littell's *The Kindly Ones* (2009).

However, I argue that the rhetorical approach has a response to such unwarranted moral relativity. After all, by assuming a "community of implied author and reader" (Riggan 1981, 36), every deviation becomes not only remarkable but intentional. The picaro, the madman, the naif, the clown: in Riggan's rhetorical approach, they all enable the reader to engage in some experimental empathy with, and perhaps even experience sympathy for, 'deviant' narrators (though the sympathy needs to be assessed on a case-by-case basis). The standards of normativity governing the extratextual world inhabited by the reader are questioned.[8] Needless to say, whereas experimental empathy with and potential sympathy for literary categories of deviant character-narrators such as picaros and others may promise some emancipatory potential, the same does not hold true for the very real ethical and legal categories of mass murderers and war criminals. Indeed, empathy is precisely what is at stake both in the rhetorical and the cognitive approach as well as in the vulgarized understanding of the banality of evil: if the perpetrator turns out to be 'all too human,' it is 'all too easy' for the reader to feel sympathy for him – and thus, it is to be apprehended, for the related ideology to be normalized as well. But Arendt's thesis is as much about the (bureaucratic) perpetrators' *lack of empathy for the*

---

6 Note that the cognitive dimension does *not*, despite first appearances, necessarily look at the individual reader in isolation; indeed, the cognitive dimension is subject to historical change and cultural variety: Vera Nünning (2004, 239) demonstrates how Dr. Primrose, the narrator of Oliver Goldsmith's *The Vicar of Wakesfield* (1766), has only been considered unreliable since the 1960s, when a "majority of critics [...] started to point out a whole range of inconsistencies between Primrose's sentimental values and the norms implicit in the structure of the text, interpreting the vicar as a self-satisfied hypocrite whose naïveté is exposed in very subtle ways."

7 This vulgarized notion entails that the perpetrators were normal human beings, just like the reader; ergo, the reader, too, might become a perpetrator in similar circumstances (which is not necessarily or entirely false). Such notions remain omnipresent in popular discourses on the Shoah.

8 The causality between engaging in experimental empathy and challenging normativity may very well be a chicken-and-egg dilemma.

victims as it is about the perpetrators' not being 'monsters' (cf. Arendt and Fest 2013, 43–45).[9]

This poses a question which could be formulated descriptively or normatively: how does (good) perpetrator fiction address the perpetrator's extraordinary position? Merely positing his unreliability will not do, since a rhetorical understanding of unreliability a priori will presume it to be a sign of the author's critical distance to his narrator.[10] This premise can only be the starting point: while it tells us something about the (at least potential) ethical function of unreliability, it tell us very little about its literary functions and manifestations.

Instead of asking whether the narrator is an object of our empathy, we could ask to what purposes he puts his own empathic faculty. Moreover, and in line with the questions of this edited volume, we may ask whether his unreliability resides in his lies; could this type of internarrational or extratextual unreliability be a rhetorical strategy that discredits even the most erudite perpetrator?[11]

I propose to look at three instances of unreliability in perpetrator fiction to offer a nuanced answer to these questions. I will discuss Maximilien Aue, the autodiegetic narrator of Jonathan Littell's *The Kindly Ones* (2009; French orig. 2006); Maximilian Schulz, the autodiegetic narrator of Edgar Hilsenrath's *The Nazi and the Barber* (2010; German orig. 1977); and the unreliable focalizers in Ian MacMillan's *Village of a Million Spirits* (2000).

In the case of *The Kindly Ones* and *The Nazi and the Barber*, the contradictions within the perpetrator's discourse are minimal. Both narrators are autodiegetic, leaving little room for contradiction within their accounts. In both novels, the signals of unreliability are generally extratextual. These similarities exist in spite of the remarkably different styles of self-representation at the beginning of the two novels. Max Schulz introduces himself as an illegitimate child, while insisting that he is of purely 'Aryan' descent. Although he tries to resolve this tension by claiming that all of his five potential fathers are purely 'Aryan' (Hilsenrath 2010, 7), Schulz's reliability becomes immediately suspect; it is undermined on account of the ideological implications that subtend this asseveration, not least because he seems blind to the possibility that the reader might disagree with this ideological framework. Why else would he authenticate his

9 To be sure, if anything is banal in the whole discussion on the nature of evil and the psychology of the perpetrator, it is the constatation that the perpetrators were not monsters but human beings.

10 The male pronoun is used deliberately here, since I can think of no female authors who have written perpetrator fiction narrated by a Nazi. A partial exception is Ulla Hahn's *Unscharfe Bilder* (2003), where the perpetrator is an intradiegetic narrator telling his story to his daughter.

11 The lie would be an instance of internarrational unreliability if it entails a contradiction within the perpetrator's discourse. By contrast, extratextual unreliability would have the content of the lie contradict the historical record that exists independently of the novel and which the reader must know well enough to note the discrepancy (cf. Hansen 2007, 242–243) – the latter is, of course, assumed in the rhetorical approach.

identity with the argument of hereditary purity? In other words, the reader is immediately alienated by the narrator's introduction. The reader's suspicion is further confirmed by Schulz's anticipation of the reader's possible demand for information on the sources providing evidence for the narrator's statements, to which Schulz cannot give a satisfactory answer (Hilsenrath 2010, 13; see McGlothlin 2014, 163–164). This anticipation of readers' possible disbelief contrasts with Schulz's blindness to the ideological difference between himself and his reader, causing even further alienation. This alienation is precisely what Aue's infamous rhetorical opening statements wish to avoid:

> Oh my human brothers, let me tell you how it happened. I am not your brother, you'll retort, and I don't want to know. And it certainly is true that this is a bleak story, but an edifying one, a real morality play, I assure you. [...] And also, this concerns you: you'll see that this concerns you. Don't think I am trying to convince you of anything; after all, your opinions are your own business. (Littell 2009, 3)

Aue seems to be alluding to the aforementioned vulgarized understanding of Hannah Arendt's thesis of the banality of evil and already intuits that the reader will disagree with his viewpoint. Aue also anticipates that the reader will want to distance him/herself from him – even before the reader knows why such distancing could be warranted (excluding, of course, the possibility that the reader has acquired paratextual knowledge about the work).

This double *rapprochement* – the appeal to normalcy and the awareness that this appeal may be met with suspicion – is immediately followed by a 'distancing' on the part of Aue: by stating that he does not want to convince the reader, he signals that he has no ulterior motive for telling his story; he will not offer an apologetic account, which the reader, or so he anticipates, would be w(e)ary of. Indeed, his arrogant attitude towards the reader emerges when he informs us that he is telling his story "to set the record straight for myself, not for you" (Littell 2009, 3). Why then go through all the trouble to emphasize his normality? The question becomes more urgent when these implicit and contradictory motives become explicit: "[t]hese notes of mine might be confused and awful too, but I'll do my best to be clear; I can assure you that they will at least be free of any form of contrition. I do not regret anything: I did my work, that's all" (Littell 2009, 5). Paradoxically, the suggestion of Aue's factual reliability relies on his moral unreliability.[12]

Clearly, both Littell's and Hilsenrath's narrators' attempts at authenticating their utterances backfire: they *must* be considered unreliable, and not just because they are Nazis. Not only do the perpetrators' self-presentations point to

[12] Note that unreliable narrators often insist on their reliability (cf. Nünning 1998, 28; Rüsen 1983, 77). In its opening sentences, Aue's account is thus not only a priori (ideologically) suspicious but constitutes an intertextual sign of unreliability as well. Schulz's opening sentences are a variation: he seems to root his reliability in an ideologically suspicious fashion (racial supremacy).

the problematic aspects of their lives, but their actual narratives also raise some questions that cannot be resolved without assuming their unreliability. Immediately after Schulz's introductory remarks, he mentions that his neighbor, Itzig Finkelstein, was born on the same day, precisely two minutes and twenty seconds after himself (Hilsenrath 2010, 8). This statement raises questions as to how a homodiegetic narrator could possess such precise information, and rightly so: soon afterwards, Max reports how his mother tells the neighbors' domestic worker that Max was precisely two minutes and twenty seconds *younger* than Itzig (Hilsenrath 2010, 12). This banal contradiction is never resolved, nor is the problem that Max's mother would have to be implausibly omniscient as well.[13] As Erin McGlothlin (2014, 160) points out, "Max is not remotely interested in giving his readers evidence for his implausible stories."

In Aue's case, we are not necessarily faced with such unresolved contradictions, nor is his apparent omniscience inexplicable: it is explained by the generic convention of the encyclopedic novel (see Ziolkowski 2017, 158; Mendelsohn 1976, esp. 1269–1271). Rather, his unreliability is due to apparent amnesia: during a visit to his mother and stepfather, he wakes up soaked in blood and finds their corpses but claims he cannot remember murdering them. While the autodiegetic narration fails to tell the reader by means of mimetic representation whether Aue is indeed the murderer, there are strong indications that he is.[14] The central issue in relation to Aue's unreliability, however, is not the question of whether or not we subscribe to his purported amnesia; if we assume that he is the killer, the omission of the murderous instance is a clear example of underreading or underreporting, but one which questions Aue's reliability throughout (cf. Phelan 2005, 34; Grethlein 2010, 572).

So Aue and Schulz are unreliable. But do they lie?

If we understand a lie to be the statement of a falsehood of which the speaker is definitely aware, then our answer must be nuanced. In the case of Aue, we cannot tell: we can only assume that he is his mother's murderer, but we have no basis for arguing whether Aue knows this and knowingly hides it from his

---

[13] The reader always has the option, of course, to choose between unreliability and other "integration-mechanism[s]," i.e. "alternative logics of resolution," when facing "textual incongruities" (Yacobi 2001, 224). In this case, the reader could opt for Yacobi's genetic integration-mechanism: "[t]he sloppy or ambivalent author, instead of tightly organizing his materials, has left incongruous elements in his text" (Yacobi 2001, 228). But this strategy cannot undo the obvious contradictions within Schulz's self-presentation: "a picaresque combination of the hyperbolic and the banal, the confessional and the implausible" (McGlothlin 2014, 160).

[14] Aside from listing the material evidence with which Aue is confronted, Jonas Grethlein offers a convincing argument based on the novel's structural intertextuality: *The Kindly Ones* incessantly alludes to Greek mythology, and shortly before the murder, Aue "visits an exhibition at the Grand Palais in Paris where he comes under the spell of a statue of Apollo, the very god who, in Aeschylus, orders Orestes to kill Clytaemestra [i.e., his mother, TV]" (Grethlein 2010, 568).

reader. After all, even if we gave him the benefit of the doubt – why would he mention these incriminating details if he believed in his innocence?[15] – Aue's own opening lines have established his status as a supreme manipulator.[16] But if we assume Aue is not lying to us, we must assume he is not lying to the police detectives, who are convinced of his guilt. Conversely, if we surmise that Aue is lying to us, we must also conclude that he lies to the police detectives. There is no difference in his status as liar across several diegetic levels.

In the case of Schulz, the matter is slightly more complicated. Shortly after adopting the identity of his murdered neighbor and emigrating to the British Mandate of Palestine, Schulz is questioned by Jewish independence fighters about his wartime activities. Their captain, Jankl Schwarz, asks whether Schulz has been in a concentration camp and whether he was in Southern Russia in 1941 – facts which Schulz does not deny. Schulz also does not deny that he was firing German weapons while in Southern Russia (Hilsenrath 2010, 375). Schulz, we know, is referring to his activities as a member of the *Einsatzgruppen*, whereas Schwarz, believing that he is talking to the erstwhile partisan Finkelstein, whom he hopes to recruit for the Israeli independence fight, assumes he used the weapons as a resistance fighter. Schulz is obviously lying through equivocation, taking advantage of the interrogator's presuppositions. Yet Schulz is, as far as we can tell, not lying to the reader: he is lying on the intradiegetic level. This makes him an unreliable narrator in the conversation with Schwarz – while his extradiegetic unreliability is due to his adherence to Nazi ideology and factual contradictions.

It should be noted that our inability to assess whether Schulz and Aue are lying *to us* is due directly to the narrative situation: both are the *sole* narrators in these fictional autobiographies. This means that the possibility of establishing unreliability is restricted to the factual contradictions within their discourse and within their self-presentation, the latter serving as a basis for arguing *why* these narrators are unreliable.[17] In the absence of other sources of information

15 Another reason for believing Aue is his factual reliability as a witness of the Shoah: "for the most part he reports on these historical events honestly and in great detail [...] appear[ing] to be as forthcoming as possible about his own participation in the genocide of the Jews" (McGlothlin 2014, 169). McGlothlin's assessment – and mine – rest on Hansen's concept of extratextual unreliability.

16 Robert Eaglestone's assessment is similar: Aue "apparently has no memory of this [...]. But, as with all the complexities of this novel, this lack of memory is not certain and may be a trick" (Eaglestone 2017, 55). Whereas Grethlein reads the novel's intertextual references to antiquity as indications of Aue's guilt as a parricide, Eaglestone reads Aue's *own* allusion to the Furies, the pursuers of parricides, as a hint at his memory/knowledge of the murder – and thus of his having lied to the reader until the novel's very end.

17 Grethlein considers Max Aue unreliable because he is "a complex character, very far from a real person," in his combination of "a great sensitivity with a rather detached attitude" and his "involvement in the cruelest crimes." Aue's "pathological sexuality and incest, according to Grethlein, merely hinder the reader's identification with this narrator, but it is implied that these characteristics add to Aue's unreliability (Grethlein

it is impossible to compare contradictions with alternative accounts. We also lack outside perspectives on the perpetrator. Thus, there is no internarrational unreliability in these novels. It should also be remarked that, in general, unreliability in the context of genocide narratives is not a device restricted to use by the perpetrators' narrational acts or to lying about the facts.

In contrast to autodiegetic narratives, multiperspectival novels may use unreliable focalization rather than (or in addition to) unreliable narration. Such is the case for *Village of a Million Spirits* (2000). This novel features various narrators: there is one impersonal heterodiegetic narrator, while there are also a number of homodiegetic passages. From its outset, the impersonal narrator outlines Magda Nowak's questionable views: she believes that Anatoly, the father of her unborn child and a Ukrainian *Trawniki* guard in Treblinka, is "as much a prisoner as the Jews even though he came out every day leading the work crews, his rifle hanging from his shoulder" (MacMillan 2000, 2). Later, we learn why Magda believes this: Anatoly himself thinks that "the Germans will never let them leave. They will kill them first" (MacMillan 2000, 74). In other words, our initial attribution of unreliability, which is grounded in ethics, may be explained by an omission in the representation of the perpetrator's mind. There is no doubt that Anatoly *does* become a victim: the SS later torture and mutilate him in order to find his stack of stolen valuables. Finally, Anatoly is executed for desertion. In addition, his hatred of the Nazis leads him to help the Jews raise money and weapons for an uprising. All of this places him in a questionable grey zone. He is a perpetrator, and he is not a Jewish victim – as the very fact that he is in a position to help them, albeit belatedly, ironically demonstrates. In this novel, unreliability is not merely tied to lying: in the case of Anatoly, it is (also) the product of substantial underreporting – we never learn why he signs up when he hates the Germans (and *not*, it seems, the Jews). Magda's view might be considered a case of misdirected empathy: for various reasons, she empathizes with her lover rather than with the Jews.

Other instances of unreliable focalization include entire passages where the narration is focalized through *Untersturmführer* ('2nd lieutenant') Joachim Voss, a serious alcoholic. This emerges from the brief passage in which he serves as narrator (MacMillan 2000, 34). More specifically, the rather 'objective' and detailed description of a gassing (horrible though that sounds) is immediately undermined by the fact that the "room darkens" (MacMillan 2000, 22). The description cannot be reliably focalized through Voss, who is looking through a window "dirtied by grease" (MacMillan 2000, 24). But neither can it be entirely reliably focalized through Berilman, a victim who, while being gassed, looks at

2010, 572). Similarly, McGlothlin pathologizes Schulz's narration: the instability of the narration (shifting from first to third person) and of the addressee (a shift not discussed in the present contribution) cause her to see Max's narrative as a further "evasion that he utilizes diegetically to circumvent punishment for his crimes" (McGlothlin 2014, 166).

Voss looking at the gassing.[18] The victim's experientiality is being undermined by the perpetrator's focalization, which in turn is undermined by both his alcoholism and the physical conditions (darkness, greased window) which impede observation.

So what of the lie? While my analysis lays no claim to completeness (the perspectives in the novel are not limited to perpetrators and bystanders; however, an analysis of the victims' perspectives goes beyond the scope of this paper), we might consider Anatoly's conspiratorial behavior (his support of the inmates' uprising) as rooted in lies – if not explicit, then through omission: as a guard, he is expected to prevent such occurrences. But this unreliable (or rather disloyal) *behavior* certainly is not sufficient to classify him to be an unreliable narrator; on the contrary, it is the only thing about him that might morally redeem him to a certain extent. His narrative unreliability lies in his self-perception as a victim, which neglects an acknowledgment of the agency that he (in contrast to the Jews) enjoys.

3. *Historical Records in a Documentary Novel*

Yet the proven method of having a tale of genocide told by and focalized through extremely unreliable perpetrators in fiction is only one way of confronting National Socialist ideology and post-war whitewashing and self-justification. A different technique consists in using the historical perpetrator's words against himself. In his documentary novel *Capesius, der Auschwitzapotheker* (*The Druggist of Auschwitz*, 2011, transl. by John Hargraves), Dieter Schlesak juxtaposes the writings of Dr. Victor Capesius, erstwhile pharmacist in Auschwitz and one of the defendants at the Frankfurt Auschwitz trial (1963–1965), with survivors' testimonies given during that trial.[19] The first two chapters thus serve no other purpose than to expose Capesius's lies; we may assume the reader already knows, to some extent, what happened when a train arrived in Birkenau. The juxtaposition of micro-fragments of narrative amounts to a narrative strategy in its own right: by not straightforwardly calling out Capesius's lies and relying on implication, Schlesak invites the reader to think along, to 'play detective.'

This is not uncommon in documentary art. Claude Lanzmann has described his own film, *Shoah* (1985), which interlaces empty and silent landscapes with

[18] Some readers will – justifiably – ask to what extent the narrative unreliability or unreliable focalization relates to the ethics of imagining and representing the gassing operation in such stirring detail. It *is* an important question, but one that would take us too far away from the topic of this essay and that cannot be granted due space within its constraints.

[19] I am referencing the German original, since my argument rests on comparing Schlesak's mediation of the court records with their original text – methodologically, the English translation (as well as *any* translation) is not suited for my purposes.

scenes of testimony, as a return to the crime scene, thus inviting us to perceive the filmmaker as a detective on the trail of the murderers (Felman and Laub 1992, 256 n.34; see also Rothberg 2000, 235). But this narrative strategy only functions, one could argue, because it draws its impact from its claims to non-fictionality. There is a strong insistence that Schlesak's novel is not fiction: the paratext on the cover (of the German original) describes the text as a documentary novel – a complex collage of narration, documentation, and retrospection. It also includes the following claim: "Auch was Adam, die einzige fiktionale Person des Buchs, berichtet, entstammt bis ins Detail den historischen Quellen" ('Everything that Adam, the sole fictional character in the novel, tells of, down to the smallest detail, corresponds to the historical sources'; Schlesak 2006; transl. mine). This is a rather bold claim: Schlesak's intertextual *mise-en-scène* – ranging from Tadeusz Borowski and Alexander Kluge to Peter Weiss – creates a highly ambivalent borderland between fictionality, fictivity, and non-fictionality (Vanassche 2018).

Indeed, these intertexts are themselves situated on the borders of fictionality and non-fictionality. By both citing *and* 'manipulating' some of his predecessors, Schlesak's *Capesius* can easily be construed as a recent instalment of the old documentary tradition. It reinvokes heated debates inspired by the gap between, on the one hand, the genre's claims to authenticity, and, on the other, the unavoidable bias that any selection and *mise-en-scène* of historical material must entail, wittingly or unwittingly – not to mention instances of fictionalization and *Verdichtung* (condensation) of the sources for aesthetic and pragmatic reasons. Yet one could just as easily argue that the genre designation – documentary novel – gives Schlesak the necessary artistic license to explore these aspects of documentary: not conveying the naked facts but presenting the literary and juridical *search* for these facts, thus their unavoidable mediation through processes of transition and canonization, omission and destruction.

We must ask, however, whether the same can be said of Schlesak's mediation of the non-fictional texts. Let us look at his manipulation of the records of the Frankfurt Auschwitz trial, which he does not explicitly signal.[20] By manipulation I do not mean unavoidable practices of compartmentalizing, selecting, and arranging the documents inherent to documentary literature, as noted above.

20 A brief note on methodology: I have compared the excerpts from Schlesak's novel with the court records, which are available on the website of the Fritz Bauer Institute (https://www.auschwitz-prozess.de). Since the time when I did my research and the writing of this contribution, the website has been visually modified; its contents are, as far as I can tell, the same. The comparison was made between the excerpts in the novel and the corresponding records; both in the novel and on the website, the court documents are identified by the eyewitness's name. The testimonies are available as machine-readable pdf files. I compared these files with the corresponding passages by entering entire sentences as they are found in *Capesius* into the search function, while allowing for changes in spelling (particularly *sz* and *ß* vs. *ss*).

There is a remarkable discrepancy between the historical records and their presentation in the novel. As with the literary intertexts, the result is a tension between fiction and non-fiction, made all the more disturbing by the non-fictional status of the court records: it is a tension between truth, lying, and fiction. If we look more closely, we can distinguish three strategies of manipulation. A brief caveat: not all of them are necessarily equally problematic.

The first strategy may be treated under the umbrella of clarification and standardization and can be subdivided into two categories. The first technique consists in Schlesak hiding the orality of the testimony by smoothing out some repetitions and anacolutha inherent in oral storytelling. A particularly good example of this is the testimony delivered by Paul Pajor (Schlesak 2006, 27–28; *"Strafsache gegen Mulka u.a." Vernehmung des Zeugen Paul Pajor* 1964, 1–2). A similar kind of standardization is to be found in grammatical 'corrections.' While several Eastern European witnesses testified in their native language, other non-native speakers testified in German. These testimonies are at times marked by linguistic peculiarities which Schlesak erases. This is again particularly evident in Pajor's testimony and its representation in *Capesius*. Schlesak even smooths out such particularities in cases in which the eyewitness was a native German speaker. Thus, Otto Wolken's Austriacisms are no longer present in the novel's representation of Wolken's testimony (Schlesak 2006, 50–55; *"Strafsache gegen Mulka u.a." Vernehmung des Zeugen Otto Wolken* 1964, 20–24). While this strategy renders certain historical constellations less visible, it is no obstacle to the poetics of investigation, since the necessary information (in particular, the origins of the witness) is provided within the account. The result is an enhancement of 'informational economy' of the text: 'excessive' text is deleted, since what matters for the purposes of the detective (as well as what matters in court) is not the eyewitness's background and not even their subjective experience of history (Assmann 2012b, 23). Rather, what matters are the historical facts that serve to condemn (or exonerate) the defendant – and these are highlighted by removing any 'distracting' patterns of speech.[21]

The second strategy begins to interfere with the records in a more profound manner. Several of the eyewitnesses testifying in Frankfurt would later publish their memoirs of the camps, even decades after the trial. In the 1990s, Mariana Adam and Ella Salomon jointly published their stories of ghettoization, deportation, and incarceration in Auschwitz with a German (and outspokenly Christian) publishing house. Adam and Salomon's memoirs are listed in the novel's

[21] An exception is made for Paisikovic's testimony, one of the few survivors of the *Sonderkommando*, who describes what he saw there: people being burnt in pits next to the crematoria, some of them alive. This rendition ("Ja... konnte nicht mehr... viele noch lebten...") strengthens the traumatizing effect of such visions (Schlesak 2006, 118). This anacoluthon, however, is not retained from the records but rather an instance of Schlesak's third strategy of manipulation (cf. *"Strafsache gegen Mulka u.a." Vernehmung des Zeugen Dov Paisikovic* 1964, 12).

bibliography – the works 'used and cited' ("[d]ie verwendete und zitierte Literatur. Die Materialien"; Schlesak 2006, 341) – which already causes us to assume that the memoirs are quoted alongside the corresponding trial records. And indeed, in some instances, it is immediately clear that the quotation must come from the memoirs, when the topic is the *trial* instead of the events in Birkenau in 1944 (Schlesak 2006, 11; see also Adam and Salomon 2001, 123). References to the trial would of course make no sense in the court records. But there are other instances where records and memoirs are intertwined without this blending being explicitly marked as such. One instance pertains to Marianne Adam's recounting of a Hungarian SS officer (it is implied that this is Capesius) performing the 'selection' on the ramp. Here, we face the illusion that Schlesak is quoting from the court recordings while the excerpt actually comes from the memoir – an illusion upheld through the immediately preceding use of other trial records (Schlesak 2006, 28; cf. Adam and Salomon 2001, 44). Occasionally, Schlesak misidentifies the source (Schlesak 2006, 78–79; cf. Müller 1979, 139–140; *"Strafsache gegen Mulka u.a." Vernehmung des Zeugen Filip Müller* 1964). As in the instances of standardization, such confusions between testimonies are not necessarily problematic: at no point does the novel say that it only uses the trial records. In the *"ère du témoin"* ('era of the witness'; Wieviorka 2013; transl. mine), the eyewitnesses have long left the courtroom (Assmann 2012a, 30) and have re-emerged – in documentary films, classrooms, interviews, and in the book market – as voices with a particular authority in describing the Shoah. In other words, a chapter entitled *Die Augen Zeugen* (the pun gets lost in translation: 'the eye witnesses,' but also: 'the eyes give testimony') may be expected to contain testimonies both inside and beyond the courtroom. By no means does the inclusion of other sources break the promise of faithfulness to the sources on the book's cover.

It is, however, the third strategy that might pose greater problems. There are various instances – in the testimonies of Ella Salomon, Otto Wolken, and Dov Paisikovic – where the statements cannot be found in either the trial records or in the memoirs listed in the novel's bibliography. While Ella Salomon's testimony contains entire paragraphs from her memoir and her testimony in Frankfurt, other paragraphs seem to have been added by Schlesak to, paradoxically, increase the story's *effet du réel*: they address and give (reconstructed) examples of the *lagerszpracha* (Schlesak 2006, 47; Adam and Salomon 2001; *"Strafsache gegen Mulka u.a." Vernehmung der Zeugin Ella Salomon* 1964).[22] In neither the court records nor the memoir of Salomon is that pidgin referred to, let alone articulated in the form of isolated lexemes. It seems that Schlesak

22 The *lagerszpracha* was a pidgin language, but no *lagerszpracha* was alike: it varied between camps and diachronically; its superstrate was German, the official language of administration and power, while the second influential language depended on the linguistic predominance in the prisoner population (cf. Oschlies 1985; 1986).

intervenes here to heighten the realism of the account. The same observation is valid for his interpolations within Jan Sikorski's testimony: here, too, Sikorski's remarks on Capesius's frowning upon the *lagerszpracha* are not found in the trial records – indeed, the *lagerszpracha* is not mentioned in that testimony at all (Schlesak 2006, 86; *"Strafsache gegen Mulka u.a." Vernehmung des Zeugen Jan Sikorski* 1964).[23] Likewise, in the use of the case of Otto Wolken, a passage is added. Here, there is less room for doubt: Schlesak explicitly says that the quote comes from the trial: "Dr. Otto Wolken beim Prozess" ('Dr. Wolken during the trial'; transl. mine) – yet the subsequent quotation is not to be found in the records (Schlesak 2006, 56; *"Strafsache gegen Mulka u.a." Vernehmung des Zeugen Otto Wolken* 1964). To be sure, if we assume that these paragraphs 'within' Salomon's, Sikorski's, and Wolken's accounts are written by Schlesak, they are still not out of line with our knowledge of the concentration camps: they depict events as we know them to have happened. The only fictional element about them is the fact that they were not historically uttered by the persons quoted. In addition to a heightened sense of realism, a textual effect, we find ourselves facing two realities: one pertaining to the events described, and one pertaining to the narrative situation and the role of authorship.

4. *Implications*

How do we deal with these discrepancies? Is Schlesak, who is confronting the lies of the perpetrator, lying to his reader? Such a claim may lack humility as well as caution. It would imply an attribution of intentionality which is difficult to establish. Schlesak may have been sloppy, may have made mistakes, but in good faith. Moreover, unlike 'classic' perpetrator fiction, in which deductive presumptions of unreliability can be corroborated with inductive elements, Schlesak's highly ambiguous counter-discourse is susceptible to negative induction: we check the listed sources for correspondences, and when we do not find them there, we cannot exclude the possibility that the statements are to be found in Schlesak's private archive – in recorded interviews which, according to Schlesak, constituted the original motive for and backbone of the novel ("Ausgangspunkt des Buchs. Die Gespräche und die erhaltenen Dokumente bilden seinen Grundstock," Schlesak 2006, 343; 'The book's premise. The conversations and the preserved documents constitute its foundation;' transl. mine).

[23] Jan Sikorski was a Polish pharmacist who was deported to Auschwitz in July 1941 and was working as a foreman in the camp's pharmacy from the winter of 1941–1942 until the evacuation of the camp in January 1945. Thus, he was an important witness concerning Capesius's duties and activities as camp pharmacist. It should be noted that the novel's representation of Sikorski's characterisation of Capesius as a proper, business-like man *is* in line with his testimony in Frankfurt. Schlesak's in(ter)ventions are minute and difficult to detect.

But the fact remains that an illusion is being created, which (at least to some extent) can be falsified. Schlesak passed away a few weeks after I gave the talk on which this contribution is based. It would be worthwhile to conduct archival research in the Archive of German Literature (Deutsches Literaturarchiv) in Marbach to look for further clues: in what manner did Schlesak fictionalize the accounts? Did he use other sources by the quoted persons, did he use other sources by third parties, or did he employ the licenses of fictionality?

For now, we must restrict ourselves to asking what consequences this procedure has for our reading of the novel. Here, too, I suggest a differentiated argumentation which basically harks back to the 'old' problem of documentary literature. Where do its 'loyalties' lie? Does it wish to document reality and reconstruct history as accurately as possible, or does it allow some degree of autonomy in relation to the facts? Can documentary draw attention to its own writing practice, and can it exist for its own sake? Can it have its cake and eat it, too? This issue has been underlying documentary theater and literature since the 1960s and 1970s and has, so it seems, not disappeared in the 'third generation' of documentary literature, even if this third generation partially avows its use of fictionality in what is presumably a self-relativizing stance (cf. Porombka 2008).

If one focuses on the 'documentary' in the documentary novel, it is easy to see how readers who come across the noted discrepancies (but then again, what ordinary reader would?) might feel cheated: the paratext promises historical accuracy, and the text does not entirely fulfill this promise. The fact that we are here dealing with the testimonies of the victims of genocide may only add to the unease with which we now (re)read the text, and this response must not be disregarded.

However, I want to point to an alternative which does not exclude the disquieting response but instead points to the precarity of both testimony (as a genre) and the archive (where testimonies are stored for us to consult). In this alternative reading, the novel mediates the mediation of the trial. After all, the fact that we have the transcripts of the Frankfurt trial is sheer lucky coincidence. German courts do not have a duty to take detailed minutes of court sessions, and judges rely on their own notes when it comes to the sentencing at the end of a trial. In the case of the Frankfurt trial, the sessions were audiotaped, and it was through the intervention of survivors, most notably Hermann Langbein, that these tapes were not destroyed but archived at the *Staatsanwaltschaft* (public prosecutor's office) in Frankfurt. They remained there, apparently largely unnoticed by journalists and historians alike, until the late 1980s, when they resurfaced in the context of the trial against Ernst August König, an erstwhile *Rottenführer* (corporal) in Birkenau (Renz 2013). Only in 2004, forty years after the trial, were the transcripts published by the Fritz Bauer Institute in Frankfurt. Moreover, as Cornelia Vismann (2000) has pointed out, court records and other mediations of the court are never neutral in themselves: they are instruments of power, they contain the interpretations of the transcribers – they structure and hierarchize historical knowledge. Practices of linguistic standardization are not restricted to Schlesak's interventions; they also occurred in court and during the transcription of the testimonies. The audio files, available at the same website as the transcripts, can be used for comparison (see also Davies 2018, 178).[24] If one remains aware of the mediation of testimony, Schlesak's novel may be said to embody this process through the 'hybridization' of fact and fiction.

Instead of calling the author a liar, we may consider to what extent narratology offers a more nuanced (and certainly more careful) approach. Moreover, if one approaches narrative unreliability rhetorically, one likewise makes assumptions about the author's intention, ascribing the unreliability of the narrator to her own willful creation. The question, however, is whether the distinction between narrator and author is as clear-cut in documentary prose as it is in classical fiction – after all, Schlesak is not inventing characters or narrators; at most, he appears to be inventing (parts of) the narration. It is risky to consider these nonfictional narrators as unreliable since this invites undue skepticism regarding their real testimony. More importantly, these people are not responsible for Schlesak's interventions. I want to propose, then, that what we are confronted with is an unreliable *narration* rather than an unreliable *narrator* – a distinction already found in transmedial narratology, particularly in film narratology (cf. Kuhn and Schmidt 2014).[25] In other words, my approach to narrative unreliability in documentary prose differs from the rhetorical approach which I find useful for autodiegetic unreliability. The unreliability does not lie in *what* is being told or in the narrator's moral and psychological constitution, but rather in a mismatch between purported and actual sources. We can document the mismatch; the intentions we may only infer. Particularly

24 In this regard, there are differences between the transcriptions: some retain the particularities of spoken (and foreign) language, others do not. The transcription of Dov Paisikovic's testimony is a case in point: during the interrogation, the judge keeps repeating Paisikovic's phrases but renders them in standard German. Decades later, the transcriber removes the same and other linguistic 'mistakes,' but does not restrict herself to 'correcting' Paisikovic's discourse: though less frequently, she also intervenes in the judge's!

25 There is another good reason for not identifying an unreliable narrator: as noted above, cognitive approaches have argued that such an identification serves as a heuristic device – readers can make sense of contradictions within the text; the unreliable narrator serves as an "integration mechanism" (Yacobi 2001, 224). In Schlesak's case, this makes no sense: the unreliability hinges not on "textual incongruities" but on intertextual incongruities (Yacobi 2001, 224). If anything, the unreliability could be seen as a disintegrating mechanism. Whether the abandoning of an anthropomorphized 'narrator' in favor of a more abstract 'narration' solves the problem entirely is a question which needs further pondering.

in the case of non-fictional narration, it may be wise to discuss poetics in a vocabulary that avoids hasty judgement.

Works Cited

Adam, Marianne, and Ella Salomon (2001) *Was wird der Morgen bringen? Zwei Jüdinnen überleben Auschwitz und finden zum Glauben an Jesus Christus*. Trans. Moshe Vogel. 3rd ed. Stuttgart: Edition Anker im Christlichen Verlagshaus.

Arendt, Hannah, and Joachim Fest (2013) *Eichmann war von empörender Dummheit. Gespräche und Briefe*. Ed. Ursula Ludz and Thomas Wild. Munich: Piper.

Assmann, Aleida (2012a) *Auf dem Weg zu einer europäischen Gedächtniskultur?* Wiener Vorlesungen im Rathaus 161. Vienna: Picus Verlag.

Assmann, Aleida (2012b) "Pathos und Passion. Über Gewalt, Trauma und den Begriff der Zeugenschaft." *Die Zukunft der Erinnerung und der Holocaust*. Ed. Aleida Assmann. Konstanz: Konstanz Univ. Press. 9–40.

Berg, Nicolas (2003) *Der Holocaust und die westdeutschen Historiker. Erforschung und Erinnerung*. Moderne Zeit: Neue Forschungen zur Gesellschafts- und Kulturgeschichte des 19. und 20. Jahrhunderts 3. Göttingen: Wallstein Verlag.

Booth, Wayne C. (1983) *The Rhetoric of Fiction*. 2nd ed. Chicago & London: Univ. of Chicago Press.

Davies, Peter (2018) *Witness Between Languages: The Translation of Holocaust Testimonies in Context*. Rochester, NY: Camden House.

Eaglestone, Robert (2017) *The Broken Voice: Reading Post-Holocaust Literature*. Oxford: Oxford Univ. Press.

Felman, Shoshana, and Dori Laub (1992) *Testimony: Crises of Witnessing in Literature, Psychoanalysis, and History*. New York & London: Routledge.

Friedlander, Henry (1995) *The Origins of Nazi Genocide: From Euthanasia to Final Solution*. Chapel Hill & London: North Carolina Univ. Press.

Grethlein, Jonas (2010) "S.S. Officers as Tragic Heroes? Jonathan Littell's *Les Bienveillantes* and the Narrative Representation of the Shoah." *Style* 44.4: 566–585.

Hahn, Ulla (2003) *Unscharfe Bilder*. Munich: Deutsche Verlags-Anstalt.

Hansen, Per Krogh (2007) "Reconsidering the Unreliable Narrator." *Semiotica* 165: 227--246.

Hilsenrath, Edgar (2010) *Der Nazi und der Friseur*. Munich: Deutscher Taschenbuch Verlag.

Hipp, Dominique (2020) *Von NS-Konzentrationslagern erzählen: Angeklagte vor Gericht über Dachau, Mauthausen, Ravensbrück und Neuengamme*. Bielefeld: transcript.

Kluge, Alexander (2000) *Chronik der Gefühle*. 2 vols. Frankfurt: Suhrkamp.

Kuhn, Markus, and Johann Schmidt (2014) "Narration in Film." *The Living Handbook of Narratology*. Hambro: Hamburg Univ. Press. Web. <https://www.lhn.uni-hamburg.de/node/64.html>. 24 Sept. 2020.

Littell, Jonathan (2009) *The Kindly Ones*. London: Chatto & Windus.

MacMillan, Ian (2000) *Village of a Million Spirits: A Novel of the Treblinka Uprising*. New York et al.: Penguin Books.

Martens, Gunther (2014) "Distant(ly) Reading Alexander Kluge's Distant Writing." *Vermischte Nachrichten: Alexander Kluge-Jahrbuch 1*. Göttingen: V&R unipress. 29–41.

McGlothlin, Erin (2014) "Narrative Perspective and the Holocaust Perpetrator: Edgar Hilsenrath's *The Nazi and the Barber* and Jonathan Littell's *The Kindly Ones*." *The Bloomsbury Companion to Holocaust Literature*. Ed. Jenni Adams. London et al.: Bloomsbury Publishing. 159–177.

Mendelsohn, Edward (1976) "Encyclopedic Narrative: From Dante to Pynchon." *MLN* 91: 1267–1275.

Müller, Filip (1979) *Sonderbehandlung: Drei Jahre in den Krematorien und Gaskammern von Auschwitz*. Ed. Helmut Freitag. Munich: Steinhausen.

Nünning, Ansgar (1998) "*Unreliable narration* zur Einführung: Grundzüge einer kognitiv-narratologischen Theorie und Analyse unglaubwürdigen Erzählens." *Unreliable Narration. Studien zur Theorie und Praxis unglaubwürdigen Erzählens in der englischsprachigen Erzählliteratur*. Ed. Ansgar Nünning. Trier: Wissenschaftlicher Verlag. 3–39.

Nünning, Ansgar (1999) "Unreliable, Compared to What: Towards a Cognitive Theory of Unreliable Narration: Prolegomena and Hypotheses." *Grenzüberschreitungen: Narratologie im Kontext/Transcending Boundaries: Narratology in Context.* Ed. Walter Grünzweig and Andreas Solbach. Tübingen: Günther Narr. 53–73.

Nünning, Vera (2004) "Unreliable Narration and the Historical Variability of Values and Norms: The Vicar of Wakefield as a Test Case of a Cultural-Historical Narratology." *Style* 38.2: 236–252.

Oschlies, Wolf (1985) "'Lagerszpracha': Zu Theorie und Empirie einer KZ-spezifischen Soziolinguistik." *Zeitgeschichte* 13: 1–27.

Oschlies, Wolf (1986) "'Lagerszpracha': Soziolinguistische Bemerkungen zu KZ-Sprachkonventionen." *Muttersprache: Vierteljahresschrift Für Deutsche Sprache* 96.1–2: 98–109.

Phelan, James (2005) *Living to Tell About It.* Ithaca & London: Cornell Univ. Press.

Porombka, Stephan (2008) "Really Ground Zero: Die Wiederkehr des Dokumentarischen." *Literatur der Jahrtausendwende: Themen, Schreibverfahren und Buchmarkt um 2000.* Ed. Evi Zemanek and Susanne Krones. Bielefeld: transcript. 267–279.

Renz, Werner (2013) "Anmerkungen zum Tonbandmitschnitt im 1. Frankfurter Auschwitz-Prozess." Tonbandmitschnitte des Auschwitz-Prozesses (1963 –1965). Ed. Fritz Bauer Institut. <http://www.auschwitz-prozess.de/materialien/T_03_Der_Tonbandmitschnitt_des_Auschwitz-Prozesses. 23 Sept. 2020.

Riggan, William (1981) *Picaros, Madmen, Naifs, and Clowns: The Unreliable First-Person Narrator.* Norman, OK: Oklahoma Univ. Press.

Rothberg, Michael (2000) *Traumatic Realism: The Demands of Holocaust Representation.* Minneapolis: Minnesota Univ. Press.

Rüsen, Jörn (1983) *Historische Vernünft. Grundzüge einer Historik I. Die Grundlagen der Geschichtswissenschaft.* Göttingen: Vandenhoeck & Ruprecht.

Schlesak, Dieter (2006) *Capesius, der Auschwitzapotheker.* Bonn: J. H. W. Dietz.

"Strafsache gegen Mulka u.a." Vernehmung der Zeugin Ella Salomon (1964) Frankfurt am Main: Fritz Bauer Institut. Web. <https://www.auschwitz-prozess.de/resources/transcripts/pdf/Salomon-Ella.pdf>.

"Strafsache gegen Mulka u.a." Vernehmung des Zeugen Dov Paisikovic. (1964) Frankfurt am Main: Fritz Bauer Institut. Web. <https://www.auschwitz-prozess.de/resources/transcripts/pdf/Paisikovic-Dov.pdf>.

"Strafsache gegen Mulka u.a." Vernehmung des Zeugen Filip Müller. (1964) Frankfurt am Main: Fritz Bauer Institut. Web. <https://www.auschwitz-prozess.de/resources/transcripts/pdf/Mueller-Filip.pdf>.

"Strafsache gegen Mulka u.a." Vernehmung des Zeugen Jan Sikorski. (1964) Frankfurt am Main: Fritz Bauer Institut. Web. <https://www.auschwitz-prozess.de/resources/transcripts/pdf/Sikorski-Jan.pdf>.

"Strafsache gegen Mulka u.a." Vernehmung des Zeugen Otto Wolken. (1964) Frankfurt am Main: Fritz Bauer Institut. Web. <https://www.auschwitz-prozess.de/resources/transcripts/pdf/Wolken-Otto.pdf>.

"Strafsache gegen Mulka u.a." Vernehmung des Zeugen Paul Pajor. (1964) Frankfurt am Main: Fritz Bauer Institut. Web. <https://www.auschwitz-prozess.de/resources/transcripts/pdf/Pajor-Paul.pdf>.

Vanassche, Tom (2018) "Intertextualität in *Capesius, der Auschwitzapotheker*: Interferenzen zwischen Fiktivität, Fiktionalität, Faktualität." *Interferenzen – Dimensionen und Phänomene der Überlagerung in Literatur und Theorie*. Ed. Sebastian Donat et al. Comparanda 17. Innsbruck: Innsbruck Univ. Press. 123–134.

Welzer, Harald, Sabine Moller, and Karolin Tschugnall (2015) *"Opa war kein Nazi." Nationalsozialismus und Holocaust im Familiengedächtnis*. 9th print. Die Zeit des Nationalsozialismus. Frankfurt am Main: Fischer Taschenbuch Verlag.

Wieviorka, Annette (2013) *L'ère du témoin*. Pluriel. Paris: Fayard.

Yacobi, Tamar (2001) "Package Deals in Fictional Narrative: The Case of the Narrator's (Un)Reliability." *Narrative* 9.2: 223–229.

Ziolkowski, Theodore (2017) *Music Into Fiction: Composers Writing, Compositions Imitated*. Studies in German Literature, Linguistics, and Culture. Rochester, NY: Camden House.

On the Authors

Katrin Althans is a DFG-sponsored postdoc research fellow at the University of Duisburg-Essen/Germany, where she is working on her second book on narratives of flight and migration in law and literature. Her research focuses on Law & Literature, migration studies, Australian and Indigenous Studies, the Gothic, literary geo- and ecocriticism, and 19th-century fiction. She is the author of *Darkness Subverted: Aboriginal Gothic in Black Australian Literature and Film* (2010) and of several articles on Indigenous Australian literature and law, the Gothic, videogames, and refugees.

Ronald G. Asch is a graduate of Tübingen University/Germany where he also completed his doctorate after having studied earlier in Kiel/Germany and in Cambridge. From 1996 to 2003 he held the chair of early modern history at the University of Osnabrück/Germany and has been teaching at the university of Freiburg/Germany for the last 17 years. Having published a study of the court of Charles I of England in 1994 his more recent publications deal inter alia with noble elites and the institution of monarchy in the early modern period. His two latest books are *Sacral Kingship between Disenchantment and Re-enchantment: The French and English Monarchies 1587–1688* (2014) and *Vor dem großen Krieg: Europa 1598-1618* (2020).

Ingo Berensmeyer is Professor of Modern English Literature at Ludwig Maximilians University Munich. His research interests are in literary theory, textual studies and book history, literary sociology, and authorship studies. He is the author of *John Banville: Fictions of Order* (2000), *Shakespeare: Hamlet* (2007), *Literary Theory* (2009), and *Literary Culture in Early Modern England, 1630–1700: Angles of Contingency* (2020). He (co-)edited the *Cambridge Handbook of Literary Authorship* (2019), a *Handbook of English Renaissance Literature* (2019), and other volumes including *Mendacity in Early Modern Literature and Culture* (2016) and *Perspectives on Mobility* (2013). Articles have appeared in journals including *Anglia, arcadia, Authorship, Comparatio, European Journal of English Studies, Études Irlandaises, New Literary History, Poetica, Poetics Today, Studies in English Literature 1500–1900*, and *Zeitsprünge*.

Dallas G. Denery II is a professor of History at Bowdoin College. He specializes in medieval and early modern intellectual and religious history, with a particular interest in skepticism and deception. He has written two books, *Seeing and Being Seen in the Late Medieval World* (2005), *The Devil Wins: A History of Lying from the Garden of Eden to the Enlightenment* (2015), as well as a variety of essays.

Monika Fludernik is Professor of English Literature at the University of Freiburg/Germany. She is also the director of the graduate school Factual and Fictional Narration (GRK 1767). Her major research interests include narratology, linguistic approaches to literature, especially metaphor studies, 'Law and Literature,' postcolonial studies and eighteenth-century aesthetics. She is the author of *The Fictions of Language and the Languages of Fiction* (1993), the award-winning *Towards a 'Natural' Narratology* (1996), *Echoes and Mirrorings: Gabriel Josipovici's Creative Oeuvre* (2000) and *Metaphors of Confinement: The Prison in Fact, Fiction and Fantasy* (2019). Among her several (co-)edited volumes are *Hybridity and Postcolonialism* (1998), *In the Grip of the Law* (2004), *Beyond Cognitive Metaphor Theory* (2011) and *Idleness, Indolence and Leisure in English Literature* (2015). Articles have appeared in, among others, *Text*, *Semiotica*, *The Journal of Historical Pragmatics*, *English Literary History*, *New Literary History*, *Textual Practice*, *ARIEL*, *The Cambridge Journal of Postcolonial Literary Inquiry*, *Diacritics*, *Poetics Today*, *Narrative*, *Style*, *The Canadian Review of Comparative Literature* and *The James Joyce Quarterly*.

Cynthia Guo is currently a doctoral candidate at the Department of Psychology at Emory University and a researcher at the Emory Infant and Child Laboratory. Her research focuses on early moral decision making from a cross-cultural perspective.

Rüdiger Heinze is Professor of American Studies at the Institute of English & American Studies of the TU Braunschweig. His major research interests are in dystopian & post-apocalyptic fiction, multilingual US-American literature, and transmedial narratology. He is the author of *Ethics of Literary Forms* (2005) and *Mosaics & Melting Pots: Children of Immigrants in US-American Literature* (2018). He is co-editor of a number of collections, among them *Unnatural Narratives, Unnatural Narratology* (2011) and *Remakes & Remaking* (2015). He is also co-editor of the series *Natural Sciences & Humanities in Dialogue* (2010–). He has published articles in various journals, among them *Storyworlds*, *Narrative*, *European Journal of American Studies*, and *Journal of Postcolonial Writing*, as well as in many collections.

Daniel Morgenroth (née Schulze) is a scholar and theater practitioner who has worked on contemporary theater, cultural histories of lying, lying studies and authenticity. Starting the season 2021/2022 he will be Artistic Director General at Gerhart-Hauptmann-Theater Görlitz-Zittau/Germany. He taught English Literature and Cultural Studies at University of Würzburg/Germany (2011–2017), worked as personal assistant to Robert Wilson (2009–2010), and was Deputy Artistic Director at Theater Konstanz/Germany (2017–2020). His publications include *Authenticity in Contemporary Theatre and Performance* (2017), *Todeslust: Zur Ontologie des Gegenwartsdramas* (2019) and *Debating with Fists: Profession-*

al Wrestling – Sport, Spectacle and Violent Drama (2014). His editorial work includes *Kulturen der Pornographie: Annäherungen an ein Massenphänomen* (2016, with Andrea Stiebritz) and *Paragrafen – Pantomimen – Partisanen: Festschrift für Christoph Nix* (2019, with Klaus Engert and Jan Hegemann). He currently works on a monograph on cultures of capitalism and counterdrafts to consumption.

Michael Navratil is a postdoctoral researcher at the university of Potsdam/Germany. He studied German, English, and philosophy at the universities of Freiburg/Germany, Oxford/UK, and the Free University of Berlin and received his PhD in German literature form the university of Potsdam in 2020. His PhD thesis *Kontrafaktik der Gegenwart. Politisches Schreiben als Realitätsvariation bei Christian Kracht, Kathrin Röggla, Juli Zeh und Leif Randt* (forthcoming in 2021) discusses counterfactual fiction as a form of political writing in contemporary German literature. His research interests include the theory of fiction, political writing, discourses of psychology and health, gender and sexuality as well as the history and mediality of drama. He is co-editor of the volumes *Daniel Kehlmann und die Gegenwartsliteratur* (2020), *Unerlaubte Gleichheit. Homosexualität und mann-männliches Begehren in Kulturgeschichte und Kulturvergleich* (2021) and *Gesundheit erzählen. Ästhetik – Performanz – Ideologie* (forthcoming in 2021). Articles have appeared in, among others, *German Life and Letters*, *Zeitschrift für deutsche Philologie*, *Sprachkunst*, *Wirkendes Wort*, *Hofmannsthal-Jahrbuch* and *Nietzsche-Studien*.

Stephan Packard is Professor for Popular Culture and its Theories at Cologne University. Research interests include semiotics; comics studies; censorship and other forms of media control; transmediality; narratology; as well as concepts of fiction and virtuality. He is co-editor of the journal *Medienobservationen* and the author of *Anatomie des Comics. Psychosemiotische Medienanalyse* (2006); other recent publications include *Charlie Hebdo: Nicht nur am 7. Januar 2015!* (2018, ed. with Wilde) and *Comicanalyse. Eine Einführung* (2019, with Rauscher, Sina, Thon, Wilde, Wildfeuer). Articles have appeared in, among others, *Frontiers of Narrative Studies*, *Beiträge zur mediävistischen Erzählforschung*, *IMAGE*, *International Journal of Comic Art*, *CLOSURE*, *Das Argument*, *Journal of Literary Semantics*, *Dogilmunhak* and *Primerjalna književnost*.

Martin Riedelsheimer is a lecturer in English Literature at the University of Augsburg/Germany. He has published on ethical questions in contemporary theater and drama and a focus of his research is contemporary fiction. In particular, he is concerned with ethics and narratology, which are also centrally discussed in his book *Fictions of Infinity: Levinasian Ethics in 21st-Century Novels* (2020). Together with Martin Middeke he is co-editing a special issue of the *Journal of Contemporary Drama in English* on the topic of Critical Theatre Ecologies (forthcoming). For a new research project he wants to investigate forms of poetic affect.

Eva Ries teaches English Literature at the University of Augsburg/Germany. Her research interests include contemporary city texts, modernist literature and narratology. She completed her PhD project, which investigates how flânerie as a technique of self contributes to the formation of ethical subjects in contemporary Anglophone city texts, in 2021 (forthcoming).

Philippe Rochat is Professor of Psychology at Emory University and director of the Emory Infant and Child Laboratory. In addition to articles and book chapters, he is the single author of 5 books: *Moral Acrobatics: How we avoid moral ambiguity by thinking in black and white* (2020, in press), *Origins of Possession* (2014/2015), *Others in Mind* (2009), *The Infant's World* (2001/2006), *Vision and Touch in Children* (1984). The thematic focus of his current research is the early sense of self, emerging self-concept, the development of social cognition and relatedness, and the emergence of a moral sense during the preschool years in children from all over the world. His research emphasizes differences in populations of children and adults growing up in highly contrasted cultural environments, as well as highly contrasted socio-economic circumstances. Rochat's overarching interest is on the specific nature and development of human self-conscious psychology. To consult publications go to: http://www.psychology.emory.edu/cognition/rochat/lab/Publications.html

Frank L. Schäfer is Professor of German Legal History and Private Law at the University of Freiburg/Germany. He is also a deputy director of the graduate school Factual and Fictional Narration (GRK 1767). His major research interests include the law of obligations, property law, legal history and narratology. He is the author of *Das Bereicherungsrecht in Europa* (2001), *Juristische Germanistik* (2008), co-author of *Repertorium der Vorlesungsquellen zu Friedrich Carl von Savigny* (2016) and co-editor of the *Materialien zum Bürgerlichen Gesetzbuch für das Königreich Sachsen*. Articles and commentaries have appeared in, among others, *Münchener Kommentar zum Bürgerlichen Gesetzbuch*, *Savigny-Zeitschrift für Rechtsgeschichte* and *Zeitschrift für Neuere Rechtsgeschichte*.

Vid Stevanović is a PhD candidate at the research training group "Globalization and Literature" at the University of Munich (LMU), where he is currently completing a thesis on 18th century It-Narratives. His research interests include economic criticism, thing-theory, structural psychoanalysis, and the literature of globalization. He is co-editor of *Literatur und Arbeit* (2018) and has recently published in *Textpraxis* and *Forschungen der Deutschen Kafka-Gesellschaft*. His most recent work includes an article on 18th-century adventure writing in the *Yearbook of Research in English an American Literature (REAL)*.

Stefan Tilg is Professor of Latin at the University of Freiburg/Germany. He is also a member and co-director of the graduate school Factual and Fictional Narration (GRK 1767). His research focuses on ancient narrative, Neo-Latin literature, and reception studies. He is the author of *Chariton of Aphrodisias and the Invention of the Greek Love Novel* (2010) and of *Apuleius'* 'Metamorphoses'*: A Study in Roman Fiction* (2014). With Eva von Contzen, he is the co-editor of the *Handbuch Historische Narratologie* (2019).

Tom Vanassche is a lecturer and researcher at the RWTH Aachen. 2008–2014 studies in Ghent and London (German, English and Comparative Literature, European Studies); 2015–2019 PhD student and researcher at the Graduate School Factual and Fictional Narration (GRK 1767) at the University of Freiburg/Germany. Major research interests: the Shoah in literature, historiography and memory, documentary literature, German-Jewish literature and intellectual history since the 18th century, ecocriticism, history of emotions. Latest publications: as an editor (with Daniela Henke) *Ko-Erinnerung. Grenzen, Herausforderungen und Perspektiven des neueren Shoahgedenkens* (2020), *Borderland Auschwitz. Lagerszpracha in Dieter Schlesak's* 'Capesius, der Auschwitzapotheker' *(2006) and its translations* (2021).